SIMPLY SENSATIONAL COOKIES

Bright Fresh Flavors, Natural Colors & Easy,
Streamlined Techniques

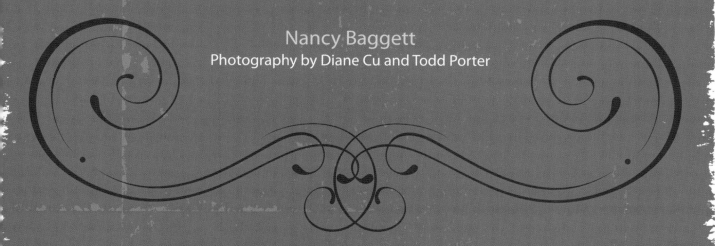

Nancy Baggett

Photography by Diane Cu and Todd Porter

WILEY

JOHN WILEY & SONS, INC.

Copyright © 2013 by John Wiley & Sons, Inc. All rights reserved.
Photography copyright 2013 by Diane Cu and Todd Porter
Cover Image: Diane Cu and Todd Porter
Cover Design: Suzanne Sunwoo
Interior Design: idesign, inc.
Published by John Wiley & Sons, Inc., Hoboken, New Jersey
Published simultaneously in Canada

Library of Congress Cataloging-in-Publication Data:

Baggett, Nancy

    Simply sensational cookies : bright fresh flavors, natural colors & easy, streamlined techniques / Nancy Baggett ;
photography by Diane Cu and Todd Porter.

    p. cm.

    Includes index.

    ISBN 978-0-470-27868-0 (cloth); 978-1-118-11056-0 (ebk); 978-1-118-11057-7-(ebk); 978-1-118-11058-4 (ebk)

    1. Cookies. I. Title.

    TX772.B29 2013

    641.86'54--dc23

    2011042968

Printed in China

10 9 8 7 6 5 4 3 2 1

CONTENTS

ACKNOWLEDGMENTS

Many people played a part in creating this book. I'm proud of it and am very grateful to all those who helped make it happen.

First, a huge thank you to Justin Schwartz, my editor, and the whole Wiley team, for being committed to quality and for making Simply Sensational Cookies the best it could possibly be. A book of this size and with full color and photography throughout is a huge undertaking for a publisher, and I am thrilled with the results. Jackie Beach, senior production editor, Joline Rivera, the book's interior designer, and Suzanne Sunwoo, the cover designer, all need to take a bow. Thanks, too, to the publicity staff, especially Claire Holzman, and to editorial assistant Eden Bunchuck for helping with many details.

I'm grateful to the enormously talented Diane Cu and Todd Porter, whose spectacular photographs for the book still take my breath away. Not only did they deliver far more than I hoped for, but they were a great pleasure to work with. Thanks, as well, to Nancy Buchanan, who so ably and cheerfully assisted us during the photo shoot.

Thanks to Judith Riven, my literary agent, for her enthusiasm, very professional representation, and steadying presence over a project that spanned more than five years.

Many thanks to my recipe testers: My kitchen assistants Linda Kirschner and Judy Silver Weisberg helped test many of the recipes, and Erica Horting also tested a number of them. Connie Hay, Sally Churgai, and Stephanie Lowell provided help as well.

Another big thank you goes to an enthusiastic group of volunteer testers who made recipes in their own kitchens, then carefully rated them for ease of preparation, taste, texture, and appearance. Their feedback was thoughtful and constructive and helped make the recipes better and more user-friendly. In alphabetical order they are: Steven Blaski, Jilda Bolton, Dixie Broyles, Sallie Buttler, Judy Carter, Susan Colletti, Pam Cote, Kit Ellis, Vicki Gensini, Monica Greaney, Rose Gulledge, Janet Holliday, Kate Marvel, Deb Melnyk, Cindy Nelson, Cindy Pauldine, Deborah Ross, Margo Sety, and Elaine Wallace.

Thank you to the friends and colleagues in my writers' group, who have been sampling and rating my recipes and critiquing my prose over literally decades. Their steadfast support and expertise has definitely made me a better writer, and perhaps a better baker and cook. I have also learned a lot from the various food editors and publishers I've written for over the years and appreciate their confidence in me and their enthusiasm for my work. Additionally, many fine cookbook authors and bakers (some I know well and others I've never met) have inspired me and shown the way towards excellence. More recently, numerous culinary bloggers and Twitter and Facebook foodie friends have shared knowledge and enthusiastically lent their support.

Finally, thanks to my wonderful family. They are my biggest advocates and enrich my professional and personal life in countless ways. They have been springboards for ideas, guinea pigs for recipes in progress, and honest (but never harsh) critics of my work. My husband, Charlie, who has been cheering me on and providing wise counsel since the very beginning, sometimes tactfully says, "It's good enough for me to eat, but not good enough to put in a cookbook!" (Obviously, he understands the taster's role very well.) The youngest fans in the family, my grandchildren Charlie and Lizzie, are my most loyal baking companions, as well as a constant reminder that cookies are not only about creating great sweet treats to eat but about bonding and sharing good times.

INTRODUCTION }

Times change. People change. Cookies do, too.

The cookie repertoire I remember from childhood was pretty different from today's. Everybody and his brother (or more likely his mother or grandmother) served up molasses-spice, gingerbread, and raisin cookies. People made lots of oatmeal cookies, sugar cookies, and date bars, as well. But except for brownies and chocolate chip cookies, the chocolate offerings were slim. And cookies tended to be quite small.

Chocolate chip cookies were very popular but came in only two basic styles—those with a bare minimum of chocolate morsels and those with fewer! Cooks were frugal then and routinely skimped on add-ins, whether nuts, fruit, or chocolate bits. My grandmother, a good baker, would have considered my One-Bowl Big Chocolate–Chocolate Chip Cookies (page 50), which call for a pound of chocolate morsels for about 30 cookies, scandalous!

I don't recollect anybody ever serving chocolate–chocolate chippers or mocha chocolate chip cookies, or any of today's interesting variations on the original Toll House theme. Nobody tossed chocolate chips into peanut butter or oatmeal cookies or brownies, either, probably because people just weren't into experimenting much. Besides that, the Nestlé morsels weren't introduced until 1939, and it took a while for folks to realize their full potential. (Butterscotch, peanut butter, and white chocolate morsels weren't even a gleam in the Nestlé product developers' eyes.)

Fast-forward to the 1980s and '90s, and the cookie scene was dramatically changed. Cookies were often large (even monsters!), and much more sumptuous than before. They were beginning to feature more complex flavor combinations and assorted morsels. Sometimes they contained several different kinds of chips, nuts, and fruits all at once. These extravagances were dubbed "Kitchen Sink" cookies; my latest version is on page 53. Big, plump white chocolate–macadamia cookies (and other white chocolate cookies, too) were the rage— my son requested them instead of a cake for his birthday parties!

Today we're moving forward again—into what could be described as the era of "high-impact cookies." Our palates are more sophisticated than ever; they've come to expect lots of "wow" power. Cookies can't just sit there on the plate or in the mouth: They have to taste and smell fabulous, look fabulous, feel fabulous on our tongue, and, yes, *sound* fabulous as they're being munched. Even the simplest, most traditional kinds, like shortbreads, butter wafers, and such, need to stand out, make a statement, and wrestle all our senses to the ground.

The kicker: Although everybody's taste buds are looking for cookies that deliver *more*, most home bakers are looking for recipes that require *less* from them. Everybody's super busy. Plus, many ardent cookie makers aren't experienced at baking. To complicate the matter even further, lots of us have now become interested in eating more less-processed, from-scratch foods and in limiting dyes and similar chemicals in our diets.

This is why, though I've authored two previous well-received cookie books, I'm compelled to tackle my favorite subject again. While my previous works mostly paid homage to popular recipes from the past, this book celebrates what's current and up and coming in cookies. There are so many new, easy, all-natural ways of heightening flavor, aroma, and texture in both classic and modern cookies, as well as methods of streamlining and simplifying preparations, that I just *have* to share them with you.

Simply Sensational Cookies is new and different in a number of ways. First, at the top left next to each recipe title you'll find a very handy doability rating from extra easy to fairly difficult, plus a few abbreviated descriptors highlighting the recipe's key attributes. These include remarks such as "very versatile," "elegance with ease," "make-ahead convenience," or "au naturel," to help you quickly assess recipes without having to read through them. Here are some other important new features.

EASY ONE-BOWL (OR ONE-SAUCEPAN) MIXING

Many of the recipes skip the traditional beating, or "creaming," of butter and sugar. Instead, the butter is quickly softened or fully melted in a microwave-safe bowl or saucepan, then the other ingredients go in. After a stirring or mixing, and, perhaps, a brief chilling, the dough gets shaped and baked.

This streamlined approach often yields much better results than creaming, because more compact dough produces cookies with more concentrated flavor and a chewy, rather than cakey, texture. It also eliminates the task of figuring out when butter is the right consistency for creaming, which is sometimes a tricky matter for newbie bakers. The old-fashioned method is probably a holdover from the days before baking soda and baking powder came along (in the 1700 and 1800s). Often, these leavening ingredients lighten cookies to the point that creaming is unnecessary.

Another streamlined approach you'll find here involves grinding certain cookie ingredients, like nuts, herbs, citrus zest, or chocolate, together with the sugar in a food processor, then incorporating the butter and flour as well. This eliminates tedious chopping by hand, quickly cuts the butter into the dry ingredients, and boosts appeal by thoroughly infusing the sugar and butter with the flavors of the nuts, herbs, and so forth. In some recipes, such as my super-easy, five-ingredient Iced Little Lemon Drops (page 47), the sugar-butter-lemon mixture actually does double-duty and serves as the base for both the dough and frosting.

FRESH, INTENSE, NATURAL FLAVORS

Simply Sensational recipes crank up flavor by taking advantage of both old and new ingredients in expected and novel ways—everything from fresh and dried herbs, sea salts, and freeze-dried berries and berry powders to citrus zests, green tea, and occasionally even ground chiles, pepper, and edible flowers get put to work! (Don't worry; most items are readily available and, when necessary, I suggest local or Internet sources.) Interestingly, people usually can't put their finger on what's unique about the various herb- and chile-enhanced cookies—they just find the faintly exotic, unfamiliar flavors surprising and highly addictive. This is certainly true of the Lavender-Lemon Garden Party Meltaways (page 92). Please banish any skepticism—lavender has an elusive, irresistible spicy-floral character that many folks discover they really love. Likewise, in the Cranberry, Orange, and Sage Cookies (page 106) the sage adds a special, unexpected flavor dimension that most folks aren't able to identify but greatly enjoy.

Thanks to freeze-dried raspberries and strawberries and berry powders now on the market, it's possible to pack far more pure, intense berry taste into cookies than ever before: My revamped chocolate-raspberry brownies are not only the fudgiest, but the fruitiest and most aromatic I've ever created. And the naturally pale pink Very Strawberry (or Very Raspberry) Sugar Dusties shortbreads (page 45), which not only contain but also are rolled in berry powder and confectioners' sugar, burst with fruit flavor.

A few recipes even benefit from naturally cooling mint leaves or hot, puckery elements in the sensory mix: The Spiced Mexican Chocolate Cookies (page 86), for example, include a little smoked paprika and cayenne, which, trust me, add wonderful warmth to the chocolate-spice taste and wow all but very timid eaters.

AU NATUREL DECORATING TECHNIQUES AND RECIPES

Decorating with bright but bland commercial sprinkles and colored sugars is traditional, but it misses a huge opportunity to build in more aroma and taste with well-flavored toppings. And it means introducing food dyes, some of which are allergens or irritants for certain people.

So, using a food processor, you can create a whole assortment of quick-to-make but highly aromatic and *naturally colorful* citrus, herb, spice, berry, and flower decorating sugars and powders that can replace the store-bought kind. Instead of just sitting there looking pretty, these naturally attractive garnishes deliver a one-two punch to the taste buds *and* the olfactory sensors every time a cookie goes to the lips. This book also serves up a large and interesting array of tempting frostings, glazes, and even nifty homemade sprinkles that get most or all of their color from natural ingredients, as well as other fresh, all-natural garnishes and finishing touches.

Of course, purchased decors and sugars are still an option: The new homemade versions just provide a tastier and possibly healthier alternative. (And most of them are surprisingly easy, too.) Since my grandchildren are always snitching the sprinkles and icings when we decorate cookies, and the whole family eats them, the au natural way has particular appeal for me.

MORE MEMORABLE AND ENTICING COOKIE TEXTURES

A significant part of the pleasure of a really good cookie is its texture, so a lot of testing has gone into ensuring that the snaps in the book really snap, the brittle wafers shatter, and the ooey-gooey cookies are exactly that. One current (delightful!) trend is cookies simultaneously serving up two textures—chewy-crispness at the edges and chewy-softness in the centers: The buttery, brown sugary Butterscotch Chewies (page 97) and Ultimate One-Bowl Chocolate Chippers (or Chunkers) on page 77 are just two good examples of this wonderfully sumptuous chewy-crispy style.

The book also picks up on a modern trend and provides assorted "crossover" cookies—ones bringing together both cracker and cookie characteristics, with really fresh, fun results. Some, like the Sweet & Crunchy Chocolate Chip Crisps (page 218) and the Sweet & Salty Peanut Crisps (page 220), are reminiscent of classic Toll House or peanut butter cookies but are light, thin, and irresistibly crisp. Some, like the Herbed Chèvre Nuggets (page 223) and the Cranberry & Fig Conserve-Stuffed Blue & Cheddar Cheese Cocktail Sandwich Cookies (page 226), have the tender texture and look of butter cookies but make great cocktail nibbles. And some, like the Oil-Cured Black Olive and Black Pepper Biscotti (page 231) and the Savory Sun-Dried Tomato & Tapenade Cocktail Rugelach (page 232), are made *exactly* the same way as classic versions, but are savory instead of sweet.

The crunchy, pleasant-to-munch-on texture of biscotti is also in demand these days, so there's a grab bag of old favorites like almond, citrus, and chocolate biscotti along with more unusual offerings like spiced espresso-orange, mocha-hazelnut, saffron, and iced gingerbread.

I've been making cookies for as long as I can remember. I don't think there's any other kitchen activity that's more fun or that creates more fond and lasting memories.

My first recollections are of helping my mother, and occasionally my grandmother, measure, mix, and bake sugar cookies and date-spice drops.

We lived in what was then a sleepy farming community in central Maryland, where most families gathered for a home-cooked meal every evening. People prepared almost all their food "from scratch," and I was expected to pitch in with tasks. The kitchen always seemed to me the most companionable, welcoming room in our house because we not only baked and cooked there but also ate most meals and sat and chatted there.

From at least our middle school years, my nearest playmate, a cousin from the adjacent farm, or my brother and I were allowed to come in and mix up a batch of raisin or oatmeal cookies whenever we liked. Besides the most obvious reward—munching on fragrant, fresh-from-the-oven goodies—we enjoyed the camaraderie and the satisfaction of completing a useful task. (Still valid reasons for baking cookies today!)

The recipes we usually made came from the backs of product boxes, and one was actually the first "saucepan cookie" I ever tried. (The butter was melted, and the remaining ingredients were then stirred in and the cookies dropped from a spoon.) The method was so foolproof and delivered such great results that it's the same one I've used to revamp many of the recipes in this book. I also yearned so much for those oatmeal cookies that when I lost the original recipe I *had* to re-create it (page 36).

The kitchen was where we gathered to prep for the major seasonal events. Every Christmas and Easter all the family bakers joined forces to ready our holiday baked goods, partly for the camaraderie and partly because a wider variety of treats could be produced.

We often gave our cookies as gifts—a nice gesture in a community where people were generous in spirit but budgets were tight. In fact, the habit of *making* rather than *buying* all my Christmas presents stuck; decades later I still don't feel ready for the holidays without several batches of homemade cookies on hand.

My mother's Christmas repertoire always included our favorite rolled sugar cookies and, sometimes, her special frosted chocolate drops, too. When I was about nine, she taught me how to ready the sugar cookies (page 30), and after that baking and decorating them was my regular contribution.

Since we didn't have a truly notable gingerbread cookie in our family collection, one year I decided to remedy that situation. After trying and rejecting both the molasses-heavy version on the Brer Rabbit bottle and the one in my mother's wooden file box, I climbed on a stool and got down the little stash of cookbooks she kept in the top of the kitchen cupboard.

It's no exaggeration to say that the seemingly unremarkable, tattered collection opened up a whole new world for me, and after that I spent a lot of my free time poring over cookie recipes and trying them out. If there is any truth to the popular notion that 10,000 hours of dedicated effort produces an expert, it could help explain my knack with cookies to this day.

BAKING COOKIES & MAKING MEMORIES TODAY

No matter the setting or lifestyle, homemade cookies, especially easy ones, can fit in and provide an opportunity to relax and unwind. Once I was grown and moved to an urban apartment, I sometimes craved

comfort food, and a batch of cookies was a perfect way to re-create the aromas and tastes of my mother's kitchen. The treats satisfied not only my own and my roommate's longings for home, but also those of the college kids who lived next door!

Later, I continued the cookie-making habit with my family and friends out in the 'burbs. Some of the all-day holiday cookie "bake-athons" undertaken with other moms and their kids when our children were young still rank among the favorite times of my child-rearing years.

These days, I mostly bake cookies with my grandchildren. The habit started when my first grandchild, Charlie, was still a toddler and just beginning to talk. If I guided his hand with mine, he was able to "help" cut out cookies and sprinkle on decorations. He quickly got the idea that the goodies had to be taken away and baked, then cooled before we ate them. After that, whenever he arrived at the front door for a visit, he'd immediately say, "Nana bake cookies?"

A few months later, the whole family was astonished when he suddenly said, "Nana, bake *gingerbread* cookies?" No one was aware he even knew that word!

Once his sister, my darling little Lizzie, came along, the three of us began baking together, often with Granddaddy or my son joining in the fun. The children have now helped make and decorate all kinds of cookies—drops, slice-and-bakes, thumbprints—in fact, every sort from chichi and fancy to homey and plain. Most recently for St. Patrick's Day, we made shamrock-shaped sandwich cookies filled with a pretty green tea–ginger buttercream (page 329)!

If you've somehow missed out on or drifted away from this simple kitchen pleasure, consider remedying that now. Today's cookies are easier and better than ever: Bake; savor; make memories that last a lifetime. Anyone can do it—I hope you will, too.

COOKIE-BAKING BASICS

BEGINNING AT THE BEGINNING

Homemade cookies are one of life's simple pleasures. They don't require a fancy kitchen or special skills, or a big investment of money or time. Many of the recipes in this book are easy enough that the cookies can literally be mixed up, baked, and ready for nibbling in less than 20 minutes—pretty nearly instant gratification! But just in case you're new to cookie baking, they always provide enough detail that you'll know exactly how to proceed.

To get you off to a good start, here are a few fundamentals and tips on ingredients, equipment, and basic techniques like measuring and mixing. (You'll also find useful tips presented right along with every recipe in the book and in each of the chapter introductions.) At the end of this chapter there is a handy Q & A section that covers common troubleshooting issues, baking ahead, and cookie packaging and shipping tips.

INGREDIENTS

Baking Soda and Baking Powder

Remember that while baking soda and baking powder are both leavenings used to lighten the texture of baked goods, they are chemically very different and aren't interchangeable. For one thing, it takes about one-third as much baking soda to do the same leavening job as baking powder, and if you go too heavy on the soda, the cookies will taste oddly bitter.

Baking powder contains both an acid and a base, and the two react and release gas in the presence of moisture and heat. As a result, it's important to store baking powder airtight in a cool spot and to use it promptly. It just naturally loses its oomph over time, so I replace mine yearly.

Baking soda is an alkali that only produces gas bubbles and lightens texture when it's combined with an acid. In a cookie dough, the acid component is most often

citrus juice, buttermilk, sour cream, honey, molasses, "American-style" (non-alkalized) cocoa powder (see more information on cocoas under the Chocolate Products section that follows), or occasionally, cream of tartar. These are required in varying amounts: Only a small quantity of strongly acidic lime juice (pH 1.8 to 2) or lemon juice (pH 2 to 2.5) is required; more of mildly acidic ingredients like honey (pH 3.5 to 5) and coffee (pH 5) are needed. But without *some* acid, the baking soda will not be activated and will lend a chemical aftertaste.

Old-fashioned recipes sometimes call for cream of tartar, an acid powder refined from wine making, to activate the baking soda. This combo is essentially like a homemade baking powder prepared with 1 part baking soda to 2 parts cream of tartar. It can substitute for baking powder in a pinch.

Baking soda sometimes clumps. Crush lumps between the fingers or with the back of a spoon until completely powdery *before* combining the baking soda with other ingredients.

Butter

I prefer to use unsalted butter and call for it throughout the book. Its taste is noticeably fresher and cleaner than that of salted butter; plus I like to control exactly how much salt I'm adding to recipes. Unsalted butter is essential in buttercream filling and frosting recipes; salted butter lends them an overly salty, off taste. Unsalted butter has a shorter refrigerator shelf life than salted butter (salt acts as a preservative), but it will keep extremely well in the freezer. Either thaw it in the refrigerator overnight or on the countertop for several hours, until the consistency specified in the recipe is reached.

A number of recipes skip the traditional creaming of the butter and sugar and instead call for either softening or fully melting the butter and then stirring in the sugar and other ingredients. If directions say to soften the butter, heat it until it is mostly soft and creamy, but still opaque and perhaps with some unmelted lumps; it should not be runny or translucent. Usually the next step is to remove the butter from the heat and continue stirring just until it is creamy-smooth. In other cases, directions call for completely melting the butter; in this case, keep heating until it is runny and translucent.

If you happen to be using frozen butter and really must thaw it in a hurry, place it in a microwave-safe bowl and microwave on *10 percent power* at 30- to 40-second intervals, checking the consistency after each microwaving interval. It's very easy to overdo it and inadvertently melt the butter completely (I know this from sad experience), so proceed slowly and gradually and stop before you think it's thawed quite enough. Be aware that butter melts unevenly in the microwave oven; it may be cold and hard in some spots, warm and runny in others. Even if you need fully melted butter, don't over-warm it, as it can raise the dough temperature and cause cookies to run and flatten too much.

Don't confuse unsalted butter with "sweet cream butter." This indicates only that the butter was churned from sweet cream, not whether salt has been added. Check the label to be sure.

If you can't obtain unsalted butter or prefer to use salted, omit any salt called for in the recipe or reduce it by at least half. Never substitute whipped butter, as it contains more air (and consequently less butter) than the same quantity of stick butter. If you must use margarine, only stick margarine will work; the tub- and soft-style products have a different moisture, fat, and air content and aren't ever suitable substitutes for butter.

Chocolate Products

This book calls for a number of different chocolate products, including unsweetened, bittersweet, semisweet, milk chocolate, white chocolate, semisweet chocolate chips (or occasionally, pistoles, disc-shaped chips), cocoa nibs (finely chopped cocoa beans), and unsweetened cocoa powder (*not* the presweetened mix for making hot cocoa). These ingredients usually can't be used interchangeably because they contain varying amounts of sugar, cocoa butter, and cacao (the chocolaty solids and natural fat, cocoa butter), all of which greatly affect the texture, taste, appearance, and flavor of cookies.

Remember that "unsweetened" and "bittersweet" chocolate are not the same. Unsweetened is basically just ground cocoa beans, which are very bitter. Bittersweet and semisweet chocolate are both sweetened with sugar, though some bittersweet blends taste fairly sweet and some semisweet chocolates seem fairly dark and bitter. (Milk chocolate, which, as the name suggests, contains milk solids, is both milder and sweeter than the other two.)

By law, chocolate called "bittersweet" must be at least 35 percent cacao, while "semisweet" must be at least 15 percent cacao. But this leaves room for great variation, and in many cookies the amount of actual chocolate incorporated needs to be precise. In such instances, I've given the recommended percentage of cacao when calling for the chocolate in the ingredient list. Problem is, some manufacturers don't post the cacao percentage on their labels. In that case you can get a fairly accurate idea of the percentage by turning to and relying on How to Guesstimate the Cacao Percentage (page 17).

To further complicate matters, two chemically different kinds of unsweetened cocoa powder are on the market: American-style, or non-alkalized (often called "natural" on the label), and Dutch-process (sometimes called Dutched or European), or alkalized. The alkalizing process not only tends to darken cocoa color and lighten its flavor, but most important, Dutching removes the natural acid. As a result, the pH of non-alkalized cocoa is usually 5.5 (slightly acidic), while the pH of Dutch-process is usually 7 (neutral) or 8 (slightly alkaline). This, of course, affects whether baking powder or baking soda should be used in the dough recipe; see the preceding

CHOCOLATE PRIMER

Chocolate tastes complex partly because it *is* more complex than most other baking ingredients. Here's some background information on why certain very precise directions in the book need to be followed carefully.

* Chocolate never needs *cooking*; it's ready to use as is or simply melted.

It melts at less than human body temperature— usually at less than 90°F! High heat not only won't speed melting, but it can also cause scorching. Heating longer or at a higher temperature won't thin out a thicker melted chocolate either; its fluidity is determined mostly by its cocoa butter or other fat content. (Since cocoa butter isn't readily available to home cooks, recipes call for incorporating a little flavorless vegetable oil when chocolate must be thinned.)

* Chocolate contains a natural starch that resists mixing smoothly with overly large amounts of liquid or with liquids that aren't pre-warmed. The occasional very specific directions calling for combining chocolate and liquids gradually and at particular temperatures encourage the blending desired. In case you've ever wondered why a ganache or similar mixture thickened rather than thinned out when cream or other liquid was added to the melted chocolate, the starch is the reason. It's also the reason chocolate scorches easily and that chocolate cookies usually need to be baked at 350°F or less.

* The percentage of cacao in the brand of chocolate used has a huge impact on final results in baked goods, so you often need to know what that number is. (See page 17 for details on determining the cacao percentage.) Though you might assume that chocolate with the highest percentage of cacao is always the best choice, that's not the case. It just needs to be in proper balance with the other ingredients.

For example, up to a point, an abundance of the natural fat, cocoa butter, is a good thing because it heightens the chocolaty taste and improves mouthfeel. But too much cocoa butter, especially in chocolate morsels or chunks added to doughs, will taste unctuous and cause the dough to run and produce overly flat cookies. (As a result, morsels and chunks specifically designed to be baking stable and used as is in cookies rarely have a cacao percentage higher than around 60 percent.) Likewise, up to a point, a chocolate loaded with the dark, intense flavoring components will boost flavor and color, but too much can yield cookies that are too bitter and harsh tasting.

discussion of baking powder and soda for details.

Chocolate is highly sensitive to heat and can burn if not melted as directed. For example, when melting chocolate and butter right on a burner, you *must* make sure to use a heavy saucepan over the *lowest temperature setting* or the chocolate may scorch. When melting chocolate in a microwave oven, melt on the power setting for the time increments specified, stopping and stirring as directed. Most important, be aware that chocolate melted in a microwave oven may be warm and *completely melted* on the *inside, before* the outside looks melted at all.

For some valuable insight into *why* chocolate has to be handled so carefully, see the Chocolate Primer sidebar on page 15.

Dried Fruits

Dried fruits such as raisins, dried sweetened cranberries, dates, currants, figs, apricots, and prunes used in cookies should be plump, moist, and fresh. To make sure they are hydrated enough not to draw moisture from the dough, many recipes call for wetting or soaking them in hot water and then draining and patting them dry before use. This simple step will go far in ensuring that your cookies stay succulent instead of becoming dry and crumbly during storage.

Eggs

All the recipes in *Simply Sensational Cookies* have been tested using large eggs. Since the texture of cookies depends on a precise ratio of sugar, fat, egg, and flour, it is best not to substitute eggs of a different size.

In recipes calling for egg whites to be beaten, the whites must be free of any yolk. Be sure the mixing bowl and beaters are also free of any traces of grease, or the whites may not fluff up properly.

In a couple of the recipes, notably the French macarons, the whites need to be separated and "aged" for at least a few days in the refrigerator. (I was skeptical

that this mattered, but when I once tried using "fresh" whites, my macarons didn't develop the expected little "feet" at the bottom.) I find it convenient to collect whites ahead and freeze them, then transfer them to the refrigerator 6 or 7 days before I make macarons.

You'll note that recipes calling for beaten whites usually direct you to start on low speed, then gradually raise the mixer speed to high. Beginning on low produces finer bubbles, which creates a more stable meringue mixture. If you have a heavy-duty stand mixture, which I recommend for macaroons and French macarons, beat the egg whites using the whisk-shaped beater.

Flour

I prefer *unbleached* all-purpose flour and have used it in all the recipes that call for white flour. I also prefer good-quality, brand-name flours, as these are thoroughly ground and pre-sifted and can normally be used without any further sifting or fluffing up. Note that in *Simply Sensational Cookies*, flour is always measured using the *dip-and-sweep* method. This means you should dip the appropriate graduated measure into the sack or canister of flour until the cup is overfull; then sweep, or level off, the mounded flour with a straight-edged spatula or knife. Don't sift or stir the flour in advance. And don't rap the cup or compact the flour by pressing it down.

Nuts

Use only fresh, good-quality nuts. All nuts rapidly become stale and may develop a noticeable rancid flavor, so taste to check freshness before adding them to doughs. If you prefer to buy nuts in more economical large quantities, freeze any that aren't used promptly. Thaw them thoroughly prior to adding them to cookie recipes. If you're in a hurry, use a microwave oven on 10 percent power; stop, stir, and check their temperature every 30 seconds to ensure they don't inadvertently

overheat and burn. Stop as soon as they feel barely room temperature to the touch, as they will continue to toast even after being removed from the microwave. Never toss still-frozen nuts into dough, as they can lower the temperature of the dough too much and prevent cookies from spreading properly.

A number of recipes call for toasting nuts, which both brings out their flavor and crisps them. In the case of hazelnuts, toasting also helps loosen the hulls (skins), which taste slightly bitter and should be removed. Instructions for hulling hazelnuts are included in recipes whenever the procedure is required, although toasted

HOW TO GUESSTIMATE THE CACAO PERCENTAGE

The cacao percentage on a package of chocolate simply indicates the percentage of cocoa bean solids and its fat, called "cocoa butter." Some chocolate bars still don't include the cacao percentage on the label, and the names of the blends, like "Special Bittersweet" or "Premium Dark," often don't shed much light on the percentage either. (Sometimes, in fact, the names seem misleading.)

But you can still use chocolate blends that don't list the cacao percentage in recipes, because there is an easy way to guesstimate the percentage for all semisweet and bittersweet bars. (The method won't work for milk chocolates or bars containing nuts.) Simply compare the *grams of sugar* per serving listed on the package with the total grams per serving listed. For example, if a "Semisweet Premium" nutrition panel lists a serving as weighing 40 grams and 20 grams are from sugar, it's a good bet the cacao percentage is around 50 percent. (Additions like vanilla and lecithin emulsifiers may account for a percent or so, but the rest of the weight has to come from the cacao.)

By the same token, if a "Rich Dark Blend" contains 40 total grams per serving and only 10 grams are from sugar, about three-quarters of the weight is from the chocolate solids and cocoa butter, meaning the cacao percentage is around 75 percent. Incidentally, as you'll discover if you do the quick ratio check routinely, many of the "semisweet," "bittersweet," or "dark" chocolates that fail to note the cacao percentage on the package are in the 45 to 50 percent cacao range.

and hulled, ready-to-use hazelnuts are becoming more and more common. I find them to be a great time- and labor-saver and well worth the extra cost.

Several recipes in *Simply Sensational Cookies* also call for almond flour—almonds that are ground powder-fine and then usually sifted to remove any coarse bits. (The product can be made at home using a food processor, but this is tedious and it is difficult to obtain the fine, flour-like consistency needed.) Supermarkets and health food stores often stock almond flour with the gluten-free baked goods, and many online vendors sell it. Keep it airtight in the refrigerator or freezer so it will stay fresh.

Spices, Herbs, Extracts, and Flavorings

The recipes in *Simply Sensational Cookies* occasionally call for dried spices and herbs. These need to be stored airtight in a cool, dark spot. Note that dried lavender can now sometimes be obtained in supermarkets along with the other offerings in the McCormick's Gourmet spice line. Unfortunately, dried spices and herbs won't keep forever, so I always take a quick sniff to check freshness before using them. Any that smell flat or musty are going to taste equally flat in cookies and should be discarded.

Fresh herbs are now usually stocked in supermarkets year-round. During the growing season, farmers' markets are an even better, less expensive source, particularly for fresh lavender and tarragon.

When recipes call for vanilla, almond, raspberry, or lemon extract and other such flavorings, use only pure, naturally flavored extracts. Not surprisingly, artificially flavored products often lend an artificial taste to baked goods, so check labels before you buy. Gourmet shops and health food stores seem to stock a wider selection of extracts than supermarkets.

One extremely useful, appealing, and potent extract you may not have encountered before is Fiori di Sicilia, or Flowers of Sicily. It has a complex vanilla-citrus-almond aroma and flavor that can greatly enhance a wide array of butter, sugar, fruit, and nut cookies. It is pricey—often $6 to $10 an ounce—but it's much more potent than the more familiar extracts, so it lasts a lot longer. (Recipes usually don't call for more than ½ teaspoon or so.) Gourmet shops sometimes carry this product, and it can be ordered from several online sources. I often purchase it at www.kingarthurflour.com.

Other frequently used flavorings include instant espresso powder or coffee granules (often dissolved in a tiny amount of water), fresh citrus zests, and freeze-dried berries and berry powders. The freeze-dried berry powders are just now coming on the scene and are enormously useful in delivering intense, natural fruit color and flavor. While the powders usually still have to be ordered online, many gourmet food store and health food shops now sell the freeze-dried berries. Page 336 gives you the quick, easy instructions for turning the berries into the powders you'll need in some recipes.

Sugar

Recipes always specify whether granulated, powdered, light brown, or dark brown sugar should be used, and these shouldn't be swapped for one another. Besides changing the look and taste, the type of sugar affects cookie texture: Brown and dark brown sugars are heavier, coarser, and contain more moisture than granulated sugar, and this can sometimes totally throw off dough consistency. Brown sugar can even cause meringue cookies to sink or go completely flat.

Avoid brown sugar that has hardened and clumped. I've learned the hard way (no pun intended) that the lumps sometimes remain even after long beating and can end up as gritty bits in the finished cookies. Also, even though some manufacturers suggest it, don't try to soften hardened brown sugar by heating it in the oven. The warm sugar will cause the butter or other fat in the recipe to overheat, soften, and perhaps run during baking. And if you try to wait until the sugar cools before adding it, it will harden again! Though it's a little tedious,

you can salvage hardened brown sugar for baking by pounding the block into small chunks with a mallet, grinding them until powdery in a sturdy food processor, then mixing in drops of cold water until it regains the typical slightly moist brown sugar consistency. (Sometimes it's easier to do this than to drop everything and run to the store!)

When powdered sugar is called for, measure it *before* sifting unless the recipe specifies otherwise.

Honey & Molasses

Occasionally, recipes in the book call for honey and molasses. In general, it's best to use clover honey or another mild-flavored honey. The neutral taste mingles better with other ingredients, plus the viscosity is fairly consistent from brand to brand. (It's often the most economical choice, too.)

Because at least one national brand of molasses sells two types—one "dark" and one "light"—several recipes specify one or the other. These terms simply indicate that one has a slightly lighter flavor and color than the other. The "dark" has a slightly more robust taste and deeper color; it should not be confused with blackstrap, which is very dark, thick, and too bitter to be satisfactory in *Simply Sensational* recipes. If your grocery store carries a product simply labeled "molasses," it will do just fine.

TECHNIQUES

Preheating the Oven

All baking times given in the book are based on results obtained using a thoroughly preheated oven. Allow at least 10 and preferably 15 minutes for preheating. Remember that opening the oven door usually drops the temperature 25° to 50°F (which is why my recipes all call for placing the oven racks in the desired positions at the same time the temperature is set). Also, keep in mind that baking times depend partly on the size of the cookies; if your cookies happen to be smaller or larger, or thinner or thicker, than normal, the baking time will necessarily change.

If you bake often, consider investing in an oven thermometer. Then you'll be sure the desired oven temperature has been reached. *A Cook's Illustrated* survey found that the thermostats in home ovens are often off by 50°F or more, dramatically affecting browning, spreading, and baking time.

Assembling and Measuring Ingredients

Cookies are among the simplest baked goods to make, but it's still wise to start by reading through each recipe and ensuring that you have the items needed. Then, take care to measure ingredients accurately: Too much or too little fat, flour, sugar, and other basics, for example, can dramatically affect cookie shape and amount of spreading, crispness, and, of course, taste.

To measure dry ingredients, use the appropriate cup from the graduated set of measures and overfill slightly. Then level off the top with a straight-edged knife or spatula. Don't stir or fluff up dry ingredients such as flour or powdered sugar first, as it will throw off the measurement. See more on measuring flour on page 16.

A 1- or 2-cup marked measuring cup with a spout works best for liquid ingredients. Be sure the cup rests on a flat surface and check the measurement from eye level.

When measuring out tablespoonfuls and teaspoonfuls of ingredients, use a standard set of measuring spoons. If your set of spoons lacks a $\frac{1}{2}$-tablespoon measure, simply measure out $1\frac{1}{2}$ teaspoons, which is in fact $\frac{1}{2}$ tablespoon. Overfill the appropriate spoon, then level off the excess with a straight-edged knife or spatula. However, note that sometimes a measuring spoon is called for and sometimes a plain flatware teaspoon or tablespoon is specified for dropping or scooping dough onto baking sheets.

Occasionally, recipes call for a "scant" $\frac{1}{4}$ teaspoon or "generous" $\frac{1}{2}$ cup of this or that ingredient. Scant means that the spoon or cup should not be quite full; generous means that it should be slightly overfull. The terms are used to compensate for the fact that the standard sets of measuring spoons and cups don't always provide a way to measure out the exact amount needed. For example, if a dough requires $\frac{3}{8}$ teaspoon of, say, salt or baking soda, rather than calling for the cumbersome $\frac{1}{4}$ teaspoon plus $\frac{1}{8}$ teaspoon, the less awkward approximation, a "generous" $\frac{1}{4}$ teaspoon is specified instead.

Since few home bakers have scales for weighing ingredients, the recipes are designed to be successful using sets of cups and spoons to measure. However, if you have kitchen scales and like to use them, here for your convenience are the weights of the most commonly called for ingredients:

Weights—Conversions for Common Ingredients

1 cup or $\frac{1}{2}$ pound butter = 8 ounces, 226.796 g

1 cup granulated sugar = 7 ounces, 198.446 g

1 cup confectioners' sugar = 4 ounces, 113.398 g

1 cup firmly packed light brown sugar = 7.5 ounces, 212.621 g

1 cup firmly packed dark brown sugar = 8.2 ounces, 232.466 g

1 cup unbleached (unsifted, dipped and scooped) all-purpose white flour = 5.1 ounces, 144.582 g

1 cup unsweetened unsifted cocoa powder = 3.4 ounces, 96.3883 g

1 large (shell removed) whole egg = 1.8 ounces, 51.0291 g

Mixing and Beating

Many of the cookies in the book skip the traditional creaming of the butter and sugar. Instead, melted butter, sugar, eggs, and flavor enhancers are all mixed together and the flour is incorporated at the very end. Not only is this approach easier, but it also normally requires only brief stirring or beating. Unless a recipe specifies otherwise, once the flour is added to the mixture, don't

Despite the conventional notion that cookies can be successfully stored airtight at room temperature for 2 or 3 weeks or longer, I've concluded that most varieties, even spicy gingerbreads, taste best within the first day or so of baking.

beat it vigorously, as this develops the flour's gluten and can cause toughness in the cookies. The direction to let the dough stand after mixing gives the flour time to absorb extra moisture and firm the dough.

Note that the instruction to "beat" means you should use a mixer, not a spoon unless this is specified.

Shaping and Baking Cookies

Cookies can be shaped in a variety of ways—by dropping or scooping, cutting into slices or bars, rolling, and so forth—and discussions and tips for each of these methods appear in the associated chapter introductions. But regardless of the method, try to keep the cookies as uniform in size and thickness as possible. Otherwise, the thinner or smaller ones will be done and beginning to burn before the bigger or thicker ones are nearly ready.

If you're baking sugar cookies or other rolled cookies in a variety of different sizes, group the larger and smaller ones on separate baking pans. Another easy way to compensate and at least partially avoid problems from uneven baking is to place any oversized cookies around the pan perimeter and undersized ones in the center. The oven heat reaches the cookies on the outside readily, so they bake the most efficiently. The ones in the center are partially shielded by the cookies around them, so they bake and brown at a slower rate.

You'll notice that every recipe includes directions on what size the cookies should be. This information enables me to provide accurate baking times and recipe yields. You can size the cookies to suit your own purposes, but will then have to determine the baking time and recipe yields yourself.

Allow at least 2 inches of space around each baking sheet so that the hot oven air can circulate freely. In some ovens, two sheets of cookies can be baked at the same time without crowding, although you'll probably need to reverse the pans from front to back about halfway through to ensure even browning. If two sheets seem cramped, bake only one pan of cookies at a time. I usually suggest this in the recipe directions.

Checking for Doneness

A minimum and maximum baking time is specified for all recipes, but a number of unpredictable factors, such as temperature of the dough, type of baking sheets, and reliability of the oven, can cause variations. As a result, the recipes always include an alternative measure of doneness, such as how brown or firm the cookies should be, to help you determine when a batch is ready. It's a good idea to check a minute or two before the cookies are supposed to be done, then bake longer, if necessary.

Cooling Cookies

Many cookies are easiest to remove from baking sheets at a particular point in their cooling process (when they are just firm enough not to tear or crumble but still flexible enough not to break). So, specific directions have been included to guide you. As soon as the cookies are firm enough, transfer them to wire racks using a thin-bladed spatula. To promote cooling, allow ample space between cookies on the racks. Then let them stand until cooled completely. If cookies inadvertently cool on the baking sheets for too long and become too brittle to remove without breaking, briefly return them to the oven to warm up a bit, then proceed.

Storing Cookies

Store cookies airtight. They should be completely cooled first, or they will release steam in the container and may become soggy or even spoil. Each recipe provides the appropriate packing instructions.

It's *always* best to store only one kind of cookie in a container, even if you're packing a variety to give as a gift. Moist, chewy cookies mixed with crispy ones will cause the crisp cookies to go limp. And spicy cookies stored with mild ones will cause the mild cookies to taste of spice. To avoid these problems when you're giving an assortment, slip each kind into its own cellophane or plastic bag and then put them all into the presentation basket, tin, or canister.

Despite the conventional notion that cookies can be successfully stored airtight at room temperature for 2 or 3 weeks or longer, I've concluded that most varieties, even spicy gingerbreads, taste best within the first few days or so after baking. (This is based on testing hundreds of different kinds and making somewhere between 13,000 and 15,000 cookies over the past several decades.) They won't spoil, but within a week the wonderful fresh flavor begins to fade, and some kinds also dry out.

Freezing helps preserve the just-baked taste, so I recommend freezing any cookies that won't be eaten within a few days. They should be packed airtight with as little headroom or airspace in the container as possible. If you plan to freeze the cookies for more than a week or so, it's best to double-wrap them or use heavy-duty freezer bags. Otherwise they will begin to pick up freezer flavors. Even when carefully wrapped, most cookies begin to taste less vibrant and even stale if frozen for more than 2 months or so.

Don't forget to label and date cookies before you stash 'em away. Unless you like mysteries and surprises, of course.

EQUIPMENT

Baking Sheets

I find that the best baking sheets for cookies are plain (light or medium metallic finish) aluminum with one or more very narrow rims. Non-reflective finishes, especially dark-colored ones, tend to absorb too much heat and cause overbrowning. Deep rims, such as those around jelly roll pans, can interfere with the circulation of hot air over the tops of cookies and curtail browning, though they will do if that's what you have. The newer sheets containing two layers of metal sandwiched together interfere with proper heat conduction and browning, too. Unless your oven tends to run very hot or burns everything on the bottom, avoid this kind of sheet.

Aluminum cookie sheets are readily available in two weights, medium and very light weight. The sturdier medium-weight sheets not only last longer but also hold and distribute heat more evenly. This helps prevent cookies from burning on the bottom or browning unevenly. The thin, flexible, lightweight sheets heat up and bake cookies quite rapidly, which promotes maximum browning and crispness but the cookies have to be very carefully watched and pans often have to be reversed during baking. It's possible to minimize the chance of burning by stacking one lightweight sheet on top of another and using them as a single, heavier unit.

Although you can certainly use several different kinds of baking sheets at once, remember that each may produce a slightly different degree of brownness and require a different baking time. If you want all cookies in a batch to look uniform, bake them on the same kind of sheet.

Cookie Cutters

A number of recipes call for cookie cutters of a particular

size and shape. This is simply to indicate how I prepared the cookies and liked them, not to curb your creativity or cramp your style. It's fine to substitute the cutter you have and come up with whatever looks you like.

Electric Mixer

Although many doughs in *Simply Sensational Cookies* are mixed by hand, some recipes do require an electric mixer. Stand mixers normally beat ingredients more quickly and efficiently than do handheld models. They are also more convenient to use, since they free up both hands for working at other tasks. Small handheld mixers will do a perfectly satisfactory job on quick mixing tasks, but they may not be powerful enough for beating the meringue mixtures needed for macaroons and French macarons. (These should be beaten with a whisk beater, not a paddle.)

Food Processor and Spice Grinder

You'll need a standard-size (or larger) food processor for some of the recipes in this book. It's the only way to puree or finely grind certain ingredients, and it's the best way to quickly cut cold butter into some doughs. A processor also makes quick work of chopping tasks, though the items won't be particularly evenly chopped. When the bits of nuts, chocolate, and so forth must be uniform, recipes direct you to chop by hand.

A few recipes suggest using a coffee or spice grinder, as the thinner, faster-moving blade is much more efficient than a food processor at grinding hard, small items like seeds and whole spices. In a pinch, you can use a processor, but it will take 4 or 5 minutes or more to do what a grinder can accomplish in 1 minute!

Measuring Cups and Spoons

Have on hand at least one set of graduated plastic or metal measuring cups for measuring dry ingredients. The most convenient sets include $\frac{1}{4}$-, $\frac{1}{3}$-, $\frac{1}{2}$-, $\frac{2}{3}$-, $\frac{3}{4}$-, and 1-cup measures, but many have fewer, usually $\frac{1}{4}$-, $\frac{1}{3}$-, $\frac{1}{2}$-, and 1-cup measures. The smaller sets will work, but you'll have to do a little math and more measuring. A glass or plastic 1- or 2-cup marked measuring cup is designed for measuring liquids but is not recommended for dry ingredients. You need a graduated set of measuring spoons, too. I prefer the ones that include a $\frac{1}{2}$ tablespoon spoon, but these are hard to find. Remember that without one, you'll just need to measure out $1\frac{1}{2}$ teaspoons instead (1 tablespoon equals 3 teaspoons).

Spatulas

A thin-bladed metal spatula (sometimes called a pancake turner) is the best choice for removing most cookies from baking sheets. (The blades of plastic or wooden spatulas are often too thick to wedge under thin cookies and lift them up neatly.) Use a spatula with a blade wider than the cookies or they may break apart or sag at the edges when lifted.

You also need a rubber or plastic spatula (sometimes called a scraper) for scraping down the sides of the mixing bowl and for folding fragile mixtures such as beaten egg whites.

Timer

While not absolutely essential, a timer comes in handy when baking cookies. It's easy to become preoccupied with readying one pan and to forget another in the oven until it's too late.

Today, many ovens and microwave ovens have a built-in digital timer you can set. Otherwise, consider purchasing an inexpensive electric or battery-powered digital timer. The older, mechanical wind-up types can also be used, but they are often less accurate and harder to read.

HANDY COOKIE-BAKING QUESTIONS & ANSWERS

Q. My cookies came out too flat and some ran together. What went wrong?

A. This can happen for a number of different reasons. If dough stands in an overheated kitchen, it may become too warm. Then, the butter in it softens excessively—and the cookies run—as soon as the pan hits the oven. Especially when your kitchen heats up, refrigerate rich buttery doughs and take out and shape portions as needed. Recipes in this book often remind you to refrigerate dough that becomes warm and soft.

Another common cause of excessive cookie spreading is using baking sheets that are too warm. Let them cool thoroughly between batches. (In the winter I put pans out on my deck for a few minutes to cool them quickly.) Of course, cookies can also run together if they're placed

too close together on baking sheets, so pay attention to how far apart the recipe says to space them.

If you have a problem with several different cookies from the book spreading too much, it may be that you're not measuring the flour correctly. See the details on page 16 on how to measure flour using the dip-and-sweep method.

Cookies may also run and flatten if a diet spread or tub margarine is used in place of butter. If you feel you must use margarine, choose *regular stick margarine*, never tub-style spreads. "Light," "diet," and soft spreads just won't work.

Chocolate chunks that have a high cacao percentage (more than about 60 percent) are usually iffy choices for adding to cookies, because they melt and run and can cause the cookies to spread out, too. Be sure to follow recipe directions on the type and amount of chopped chocolate you add. (Chocolate morsels are formulated to be baking-stable and keep their shape during baking, so they usually don't cause any problems.)

Q. My cookies often burn. What can I do?

A. Oven thermostats are often inaccurate, so the temperature may actually be higher than what you selected. If you don't have an oven thermometer to check, use the trial-and-error method and lower the setting until you get better results. If the cookies burn unevenly, the oven likely has hot spots, in which case repositioning and turning the pans several times during baking will help. It also helps to use heavy, light-colored baking sheets, or, in a pinch, two thin pans stacked together. Air-cushioned pans don't conduct heat well so I don't normally recommend them, but they may be the solution if your oven runs superhot or the cookies burn only on the bottom.

Q. Help! My cookies stuck to the pans, then broke when I tried to remove them.

A. Some cookies—for instance, meringues and others loaded with egg whites, or those with lots of chocolate or candy bits—tend to stick tenaciously. To head off trouble, recipes for sticky doughs often call for lining the pans with baking parchment or a silicone mat or perhaps aluminum foil, instead of greasing them. So, start by prepping the pans as directed.

Another key to cookie removal is using a wide, thin-bladed spatula *at the right moment*—when the rounds have cooled and firmed up some but are not completely cold and brittle. The recipes note how long the cookies should stand, but if you inadvertently let a pan get too cool, return it to the oven for a couple of minutes to re-warm and soften the cookies before trying to remove them.

Q. I've read that the butter temperature is a key to success in cookie baking. But how do I know when the temperature is right?

A. Many cookie recipes in this book actually call for melted butter, so the mixing is much less tricky than when the butter and sugar must be beaten, or creamed, together. Recipes that do call for the traditional creaming usually specify "slightly softened" butter, which is soft enough to beat readily but also firm enough to hold some shape and fluff up a bit. A "press test" is a good way to check for the right consistency: Press down on the butter with a fingertip; a little pressure should make an indentation that stays in the surface. If the butter is too hard to press, let it warm up a little longer. If it's squishy-soft, return it to the fridge to firm up a bit, then test again.

A number of cookies in the book call for cold, firm butter. In this case, it's usually cut (not beaten) into other ingredients using a food processor. Here, the butter should feel cold and should not give when you press the surface.

Q. I like to make holiday cookies ahead. Any advice?

A. Despite the conventional wisdom that cookies are great keepers, I've found that they keep much better in the freezer than just stashed in a pantry. The flavor is brighter and cleaner, and they stay moister. This makes perfect sense when you consider that many cookies have lots of butter, nuts, and dried fruits that can taste stale if left standing at room temperature for long. Most cookies freeze well (when packed airtight) for up to 2½ months.

When readying cookies for the freezer, follow these rules: Always let the cookies cool completely first. Pack each kind in a separate airtight container (otherwise the mild cookies will pick up the flavors of the spicy ones, and crispy cookies will pick up moisture from the soft ones). Label and date the containers so you know what's what. When thawing, loosen the lid or open the bag slightly so that condensation doesn't form as the cookies warm up.

Q. Got any tips for mailing cookies?

A. Sturdy, not-too-thin cookies are the best candidates for shipping; those at least ¼ to ⅜ inch thick generally hold up well without special packaging. Skip all varieties that are crumbly, very tender, brittle, or that have sticky fillings or toppings. For rolled cookies, chose compact forms like bells, balls, ovals, and only plump rounded people or animal shapes. (I once shipped an assortment with some very pointy stars, elves with peaked caps, and deer with antlers. Nearly every one of these had the pointy pieces broken off!)

Plastic boxes and metal tins both make fine storage containers. To keep the individual varieties separated, put them in cellophane or plastic bags first. A friend of mine also has great success packing her round wafers in recycled Pringles cans, though the look is strictly utilitarian.

Pack your cookie containers in larger boxes padded with Styrofoam bits, plastic bubbles, popcorn, or other airy filler to protect against bumps and thumps. If your cookies have far to go, consider shipping via air for freshest taste and minimum breakage.

Q. My cookies came out dry and crumbly. What did I do wrong?

A. Some very appealing tender or fragile cookies are on the crumbly side, but a dry-as-dust texture is usually the result of mishandling. Overbaking is the most common problem, which is a good reason to use a timer set to several minutes less than the recipe calls for. You can then bake longer, if necessary. Remember, too, that baking continues a minute or two after cookies are removed from the oven.

Another cause of crumbly texture is adding in extra flour or overly dry dried fruit. See page 16 for more information on this subject. And be sure you're actually measuring out the dry ingredients correctly. Flour should not be packed down during measuring; see page 20 for details.

EXTRA-EASY COOKIES }

This chapter serves up a nice variety of easy bake-from-scratch recipes that go together quickly and feature fairly short or short ingredient lists. It's a handy place to start when your time or expertise is limited, but you're hungry for strictly homemade goodies and top-notch taste. You'll find everything from homey drops to assorted hand-shaped cookies, and even some savory two- or three-ingredient savory Herbed Parmesan Wafers.

Some recipes simultaneously trim prep time *and* boost taste by taking advantage of certain ready-to-use products. For example, in the Nutellos, Nutella spread makes it possible to deliver rich chocolate-hazelnut appeal without melting any chocolate or toasting and grinding any nuts. In the Five-Spice Snaps, commercial five-spice powder lends complex, gratifyingly spicy taste and aroma but requires measuring out only one premixed spice blend.

Other cookies, like the One-Bowl Brown Sugar Drops and One-Pot Honey-Oatmeal Drop Cookies, minimize muss and fuss by relying on streamlined mixing and simple drop shaping. The Iced Little Lemon Drops trim time with a clever two-birds-with-one-stone technique: The beaten butter-sugar-lemon mixture is divided and does double-duty in both the dough and the icing.

Keep in mind that this chapter isn't the only place to look for extra-easy recipes: You'll find them throughout the book, especially in the No-Bake, Semi-Homemade, and Drop Cookies chapters.

1 cup (2 sticks) unsalted butter, slightly softened and cut into chunks

½ cup granulated sugar, plus ¼ cup for garnish

1 large egg, at room temperature

2 teaspoons vanilla extract

½ teaspoon salt

2 cups plus 2 tablespoons unbleached all-purpose white flour, plus more if needed

Tip

To ensure that the cookies bake evenly, be sure to press the balls into rounds that are evenly thick.

SWEET & SIMPLE SUGAR COOKIES

Sweet and simple sums it up nicely: These are sweet enough that children will love them, yet not so sugary that grown-ups will cringe! They are also wonderfully buttery and crisp to the point you can actually hear a little crunch with every bite. They are also good keepers.

While these are splendid on their own, they are excellent paired up and used to create ice cream, buttercream, jam, or even Nutella sandwiches. If preparing the sandwiches, you may want to make the cookies a bit smaller than what's called for—unless you like supersized servings.

Baking Preliminaries: Position a rack in the middle of the oven; preheat to 350°F. Grease several large baking sheets or coat with nonstick spray.

In a large bowl, vigorously beat together the butter and ½ cup sugar until well blended and smooth. Add the egg, vanilla, and salt to the bowl; beat for 2 minutes or until the mixture is lightened in color and texture. Scrape down the sides as needed. Beat or stir in the flour just until evenly incorporated. Let stand to firm up for 5 minutes if too soft to shape. If the dough is still soft, work in up to 1½ tablespoons more flour.

With well-greased hands, pull off dough portions and shape into scant 1-inch balls. (Alternatively, scoop up balls of dough using a 1¼-inch-diameter spring-loaded scoop.) Space them about 2½ inches apart on the baking sheets. Grease the bottom of a large flat-bottomed glass and dip it into the ¼ cup sugar. Press down on a ball to flatten it into a scant 2¼-to 2½-inch, evenly thick round. Repeat, dipping the glass in the sugar, then flattening the balls. As needed, wipe excess sugar from the glass and re-grease the surface.

Bake (middle rack) one sheet at a time for 8 to 12 minutes or until the cookies are lightly tinged at the edges. Transfer the baking sheets to wire racks; let stand until the cookies firm up slightly, about 4 minutes. Using a wide spatula, transfer the cookies to the wire racks. Let cool.

Yield: Makes about forty 2⅔-inch cookies

Storage: Store these, airtight, for up to 1 week. They can be frozen, airtight, for up to 1 month.

CHOCK-FULL-OF-CHIPS TOLL HOUSE–STYLE DROP COOKIES

You'll be hard pressed to find an easier traditional-style chocolate chip cookie recipe anywhere—and certainly not one yielding cookies this good! These are buttery, pleasingly brown sugary, noticeably crispy, and, as the name suggests, just loaded with chocolate morsels. (If for some reason you don't care for cookies chock-a-block with chips, feel free to cut back.)

For a gentle brown sugar taste, use light brown sugar; for a fuller, deeper flavor, darker dough color, and slightly more compact texture, go with the dark brown.

1 cup (2 sticks) unsalted butter, cut into chunks

¾ cup plus 2 tablespoons packed light or dark brown sugar

1 large egg, at room temperature

2 teaspoons vanilla extract

½ teaspoon salt

2 cups plus 1 tablespoon unbleached all-purpose white flour, plus more if needed

1½ to 2 cups (up to one 10-to 11-ounce bag) semisweet or bittersweet chocolate morsels

Baking Preliminaries: Position a rack in the middle of the oven; preheat to 350°F. Grease several large baking sheets, or coat with nonstick spray, or line with baking parchment.

In a large microwave-safe bowl with the microwave on medium power, heat the butter just until softened, but not melted or runny, stopping and stirring every 20 seconds. (Alternatively, warm the butter over medium heat in a medium saucepan, stirring, until softened but not melted or runny. Remove from the heat.) Continue stirring until completely creamy-smooth and cooled to warm.

Vigorously stir the brown sugar into the butter until well blended, mashing out any sugar lumps with the back of the spoon. Vigorously stir in the egg, vanilla, and salt until the mixture is well blended. Stir in the 2 cups plus 1 tablespoon flour and morsels just until evenly incorporated. If the dough is very soft, stir in 1 more tablespoon flour.

Drop the dough by heaping 1-tablespoon measuring spoons, spacing about 2½ inches apart on the baking sheets. (Alternatively, scoop up the dough with a 1½-inch-diameter spring-loaded scoop.) With greased fingertips, pat down the tops to even the mounds slightly.

Bake (middle rack) one sheet at a time for 8 to 12 minutes or until the cookies are barely tinged all over and slightly darker at the edges. Rotate the pans from front to back about halfway through if needed for even browning.

Transfer the baking sheets to wire racks. Let stand until the cookies firm up slightly, about 3 minutes. Using a wide spatula, transfer the cookies to cooling racks. Let cool completely before packing airtight.

Yield: Makes thirty to thirty-five 2¾- to 3-inch cookies

Storage: Store these, airtight, for up to 1 week. They can be frozen, airtight, for up to 1 month.

Cookie Jar Wisdom
True sacrifice is offering someone else the last chocolate chip cookie in the jar.

1 cup (2 sticks) cold unsalted
    butter, cut into chunks
1⅓ cups smooth or chunky peanut
    butter
1⅓ cups packed light brown sugar
¾ teaspoon baking soda
⅛ teaspoon salt
2 large eggs, at room temperature
2 cups quick-cooking (not instant)
    oats
2 cups unbleached all-purpose
    white flour
    1½ to 2 cups (up to one 10- to
    11-ounce bag) semisweet or
    milk chocolate morsels

PEANUT BUTTER–OATMEAL CHIPSTERS

Peanut butter, oats, and chocolate chips—I probably don't need to say much more! These are unfussy and rustic looking, full of peanut and oat flavor and, due to the ample addition of *milk* chocolate morsels, a little mellower than some chocolate chip cookies. Children seem especially fond of these.

If you are interested in slipping more whole wheat flour into your baking, see the variation at the end of the recipe.

Baking Preliminaries: Place a rack in the middle of the oven; preheat to 350°F. Line several large baking sheets with baking parchment.

In a large microwave-safe bowl, melt the butter on 50 percent power, stopping and stirring every 30 seconds until mostly melted and runny. (Alternatively, in a large heavy saucepan over medium heat, melt the butter until mostly melted and runny, stirring. Remove from the heat.) Stir the butter until fully melted. Vigorously stir in the peanut butter, brown sugar, baking soda, and salt until evenly incorporated and free of lumps. Let cool until warm to the touch.

Vigorously stir in the eggs, then the oats; let stand for 5 minutes so the oats can hydrate. Thoroughly stir in the flour and morsels. If the dough is soft, refrigerate it for 10 to 15 minutes, until firmed up slightly. Using a 2-inch-diameter spring-loaded scoop or heaping soupspoon, drop the dough into 2-inch mounds, spacing about 2½ inches apart. Using a lightly greased table fork, press down on the cookies to form a crisscross pattern in the tops.

Bake (middle rack) one sheet at a time for 11 to 14 minutes or until the cookies are lightly tinged with brown all over and barely firm when pressed in the center top. Transfer the baking sheets to wire racks. Let stand to firm up for about 3 minutes. Using a wide spatula, transfer the cookies to the wire racks. Cool completely. Cool the baking sheets between batches to prevent the cookies from spreading too much.

Yield: Makes thirty to thirty-five 2¾- to 3-inch cookies

Storage: Store these, airtight, for up to 1 week. They can be frozen, airtight, for 3 to 4 weeks.

Variation: Whole Wheat–Peanut Butter–Oatmeal Chipsters Replace 1 cup of the white flour with 1 cup of white whole wheat flour or regular whole wheat flour. Add 1 teaspoon vanilla extract when the eggs are added.

Extra Easy
Quick one-bowl,
one-spoon mixing.
Easy drop or scoop shaping.

14 tablespoons (2 sticks minus
    2 tablespoons) cold unsalted
    butter, cut into chunks
1 cup packed brown sugar, dark
    preferred
1 large egg, at room temperature
2½ teaspoons vanilla extract
½ teaspoon salt
¼ teaspoon baking soda
2 cups unbleached all-purpose
    white flour
1 cup butterscotch or peanut
    butter morsels, or a
    combination

ONE-BOWL BROWN SUGAR DROPS

Brown sugar is one of those flavors that almost everybody likes, but especially kids. Here it's accented with either butterscotch or peanut butter morsels—or if you can't decide between the two, use half of each.

The dough gets quickly mixed together in one bowl and is simply dropped from a spoon or scoop. The recipe is a good one for beginning bakers: My seven- and eight-year-old grandchildren made these with just a little assistance from me and were thrilled with the results.

Baking Preliminaries: Position a rack in the middle of the oven; preheat to 350°F. Grease several baking sheets or coat with nonstick spray.

In a large microwave-safe bowl with the microwave on 50 percent power, heat the butter just until softened but not melted or runny, stopping and stirring every 30 seconds. (Alternatively, warm the butter over medium heat in a medium saucepan, stirring, until softened but not melted or runny. Remove from the heat.) Continue stirring until the butter is completely creamy-smooth and cooled to warm.

Vigorously stir the brown sugar into the butter until well blended, mashing out any sugar lumps with the back of the spoon. Stir in the egg, vanilla, salt, and baking soda until thoroughly incorporated. Stir in the flour and morsels just until evenly incorporated. Drop the dough with a 1½-inch-diameter spring-loaded scoop or by heaping measuring tablespoonfuls, spacing about 2 inches apart.

Bake (middle rack) one sheet at a time for 8 to 12 minutes or until the cookies are barely tinged and almost firm when pressed in the middle; be careful not to overbake. Transfer the baking sheets to wire racks, and let stand until the cookies firm up just slightly, about 2 minutes. Using a wide spatula, transfer them to the wire racks. Let cool completely.

Yield: Makes about thirty 2½-inch cookies

Storage: Store these, airtight, for up to 1 week. They can be frozen, airtight, for 3 to 4 weeks.

Extra Easy
One-pot mixing.
Easy drop or scoop shaping.

1½ cups (3 sticks) unsalted butter, cut into chunks

1⅔ cups packed dark or light brown sugar

⅓ cup clover honey or other mild honey

¼ teaspoon regular table salt or ¾ teaspoon coarse crystal salt, divided

4 cups old-fashioned rolled oats

1½ teaspoons baking powder

1¾ cups unbleached all-purpose white flour

ONE-POT HONEY-OATMEAL DROP COOKIES (WITH OR WITHOUT COARSE SALT)

These are mild and homey. They are also chewy and mellow, with the taste of butter, brown sugar, and honey coming through clearly. They make a great snack for anybody, anytime. You can prepare them even when you're out of eggs. And you need only one pot for mixing and a spoon for stirring.

Note that this recipe gives you the option of topping the cookies with coarse crystal salt, a contemporary touch that balances the slight sweetness of the honey nicely. However, if you're a traditionalist or simply find a salt garnish distracting, feel free to leave it out.

Baking Preliminaries: Position a rack in the middle of the oven; preheat to 325°F. Generously grease several large baking sheets or coat with nonstick spray.

In a very large saucepan or pot, melt the butter until fluid over medium heat, stirring. Remove from the heat. Stir the sugar, honey, and salt into the butter; if using regular table salt, add it all, if using coarse crystal salt, add ⅛ teaspoon and reserve the remainder for garnishing the cookies. Continue stirring the mixture, mashing out any lumps of sugar until completely smooth. Thoroughly stir in the oats and baking powder. Let the dough stand until cooled slightly.

Stir the flour into the dough until evenly incorporated. Let it stand to firm up for 5 to 10 minutes. Using soupspoons or a 1½-inch-diameter ice cream scoop, scoop up the dough and drop in even 1½-inch mounds, spacing 2 inches apart. Pat down the mounds into 2-inch rounds. If garnishing with coarse salt, add a few crystals to the cookie tops.

Bake (middle rack) one sheet at a time for 10 to 13 minutes or until the cookies are brown at the edges and lightly tinged on top; watch carefully, as they may brown very rapidly at the end. Transfer the baking sheets to wire racks. Let the cookies firm up for about 2 minutes. Using a wide spatula, transfer the cookies to the wire racks. Let cool completely.

Yield: Makes forty to forty-five 2½- to 3-inch cookies

Storage: Store these, airtight, for up to 1 week. They can be frozen, airtight, for up to 1 month.

Extra Easy
One-pot mixing.
Easy drop or scoop shaping.

¾ cup (1½ sticks) unsalted butter,
   cut into chunks
2 cups old-fashioned rolled oats
   Scant 1½ cups packed light or
   dark brown sugar
½ teaspoon baking soda
¼ teaspoon ground cinnamon
⅛ teaspoon salt
1 large egg, at room temperature
1 cup dark, seedless raisins, rinsed,
   drained, and patted dry on
   paper towels, optional
1¼ cups unbleached all-purpose
   white flour, plus more if
   needed

OLD-FASHIONED FARMHOUSE OATMEAL COOKIES

When I was a child, my cousin who lived next door and I usually rode our horses after school. But when the weather was too rainy or cold to go out, we often made cookies instead.

Oatmeal cookies much like these were usually our choice, partly because all the very simple ingredients were staples in our families' country kitchens, and partly because the recipe was easy enough for us to make without adult supervision. The finished cookies were mild and comforting, crunchy-crisp, and generous in size. They were also attractive enough that we could feel proud of our handiwork.

The original recipe somehow got lost over the years, and I missed the cookies so much that I eventually had to re-create them. These are as good (well, almost!) as the ones I remember.

Baking Preliminaries: Position a rack in the middle of the oven; preheat to 350°F. Grease several baking sheets or coat with nonstick spray.

In a large heavy saucepan over medium heat, melt the butter, stirring, until completely melted and runny. Remove from the heat. (Alternatively, in a large microwave-safe bowl, microwave the butter on 50 percent power, stopping and stirring every 25 seconds, just until melted and runny.)

Thoroughly stir the oats and 1 tablespoon water into the butter. Let stand for 5 minutes so the oats can hydrate. Vigorously stir in the sugar, baking soda, cinnamon, and salt until thoroughly incorporated. Vigorously stir in the egg, and raisins (if using), then the flour until very well blended. If the dough is very soft, stir in 1 to 2 tablespoons more flour. If it is still soft, let stand to firm up for 5 minutes.

Using a 1½-inch-diameter spring-loaded scoop or heaping measuring tablespoon form the dough into uniform mounds, spacing 2½ inches apart on the baking sheets to allow for spreading. Using your fingertips, pat down the mounds just slightly.

Bake (middle rack) one sheet at a time for 7 to 10 minutes or until barely firm in the center tops, tinged with brown, and slightly darker at the edges. Transfer the baking sheets to wire racks. Let the cookies stand on the pans to firm up for 3 minutes, then transfer them to the wire racks using a spatula. Cool completely before packing for storage.

Yield: Makes thirty 2¾-inch plain cookies, about 35 with raisins

Storage: Store these, airtight, for up to 1 week. They can be frozen, airtight, for up to 1 month.

HERBED PARMESAN WAFERS

If you've not come upon a Parmesan wafer recipe before, you may find it hard to believe that something so simple could be so tasty! On the other hand, if you like Parmesan cheese, you will quickly realize that there is nothing *not* to like in these brittle-crisp and savory wafers.

They are also attractive, with a see-through, bubbled look and thinness reminiscent of old-fashioned lace cookies. (Fortunately, they are a little less fragile and much easier to make than lace cookies!)

Serve these along with a soup (they're especially good with tomato soup) or a salad or as a before-dinner nibble. Note that they are completely gluten-free.

The only key to success with these is to use fresh, good-quality Parmesan cheese. The black pepper is optional; add it amply, sparingly, or not at all depending on whether you want the crackers to have a little kick of heat.

The recipe may be doubled, if desired.

1⅓ cups freshly shredded Parmesan cheese
1 teaspoon finely chopped fresh chives or 1 teaspoon dried chives or basil leaves
Freshly and coarsely ground black pepper, optional

Baking Preliminaries: Position a rack in the upper third of the oven; preheat to 375°F. Line two large baking sheets with nonstick foil or with foil sprayed with nonstick spray.

In a medium bowl, stir together the cheese and herbs. Using a 1-tablespoon measuring spoon filled about two-thirds full, scoop up the mixture and place in 2- to 2½-inch mounds about 2 inches apart on the sheets. Pat or spread out the shreds so they are evenly spaced and spread out into rounds. Grind black pepper over the tops, if desired.

Bake (upper rack) one pan at a time for 6 to 9 minutes; reverse the pan from front to back about halfway through, continuing until the wafers are bubbly and just slightly golden colored. Remove from the oven and let firm up for about 2 minutes. Using a wide spatula, transfer the crisps to paper towels and let stand until thoroughly cooled.

Yield: Makes about twenty-five 2½- to 3-inch wafers

Storage: Store these, airtight and refrigerated, for 3 to 4 days; let return to room temperature before serving. They can be frozen, airtight, for up to 1 month.

1 cup Nutella chocolate-hazelnut spread, at room temperature
5 tablespoons unsalted butter, slightly softened and cut into chunks
3 tablespoons unsweetened natural (non-alkalized) cocoa powder or Dutch-process cocoa powder
1 teaspoon baking powder
1⅓ cups unbleached all-purpose white flour
About ⅓ cup clear crystal sugar, turbinado sugar, or other coarse granulated sugar for garnish

Tip
Note that no eggs are needed for these cookies. And the only sugar required is used as a garnish.

NUTELLOS THREE WAYS (CHOCOLATE-HAZELNUT COOKIES)

You probably already guessed—this recipe features Nutella. (In case you haven't heard of it, it's a smooth chocolate-hazelnut spread often stocked in supermarkets near the peanut butter or other nut spreads.) This European ingredient serves as a handy time-saver, lending full-bodied hazelnut flavor while obviating the task of toasting, hulling, and grinding any nuts. Instead, you just measure out and stir a cup of the spread right into the dough.

As the title and photo indicate, you can readily create three different cookies with this recipe—simple rounds, sandwiches, and thumbprints.

Baking Preliminaries: Position a rack in the middle of the oven; preheat to 325°F. Set out two large baking sheets.

In a large bowl, with a mixer on medium speed, beat the Nutella, butter, cocoa powder, baking powder, and 3 tablespoons water until well blended. On low speed, beat in about half the flour. Beat or stir in the remaining flour just until smoothly incorporated. If the dough is too dry and crumbly to hold together, beat or stir in a little more water.
Pull off scant 1-inch dough portions and shape into balls. Roll them in a saucer of the crystal sugar until coated. Space them about 2 inches apart on the sheets. Press down into 2-inch evenly thick rounds with a palm.

Bake (middle rack) one pan at a time for 12 to 16 minutes or until the cookies are barely firm when pressed in the center top.

Transfer the pan to a wire rack. Let the cookies stand until cooled completely. For sandwiches, spread nutella between cookie pairs.

Yield: Makes thirty-five to forty 2¼-inch cookies

Storage: Store these, airtight and packed in a single layer, at room temperature for up to 1 week. They can be frozen, airtight, for up to 2 months; thaw completely before serving.

Variation: Nutellos Raspberry Thumbprint Cookies Make the dough, then shape into balls and roll in sugar as directed. Press a deep indentation into the center top of each ball with your thumb or knuckle. Put ½ teaspoon seedless raspberry jam or preserves in each cookie. (Don't use jelly, which tends to run.) Bake as directed, except increase the baking time by 1 to 2 minutes. Let the cookies cool until the filling sets, at least 1 hour, before packing for storage.

Extra Easy
One-bowl, one-spoon mixing.
Short ingredient list.

1½ to 2 cups (up to one 10- to
   11-ounce bag) semisweet
   chocolate morsels, divided
1 14-ounce can sweetened
   condensed milk, at room
   temperature
2 teaspoons vanilla extract
1 large egg, at room temperature
1⅓ cups unbleached all-purpose
   white flour, plus more if
   needed

Tip
Be sure to use sweetened condensed
milk and not evaporated milk in the
recipe. Evaporated milk is not sweet
or thick enough and will not work!

SUPER-FAST FUDGIES

This recipe is particularly handy when you're in a hurry or you want to bake some cookies but have no butter or sugar on hand. It's also a good starter recipe for children or grown-up beginning bakers. As the name suggests, fudgies are moist, rich, and fudge-like.

You can tweak this recipe for slightly more sophisticated palates; see the variation at the end of the recipe.

Baking Preliminaries: Position a rack in the middle of the oven; preheat to 350°F. Line several baking sheets with baking parchment or coat heavily with nonstick spray.

In a large microwave-safe bowl, microwave a generous ¾ cup chocolate morsels on 100 percent power for 45 seconds. Stir well, then microwave on 50 percent power, stopping and stirring every 20 seconds, until the chocolate melts completely. (Alternatively, in a large heavy saucepan warm ¾ cup morsels over lowest heat, stirring constantly, until they mostly melt. Immediately remove from the burner and stir until completely melted.)

Vigorously stir the condensed milk and vanilla into the chocolate. Let cool till warm, then vigorously stir in the egg until evenly blended. Stir in the flour and the remaining morsels just until evenly incorporated. If the dough is very soft, stir in 1 tablespoon more flour and let stand for several minutes to firm up slightly; don't worry if it still seems soft. Drop the dough by heaping measuring tablespoonfuls, spacing about 2 inches apart on the baking sheets.

Bake (middle rack) one pan at a time for 6 to 8 minutes or until barely firm when pressed in the center top; be careful not to overbake. Let the cookies cool and firm up for 5 minutes before transferring them to racks; they are too tender to move when hot. Using a spatula, transfer the cookies to racks; let stand until completely cooled.

Yield: Makes about thirty-five 2½-inch cookies

Storage: Store these, covered and in a cool place, for 3 to 4 days. They can be frozen, airtight, for up to 1 month.

Variation: Orange-Pecan Fudgies Add 1 teaspoon finely grated orange zest and ½ cup chopped pecans when adding the vanilla.

FLOURLESS PEANUT BUTTER COOKIES

Flourless peanut butter cookie recipes have been circulating around for a number of years, and they are especially popular now that more and more folks are going gluten-free. I've found many versions too sweet, so I have reduced the amount of sugar in this recipe. The original cookies also seemed a little plain, so I've jazzed these up with chocolate morsels or chopped peanuts. As you might guess, they are rich, dense, and very peanut buttery. Since they lack gluten, they are also on the tender, crumbly side, so they need to be stored flat in a single layer and handled gently.

In a large bowl, using a fork, lightly beat the eggs. Vigorously stir in the brown sugar until the mixture is well blended and lump-free; press out any lumps with the back of a spoon. Vigorously stir in the peanut butter and chocolate morsels (if using) until smoothly incorporated. Refrigerate, covered, for 30 to 40 minutes to firm up slightly.

2 large eggs, at room temperature
1⅓ cups packed light brown sugar
2 cups smooth or chunky peanut
  butter
1 cup (one 6-ounce package)
  semisweet chocolate morsels,
  optional
½ cup chopped salted peanuts for
  garnish, optional

Baking Preliminaries: Position a rack in the middle of the oven; preheat to 350°F. Line several large baking sheets with baking parchment. With greased hands, divide the dough in quarters, then divide each quarter into 8 equal balls. If the peanut garnish is being used, put the peanuts in a small bowl and lightly press the tops of the balls into the peanuts. Space the balls about 2½ inches apart on the baking sheets, nut side up if peanuts were used. Making a crisscross with a greased table fork, press the balls into 2-inch rounds.

Bake (middle rack) one sheet at a time for 10 to 13 minutes, just until the cookies are beginning to feel firm when pressed in the center; be very careful not to overbake. Transfer to a wire rack; let stand until cooled completely.

Yield: Makes thirty-two 2¾-inch cookies

Storage: Store these in an airtight container packed flat with wax paper between the layers, at room temperature for up to 1 week. They can be frozen, airtight, for up to 1½ months; let come to room temperature before serving.

½ cup packed dark brown sugar
2½ to 3 teaspoons five-spice
   powder, to taste
¼ teaspoon baking soda
¼ teaspoon salt
½ cup dark corn syrup
1 large egg, at room temperature
2½ tablespoons corn oil or other
   flavorless vegetable oil
1 cup unbleached all-purpose
   white flour

Tip

The snaps need to be lifted off the baking sheets with a very thin-bladed spatula as soon as they are cool and firm enough not to tear—just 30 to 40 seconds. Once they cool, they'll stick to the pan and turn brittle, but you can remedy this by returning them to the oven for a couple of minutes to warm up again.

FIVE-SPICE SNAPS

These large fragrant snaps are an interesting change of pace from classic gingersnaps because Asian five-spice powder and corn syrup stand in for the usual ginger and molasses. The cookies not only snap when you bite into them, but—dare I say it—are also a snap to make! They are also light, aromatic, and nearly fat-free.

As the name suggests, five-spice powder contains a mix of five spices, usually star anise, cinnamon, cloves, fennel seeds, and Sichuan pepper. The flavor varies a bit from brand to brand, but it usually produces a slightly exotic but tempting gingersnap taste. Depending on the pungency of the spice mixture you have on hand, you can adjust the amount added.

Baking Preliminaries: Position a rack in the middle of the oven; preheat to 350°F. Generously grease several large baking sheets or generously coat with nonstick spray.

In a large bowl, thoroughly stir together the brown sugar, five-spice powder, baking soda, and salt until well blended. Vigorously stir in the corn syrup, egg, and oil until the mixture is well blended and smooth. Stir in the flour just until evenly incorporated. If the mixture is very soft, let it stand to firm up for 5 minutes. Drop the dough by heaping measuring teaspoonfuls, spacing about 3 inches apart on the baking sheets to allow for a lot of spreading.

Bake (middle rack) one sheet at a time for 8 to 12 minutes or until the cookies feel almost firm when pressed in the middle, and are tinged with brown and slightly darker at the edges. Set the baking sheet on a wire rack, and let stand until the cookies firm up just slightly, about 1 minute. Using a wide spatula, immediately transfer the cookies to wire racks. Let cool.

Yield: Makes thirty-five to forty 3-inch snaps

Storage: Store these, airtight, for up to 1 week. They can be frozen, airtight, for 3 to 4 weeks.

10 tablespoons (1¼ sticks) unsalted butter, softened and cut into chunks
1 7- to 8-ounce package or can almond paste, cut or spooned into chunks
5 tablespoons granulated sugar
¼ teaspoon salt
1 large egg, at room temperature
1 cup chopped blanched slivered almonds, divided
1¼ cups unbleached all-purpose white flour

Cookie Jar Wisdom
Surveys say 100 out of every 90 people prefer homemade cookies.

ALMOND WAFERS (OR ALMOND JAMPRINTS)

Light and simple yet full of almond flavor, these slightly chewy rounds are great when you're looking for a not-too-sweet, understated cookie to go with tea, or perhaps with a bowl of fruit or sorbet. They are a nice, slightly dressy change of pace from traditional sugar cookies, and can be turned into jamprints if desired. (See the variation below.)

Baking Preliminaries: Position a rack in the middle of the oven; preheat to 350°F. Line two large baking sheets with baking parchment or spray with nonstick spray.

In a large bowl, with a mixer on medium speed, beat the butter, almond paste, sugar, and salt until well blended and smooth. Beat in the egg until thoroughly incorporated. On low speed, beat in about two-thirds of the almonds and half the flour, just until the mixture comes together. Beat or stir in the last of the flour just until evenly incorporated.

Pull off scant 1-inch portions of dough and shape into balls. Put the remaining almonds in a shallow bowl. Dip the tops of each ball into the nuts, then space them, nut side up, about 2½ inches apart on the baking sheets. With a greased palm, press the balls into 2½-inch-diameter rounds.

Bake (middle rack) for 11 to 15 minutes, until the wafers are lightly tinged all over and slightly darker at the edges. Transfer the pan to a wire rack. Let stand until cooled completely before packing the wafers airtight.

Yield: Makes thirty to thirty-five 2¾-inch wafers

Storage: Store these, airtight at room temperature, for up to 1 week. Or freeze, airtight, for up to 2 months; thaw completely before serving.

Variation: Almond Jamprints Prepare the dough exactly as directed. Once the nut-coated balls are placed on the baking sheets, press a well into the center of each ball using a thumb or knuckle. Put about ½ teaspoon apricot, cherry, or peach jam into each well; don't overfill the wells. Bake at 350°F for 14 to 18 minutes, or until tinged with brown at the edges.

1 cup (2 sticks) unsalted butter, cool but slightly softened and cut into chunks

1 cup vanilla powdered sugar (page 327) or regular powdered sugar, divided

2 teaspoons vanilla extract
Generous ⅛ teaspoon salt

2 cups plus 1 tablespoon unbleached all-purpose white flour, plus more if needed

Tip

If you have vanilla powdered sugar on hand, do use it instead of plain powdered sugar for an even more sublime flavor and aroma with no extra work. I always keep a jar around, and this is a favorite way to use it.

VANILLA BUTTER BALLS

These delectable powdered sugar–dusted treats are reminiscent of Mexican wedding cookies, but without the nuts. They have an amazingly tender, melt-in-the-mouth texture and a mild yet delightful butter-vanilla flavor. The recipe is convincing evidence that simple ingredients handled simply can be superb.

Baking Preliminaries: Position a rack in the middle of the oven; preheat to 350°F. Line two large baking sheets with baking parchment.

In a large bowl, with a mixer on low, then medium, speed, beat the butter, ½ cup powdered sugar, vanilla, and salt until well blended and smooth. On low speed, beat in 1 cup plus 1 tablespoon flour just until the mixture begins to mass. Knead in the remaining 1 cup flour by hand. If the dough seems too soft or greasy, work in up to 1 tablespoon extra flour; if slightly dry and crumbly, work in a teaspoon or two of water.

Pull off scant 1-inch portions and shape into balls. Space about 2 inches apart on the baking sheets.

Bake (middle rack) one sheet at a time for 12 to 16 minutes, until the cookies are just lightly tinged at the edges.

Transfer the pan to a wire rack. Let the cookies stand until cooled; they are too tender to handle while warm. Put the remaining ½ cup powdered sugar in a bowl and, working with three or four cookies at a time, roll them in the sugar until coated all over.

Yield: Makes thirty to thirty-five 2-inch balls

Storage: Store these, covered and at room temperature, for up to 1 week. They can be frozen, airtight, for 2 months; thaw completely before serving.

5 tablespoons unsalted butter,
   softened and cut into chunks
¼ cup corn oil or other flavorless
   vegetable oil
   Generous 1 cup powdered
   sugar, divided
¼ teaspoon baking soda
   Generous ¼ cup freeze-dried
   strawberry powder or
   raspberry powder (page 336),
   divided
1⅓ cups unbleached all-purpose
   white flour

VERY STRAWBERRY (OR VERY RASPBERRY) SUGAR DUSTIES

If you can imagine the popular buttery, powdered sugar–dusted butter cookies flavored inside and out with pure, natural strawberry or raspberry powder, you'll have a good idea of these dainty, tender-crisp little cookies. The powder, which can either be bought online or quickly prepared from freeze-dried berries using the recipe on page 336, gives them a distinctive, intense fruitiness. It also lends a bit of natural berry color and aroma to the powdered sugar coating. Folks who have never eaten cookies prepared with freeze-dried berry powder are usually enthralled by these.

Baking Preliminaries: Position a rack in the middle of the oven; preheat to 350°F. Line two large baking sheets with baking parchment.

In a large bowl, with a mixer on low, then medium, speed, beat the butter, oil, ⅔ cup powdered sugar, baking soda, 3 tablespoons freeze-dried berry powder, and 2 tablespoons water until well blended and smooth. On low speed, beat in the flour just until evenly incorporated. If the mixture is dry and crumbly, gradually work in enough water for it to hold together without being wet.

Pull off dough portions and shape them into ¾-inch balls. Space about 1½ inches apart on the baking sheets.

Bake (middle rack) one pan at a time for 12 to 16 minutes or until the cookies are just lightly tinged with brown at the edges.

Transfer the pan to a wire rack. Let the cookies stand until cooled completely, as they are too tender to handle while warm. Stir together the remaining powdered sugar and remaining berry powder in a bowl and, working with three or four cookies at a time, gently stir them into the sugar until coated all over. If any sugar is left over, sift it over the cookie tops.

Yield: Makes about twenty-five 2-inch cookies

Storage: Store these, covered and at room temperature, for up to 1 week. They can be frozen, airtight, for 2 months; thaw completely before serving.

Very finely grated zest (yellow part of the peel) and juice of 2 medium-large lemons
¾ cup (1½ sticks) unsalted butter, softened and cut into chunks
2 cups powdered sugar, divided, plus more if needed
Generous ¼ teaspoon baking soda
1½ cups unbleached all-purpose white flour
Extra lemon zest for garnish, optional

Tip

Don't assume that because the amount of baking soda in the recipe is modest, you can leave it out or substitute baking powder. Baking soda neutralizes the acid in the lemon juice. This helps promote browning and also contributes to the light, crisp texture.

ICED LITTLE LEMON DROPS

I love these! It's always hard to beat the flavor, fragrance, and zing of fresh lemons, and in this streamlined five-ingredient recipe the ample amount of butter heightens their appeal even further. They are crisp and richly citrusy, with a puckery lemon-butter icing that's both gratifying and effortless.

To keep preparations simple, the icing uses some of the same butter, juice, and zest mixture that's beaten together for the dough. You just set some of it aside, then add powdered sugar and a little more lemon juice to make the topper.

Baking Preliminaries: Position a rack in the middle of the oven; preheat to 325°F. Line two large baking sheets with baking parchment.

Put the lemon zest in a large mixing bowl; reserve the juice separately in a cup. Add the butter, 3 tablespoons of the reserved lemon juice, and 1 cup powdered sugar to the mixing bowl. Beat on low, then medium, speed until lightened in color and fluffy, about 1½ minutes. Measure out 2 tablespoons of the beaten butter mixture and reserve in a small deep bowl; it will be used to make the icing.

On low speed, thoroughly beat the baking soda into the butter mixture left in the large bowl. Then beat in the flour just until evenly incorporated. If the dough is very soft, let it stand for 5 minutes.

Drop the dough by heaping measuring teaspoonfuls, spacing about 2 inches apart on the baking sheets; keep the cookies small.

Bake (middle rack) one pan at a time for 9 to 12 minutes, until the cookies are tinged with brown at the edges and just firm when pressed in the center top. Transfer the pan to a wire rack. Let the cookies stand until firmed up, about 3 minutes. Then transfer to racks. Let cool.

Stir 1½ tablespoons of the reserved lemon juice and the remaining 1 cup powdered sugar into the reserved 2 tablespoons butter mixture until very well blended. If necessary, thin the icing with more lemon juice or with water, stirring well, until it is fluid but not runny. Stir in a little more powdered sugar if the icing is too runny to hold some shape. Dip the cookie tops into the icing, shaking off the excess. For a thicker layer of icing, dip them twice. Garnish with a pinch of extra zest, if desired. Let the cookies stand until the icing sets, 30 to 40 minutes.

Yield: Makes about thirty 2½-inch iced cookies

Storage: Store these, airtight, in a single layer.

DROP COOKIES }

Drop cookies rightly have a reputation for being super easy to make because they're formed by simply dropping dough onto baking sheets. Since they look casual and rough-hewn, they tend to feature streamlined mixing and skip fussy garnishing, too. You'll find a large and varied collection in this chapter.

Hearty, homey recipes you can really sink your teeth into—like Ultimate One-Bowl Chocolate Chippers, Peanut Butterscotchies, and Carrot Drop Cookies with Cream Cheese Glaze—abound in this chapter. But you'll also find more sophisticated choices, like Bittersweet Chocolate Cracks. My Pink Peppercorn and Rose Water Macaroons are, obviously, out on the cookie edge!

Actually, many recipes in the chapter give you the option of scooping as well as dropping the cookies. With most doughs, shaping with a spring-release ice cream scoop is as easy as dropping with a spoon, but it lends a more uniform, rounded look. You'll notice that directions always specify using a 1¼-inch-, 1½-inch-, or a 2-inch-diameter scoop. While these sizes may sound similar, they aren't—the 1¼-inch scoop produces fairly small cookies, the 1½-inch scoop produces medium-size cookies, and the 2-inch, very large ones. If you bake

cookies a lot, consider investing in sturdy spring-loaded scoops in these sizes.

When recipes call for spoons for dropping, directions always indicate exactly what sort of spoon to use—a measuring teaspoon or tablespoon; or an ordinary tableware teaspoon; or, occasionally, a flatware soupspoon (which is typically slightly more ample than the tableware teaspoon). Instructions also detail whether the dough should be heaped (forming a high mound) or rounded (slightly mounded) or leveled. These details help ensure that your cookies are the size intended and will therefore bake in the time specified and make the number of cookies indicated. You can certainly make your cookies larger or smaller, if desired—just remember that the baking times and yields given in the recipe will no longer apply.

Just in case you're completely unfamiliar with the cookie-dropping process, let me answer a question an enthusiastic, earnest, and precise young baker once posed: How far should the cookies be dropped?! It's not really critical, but I find that holding the spoon or scoop 1½-to 2inches above the baking sheet works well.

Easy
One-bowl or one-pot mixing.
Dropped or scooped
shaping.

- 1 cup (2 sticks) unsalted butter, cut into chunks
- 2⅔ cups (16 ounces) semisweet chocolate morsels, divided
- 1 cup packed light or dark brown sugar
- ½ cup granulated sugar
- 2 large eggs, at room temperature
- 2½ teaspoons vanilla extract
- ¾ teaspoon instant espresso powder (or 1 teaspoon instant coffee granules) dissolved in 1 teaspoon hot water
- 1 teaspoon baking powder
- ½ teaspoon baking soda
- ¾ teaspoon salt
- 2¼ cups unbleached all-purpose white flour
- 1 cup chopped walnuts or pecans, optional

Tip
Cool the baking sheets between batches or the cookies may spread too much.

Tip
A little espresso or coffee powder is incorporated to add depth to the chocolate flavor but it doesn't stand out enough to warrant calling these mocha cookies.

ONE-BOWL BIG CHOCOLATE–CHOCOLATE CHIP COOKIES

These big, tender-chewy chocolate cookies take a pound of chocolate morsels—that's about 800 chips, in case you're counting! Most are used whole—folded in—but some are melted in to enrich the dough. The easy one-bowl mixing yields decidedly crispy-chewy cookies.

In a large microwave-safe bowl with the microwave on high power, melt the butter just until completely melted and runny, about 1 minute. (Alternatively, put the butter in a very large saucepan and melt it until runny, stirring, over medium heat. Remove the pan from the heat.)

Stir ⅔ cup chocolate morsels into the butter until completely melted. Vigorously stir in the brown and granulated sugars until well blended. When the mixture has cooled to warm, stir in the eggs, vanilla, espresso mixture, baking powder, baking soda, and salt until well blended and smooth. Stir in the flour, then nuts (if using) and remaining chocolate morsels just until evenly incorporated. If the dough is crumbly, gradually mix in a teaspoon or two of water until it holds together.

Cover and refrigerate about 15 minutes, until the dough is just slightly cooled.

Baking Preliminaries: Position a rack in the middle of the oven; preheat to 350°F. Grease several baking sheets or coat with nonstick spray. Using a 1½-inch diameter ice cream scoop or two soupspoons put 1½-inch mounds of dough about 3 inches apart on the baking sheets. With a greased palm, pat them down just slightly.

Bake (middle rack) one sheet at a time for 10 to 15 minutes or until the cookies feel almost firm when pressed in the middle. Transfer the baking sheet to a wire rack. Let the cookies firm up just slightly, about 2 minutes. Using a wide spatula, transfer the cookies to wire racks. Let stand until completely cooled.

Yield: Makes about thirty 3-inch cookies

Storage: Store these, airtight, for up to 1 week. They can be frozen, airtight, for 3 to 4 weeks; thaw before serving.

28 Andes mints (4.67-ounce package)
8   ounces bittersweet (not unsweetened) or semisweet chocolate, broken up or coarsely chopped
2   tablespoons unsalted butter, cut into chunks
$\frac{1}{3}$ cup granulated sugar
2   large eggs, at room temperature
$\frac{1}{4}$ teaspoon baking soda
$\frac{1}{8}$ teaspoon salt
$\frac{2}{3}$ cup unbleached all-purpose white flour

Tip

The recipe is designed to use one entire package of the mints, so don't let anyone snack while you're making these!

CHOCOLATE–ANDES MINT DROPS

Andes chocolate-mint candies are used both in the dough and on top of these novelty cookies, and they lend a very pronounced and unique mint flavor and eye-catching look. They will please chocolate-mint fans in general and will drive Andes mint fans, in particular, completely wild. They are dense, rich, and candy-like, so keep them on the small side.

Baking Preliminaries: Position a rack in the middle of the oven; preheat to 325°F. Line several large baking sheets with baking parchment.

Coarsely chop 20 mints; cut the 8 remaining mints crosswise into thirds and set aside separately for garnish.

In a medium microwave-safe bowl, melt the bittersweet chocolate (not the chopped mints) and butter in a microwave oven on 50 percent power, stopping and stirring at 30-second intervals, until the chocolate mostly melts. (Alternatively, in a medium heavy saucepan warm the chocolate and butter over lowest heat, stirring frequently, until mostly melted. Immediately remove from the burner, stirring.) Stir until completely melted. Thoroughly stir the chopped mints into the chocolate mixture.

In a large mixer bowl (using the whisk beater, if available) with the mixer on medium speed, beat together the sugar, eggs, baking soda, and salt until blended. Gradually raise speed to high; beat for 4 to 5 minutes, until the mixture is thick, foamy, and lightened. On low speed, beat in the flour, then the melted chocolate mixture. Let the dough stand to firm up for 10 minutes. Using teaspoons, drop the cookies into twenty-four 1-inch mounds, spacing about 2 inches apart on the baking sheets.

Bake (middle rack) for 7 to 9 minutes or until cookies feel just firm on the edges but still slightly soft in the middle. Top each cookie with a third of a mint; return to the oven for 1 minute to partially melt. Then immediately remove from the oven. Let sheets stand for 2 minutes so cookies can firm up, then transfer them to wire racks. Let cool thoroughly.

Yield: Makes twenty-four 2$\frac{1}{4}$-inch cookies

Storage: Store these, airtight, for up to 1 week. They can be frozen, airtight, for up to 1 month.

1 cup (2 sticks) unsalted butter,
    cut into chunks
1⅓ cups packed light brown sugar
2 large eggs, at room temperature
2 teaspoons vanilla extract
½ teaspoon baking soda
½ teaspoon salt
1½ cups white rice flour
½ cup brown rice flour
½ cup cornstarch
    1½ to 2 cups (up to one 10- to
    11-ounce bag) semisweet
    chocolate morsels

Tip
While vigorously stirring wheat flour
doughs tends to make them tough,
extra stirring helps keep rice flour
doughs from being crumbly. For
best texture do not omit the brown
rice flour and stir it in very vigorously.

GLUTEN-FREE CLASSIC-STYLE CHOCOLATE CHIP COOKIES

As a rule, I'm not overjoyed with gluten-free baked goods. While they are a boon to those, like my daughter-in-law, who must avoid gluten, they usually seem, um, "lacking" to folks used to ordinary wheat flour–based recipes. These, I'm pleased to say, are not your typical gluten-free cookies: Often, they even pass for "regular" cookies. The only noticeable differences are a slightly more crumbly texture and a tendency to dry out a bit as they stand. (Freezing them can't alleviate this problem.) The good news for our family is that when I bake these, everybody can dig in and enjoy them. The bad news is that my daughter-in-law has to battle to stash any away for herself.

Baking Preliminaries: Position a rack in the middle of the oven; preheat to 350°F. Grease several baking sheets or coat with nonstick spray; or line them with baking parchment.

In a large microwave-safe bowl with the microwave on 50 percent power, heat the butter until very soft but not melted or runny, stopping and stirring every 20 seconds. (Alternatively, warm the butter over medium heat in a medium saucepan, stirring, until softened but not melted or runny. Remove from the heat.) Continue stirring until completely creamy-smooth.

Vigorously stir in the sugar until well blended; mash out any lumps and stir until cooled to barely warm. Vigorously stir in the eggs, vanilla, baking soda, and salt until the mixture is well blended and smooth. Very vigorously stir in the white and brown rice flours, cornstarch, then the chocolate morsels until evenly incorporated. Let stand to firm up for about 5 minutes.

Using a 1½-inch diameter spring-loaded scoop, or heaping soupspoons, drop mounds of dough about 3 inches apart on the baking sheets. Bake (middle rack) one sheet at a time for 10 to 12 minutes or until the cookies are tinged with brown and feel almost firm when pressed in the middle. Let stand until firmed up just slightly, about 2 minutes. Using a wide spatula, transfer the cookies to wire racks. Cool completely. Cool the baking sheets between batches or the cookies may spread too much.

Yield: Makes thirty to thirty-five 3-inch cookies

Storage: Store these, airtight, for up to 1 week. They can be frozen, airtight, for 3 to 4 weeks.

1¼ cups chopped pecans

1¼ cups shredded or flaked
   sweetened coconut

½ cup unbleached all-purpose
   white flour

½ teaspoon baking powder

½ teaspoon salt

3 cups (about 18 ounces)
   semisweet chocolate morsels,
   divided

5½ tablespoons unsalted butter,
   cut into chunks

¼ cup smooth peanut butter

2 teaspoons vanilla extract

1 tablespoon instant espresso
   powder dissolved in
   1 tablespoon hot water

4 large eggs, at room temperature

¾ cup granulated sugar

1 9-ounce package peanut
   butter morsels, Reese's brand
   preferred

1 cup (about 6 ounces) good-
   quality white chocolate
   morsels

KITCHEN SINK CHOCOLATE-NUT TRIPLE CHIPSTERS

I admit it—these are rich, extravagant, everything-but-the-kitchen-sink cookies. Besides the three kinds of morsels delivering taste and texture, pecans, coconut, peanut butter, and espresso powder also contribute to the unique flavor. The cookies also have an irresistible succulence and chewiness. I believe you'll find these worth the calories, as well as the little extra effort required to assemble the ingredients and beat the batter.

Baking Preliminaries: Position a rack in the middle of the oven; preheat to 325°F. Line several large baking sheets with baking parchment.

Spread the pecans and coconut on a large rimmed baking sheet. Toast in the oven, stirring every 3 or 4 minutes, until the coconut begins to brown. Continue toasting, stirring every 2 minutes to redistribute the mixture, until nicely browned, 11 to 15 minutes total. Stir the flour, baking powder, and salt into the coconut-nut mixture; set aside until cooled. In a medium heavy saucepan over lowest heat, warm 1½ cups semisweet chocolate morsels and the butter, stirring constantly, until mostly melted. Immediately remove from the heat; stir until completely melted. Vigorously stir in the peanut butter, vanilla, and coffee mixture until smooth.

With a mixer on low, then medium, speed (using a whisk-shaped beater if available), beat together the eggs and sugar for about 2 minutes, until very foamy. Raise speed to high and beat for 4 to 6 minutes, until the mixture is lightened, thickened, and drops in ribbons from the beater. Reduce the mixer speed to low; slowly beat in the chocolate–peanut butter mixture until evenly incorporated. Stir in the coconut-flour mixture, the remaining semisweet chocolate and peanut butter morsels, and the white chocolate morsels until evenly mixed. Using a 2-inch-diameter ice cream scoop filled not quite full (or scant 2 tablespoons dough), form mounds, spacing about 2½ inches apart.

Bake (middle rack) one sheet at a time, rotating the pan from front to back halfway through, for 10 to 14 minutes or until the cookies are cracked and almost firm at the edges but still soft in the center; don't overbake. Slide the paper, cookies still attached, onto a wire rack. Let the cookies cool, then peel them from the paper.

Yield: Makes about thirty 3-inch cookies

Storage: Store these, airtight, for 3 days. They can be frozen, airtight, for 1 month.

Fairly Easy
Sophisticated taste, yet fairly
simple preparation.
Easy shaping—dropped from
a spoon.

12 ounces 60 to 70 percent cacao
    semisweet or bittersweet
    chocolate, divided
3   tablespoons unsalted butter
2   large eggs, at room temperature
½   cup plus 1 tablespoon
    granulated sugar
2   teaspoons vanilla extract
¼   teaspoon baking powder
⅛   teaspoon salt
1   tablespoon Grand Marnier,
    cognac, or cooled brewed
    coffee
¼   cup unbleached all-purpose
    white flour

Tip
This recipe calls for baking
parchment because it keeps the
cookies from sticking and scorching.
Don't try to bake them without it.

BITTERSWEET CHOCOLATE CRACKS

With 12 ounces of chocolate in about two dozen cookies, these dark, rich, almost gooey bittersweet rounds (named for their dramatic surface cracks) pack a powerful chocolate punch. I've seen numerous versions similar to this recipe circulating—it's no wonder they're popular!

The particular chocolate used is really the key to the character of these cookies, so pick whatever blend pleases you that falls within the 60 to 70 percent cacao range. Some choices in this range are on the bitter and bold side; some are enticingly spicy or fruity; some are surprisingly mellow and smooth—and they will all work. But don't use a brand with a higher cacao content than what's called for; the chocolate will be more prone to melting, which can cause cookies to flatten too much during baking.

Baking Preliminaries: Position a rack in the middle of the oven; preheat to 350°F. Line two large baking sheets with baking parchment.

Coarsely chop 7 ounces of chocolate. In a small heavy saucepan over lowest heat, stir together the chopped chocolate and the butter. Stirring constantly, warm until the chocolate is partly melted. Immediately remove from the heat. Stir occasionally until the chocolate completely melts and the mixture cools to warm.

With a mixer on low, then medium, speed (and using a whisk-shaped beater if available), beat together the eggs, sugar, vanilla, baking powder, and salt. Raise speed to high and beat for 8 to 12 minutes, until the mixture is as thick as sour cream, airy, and lightened in color. Reduce the mixer speed to low; slowly beat in the warm butter-chocolate mixture and Grand Marnier until evenly incorporated. Add the flour, beating just until evenly incorporated; scrape down the bowl as needed. Chop the remaining 5 ounces chocolate into chocolate morsel–size pieces, then stir them into the batter just until evenly distributed.

Drop the dough by rounded measuring tablespoonfuls, spacing 2 inches apart on the sheets.

Bake (middle rack) one sheet at a time, rotating the sheets from front to back halfway through, for 9 to 13 minutes or until almost firm when pressed on top; don't overbake. Slide the paper and cookies onto a wire rack. Let stand until they cool, then peel them from the parchment.

Yield: Makes about twenty-five 2½-inch cookies

Storage: These are best when very fresh but will keep, airtight and at room temperature, for 2 days. They can be frozen, airtight, for up to 1 month; thaw completely before serving.

1¼ cups unsweetened natural (non-alkalized) cocoa powder
¾ cup sour cream or light sour cream
2 sticks (1 cup) unsalted butter, softened and cut into chunks
2⅓ cups granulated sugar
2 large eggs, at room temperature
1 teaspoon baking soda
1 teaspoon salt
3 cups unbleached all-purpose white flour, divided
1 tablespoon vanilla extract Marshmallow Vanilla Crème Filling, Raspberry Crème Filling, Mocha-Orange Crème Filling, or Mint Crème Filling (page 320) to fill the pies

CHOCOLATE WHOOPIE PIES

A favorite in both Pennsylvania Dutch country and New England, whoopie pies were one of America's first supersized cookies. Like the equally gigantic moon pies, whoopies date back to the early twentieth century. But whoopies are more cakey—in fact, one popular story of their origin describes a home baker readying the hamburger bun–size rounds from dollops of leftover cake batter. As for the history of their name, the long-defunct Berwick Cake Factory in Boston's Roxbury section, where the sweets were once made, does gives a clue; an old picture of the building clearly shows the words "Whoopee! Pies," imprinted on the side.

Though the cake batter tale is unsubstantiated, the pies do indeed taste like cakes sandwiched around frosting. The following recipe is for chocolate whoopies, the most popular flavor, though the batter can be modified slightly to complement four different filling versions. (The filling recipe, plus four variations are on page 320.)

Lately, some pastry shops have been turning out fancier "mini whoopies," prepared by baking the batter in madeleine pans. I give instructions for readying both the classic and more upscale versions below.

Baking Preliminaries: Position a rack in the middle of the oven; preheat to 375°F. Grease two large baking sheets or coat with nonstick spray. Or if preparing madeleine mini whoopies, spray the molds in the pan generously with nonstick spray.

In a small deep bowl, stir 1 cup boiling water into the cocoa until smooth and well blended. Let cool till warm to the touch, then stir or whisk in the sour cream until smoothly incorporated.

In a large bowl, beat the butter and sugar on medium speed until very well blended, smooth, and lightened in color, about 2 minutes. On low speed, add the eggs, baking soda, and salt, beating until evenly incorporated. Beat in 2 cups flour, scraping down the sides as needed. Gradually beat in the cocoa–sour cream mixture and vanilla until smoothly incorporated. Stir or beat in the remaining flour until evenly incorporated, scraping down the bowl as needed.

For regular whoopie pies, drop scant ¼-cup mounds of dough 3 inches apart on the baking sheets. For madeleine pan mini whoopies, fill the greased madeleine molds about three-quarters full.

Bake (middle rack) until the whoopies are springy to touch and a toothpick inserted in the center comes out clean, 7 to 11 minutes. (The time for the madeleine cakes varies greatly depending on the metal used for the pan.) Cool the pans on racks for 2 minutes. Using a wide spatula, transfer the whoopies to racks to cool; for madeleine mini whoopies gently run a knife underneath them to loosen, then transfer to racks to cool.

Prepare the filling as directed on page 320. Lay out half the whoopies, underside up, on a wax paper–lined large rimmed tray or pan. For full-size whoopies, spread enough filling on the cakes to yield a $\frac{1}{3}$-inch-thick layer, or as desired. Top each cake with a similar-size one, pressing them together until the filling squeezes out to the edges.

Yield: Makes about twelve 3- to 3½-inch whoopie pie sandwiches or 24 madeleine-shaped whoopies

Storage: Store these, airtight at room temperature, for up to 1 week. They can be frozen, packed in individual bags, for up to 1 month; let come to room temperature before serving.

Variation: Chocolate-Raspberry Whoopies Add 1 teaspoon raspberry extract along with the vanilla.

Variation: Chocolate-Orange Whoopies Add 1 teaspoon finely grated orange zest along with the vanilla.

Variation: Chocolate-Mint Whoopies Add 1 teaspoon crème de menthe, spearmint, or peppermint extract along with the vanilla.

1 cup (2 sticks) unsalted butter,
   cut into chunks
1 cup coarsely chopped salted
   macadamia nuts
   Scant 1 cup packed light brown
   sugar
2 tablespoons light or dark corn
   syrup
2 teaspoons vanilla extract
½ teaspoon baking soda
½ teaspoon salt
1 large egg, at room temperature
1⅔ cups unbleached all-purpose
   white flour
1½ cups (9 ounces) good-quality
   white chocolate morsels, or
   chopped white chocolate

Tip

Be sure not to leave out the corn
syrup; while the small amount might
not seem important, it helps keep
the cookies moist and chewy.

Tip

For even more sumptuous cookies
with a fruity, chewy pineapple twist
see the variation at the end of the
recipe.

BUTTERY WHITE CHOCOLATE–MACADAMIA DROP COOKIES

This recipe updates the white chocolate and macadamia nut cookies that
were the rage several decades ago. The cookies are fairly large, chewy, and
nutty-crisp. The recipe first calls for browning the butter in a saucepan and
then toasting the nuts in the bubbling-hot fat. These steps bring out the
flavor of both the butter and the macadamias and yield cookies considerably
richer-tasting than older versions (that may seem hard to believe!).

Baking Preliminaries: Position a rack in the middle of the oven; preheat
to 350°F. Line two large baking sheets with baking parchment.

In a medium heavy saucepan over medium heat, bring the butter to a
boil. Adjust the heat so it bubbles gently. Stirring the bottom frequently,
gently boil for 3 minutes. Stir in the macadamias; the mixture will foam
up. Cook, stirring, for 30 seconds to 1 minute longer or just until the
butter turns fragrant and the nuts just start to brown; check frequently
and immediately remove the pan from the heat when the butter or nuts
start to darken.

Stop the cooking by turning the mixture out into a large heatproof
bowl. Let cool to just warm to the touch, about 10 minutes. Then stir
in the sugar, corn syrup, vanilla, baking soda, and salt until thoroughly
incorporated. Vigorously stir in the egg. Stir in the flour, then the white
chocolate morsels or chunks until evenly incorporated.

If the dough seems too stiff to drop, stir in a teaspoon or two of water;
if too wet, let it stand to cool for a few minutes longer. Using heaping
soupspoons, drop the dough into 2-inch-diameter mounds (or use an
over-filled 2-inch-diameter ice cream scoop), spacing 2¾ inches apart.

Bake (middle rack) one pan at a time for 11 to 15 minutes or until the
cookies are just light golden all over, slightly darker around the edges,
and almost firm when pressed in the middle; don't overbake. Let the
cookies stand to firm up slightly, about 2 minutes. Using a wide spatula,
transfer them to wire racks. Cool completely.

Yield: Makes twenty-five to thirty 3-inch cookies

Storage: Store these, airtight, for up to 1 week. They can be frozen,
airtight, for 3 to 4 weeks.

Variation: Pineapple, Macadamia, and White Chocolate Drop Cookies
Add 1 teaspoon grated lemon zest when adding the vanilla. Fold in 1
cup finely chopped dried cranberry rings when adding white chocolate
morsels.

1½ to 2 cups (up to one 10-
   to 11-ounce bag) butterscotch
   morsels, divided
1 cup (2 sticks) unsalted butter,
   cut into chunks
1½ cups smooth or chunky peanut
   butter
1 cup packed light brown sugar
1 teaspoon baking soda
2 large eggs, at room temperature
2⅓ cups unbleached all-purpose
   white flour

Tip

Butterscotch morsels don't melt as
quickly as chocolate chips, so they
will require more microwaving and
stirring than is normally needed for
chocolate morsels.

PEANUT BUTTERSCOTCHIES

A riff on the classic peanut butter cookie, these have a rich peanut butter and butterscotch taste, a pleasing sandy and tender texture, and accenting morsels of butterscotch here and there. They are great when you crave peanut butter cookies but want something a little different.

In a large microwave-safe bowl, microwave ⅔ cup morsels and half the butter on high power for 1 minute. Stir well, then microwave on 50 percent power, stopping and stirring every 30 seconds, until mostly melted, 1 to 1½ minutes longer. Stir and mash the morsels against the bowl sides until fully melted. Vigorously stir in the remaining butter until melted.

Stir the peanut butter, brown sugar, and baking soda, then the eggs, into the butter mixture until evenly incorporated. Stir in the flour and the remaining morsels until evenly incorporated. Cover and refrigerate the dough until cool and firm, at least 45 minutes and up to 24 hours if desired. (Let cold, stiff dough warm up slightly before using.)

Baking Preliminaries: Position a rack in the middle of the oven; preheat to 350°F. Grease several large baking sheets or coat with nonstick spray; or line them with baking parchment.

Using a 1½-inch-diameter spring-loaded ice cream scoop or heaping 1-tablespoon measure, drop the dough into uniform mounds, spacing about 3 inches apart on the baking sheets. With the tines of a well-greased fork, form a crisscross in each mound, pressing each into about a 2¼-inch round.

Bake (middle rack) one sheet at a time for 9 to 13 minutes or until the cookies are lightly browned at the edges but still slightly soft and underdone in the centers. Transfer the baking sheet to a wire rack. Let the cookies firm up for 4 minutes. Using a wide spatula, transfer them to wire racks. Cool completely before packing for storage.

Yield: Makes forty-five to fifty 3-inch cookies

Storage: Store these, airtight, for up to 1 week. They can be frozen, airtight, for up to 1 month.

ONE-BOWL WHITE CHOCOLATE–CRANBERRY DROP COOKIES

Almost anyone who's ever tried white chocolate and cranberries together will tell you it's a winning combination. The mild, creamy-sweet white chocolate and zingy-tasting fresh berries balance one another nicely, plus they provide a pretty eye-catching color contrast. In this recipe, orange zest and spices also heighten the full-bodied flavor and dried cranberries add chew, so these drops seem special and festive even though they are fairly fuss-free.

Since fresh cranberries are in our stores in late autumn, people seem to think of these as mostly Thanksgiving and Christmas cookies. But frozen cranberries will work just as well in the recipe, and they make it possible to enjoy these in other seasons, too (which I do!).

¾ cup (1½ sticks) unsalted butter, cut into chunks

1 cup minus 2 tablespoons granulated sugar

1 cup sweetened dried cranberries

1 large egg
Grated zest (orange part of the peel) of 1 small orange

2 teaspoons vanilla extract

1 teaspoon baking powder

½ teaspoon ground cinnamon

½ teaspoon ground ginger
Scant ½ teaspoon salt

1⅔ cups unbleached all-purpose white flour

1½ to 2 cups (up to one 10- to 11-ounce bag) white chocolate morsels

⅔ cup chopped fresh or frozen (partially thawed) cranberries

Baking Preliminaries: Position a rack in the middle of the oven; preheat to 350°F. Line several baking sheets with baking parchment.

In a large microwave-safe bowl with the microwave on 50 percent power, melt the butter just until mostly melted and fluid; stop and stir every 20 to 30 seconds. Vigorously stir in the sugar until the butter completely melts; mash out any lumps as necessary. Stir in the dried cranberries. Let cool till warm. Stir in the egg, orange zest, vanilla, baking powder, cinnamon, ginger, and salt until the mixture is well blended and smooth. Stir in the flour and morsels just until evenly incorporated. Gently fold in the fresh cranberries until evenly incorporated. If the dough is crumbly, gradually stir in a few teaspoons of water until it holds together; if too soft, stir in a few teaspoons of flour.

Using a medium (1½-inch) spring-loaded ice cream scoop or heaping soupspoon, drop the dough into mounds about 2½ inches apart on the sheets. Bake (middle rack) one sheet at a time for 11 to 13 minutes or until the cookies are tinged with brown and feel almost firm when pressed in the middle.

Remove from the oven; let stand until the cookies firm up just slightly, about 2 minutes. Using a wide spatula, transfer the cookies to wire racks. Cool completely. Cool the baking sheets between batches or the cookies may spread too much.

Yield: Makes about thirty-five 2½-inch cookies

Storage: Store these, airtight, for up to 1 week. They can be frozen, airtight, for 3 to 4 weeks.

¾ cup (1½ sticks) unsalted butter,
   cut into chunks
2½ ounces unsweetened chocolate,
   coarsely broken up or chopped
1 cup granulated sugar
1 tablespoon instant espresso
   powder dissolved in
   1 tablespoon warm water
1 large egg, at room temperature
2 teaspoons vanilla extract
1 teaspoon baking powder
   Scant ½ teaspoon salt
1½ cups unbleached all-purpose
   white flour, plus more if
   needed
   1½ to 2 cups (up to one 10- to
   11-ounce bag) white chocolate
   morsels

Cookie Jar Wisdom
I don't drown my sorrows;
I suffocate them with
chocolate chip cookies.
              Author unknown

ONE-BOWL MOCHA–WHITE CHOCOLATE CHIP COOKIES

Mocha and white chocolate are another of those match-made-in-heaven baking combinations. For some reason, mocha and white chocolate marry even better than dark and white chocolates. The white chocolate creaminess smoothes the coffee bitterness, while the coffee flavor boosts the appeal of the chocolate. The cookies taste vaguely like café au lait, only more complex and satisfying.

Despite the complex flavor blend, this recipe is one of those one-bowl wonders. When I want the decadence of chocolate–white chocolate chip cookies but am also yearning for something both easy and a little different, I turn to these.

Baking Preliminaries: Position a rack in the middle of the oven; preheat to 350°F. Grease several baking sheets or coat with nonstick spray; or line them with baking parchment.

In a large microwave-safe bowl with the microwave on 50 percent power, melt the butter and chocolate just until mostly melted, stopping and stirring every 30 seconds. Then vigorously stir until the butter and chocolate completely melt. Thoroughly stir in the sugar and espresso-water mixture. Let cool till warm. Vigorously stir in the egg, vanilla, baking powder, and salt until the mixture is well blended and smooth. Stir in the flour and white chocolate morsels just until evenly incorporated. If the dough is slightly soft, let stand to firm up for 5 to 10 minutes. Stir in 1 tablespoon more flour to stiffen the dough more, if necessary.

Using a 1½-inch-diameter spring-loaded ice cream scoop or heaping soupspoon, drop the dough into mounds about 2½ inches apart on the baking sheets. Bake (middle rack) one sheet at a time for 9 to 12 minutes, until the cookies are lightly tinged with brown and not quite firm when pressed in the middle.

Let stand until the cookies firm up just slightly, about 2 minutes. Using a wide spatula, transfer the cookies to wire racks. Cool completely. Cool the baking sheets between batches or the cookies may spread too much.

Yield: Makes about thirty 2½- to 3-inch cookies

Storage: Store these, airtight, for up to 1 week. They can be frozen, airtight, for 3 to 4 weeks.

Easy
One-bowl mixing.
Simple drop-from-a-spoon shaping.
Gluten-free.

1 14-ounce package flaked or shredded sweetened coconut
⅔ cup egg whites (3 or 4 large), at room temperature and free of yolk
¼ teaspoon cream of tartar or ¼ teaspoon fresh lemon juice
⅔ cup granulated sugar
1¼ teaspoons vanilla extract
⅛ teaspoon almond extract or ⅛ teaspoon coconut extract, optional
⅛ teaspoon salt

Tip
Gussy up the macaroons by dipping their tops in chocolate ganache; people will swoon over these! Simply let the macaroons cool, then follow the ganache preparation and dipping directions on page 318.

Tip
Even though it adds a step, don't skip toasting the coconut because this brings out the flavor and aroma.

TOASTED COCONUT MACAROONS

Some macaroons are compact, dainty, and understated; others, like these classics, are large, fluffy-puffy, and loaded with coconut. There will always be a place for them in our hearts and on our tables—maybe even more so now that many folks are going gluten-free.

These are easy, succulent, and well flavored. Note that the basic recipe can be easily tweaked to create macaroons with an exotic feel; see the variations at the end.

Baking Preliminaries: Position a rack in the middle of the oven; preheat to 325°F. Line several baking sheets with baking parchment.

On a large rimmed baking sheet, toast the coconut for 10 to 14 minutes, stirring every 3 or 4 minutes to redistribute, until just tinged with brown all over. Let cool.

In a large grease-free bowl with the mixer on low speed (and using a whisk-shaped beater if available), beat together the egg whites and cream of tartar until frothy. Raise the speed to medium. Beat just until the mixture is opaque and forms soft peaks, about 1½ minutes. Gradually raise speed to high and, 2 tablespoons at a time, add the sugar; beat for 20 seconds after each addition. Add the vanilla, almond extract (if desired), and salt. Beat until the mixture stands in glossy peaks, about 1 minute longer. Fold in the coconut until evenly incorporated. Drop the macaroons by heaping soupspoons into 2-inch mounds, spacing about 2½ inches apart on the baking sheets.

Bake (middle rack) for 14 to 18 minutes, until lightly tinged with brown on top and barely firm when lightly pressed at the edges. Set aside to firm up slightly. Using a spatula, transfer to wire racks. Let cool.

Yield: Makes thirty to forty 2½- to 2¾-inch macaroons

Storage: Pack the macaroons airtight with wax paper between the layers. Store in a cool spot but not refrigerated. They will keep for several days. They can also be frozen, airtight, for up to 1 month.

Variation: Orange-Ginger-Coconut Macaroons Add 2 teaspoons finely grated orange zest, incorporate along with the sugar. Add ¼ cup finely chopped crystallized ginger along with the coconut.

Variation: Pink Peppercorn Macaroons Add 1 tablespoon rose water and 2 tablespoons finely crushed pink peppercorns when the vanilla is added.

¾ cup (1½ sticks) unsalted butter,
   cut into chunks
1 cup packed light or dark brown
   sugar
⅔ cup granulated sugar
2 cups old-fashioned rolled oats
1½ cups flaked or shredded
   sweetened coconut
2 large eggs, at room temperature
2½ teaspoons vanilla extract
1½ teaspoons baking powder
¾ teaspoon salt
2 cups unbleached all-purpose
   white flour

Cookie Jar Wisdom
A cookie in the hand is
worth way more than two in
somebody else's hand.

OATMEAL-COCONUT NUBBIES

"Comforting" is the key word to describe these simple yet irresistible drop cookies. At my house they disappear before they're even cool enough to put away! They are the kind of treat a favorite relative might keep stashed in an old stoneware cookie jar and give out "just because."

Make these to satisfy a sudden cookie craving or for an impromptu family baking session; they call for only basic kitchen staples and equipment and easy techniques. Very young kids can help, and older ones can proudly ready these all by themselves. They're a good choice for grown-up beginning bakers, too.

These don't need dressing up, but, if you insist, stir in a cup of chocolate, butterscotch, or peanut butter morsels just before baking. In this case, increase the baking time by a minute or two.

Baking Preliminaries: Position a rack in the middle of the oven; preheat to 350°F. Grease several large baking sheets or coat with nonstick spray.

In a large microwave-safe bowl with the microwave on 50 percent power, heat the butter until very soft but not melted or runny, stopping and stirring every 20 seconds. (Alternatively, warm the butter over medium heat in a medium saucepan, stirring, until softened but not melted or runny. Remove from the heat.) Stir until creamy-smooth.

Vigorously stir in the brown and granulated sugars until the mixture is well blended and only slightly warm to the touch. Stir in the oats and coconut, then the eggs, vanilla, baking powder, and salt until evenly incorporated. Stir in the flour, just until evenly incorporated. If the dough is soft, let it stand for 5 minutes; if dry, stir in 2 teaspoons water.

Drop the dough into even mounds with a 1½-inch-diameter spring-loaded ice cream scoop or by heaping tablespoonfuls, spacing about 2 inches apart on the baking sheets.

Bake (middle rack) one sheet at a time, for 9 to 12 minutes or until the cookies feel almost firm when pressed in the center top; be careful not to overbake. Transfer the baking sheet to a wire rack; let stand until the cookies firm up just slightly, about 2 minutes. Using a wide spatula, transfer the cookies to wire racks. Let cool.

Yield: Makes about thirty 2½-inch cookies

Storage: Store these, airtight, for up to 1 week. They can be frozen, airtight, for up to 1 month.

SPICED OATMEAL-RAISIN DROPS

Oatmeal-raisin cookies are comfort food with a capital C. As I was growing up, nearly everybody had a relative or friend who baked them. Perhaps because they are fairly wholesome, economical, and quick, today's home bakers still bake them, too. These oatmeal-raisin drops are gently, pleasantly spiced, chewy-soft, moist, and generously studded with raisins. They are one of my old favorites.

The recipe is from my grandmother's file box. I've left the basic ingredients and proportions pretty much alone but have updated the preparation method a good bit. First, it's easier to mix the spices, salt, and soda right in with the butter and sugar instead of in a separate bowl with the flour. More important, this seemingly simple step brings the spices into direct contact with the butter and infuses it with their flavors—which heightens overall appeal.

In addition, directions call for plumping the raisins by rinsing them under hot water and for letting the oats stand and hydrate for a few minutes. This counteracts the tendency of these two dry ingredients to draw moisture from the cookies after they bake. The result: cookies that stay satisfyingly succulent rather than becoming crumbly as they stand.

1 cup (2 sticks) unsalted butter, slightly softened and cut into chunks
1½ cups packed light brown sugar
1½ teaspoons ground cinnamon
½ teaspoon ground cloves
½ teaspoon baking soda
½ teaspoon salt
2 large eggs, at room temperature
3½ cups old-fashioned rolled oats
1¼ cups dark seedless raisins, rinsed under hot water and drained
1⅓ cups unbleached all-purpose white flour

Baking Preliminaries: Position a rack in the middle of the oven; preheat to 350°F. Grease several baking sheets or coat with nonstick spray.

In a large bowl with a mixer on medium speed, beat together the butter, sugar, cinnamon, cloves, baking soda, and salt until well blended and smooth, about 2 minutes. Beat in the eggs until smoothly incorporated, then thoroughly stir in the oats and raisins. Let stand for 5 minutes so the oats and raisins can hydrate. Stir in the flour until evenly incorporated.

Using a heaping soupspoon or 1½-inch-diameter spring-loaded ice cream scoop, drop the dough, spacing about 2 inches apart on the baking sheets.

Bake (middle rack) one sheet at a time, for 9 to 13 minutes or until the cookies are lightly tinged with brown; don't overbake. Let stand until the cookies firm up just slightly, about 2 minutes. Using a wide spatula, transfer the cookies to cooling racks. Cool completely. Cool the baking sheets between batches or the cookies may spread too much.

Yield: Makes about thirty-five 2½-inch cookies

Storage: Store these, airtight, for up to 1 week. They can be frozen, airtight, for 3 to 4 weeks.

Easy
Easy bowl-and-spoon mixing.
Gluten-free.

3½ cups gluten-free old-fashioned
   rolled oats, divided
1½ cups (3 sticks) unsalted butter, cut
   into chunks
1⅓ cups packed light brown sugar
¼ cup light or dark corn syrup
1 tablespoon ground cinnamon
1 teaspoon baking powder
½ teaspoon salt
1 cup dark seedless raisins, rinsed
   under hot water and drained
2 large eggs, at room temperature
⅔ cup *each* white rice flour and
   brown rice flour
½ cup chopped walnuts, optional

Tip
Depending on the brand of oats and
rice flours, the dough may stiffen a
bit or seem very soft. If necessary,
add a small amount of extra flour,
but for cookies that stay moist don't
overdo it!

GLUTEN-FREE OATMEAL-RAISIN COOKIES

This recipe takes the typical nubby, homey raisin-oatmeal cookie and
substitutes white and brown rice flours for treats that are suitable for those
with gluten allergies. The brown sugar, cinnamon, and raisins complement
the gentle grain goodness of the oats and rice very nicely—so these don't
have that typical health food taste. They also stay moister than many gluten-
free cookies, owing to the corn syrup in the recipe and the fact that the
dough starts out fairly soft and moist.

Be sure to use gluten-free oats in this recipe.

Baking Preliminaries: Position a rack in the middle of the oven; preheat
to 350°F. Grease several large baking sheets or coat with nonstick spray.

Grind 2 cups oats to a powder in a food processor. In a very large
saucepan or pot, melt the butter until runny over medium heat, stirring.
Remove from the heat. Stir the sugar, corn syrup, cinnamon, baking
powder, and salt into the butter, mashing any lumps of sugar until
completely smooth. Vigorously stir in the ground and whole oats, raisins,
then eggs; let stand for 5 minutes.

Vigorously stir the rice flours and walnuts (if using) into the dough until
evenly incorporated. Let stand until firmed up a bit, about 10 minutes.
If the dough is still very soft, stir in up to 2 tablespoons more white rice
flour, but not more. Using a 1½-inch spring-loaded ice cream scoop or a
heaping 1-tablespoon measure, scoop up the dough and place in even
mounds on the baking sheets, spacing 2 inches apart. If the dough is
firm enough that it stands in mounds, press them down until flattened to
about 2 inches in diameter.

Bake (middle rack) one sheet at a time, for 10 to 13 minutes or until
the cookies are brown at the edges and lightly tinged on top; don't
overbake. Transfer the baking sheet to a wire rack. Let the cookies firm
up for about 2 minutes. Using a wide spatula, transfer the cookies to wire
racks. Let cool completely.

Yield: Makes about thirty-five 2½-inch cookies

Storage: Store these, airtight, for up to 1 week. They can be frozen,
airtight, for up to 1 month.

Extra Easy
Easy one-bowl, one-spoon mixing.
Make-ahead dough.
Easy yet decorative shaping.

PEANUT BUTTER CRISSCROSSES

This is the classic American peanut butter cookie at both its best and its easiest: full-bodied peanutty flavor, crisp-chewy texture, and dough that is mixed together in one bowl with one spoon. Decorated with the usual crisscross marks on top, these are attractive, too. The recipe is a good one for beginning bakers.

In a large microwave-safe bowl, with the microwave on 50 percent power heat the butter until very soft but not melted or runny, stopping and stirring every 30 seconds. (Alternatively, warm the butter over medium heat in a medium saucepan, stirring, until softened but not melted or runny. Remove from the heat.) Continue stirring until completely creamy-smooth and very soft. Vigorously stir the peanut butter, brown and granulated sugars, baking soda, and salt into the butter until evenly incorporated. Vigorously stir in the eggs and vanilla until well blended. Stir in the flour until evenly incorporated. Cover and refrigerate the dough until cool and firm, at least 45 minutes and up to 24 hours if desired. (Let cold, stiff dough warm up slightly before using.)

1   cup (2 sticks) unsalted butter, cut into chunks
1¼ cups smooth or chunky peanut butter
1   cup packed light brown sugar
¾   cup granulated sugar
¾   teaspoon baking soda
¼   teaspoon salt
2   large eggs, at room temperature and beaten with a fork
2   teaspoons vanilla extract
2½ cups unbleached all-purpose white flour
    Chopped peanuts for garnish, optional

Baking Preliminaries: Position a rack in the middle of the oven; preheat to 375°F. Grease several large baking sheets or coat with nonstick spray.

Using a heaping 1½-inch-diameter spring-loaded ice cream scoop or heaping soupspoon, drop the dough into uniform mounds, spacing about 2½ inches apart on the baking sheets. With the tines of a well-greased fork, form a crisscross in the top of each, pressing the dough down into 2-inch rounds. (If garnishing with peanuts, press down in one direction with the fork, top with some peanuts, then press down in the other direction to embed them.) Wipe off and re-grease the fork as needed. Bake (middle rack) one sheet at a time, for 9 to 11 minutes or until the cookies are just barely tinged at the edges but still slightly soft in the centers. Transfer the baking sheet to a wire rack. Let the cookies firm for 5 minutes. Using a wide spatula, transfer them to wire racks. Cool completely before packing for storage.

Yield: Makes forty to forty-five 3-inch cookies

Storage: Store these, airtight, for up to 1 week. They can be frozen, airtight, for up to 1 month.

Easy
One-saucepan, one-spoon mixing.
Great aroma, spicy taste.

1 cup (2 sticks) unsalted butter, slightly softened and cut into chunks

1½ cups packed light brown sugar

2½ teaspoons ground cinnamon, plus a little more for optional garnish

½ teaspoon ground nutmeg or ground allspice

2 teaspoons baking powder

½ teaspoon salt

2 cups finely chopped or grated carrots (about 4 medium)

1 cup chopped walnuts, optional

1 cup seedless dark or golden raisins, rinsed in warm water, well drained, and patted dry, optional

2 large eggs, at room temperature and lightly beaten with a fork

2½ cups unbleached all-purpose white flour

Cream Cheese Glaze (page 322) for garnish

Tip
Quickly ready the carrots by chopping coarse slices or chunks in a food processor until finely chopped.

CARROT DROP COOKIES WITH CREAM CHEESE GLAZE

Yes indeed, these drop cookies will remind you of carrot cake. Only here the taste is in the form of convenient eat-out-of-hand cookies. These are fragrant, spicy, moist, and appealingly chunky-chewy with nuts and raisins. (Although most grown-ups consider the nuts and raisins essential in these cookies, some kids—including my grandchildren—prefer them plain. In this case, feel free to leave them out.)

Baking Preliminaries: Position a rack in the middle of the oven; preheat to 375°F. Grease two large baking sheets or coat with nonstick spray.

In a large heavy saucepan over medium heat, melt the butter until mostly melted and runny, stirring. Remove from the heat; stir until completely melted and fluid. Vigorously stir in the sugar, cinnamon, nutmeg, baking powder, and salt. Thoroughly stir in the carrots, nuts (if desired), and raisins, if using. Vigorously stir in the eggs, then fold in the flour until evenly incorporated. Using soupspoons, drop 1¼-inch mounds of dough
2½ inches apart on baking sheets.

Bake (middle rack) one sheet at a time for 12 to 16 minutes or until the cookies are lightly browned all over and springy to the touch. Let the cookies stand on the sheets for 2 minutes, then transfer them to the racks to cool completely.

Prepare the Cream Cheese Glaze as directed. Dip the tops of the cooled cookies into the glaze, shaking off the excess, or generously swirl it on with a knife, if preferred. If desired, garnish the tops further by sprinkling a little nutmeg or cinnamon over the glaze before it sets. Let stand until the glaze sets.

Yield: Makes about thirty-five 2½-inch cookies

Storage: Store these, packed airtight in a single layer at room temperature, for up to 1 week. They can be frozen for up to 1 month.

3 large eggs, at room temperature and beaten with a fork

½ cup corn oil, canola oil, or other flavorless vegetable oil

½ cup clover honey or other mild-flavored honey

⅓ cup lekvar (prune filling) or one 4-ounce jar baby food prunes

1 cup packed light brown sugar

1 tablespoon ground cinnamon

1 teaspoon baking soda

½ teaspoon salt

2 cups old-fashioned rolled oats

1⅓ cups seedless dark or golden raisins or sweetened dried cranberries, or a combination of raisins and cranberries

1½ cups unbleached all-purpose white flour

1 cup whole wheat flour

1 cup chopped walnuts or almonds, or a combination

GOOD AND GOOD-FOR-YOU HONEY-GRANOLA COOKIES

Containing the fruits, grains, nuts, and honey often featured in granola, these big, soft, homespun cookies are both healthful and full of fiber, yet remarkably appealing. They contain a secret ingredient that you may not want to mention but shouldn't leave out—prunes! Either lekvar, a prune filling often sold with the baking supplies in Jewish markets, or a jar of baby food prunes will do. Either adds subtle flavor and moistness but no pruney taste, although I, personally, love Danish with prune filling so wouldn't object to this ingredient anyway.

Note that these could stand in for a bowl of breakfast granola for those too rushed to sit down and eat.

Baking Preliminaries: Position a rack in the middle of the oven; preheat to 350°F. Line several large baking sheets with baking parchment or spray with nonstick spray.

In a large bowl, very thoroughly stir together the eggs, oil, honey, lekvar, sugar, cinnamon, baking soda, and salt. Stir in the oats and dried fruit; let stand to hydrate for 5 minutes. Stir in the flours and nuts just until evenly incorporated. If the dough seems dry and stiff, stir in up to 2 tablespoons water.

Scoop up the dough using a nonstick spray–coated (or well-oiled) 2-inch-diameter (or similar large) spring-loaded ice cream scoop, spacing the portions about 2½ inches apart on the baking sheets. Oil or coat the scoop with more nonstick spray as needed to prevent the dough from sticking. (Alternatively, using a heaping soupspoon, drop the dough into scant 2-inch mounds. (With a greased palm, flatten the cookies into 3-inch rounds.)

Bake (middle rack) one sheet at a time for 10 to 13 minutes, just until the cookies are lightly browned at the edges and feel barely firm when pressed in the center. Let the cookies firm up for about 3 minutes, then transfer to a wire rack and cool completely.

Yield: Makes about twenty-five 3½-inch cookies

Storage: Store these, airtight and at room temperature, for up to 1 week. They can be frozen, airtight, for up to 1½ months; let come to room temperature before serving.

¾ cup (1½ sticks) unsalted butter, slightly softened

1 cup granulated sugar, plus about 2 tablespoons for garnish

1 tablespoon ground ginger

1 teaspoon baking soda

1 teaspoon ground cinnamon

½ teaspoon salt

Generous ¼ teaspoon ground cloves

1 large egg, at room temperature

¼ cup molasses

2 cups unbleached all-purpose white flour, plus more if needed

¼ cup very finely chopped crystallized ginger

Tip

These need to be lifted off the baking sheets as soon as they are firm enough not to tear or buckle; otherwise they will stick. If they inadvertently cool too much and stick to the pan, simply return the pan to the oven to warm them again. Don't try to lift them off when they are cold, as they will be brittle and might break.

DOUBLE-GINGER GINGERSNAPS

These are wonderful gingersnaps—crisp and light-textured, rustically handsome, and full of satisfying ginger flavor. The recipe is from one of my food writer friends, Connie Hay, who says ginger cookies are among her favorites. It shows!

Baking Preliminaries: Position a rack in the middle of the oven; preheat to 350°F. Set out two large ungreased baking sheets.

In a large bowl with a mixer on medium speed, beat the butter, 1 cup sugar, the ginger, baking soda, cinnamon, salt, and cloves until fluffy and well blended, about 2 minutes. Add the egg and molasses, beating until evenly incorporated; scrape down the bowl as needed. Beat or stir in the flour until evenly incorporated. Stir in the crystallized ginger. If the dough is overly soft, stir in up to 1½ tablespoons more flour.

Using a rounded 1-tablespoon measuring spoon, drop the dough onto ungreased cookie sheets, spacing about 2 inches apart. Grease your fingertips and dip into the remaining 2 tablespoons granulated sugar. Pat down the cookie tops with your fingertips until just barely flattened, dipping into the sugar before each cookie.

Bake (middle rack) one sheet at a time for 9 to 12 minutes, until the rounds are just slightly darker at the edges. Cool on the baking sheet for 1 minute, then immediately transfer to a cooling rack using a wide-bladed spatula. Let cool thoroughly.

Yield: Makes forty to forty-five 2½-inch cookies

Storage: Store these, airtight, for up to 10 days. They can be frozen, airtight, for up to 2 months.

HAND-SHAPED COOKIES }

Many attractive and varied looks are possible when you hand shape cookies—the result all depends on the shaping technique. Admittedly, even the easiest hand shaping takes a tad more time than dropping a dough but the reward is more handsome treats, from wafers, buttons, and domes to crisscross cookies and even uniform rounds paired to form sandwiches. The overall effect can vary widely, too, from fairly plain, like the Crispy-Soft Cinnamon-Vanilla Monster Cookies, to somewhat fancy, like the Toasted Coconut Tuiles.

Hand shaping cookies is also fun—especially for kids, who always seem to enjoy getting their hands into and playing with dough. Some grown-ups find the hand-crafting part enjoyable, too, especially when they're working alongside their favorite young bakers.

The most basic technique is rolling dough portions into balls. These often just get placed on sheets and baked; depending on their consistency they may retain much of their original shape, like the Orange Dusties,

or flatten out some, like the Bouchon Bakery–Style Dark Double-Chocolate Chippers.

Pay close attention to what size the dough portions should be and even use a ruler to check if you're not sure how large or small a 1- or 2-inch ball really is. Perhaps surprisingly, when people just "guesstimate," they are often *wildly off*, throwing baking times and yields off, too.

Sometimes, the cookies are further shaped and festively decorated with follow-up steps, like rolling or dipping the balls into sugar, nuts, or coconut, or flattening them with a palm, bottom of a glass, or crisscross of a fork. These extra touches lend lots of pizzazz but require no special skills and, usually, little effort.

Note that while slice-and-bake cookies and biscotti involve some initial hand shaping, both of these kinds are finished by cutting a dough log into slices, and, in the case of biscotti, double baking. So, each of these types appears in its own chapter.

ULTIMATE ONE-BOWL CHOCOLATE CHIPPERS (OR CHUNKERS)

If you're one who feels that ready-to-use semisweet chocolate morsels produce perfectly delicious chocolate chip cookies, then use whatever brand of semisweet or bittersweet morsels you like for these crisp-on-the-edge, chewy-in-the-middle cookies. If, on the other hand, you prefer chunks of premium chocolate, feel free to substitue chopped chocolate.

In this case, don't use chocolate with a cacao percentage higher than 65 percent or the cookies may flatten too much. (See the Chocolate Primer on page 15 for details.)

¾ cup (1½ sticks) unsalted butter, cut into chunks
⅔ cup packed light brown sugar
½ cup granulated sugar
1 large egg, at room temperature
2 teaspoons vanilla extract
Scant ½ teaspoon salt
Generous ¼ teaspoon baking soda
1¾ cups unbleached all-purpose white flour, plus more if needed
1½ to 2 cups (up to one 10- to 11-ounce bag) semisweet or bittersweet chocolate morsels, or substitute 1½ to 2 cups chopped (⅛- to ¼-inch pieces) semisweet or bittersweet (50 to 65 percent cacao) chocolate bars, disks, or pistoles

Baking Preliminaries: Position a rack in the middle of the oven; preheat to 350°F. Grease two large baking sheets or coat with nonstick spray; or line them with baking parchment.

In a large microwave-safe bowl with the microwave on 50 percent power, heat the butter until very soft but not completely melted or runny, stopping and stirring every 30 seconds. (Alternatively, warm the butter over medium heat in a medium saucepan, stirring, until softened but not melted or runny. Remove from the heat.) Continue stirring until completely creamy-smooth and cooled to barely warm.

Vigorously stir the sugars into the butter, mashing out any lumps with the back of the spoon and stirring until well blended. Let cool to barely warm. Vigorously stir in the egg, vanilla, salt, and baking soda until the mixture is well blended and smooth. Stir in the flour just until evenly incorporated. Lightly fold in the chocolate morsels or chunks; excess stirring may cause melting. If the dough is too soft to shape, stir in up to 2 tablespoons more flour to stiffen it slightly. On a sheet of wax paper with greased hands divide the dough into quarters. Then shape each into 6 or 7 balls, spacing 2½ inches apart on the baking sheets. Pat down tops just slightly.

Bake (middle rack) one sheet at a time until lightly tinged with brown and are not quite firm when pressed in the middle, 10 to 13 minutes. Let stand to firm up, about 2 minutes. Using a wide spatula, transfer to wire racks. Cool completely.

Yield: Makes twenty-four to twenty-eight 2½- to 3-inch cookies

Storage: Store these, airtight, for up to 1 week. They can be frozen, airtight, for 3 to 4 weeks.

Tip

Thoroughly cool the baking sheets between batches so the cookies don't spread too much.

6 tablespoons unsalted butter, cut
into chunks
8 ounces 60 to 70 percent cacao
chocolate bars, coarsely
chopped or broken into pieces
⅓ cup mint-scented granulated
sugar (page 338) or ⅓ cup
granulated sugar
1 teaspoon baking powder
½ teaspoon peppermint, spearmint,
or crème de menthe extract
or 1 tablespoon very finely
pulverized dried mint leaves
Scant ¼ teaspoon salt
3 large eggs, at room temperature
1½ cups unbleached all-purpose
white flour
1 cup (6 ounces) chocolate-mint
morsels or ⅔ cup chopped
Andes mint candies
½ cup powdered sugar, plus more
as needed for coating cookies

CHOCOLATE-MINT CRACKLES

At one point while testing a lot of cookie recipes for the book, I gathered up some samples and sent them to my editor, Justin Schwartz. Since the crackles were rolled in powdered sugar, I worried about shipping them, but Justin is a chocolate and mint fan, so I sent them anyway.

He later reported that they had arrived, "Just fine!" Even better, he and some other Wiley staff members who tasted these thought they tasted, "just fine," too.

Crackles are named for the dramatic, dark surface cracks that develop as powdered sugar–coated balls of chocolate dough expand and develop fissures during baking. This refreshing double-chocolate version boasts not only a dark, fudgy mint dough, but it also is enlivened with chocolate-mint morsels or chopped mint-flavored chocolate candies.

Baking Preliminaries: Position a rack in the middle of the oven; preheat to 325°F. Line several large baking sheets with baking parchment.

Combine the butter and chocolate in a large microwave-safe bowl. Microwave on high power for 1 minute, then stir well. On medium power continue microwaving, stopping and stirring every 30 seconds, until the mixture partially melts. (Alternatively, in a large saucepan warm the butter and chocolate over low heat, stirring constantly, until mostly melted. Immediately remove from the heat.)

Stir the chocolate mixture until completely melted. Stir the sugar, baking powder, extract, and salt into the mixture until well blended. Let cool to barely warm (otherwise the eggs may cook when added).

One at a time, vigorously stir the eggs into the chocolate mixture. Stir the flour into the chocolate mixture just until well blended. If the dough is crumbly, gradually mix in a teaspoon or two of water until it holds together. Cover and refrigerate the dough until cooled, but not cold and stiff, 20 to 30 minutes. Stir in the chocolate morsels until evenly incorporated. Continue chilling the dough, covered, until firm enough to handle, at least 3 hours and up to 24 hours.

Put the powdered sugar in a deep bowl. Divide the dough in quarters; divide each quarter into 8 or 9 equal portions. Roll the portions between the palms into 1¼-inch balls. Working with a few balls at a time, drop them into the powdered sugar and rotate the bowl until they are heavily coated and no chocolate shows through. Transfer them to baking sheets, spacing about 1½ inches apart. As necessary, wipe the chocolate buildup from your hands. Repeat the process, replenishing the powdered sugar bowl as needed.

Bake (middle rack) one sheet at a time for 8 to 10 minutes or until just beginning to feel firm on the surface but still soft inside when pressed in the center top; don't overbake. The cookies will have attractive surface cracks. Let them stand for several minutes to firm up. Transfer to wire racks; cool thoroughly.

Yield: Makes thirty-five to forty 1¾-inch cookies

Storage: Store these airtight, preferably with wax paper between layers, for up to 1 week.

Tip

Mint-flavored chocolate morsels are most often available during the Christmas holidays. Substitute chopped Andes mints if necessary.

Tip

The powdered sugar coating stands out best when applied heavily and when the dough is still cold and stiff as it goes into the oven.

Fairly Easy
Easy bowl and spoon mixing.
Gourmet taste with ease.

¾ cup unbleached all-purpose white flour
½ cup plus 1 tablespoon good-quality unsweetened Dutch-process cocoa powder, sifted after measuring, if lumpy
1 teaspoon baking powder
Generous ¼ teaspoon table salt
10 tablespoons (1¼ sticks) unsalted butter, slightly softened and cut into chunks
⅔ cup packed dark brown sugar
2 tablespoons granulated sugar
2 teaspoons molasses
2 teaspoons vanilla extract
1 large egg, at room temperature
3½ ounces 55 to 70 percent cacao semisweet or bittersweet chocolate, chopped into morsel-size chunks (generous ½ cup)
⅔ cup (3½ ounces) gourmet-quality semisweet or bittersweet chocolate morsels (do not substitute chocolate chunks)

BOUCHON BAKERY–STYLE DARK DOUBLE-CHOCOLATE CHIPPERS

For those yearning for the to-die-for taste of Bouchon Bakery's big, dark, double-chocolate chunk cookies but unable to make a trip to Napa Valley or New York City, there are two solutions. Williams-Sonoma stores sell the makings for these goodies in convenient, but very pricey, gourmet kits. (In case you're skeptical about the quality of cookies from a box mix, don't be: These are gourmet treats—and almost as tempting as the truly memorable ones I purchased right from the ovens at the Napa bakery.)

The other solution is to create your own cookies following my knockoff recipe here. Let me note right now that it's not *identical* to the Bouchon version. This would require using *exactly* the same kinds of cocoa powder, chocolate morsels, chocolate chunks, brown sugar, molasses, and flour, and in exactly the same proportions. Actually duplicating *all* the ingredients would, in fact, be impossible, because the bakery uses a special, custom-blend alkalized "cocoa noir" cocoa powder that's manufactured exclusively for the bakery's use.

That said, if you're simply willing to hunt down and use the gourmet-quality bittersweet chopped chocolate, the chocolate morsels, and the cocoa powder called for here, your cookies will be very similar to the Bouchon ones—maybe even better. There is nothing the least bit tricky about the mixing and shaping method (it's quite routine); the ingredients are the key to success. But be aware that just switching among the various cocoas will change the taste, aroma, and even cookie color slightly. Different kinds of morsels and chopped chocolate affect flavor, too, so have fun experimenting.

The recipe may be doubled if you wish.

Baking Preliminaries: Position a rack in the middle of the oven; preheat to 350°F. Line several large baking sheets with baking parchment.

In a medium bowl, thoroughly stir together the flour, cocoa powder, baking powder, and salt. In a mixer on medium speed, beat the butter until well blended and smooth, about 1 minute. Add the brown and granulated sugars, molasses, and vanilla; beat until thoroughly incorporated and the mixture is well blended. Beat in the egg until thoroughly incorporated. Add the flour mixture, beating or stirring, just until evenly incorporated. Stir in the chopped chocolate and chocolate morsels.

If the dough seems soft, let it stand to firm up for 5 to 10 minutes. If

the dough is crumbly, gradually mix in a teaspoon or two of water until it holds, together. On a sheet of wax paper, with well-greased hands, divide it in half. Then shape each half into 8 or 9 equal balls, spacing about 3 inches apart on the baking sheets. With a lightly greased palm, press down until the balls just slightly flatten.

Bake (middle rack) one sheet at a time for 8 to 11 minutes, just until the cookies are beginning to feel firm when pressed at the edges; be very careful not to overbake. Transfer to a wire rack and let stand for 3 or 4 minutes. Transfer the cookies to racks and let cool completely.

Yield: Makes sixteen to eighteen 2½- to 3-inch cookies

Storage: These are best fresh but will keep, airtight and at room temperature, for up to 3 days. They can be frozen, airtight, for up to 1½ months; let come to room temperature before serving.

Cookie Jar Wisdom
Anybody who says they don't like chocolate chip cookies is either lying or an alien.

Tip

Do not try to substitute all chocolate chunks or all chocolate morsels for the combination of the two. And carefully follow the guides on what the cacao percentages should be. The high cacao percentage of chocolate chunks means that, unlike chocolate morsels, they are not "baking stable." Instead, they will run and flow during baking and cause some flattening of the cookies. Some flow is good, but you don't want too much, so the cacao percentage shouldn't be overly high. Also, if you use too many chunks and skip the chips, your cookies will likely be too soft and too thin. (Check out the Chocolate Primer on page 15 for more information.)

1½ cups (3 sticks) unsalted butter, slightly softened and cut into chunks

1⅓ cups powdered sugar

¼ cup cornstarch

2 teaspoons vanilla extract

¾ teaspoon almond extract or ½ teaspoon lemon extract

Generous ¼ teaspoon salt

2⅓ cups unbleached all-purpose white flour

Assorted buttercream frostings, optional

Tip

For a quick, understated garnish, add a few zig-zags of the Glossy Chocolate Drizzle, page 314, to the cookie tops following the directions in that recipe.

EASY VANILLA MELTAWAYS

The word "meltaway" is usually a tip-off that the cookies have a noticeably smooth-crisp, melt-in-your mouth texture—which these delightful cookies definitely have. In case you wonder, the distinctive texture comes from the cornstarch and powdered sugar.

These are simple, a bit delicate, light yet buttery, and a nice, less sweet substitute for regular sugar cookies. I like to serve them with fruit compotes, sorbets, or ice cream. They can also be dressed up by swirling on a pretty array of buttercream frostings, for stunning yet very doable party cookies.

Baking Preliminaries: Position a rack in the middle of the oven; preheat to 325°F. Line several large baking sheets with baking parchment.

Combine the butter, powdered sugar, cornstarch, extracts, and salt in a large bowl. Beat with a mixer on low, then medium, speed until blended and completely smooth. Gradually add the flour, beating on low or stirring it in until smoothly incorporated. Stir in the last of it if the mixer motor labors.

If the dough looks dry and doesn't hold together well, gradually add up to 1 tablespoon or so of water, kneading or beating until the mixture just holds together when squeezed between the fingertips.

Working on wax paper, shape the dough into an evenly thick disk, then divide it into quarters. Divide each quarter into 12 equal portions. Shape the portions into balls, spacing about 2 inches apart on the baking sheets. Flatten the balls into 1½-inch-diameter, evenly thick rounds with your palm.

Bake (middle rack) one pan at a time for 15 to 18 minutes or until just firm when pressed in the center top, faintly tinged at the edge, and browned on the bottom (gently lift one slightly with a spatula to check). Transfer the pan to a wire rack. Let cool completely; the cookies are too tender to move while hot.

To decorate (optional): Top the thoroughly cooled cookies with a swirl or piped rosette of three or four different flavors and colors of buttercream frostings (pages 321-332), following the directions in the frosting recipes.

Yield: Makes forty-eight 2- to 2¼-inch cookies

Storage: Store these, airtight and at room temperature, for up to 10 days. They can be frozen, airtight, for up to 1½ months.

1 cup (about 3 ounces) dried cherries
1½ tablespoons kirsch (clear cherry brandy) or fresh orange juice
12 ounces bittersweet or semisweet chocolate, divided
¼ cup (½ stick) unsalted butter, cut into chunks
⅔ cup granulated sugar
¼ cup unsweetened natural (non-alkalized) cocoa powder or Dutch-process cocoa powder, sifted after measuring, if lumpy
½ teaspoon baking powder
½ teaspoon almond extract
⅛ teaspoon salt
2 large eggs, at room temperature
½ cup plus 1 tablespoon unbleached all-purpose white flour

Cookie Jar Wisdom
Cookie Way to 5 Fruits 'n' Veggies a Day: Pumpkin cookies, carrot cookies, chocolate cherry cookies, and raspberry brownies.

DARK CHOCOLATE–CHOCOLATE CHUNK CHERRY COOKIES

Chocolate and cherries: I probably don't need to say anything more about this astonishingly appealing pair! But I'll add that these cookies are devastatingly decadent and deeply, intensely chocolaty, yet somehow light, with a bit of chew, too. They are best eaten fresh, as they do dry out quickly, but frankly, I don't think this will be a problem!

Baking Preliminaries: Position a rack in the middle of the oven; preheat to 350°F. Line several large baking sheets with baking parchment.

In a small deep bowl, stir together the cherries and kirsch. Set aside for at least 10 minutes so the cherries can rehydrate.

Break up or very coarsely chop 6 ounces chocolate. In a large microwave-safe bowl, melt the chocolate and the butter in the microwave on 100 percent power for 1 minute. Stir well. If necessary, continue microwaving on 50 percent power, stopping and stirring every 20 seconds, just until barely melted and smooth. Stir the sugar, cocoa powder, baking powder, almond extract, and salt into the chocolate mixture until well blended. Stir in the cherries (and any unabsorbed liquid). Let cool till warm. One at a time, vigorously stir in the eggs until well blended. Stir in the flour just until evenly incorporated. Chop the remaining 6 ounces chocolate into morsel-size pieces. Stir half into the dough. Put the remainder in a shallow bowl to use for garnish.

Cover and refrigerate the dough until firm enough to shape into balls, at least 45 minutes and up to 2 hours. (If it becomes too cold and stiff to shape, let it warm up slightly.) Pull off portions and shape into 1-inch balls. Press the top of each into the chocolate pieces, then lay them, chocolate pieces up, about 2 inches apart on the baking sheets.

Bake (middle rack) one pan at a time for 9 to 11 minutes or until cookies are puffed and just barely firm when pressed on top. Remove from the oven; let cookies stand to firm up slightly, about 2 minutes. Then, using a wide spatula, transfer to wire racks. Cool thoroughly and let stand until the chocolate chunks begin to set up, at least 1 hour. (Or speed this by refrigerating cookies.)

Yield: Makes thirty to thirty-five 2-inch cookies

Storage: Store these, airtight, for several days. They can be frozen for up to 1 month.

3   cups (18 ounces) 50 to 60
     percent cacao semisweet
     chocolate morsels, divided
¾ cup (1½ sticks) unsalted butter,
     just slightly softened and cut
     into chunks
1   cup granulated sugar
6   tablespoons unsweetened
     natural (non-alkalized) cocoa
     powder or Dutch-process
     cocoa powder
1½ teaspoons ground cinnamon
1   teaspoon ground allspice
     Finely grated zest (orange part
     of the peel) from 1 medium
     orange
¼ to a scant ½ teaspoon ground
     cayenne pepper, to taste
2   cups unbleached all-purpose
     white flour

Tip

Beware—the heat of cayenne
gradually intensifies as the cookies
stand for a day or two!

Tip

Add a little pizzazz by accenting
these rounds with the Glossy
Chocolate Drizzle, page 314.

ORANGE FIRE-AND-SPICE CHOCOLATE SHORTBREADS

These are not your typical understated shortbreads! In fact, since they feature not only chocolate and chocolate chips but also cayenne pepper, orange, cinnamon, and allspice, they are at the other end of the spectrum from the comforting classic butter versions most folks are familiar with. Instead, though they look fairly ordinary, they are deeply chocolaty and slightly exotic tasting, and they provide a tingly little after-burn.

Most people don't even notice the cayenne at first—it takes a few seconds to slowly, quietly kick in. If you wish to dial down the temperature, add only the minimum ¼ teaspoon called for; it will add depth and a hint of heat but won't put off timid tasters. For noticeable fire, use a heavier hand—a scant ½ teaspoon cayenne will please more adventuresome eaters.

Baking Preliminaries: Position a rack in the middle of the oven; preheat to 350°F. Line several large baking sheets with baking parchment.

Combine 2 cups chocolate morsels and the butter in a large microwave-safe bowl. Microwave on high power for 1 minute, then stir. If necessary, continue microwaving on medium powder, stopping and stirring at 20-second intervals until mostly melted. (Alternatively, melt 2 cups chocolate morsels and the butter in a large saucepan over low heat, stirring constantly, until partly melted. Immediately remove from the heat.) Stir until completely melted and cooled slightly.

Thoroughly stir the sugar, cocoa, cinnamon, allspice, orange zest, and cayenne into the melted chocolate mixture. Thoroughly stir in the flour, then let the dough cool for 5 minutes. If the mixture is dry and crumbly, gradually mix in a little water until the dough holds together. Stir in the remaining 1 cup chocolate morsels just until incorporated; excessive stirring can cause them to start melting.

Divide the dough into quarters. Divide each quarter into 8 equal balls, spacing about 2½ inches apart on the baking sheets. Pat down until just flattened.

Bake (middle rack) one sheet at a time for 9 to 12 minutes, just until the cookies are beginning to feel firm when pressed in the center; be very careful not to overbake. Transfer to a wire rack, let cool.

Yield: Makes thirty-two 2½-inch cookies

Storage: Store these, airtight and at room temperature, for up to 10 days. They can be frozen, airtight, for up to 1½ months; let come to room temperature before serving.

12   ounces 60 to 70 percent cacao
      semisweet or bittersweet
      chocolate, coarsely chopped
      (2½ cups)
½   cup (1 stick) cold unsalted butter,
      cut into chunks
¾   cup plus 2 tablespoons
      granulated sugar
6½   tablespoons unsweetened
      natural (non-alkalized)
      cocoa-powder or Dutch-
      process cocoa powder
2   tablespoons finely chopped
      cocoa nibs, optional
2   teaspoons ground cinnamon
      Finely grated zest (orange part
      of the peel) from 1 small
      orange
½   teaspoon baking soda
¼   teaspoon ground cayenne
      pepper, or more to taste
¼   teaspoon ground smoked
      paprika, optional
⅛   teaspoon salt
2   cups unbleached all-purpose
      white flour
2   large eggs, at room
      temperature, lightly beaten
      with a fork
      About 3 tablespoons crystal,
      sparkling, or sanding sugar or
      turbinado or other translucent
      crystal sugar

SPICED MEXICAN CHOCOLATE COOKIES

These very dark, spiced chocolate cookies take their inspiration from Mexican chocolate. Typically, it has a distinctive sandy texture and is made with roasted and ground cocoa nibs, coarse sugar, roughly ground cinnamon, and sometime other spices also. (The tradition of combining chocolate with other flavoring elements dates back centuries: In 1519, when Cortes arrived in what is now Mexico City, he found the Aztec emperor Montezuma drinking a frothy, heavily spiced chocolate beverage from golden goblets.)

Note that this recipe includes a little hit of cayenne pepper, which lends a slight piquancy that's extremely pleasing. To reproduce the slightly smoky flavor of Oaxaca-style chocolate, add a little optional smoked paprika, too. The crystal sugar garnish lends the cookies a toothsome, slightly crunchy-gritty texture typical of many Mexican chocolates.

Baking Preliminaries: Position a rack in the middle of the oven; preheat to 350°F. Line several large baking sheets with baking parchment.

Combine the chocolate and butter in a large microwave-safe bowl. Microwave on high power for 1 minute. Stir well. On 50 percent power continue microwaving, stopping and stirring every 30 seconds, until mostly melted. Stir until completely melted and cooled to warm.

Thoroughly stir the sugar, cocoa, cocoa nibs (if using), cinnamon, orange zest, baking soda, cayenne, smoked paprika (if using), and salt into the chocolate-butter mixture until evenly incorporated. Thoroughly stir in a generous half of the flour, then the eggs, then the remaining flour until evenly incorporated. If the dough is crumbly, gradually work in a teaspoon or two of water until it holds together. If the dough seems too soft, let it stand to firm up for 5 minutes.

Divide the dough into quarters. Then divide each into 9 or 10 equal portions, shaping into balls. Dip the tops of the balls into a saucer of coarse sugar, then space, sugar side up, about 2½ inches apart on the baking sheets. Using the bottom of an oiled drinking glass, press down until flattened into 2½-inch rounds.

Bake (middle rack) one sheet at a time for 11 to 14 minutes, just until the cookies are firm when pressed in the center; don't underbake. Let cool on the pans for 5 minutes. Transfer to wire racks; cool completely.

Yield: Makes thirty-six to forty 3-inch cookies

Storage: Store these, airtight and at room temperature, for up to 10 days. Or freeze, airtight, for up to 1½ months; serve at room temperature.

½ cup (1 stick) cold unsalted butter, cut into chunks

1¼ cups granulated sugar

¼ cup unsweetened natural (non-alkalized) cocoa powder

2 teaspoons instant coffee granules

¼ teaspoon baking soda

¾ cup smooth or chunky peanut butter

1 large egg, at room temperature
Enough very overripe banana to yield ¼ cup coarsely mashed pulp (about 1 small banana)

1½ cups unbleached all-purpose white flour

1½ cups (9 ounces) semisweet or bittersweet chocolate morsels, divided

CHOCOLATE CHIP, PEANUT BUTTER, AND BANANA SOFTIES

The chocolate, peanut butter, and banana complement one another nicely in these plump, decadent, and handsome cookies. In one bite you notice the chocolate, in the next the banana, then in another the peanut butter—the subtle interplay is delightful.

These are chewy-soft when first baked, then soften a bit more during storage. They aren't usually around long at my house, though, because we just can't stop eating them! For a totally over-the-top treat, turn these into sandwich cookies following the variation at the end.

Baking Preliminaries: Position a rack in the middle of the oven; preheat to 350°F. Line several large baking sheets with baking parchment.

In a large mixing bowl with a mixer on medium speed, beat the butter, sugar, cocoa, coffee granules, and baking soda until very well blended, about 2 minutes. Add the peanut butter, egg, and banana and beat until smoothly and evenly incorporated, scraping down the bowl sides as necessary. With the mixer on low, then medium, speed, beat in half the flour until thoroughly incorporated. Add the remaining flour and ½ cup morsels and beat or stir in until evenly incorporated. Put the remaining morsels in a shallow bowl.

Working on wax paper, divide the dough into quarters, then divide each quarter into 8 equal balls. Roll the balls in the remaining chocolate morsels until lightly studded; pat and press the morsels into the balls to imbed them slightly. Space 2½ inches apart on the baking sheets. Flatten into 2½-inch rounds with a palm.

Bake (middle rack) one sheet at a time for 10 to 13 minutes, just until the cookies feel barely firm when pressed in the center. Let the cookies firm up for about 3 minutes, then transfer to a wire rack and cool completely.

Yield: Makes thirty-two 2½- to 2¾-inch cookies

Storage: Store these, airtight and at room temperature, for up to 1 week. They can be frozen, airtight, for up to 1½ months; serve at room temperature.

Variation: Softies Sandwich Cookies Pair up the cookies, spreading the bottoms with a ¼- to ⅓-inch-thick layer of Mocha-Orange Crème or Peanut Butter Crème fillings, page 320, then covering with tops and squeezing together lightly.

1 cup smooth peanut butter
1 cup (2 sticks) unsalted butter, slightly softened
1⅔ cups packed light or dark brown sugar
2 large eggs, at room temperature
½ cup unsweetened natural (non-alkalized) cocoa powder or Dutch-process cocoa powder
2 teaspoons vanilla extract
1 teaspoon baking powder
¼ teaspoon salt
2¼ cups unbleached all-purpose white flour
6 ounces milk chocolate or semisweet chocolate morsels, processed or chopped very fine (⅛-inch bits)

Cookie Jar Wisdom
Cookie Equation: The number of chocolate chips in cookies is inversely proportional to the number of minutes it takes before they disappear.

PEANUT BUTTER–FUDGE CHIP CRISSCROSSES

The chocolate–peanut butter synergy is particularly pleasing in these cookies: Sometimes they taste a little more nutty to me, sometimes a tad more chocolaty, but mostly, the two flavors work in harmony to create a combo that's better than either flavor alone. These are rich and satisfying in the same way that really good classic peanut butter crisscrosses are, yet the taste is unique, more complex, and, in my opinion, more interesting.

Actually, it took a good deal of fine-tuning to get the chocolate and peanut butter flavors to balance and function as one. I usually prefer semisweet chocolate over milk chocolate in cookies, but here the milder taste of the milk chocolate morsels seems to blend in better and sing rather than shout too loudly. But, if you really want a stronger chocolate presence or just find it more convenient to use semisweet morsels, go for it!

Baking Preliminaries: Position a rack in the middle of the oven; preheat to 350°F. Grease several large baking sheets or coat with nonstick spray.

In a large mixer bowl with the mixer on low, then medium, speed, beat together the peanut butter, butter, and sugar until well blended and smooth. Beat in the eggs until smoothly incorporated. Add the cocoa powder, vanilla, baking powder, and salt. Beat on low, then medium, speed until very well blended and lightened in color, about 2 minutes. On low speed, beat in the flour and chocolate morsels just until thoroughly incorporated; if the motor labors, complete the mixing with a large wooden spoon. If the dough is crumbly, gradually mix in a teaspoon or two of water until it holds together.

Divide the dough into quarters. Divide each quarter into 8 equal balls. Space about 2½ inches apart on the baking sheets. With a lightly greased fork, form a crisscross on the cookie tops, pressing each down until about 2½ inches in diameter.

Bake (middle rack) one pan at a time for 7 to 11 minutes or until the cookies are not quite firm when pressed in the center top; be careful not to overbake. Transfer the pan to a cooling rack. Let the cookies stand for 3 to 4 minutes; they will be too tender to move at first. Using a wide spatula, transfer the cookies to wire racks. Let stand until thoroughly cooled.

Yield: Makes thirty-two 2¾-inch cookies

Storage: Store these, airtight, for up to 1 week. They can be frozen, airtight, for up to 1½ months.

3½ cups unbleached all-purpose
     white flour
1⅔ cups granulated sugar
1½ tablespoons ground cinnamon
1½ tablespoons ground ginger
1½ tablespoons ground cloves
2   teaspoons baking powder
     Scant ½ teaspoon salt
1   cup corn oil or other flavorless
     vegetable oil
⅓   cup light or dark molasses (not
     blackstrap)
3   large eggs, at room temperature
     and beaten with a fork
     Zest (yellow part of the peel) of
     1 large lemon and/or
     ½ teaspoon lemon extract

Tip

For extra fragrance and flavor,
garnish the cookies with a sprinkling
of lemon or orange decorating sugar
(page 333) just before they go in
the oven.

BIG MOLASSES-SPICE FLATS

Rustic and homespun-looking, these large flat cookies have a crispy-chewy texture and lovely fragrance. The molasses, a trio of spices, and the lemon all mingle together to give them robust flavor. They always win compliments from spice cookie fans, and are also popular with those who don't care for or (more likely) can't eat butter.

Baking Preliminaries: Position a rack in the middle of the oven; preheat to 350°F. Grease several large baking sheets or line with baking parchment.

In a large bowl, thoroughly stir together the flour, sugar, cinnamon, ginger, cloves, baking powder, and salt. In a deep medium bowl, using a fork or whisk, beat together the oil, molasses, eggs, zest, and/or extract until well blended. Vigorously stir the oil mixture into the flour mixture until thoroughly incorporated. If the dough is very soft, stir in up to 2 tablespoons more flour until evenly incorporated.

Turn the dough out onto a sheet of wax paper. Divide it into quarters. Form each quarter into 8 balls, spacing them about 3 inches apart on baking sheets. Press down on the balls with the oiled bottom of a large flat drinking glass until about 2½ inches in diameter.

Bake (middle rack) one sheet at a time for 9 to 12 minutes, just until the cookies are beginning to brown at the edges; be careful not to overbake. Let stand to firm up for 3 minutes. Transfer to wire racks; let stand until cooled completely.

Yield: Makes thirty-two 3½-inch cookies

Storage: Store these, airtight and at room temperature, for up to 10 days. They can be frozen, airtight, for up to 2 months; let come to room temperature before serving.

1 cup (2 sticks) unsalted butter, slightly softened

⅔ cup corn oil, canola oil, or other flavorless vegetable oil

¾ cup powdered sugar

⅔ cup packed light brown sugar

2 teaspoons baking powder

¾ teaspoon ground cinnamon, Saigon cinnamon preferred

½ teaspoon salt

1 large egg plus 1 large egg yolk, at room temperature

2½ teaspoons vanilla extract

3⅔ cups unbleached all-purpose white flour

⅓ cup granulated sugar combined with 1 teaspoon cinnamon for garnish

CRISPY-SOFT CINNAMON-VANILLA MONSTER COOKIES

At first glance these monster cookies look traditional, maybe ordinary, but they have a whisper-crisp texture and a gentle, kid-pleasing flavor that make them quite special. They are quietly handsome and, particularly if fresh, gourmet-quality cinnamon is used, their taste and aroma linger in memory long after the last crumbs are gone. They may well become a family favorite. Just in case you're curious, the oil in the cookies helps produce their tender yet crispy texture.

Baking Preliminaries: Position a rack in the upper third of the oven; preheat to 350°F. Grease several baking sheets or line with baking parchment.

In a large mixer bowl with the mixer on medium speed, beat together the butter, oil, powdered and brown sugars, baking powder, cinnamon, and salt until very light and fluffy, about 2 minutes. Scrape down the bowl as needed.

Beat in the egg and yolk and the vanilla until very well blended and smooth. On low speed, beat in a generous half of the flour. Beat or stir in the remainder of the flour until evenly incorporated. Refrigerate the dough for 10 to 15 minutes to firm up slightly. Put the sugar-cinnamon mixture in a shallow bowl.

Working on wax paper, divide the dough in half, then divide each half into 12 equal balls. Space them about 3 inches apart on the baking sheets. Lightly coat the bottom of a large flat-bottomed jar with vegetable oil. Dip the oiled surface into the garnishing sugar, then press down on a ball to form an evenly thick 3½-inch round. Continue, dipping the jar into sugar between each cookie, and oiling it after every 2 or 3 cookies. (If the sugar builds up, wipe it off, re-oil the jar bottom, and continue.) Lightly sprinkle the cookies with additional cinnamon-sugar.

Bake (upper rack) one pan at a time for 8 to 10 minutes or until the cookies are just light golden brown around edges; don't overbake. Turn the pan from front to back about halfway through baking to ensure even browning. Transfer the pan to a cooling rack. Let stand until the cookies firm up, about 2 minutes. Then, using a wide spatula, transfer them to wire racks. Let stand until completely cooled.

Yield: Makes twenty-four 4½-inch cookies

Storage: Store these, airtight, for up to 10 days. They can be frozen, airtight, for up to 2 months.

1½ cups powdered sugar

¼ cup cornstarch

¼ cup washed, patted dry, and chopped fresh rose petals or 2 tablespoons finely chopped fresh, very tender lavender blooms and bracts (no stems)

1 tablespoon finely grated lemon zest (yellow part of the peel) Generous ¼ teaspoon salt

2½ cups unbleached all-purpose white flour, plus more if needed

1½ cups (3 sticks) cool and firm unsalted butter, cut into pats

1 tablespoon rose water for rose cookies or 2 teaspoons vanilla for lavender cookies

¾ teaspoon lemon extract Rose or lavender buttercream (page 330)

Tip

For an even more elaborate presentation and larger yield, make the recipe in the rose, lavender, and tarragon or basil flavors, then serve the pink, lavender, and green frosted meltaways all together on a tray.

ROSE OR LAVENDER-LEMON GARDEN PARTY MELTAWAYS

These strike me as the ultimate spring or summer garden party cookies. They've got a romantic garden look and lovely floral or herb flavors to match. For one thing, the recipe calls for tossing chopped rose petals (yes, that's right, fresh-from-the-garden rose petals!), or lavender blooms and bracts (the flower heads), into the dough. These lend a unique bouquet and taste: In the case of the rose version, it's subtle and elusive; in the case of the lavender it's fairly bold and distinct. (The same recipe can also be modified slightly to create equally attractive tarragon-lemon, or basil-lemon cookies; see the variations at the end.) Don't try to substitute dried rose petals or herbs—they are a bit too coarse and dry to work well.

The tender, not-too-sweet cookies are also designed to be presented with a matching extremely flavorful and pretty rose or lavender buttercream (page 330). The soft pink or lavender (or if making mint, tarragon, or basil cookies, pastel green) toppings are particularly eye-catching piped into rosebud-shaped or traditional rosettes using a pastry bag fitted with a ½-inch-diameter open star tip, but they can be swirled on with a knife if preferred.

To complete the garden theme and create even more visual impact, just before serving I like to sprinkle the cookie tops with a little floral "confetti" or garnish with tiny flower petals or blooms. For the confetti, I simply chop rose petals into small shreds; I use the tiny bright lavender blooms (plucked from the bracts) as is. Other suitable petals and whole edible flower options include fresh tiny pansies, rosebuds, pinks (aka dianthus), Johnny-jump-ups, and real violets (not African violets). (Keep in mind that many flowers, including African violets, are inedible or taste unpleasant so can't be used.) Remember that fresh flowers, whole or chopped, start to fade in about an hour. And use only unsprayed flowers, of course.

Baking Preliminaries: Position a rack in the middle of the oven; preheat to 325°F. Line several large baking sheets with baking parchment.

In a food processor, process the powdered sugar, cornstarch, rose petals or lavender, zest, and salt until very well blended, about 2 minutes. Carefully scrape up the mixture from the bottom and down from the sides; then process 2 minutes longer or until the petals or herb bits are very fine but not pureed.

Add 1 cup flour to the processor. Sprinkle the butter pats, then the rose water or vanilla and lemon extract over the top. Process in on/off pulses until the butter is cut in and only very fine bits remain. Sprinkle over all but about ¼ cup remaining flour. Pulse the processor until the flour is

mostly incorporated, stopping and scraping up the bottom and down the bowl sides several times; don't overprocess.

Put half of the remaining ¼ cup flour on a large sheet of baking parchment and scrape out the processed dough onto it. Sprinkle over the remaining flour. Lightly knead with the hands just until it comes together smoothly. If the dough is crumbly, work in up to 3 teaspoons water, or for a less soft or wet dough work in up to ¼ cup more flour.

Shape the dough into an evenly thick disk, then divide it into quarters. Divide each quarter into 12 equal portions. Shape the portions into balls, spacing about 2 inches apart on the baking sheets. Pat down the balls into scant 2-inch-diameter, evenly thick rounds with a palm.

Bake (middle rack) one pan at a time for 15 to 18 minutes or until just firm when pressed in the center top and faintly tinged at the edges. Transfer the pan to a wire rack. Let cool completely; the cookies are too tender to move while warm.

To decorate with buttercream: Top the thoroughly cooled cookies with a swirl or piped rosette of the matching buttercream frosting (page 330), following the directions in the frosting recipe. Garnish the buttercream (as shown in the photo) with edible flower petals or chopped rose petal or lavender bloom "confetti," if desired.

Yield: Makes forty-eight 2¼- to 2½-inch cookies

Storage: Store these, airtight and at room temperature, for up to 10 days. They can be frozen for up to 1½ months.

Variation: Minted Meltaways Proceed exactly as for the rose petal meltaways, except substitute ⅓ cup chopped tender spearmint or peppermint leaves (no stems) for the rose petals. Process as directed until the leaves are very finely chopped but not pureed. Omit the lemon extract and add ½ teaspoon mint extract when the vanilla is added. Top the cookies with Fresh Mint Buttercream (page 332) and garnish with mint "confetti" or tiny crystallized or fresh mint leaves, if desired.

Variation: Tarragon-Lemon or Basil-Lemon Meltaways Proceed exactly as for the rose petal meltaways, except substitute ⅓ cup chopped tender tarragon or basil leaves (no stems) for the rose petals. Process as directed until the leaves are very finely chopped but not pureed. If available, add ½ teaspoon anise extract when the vanilla and lemon extracts are added. Top the cookies with the Fresh Tarragon or Basil Buttercream (page 332), and garnish with tarragon or basil "confetti," if desired.

¾ cup (1½ sticks) unsalted butter, cut into chunks

1 cup plus 2 tablespoons granulated sugar

1 large egg, at room temperature

2 tablespoons light corn syrup
Grated zest (yellow part of the peel) of 1 large lemon

¾ teaspoon lemon extract

½ teaspoon baking soda

¼ teaspoon salt

2 cups unbleached all-purpose white flour
Lemon-scented decorating sugar (page 333) for garnish, optional

Tip

Make these smaller and tuck them around lemon buttercream (page 328) for citrus sandwich cookies!

LIGHTLY LEMON SUGAR COOKIES

As the name suggests, these sugar cookies have a really delightful light lemon flavor. They are also crispy on the edges and noticeably chewy in the middle. Though the recipe *appears* to be fairly ordinary, these are in fact exceptional. They are one of my husband's favorites, and, as you might guess, he's pretty selective because he gets to sample a *lot* of different cookies!

In a large microwave-safe bowl, with the microwave on 50 percent power heat the butter until very soft but not melted or runny, stopping and stirring every 30 seconds. (Alternatively, warm the butter over medium heat in a medium saucepan, stirring, until softened but not melted or runny. Remove from the heat.) Continue stirring until completely creamy-smooth.

Vigorously stir the sugar into the butter until well blended. Let stand until cool to barely warm (otherwise the egg may cook when added). Vigorously stir in the egg, corn syrup, lemon zest, extract, baking soda, and salt. Gradually stir in the flour just until evenly incorporated. If the dough is crumbly, work in up to 2 teaspoons water until it holds together; if too soft, work in up to 1 tablespoon more flour. Cover and refrigerate until firm, at least 45 minutes and up to 24 hours. (Let very cold, stiff dough warm up slightly before using.)

Baking Preliminaries: Position a rack in the middle of the oven; preheat to 350°F. Grease several large baking sheets or coat with nonstick spray.

With greased hands, shape the dough into 1-inch balls. For more intense lemon flavor, lightly dip the cookie tops in lemon sugar. Space, sugar side up, 2½ inches apart on the baking sheets; allow room for spreading.

Bake (middle rack) one sheet at a time for 11 to 14 minutes or until tinged with brown at the edges and just barely firm when pressed in the center top. (For chewier cookies, underbake; for crisper ones, overbake slightly.) Let stand on the baking sheet for 5 minutes. Then transfer the cookies to wire racks. Cool completely before packing for storage.

Yield: Makes about forty 3-inch cookies

Storage: Store these, airtight, for up to 1 week. They can be frozen, airtight, for up to 1 month.

Easy
One-bowl,
one-spoon mixing.
Shaped by
rolling into balls.

¾ cup (1½ sticks) cold unsalted butter, cut into chunks
1 cup granulated sugar
1 teaspoon baking powder
1 teaspoon ground nutmeg, freshly grated preferred
1 teaspoon ground cinnamon
½ teaspoon salt
3 tablespoons heavy cream, plus more if needed
2 tablespoons dark rum; or 2 tablespoons fresh orange juice and ¼ teaspoon rum or brandy extract; or ⅛ teaspoon almond extract
3 large egg yolks, at room temperature
2 teaspoons vanilla extract
2½ cups unbleached all-purpose white flour
1½ tablespoons granulated sugar combined with ½ teaspoon ground nutmeg for garnish

Tip

Freshly grated nutmeg really gives these cookies a nice flavor boost. (Grate some of the rest of the nutmeg over your eggnog to enhance it, too.)

EGGNOGGINS

These gently flavored sugar cookies don't contain eggnog; they just have its characteristic appealing cream, egg, and spice flavors. My family's eggnog has always been spiked with a little rum or blended whiskey, so I like it in this recipe. But feel free to omit it if you wish to cater to children's tastes or prefer to avoid alcohol.

Eggnoggins are actually good anytime, but they are particularly popular at Thanksgiving and Christmas—when eggnog itself is on minds and menus of many.

Baking Preliminaries: Position a rack in the middle of the oven; preheat to 325°F. Line several baking sheets with baking parchment.

In a large microwave-safe bowl, with the microwave on 50 percent power heat the butter until soft but not melted or runny, stopping and stirring every 30 seconds. (Alternatively, warm the butter over medium heat in a medium saucepan, stirring, until softened but not melted or runny. Remove from the heat.) Continue stirring until completely creamy-smooth.

Vigorously stir the sugar, baking powder, nutmeg, cinnamon, and salt into the butter until well blended. Let cool till warm. Stir in the cream and rum, then the egg yolks one at a time, then the vanilla, until the mixture is well blended. Stir in the flour until evenly incorporated. If the dough is dry and crumbly, stir in a little more cream. Refrigerate for 10 to 15 minutes to firm up.

On wax paper, divide the dough into quarters. Then divide each quarter into 12 equal balls. Space about 2½ inches apart on baking sheets; pat down into 2-inch rounds. Sprinkle with the sugar-nutmeg garnish.

Bake (middle rack) one pan at a time for 15 to 18 minutes or until the cookies are tinged with brown at the edges and just barely firm when pressed in the center top. Remove the pan from the oven; let the cookies stand to firm up for 2 to 3 minutes. Using a wide spatula, transfer the cookies to wire racks. Let cool.

Yield: Makes forty-eight 2¼-inch cookies

Storage: Store these, airtight, for up to 1 week. They can be frozen, airtight, for 3 to 4 weeks.

½ cup dark corn syrup
½ cup packed light or dark brown
    sugar
1 large egg, at room temperature
1 cup (2 sticks) unsalted butter,
    melted and cooled
2 teaspoons vanilla extract
1½ teaspoons baking powder
¼ teaspoon salt
2⅓ cups unbleached all-purpose
    white flour
    1½ to 2 cups (up to one 10-
    to 11-ounce bag) butterscotch
    morsels, divided

Tip

To quickly bring a refrigerated egg to room temperature, set it in a cup of warm water. Let stand for 1 minute, then replace the water with hot tap water. Let stand until the egg is needed.

BUTTERSCOTCH CHEWIES

The dark corn syrup, brown sugar, and abundance of butter in this recipe lend these large homey rounds great succulence and chew. They are just short of gooey-soft in the centers; the edges are chewy-crisp. The cookies are always kid pleasers.

In a large bowl, vigorously stir together the corn syrup, brown sugar, egg, butter, vanilla, baking powder, and salt until very well blended and the sugar dissolves. Stir in the flour and 1 cup morsels just until the flour is evenly incorporated. Cover and refrigerate the dough for 30 to 45 minutes (no longer), until just slightly firm. Put the remaining morsels in a shallow saucer.

Baking Preliminaries: Position a rack in the middle of the oven; preheat to 350°F. Coat several large baking sheets with nonstick spray or line with baking parchment.

On a sheet of wax paper, divide the dough into quarters. With well-greased hands, divide each quarter into 8 equal balls. Lightly dip the top of each ball into the morsels until a few pieces are imbedded. Space the balls, morsel side up, about 2½ inches apart on the baking sheets, patting them down just until flat on top.

Bake (middle rack) one sheet at a time for 10 to 12 minutes or until the cookies are lightly browned; they should look moist and just slightly underdone in the centers. Transfer the baking sheet to a wire rack. Let the cookies firm up for 5 minutes. Using a wide spatula, transfer them to wire racks. Cool completely before packing for storage.

Yield: Makes twenty-four 2½-inch cookies

Storage: Store these, airtight, for up to 1 week. They can be frozen, airtight, for up to 1 month.

Easy one-bowl, one-spoon mixing.
Simple hand shaping—
rolled into balls,
then flattened.

1 cup (2 sticks) unsalted butter,
   cut into chunks
1 cup chopped pecans, plus 36
   perfect halves for garnish
¾ cup powdered sugar
¼ cup packed light brown sugar
   3 to 4 tablespoons light cream
   or half-and-half, plus more if
   needed
2 teaspoons vanilla extract
   Scant ½ teaspoon salt
2 cups unbleached all-purpose
   white flour

{ **Cookie Jar Wisdom**
When life is bad and getting
worse, keep a cookie in your
purse.

BEST-EVER BROWNED BUTTER–PECAN SHORTBREAD DOMES

I love pecan shortbread cookies and think this may be my best version ever. Browning the pecans in brown butter not only toasts the nuts but also permeates the butter with their sweet, earthy flavor. A perfect pecan half, not only looks pretty, but adds crunch and one more big, satisfying bite of pecan.

These are tender, rich, and super mellow. Just thinking about them makes me want to go bake!

Baking Preliminaries: Position a rack in the upper third of the oven; preheat to 350°F. Grease several baking sheets or line with baking parchment.

In a medium heavy saucepan over medium heat, bring the butter to a boil; it will be foamy. Adjust the heat so it bubbles gently. Cook, stirring the bottom frequently, until the butter turns fragrant and golden, 3 to 4 minutes; watch carefully to avoid burning. Stir in the pecans; it's normal for the mixture to foam up. Let return to a gentle boil. Cook, watching carefully, for up to 2 minutes; if the pecans begin to darken, immediately remove the pan from the heat. Let cool till warm, about 15 minutes. (Or speed cooling by placing the pan in a bowl of ice water.)

Stir the powdered and brown sugars, 3 tablespoons cream, vanilla, and salt into the cooled butter-pecan mixture until smoothly incorporated. Stir in the flour until fully incorporated. If the mixture is crumbly, work in more cream until it holds together nicely but is not wet.

Divide the dough into thirds. Divide each third into 12 equal balls, spacing about 2½ inches apart on the baking sheets. Press a pecan half firmly into each ball; if the edges of the rounds crack, just push them back together again.

Bake (upper rack) one pan at a time for 13 to 17 minutes or until the cookies are just light golden all over and slighter darker at the edges. Turn the pan from front to back about halfway through baking to ensure even browning. Transfer the pan to a cooling rack. Let the cookies firm up, 5 minutes; they are too tender to move while hot. Using a wide spatula, transfer them to wire racks. Let cool completely.

Yield: Makes thirty-six 2½-inch cookies

Storage: Store these, airtight, for up to 10 days. They can be frozen, airtight, for up to 2 months.

Fairly Easy
Easy food processor mixing.
Store-bought or
shortcut filling options.

2 cups lightly packed shredded or flaked sweetened coconut, divided

⅔ cup packed light or dark brown sugar

¼ teaspoon salt

1 cup (2 sticks) cool and firm unsalted butter, cut into chunks

1 large egg, at room temperature

2 teaspoons vanilla extract

½ cup cornstarch

2 cups unbleached all-purpose white flour, divided

1 batch Homemade Dulce de Leche (page 323) or about 2 cups purchased dulce de leche

Tip

Create slightly more unusual chocolate dulce de leche sandwiches. Simply ready them using the chocolate filling on page 315. For an even more pronounced chocolate flavor, use the chocolate ganache filling on page 318.

COCONUT ALFAJORES WITH DULCE DE LECHE

Alfajores are wildly popular in a number of Latin American countries, and with good reason. Normally they are presented as sandwich cookies filled with a rich, sweet milk caramel called "dulce de leche." This gives them a unique succulence and chewy-gooey goodness. Here the flavor is further enhanced by adding toasted coconut for extra taste, texture, and visual appeal.

Baking Preliminaries: Position a rack in the middle of the oven; preheat to 325°F. Grease several large baking sheets or coat with nonstick spray.

On a rimmed baking sheet toast the coconut (middle rack), stirring every 3 minutes, until lightly browned, about 10 minutes. Let cool.

In a food processor, process half the coconut, the brown sugar, and salt until the coconut is very finely chopped. Add the butter, egg, and vanilla. Process in on/off pulses until the butter is cut in and the mixture is crumbly. Add the cornstarch and half the flour. Process in pulses until the ingredients are evenly blended and the mixture just starts to come together.

Turn out the dough onto a sheet of wax paper. Gradually knead in the remaining flour until evenly incorporated. If the dough is dry, work in up to 1 tablespoon water; if too wet, work in up to 2 tablespoons flour.

Divide the dough into quarters, then divide each quarter into 12 balls. Space about 2½ inches apart on the baking sheets. Pat down with a greased palm until flattened into 2¼-inch rounds.

Bake (middle rack) for 7 to 10 minutes or until the cookies are just barely firm when pressed in the center top. Remove from the oven, and let the cookies stand to firm up for 3 or 4 minutes. Transfer to wire racks using a wide-bladed spatula. Let thoroughly cool.

Assemble the sandwiches: Spread enough dulce de leche on the underside of a cookie to produce a ¼- to ⅓-inch-thick layer. Cover with another cookie, underside down. Press down until the filling squeezes out to the edges. Repeat to ready all the sandwiches. Garnish by patting the remaining coconut into the filling at the cookie edges all the way around.

Yield: Makes twenty-four 2¾-inch cookie sandwiches

Storage: Store these, airtight and refrigerated, for up to 1 week. They can be frozen, airtight, for up to 1 month; let thaw before serving.

1 cup lightly packed flaked or
   shredded sweetened coconut
6½ tablespoons unsalted butter,
   cut into chunks
⅓ cup egg whites (about 3 large), at
   room temperature and free of
   yolk
   Generous pinch of salt
¾ cup plus 2 tablespoons
   powdered sugar
1 teaspoon vanilla extract
¼ teaspoon coconut extract (not
   imitation), or substitute
   ⅛ teaspoon almond extract
   and ⅛ teaspoon vanilla extract
½ cup unbleached all-purpose
   white flour

Tip

Be sure to have some wine bottles
or rolling pins at hand so the tuiles
can be draped over them while
still warm and pliable. Since you
must work quickly, bake only 5 or 6
cookies at once.

TOASTED COCONUT TUILES

These very crisp, thin coconut-flavored wafers are shaped somewhat like the curved tiles (*tuiles* in French) covering the roofs in parts of France. The wafers are formed by spreading out small amounts of batter onto the baking sheets with a table knife. When the wafers come off the baking sheets they are immediately draped over a curved surface such as a rolling pin or wine bottle to set their shape.

Baking Preliminaries: Position one rack in the middle of the oven and one in the upper third; preheat to 325°F. Line several baking sheets with baking parchment.

On a large rimmed baking sheet, toast the coconut (middle rack) for 6 to 8 minutes, stirring frequently to redistribute and promote even toasting, until just tinged with brown. Meanwhile, in a microwave-safe bowl, melt the butter on 50 percent power, stopping and stirring every 30 seconds, until very soft and partly melted. (Alternatively, partially melt the butter in a saucepan over medium-low heat, stirring constantly. Remove from the heat.) Stir until melted, then let cool till warm.

Using a whisk, in a large grease-free bowl, beat together the egg whites and salt until frothy and opaque. Gradually whisk in the sugar, then the vanilla and coconut extracts. Sift the flour over the batter; fold in gently. Whisk in the cooled butter until evenly incorporated.

Drop the batter by heaping teaspoonfuls onto each baking sheet, spacing 3½ inches apart. Using a table knife, spread out the rounds until about 3 inches around or until the batter is thin enough to see through in spots. Generously sprinkle the toasted coconut over the rounds.

Bake (upper rack) one pan at a time for 6 to 8 minutes; reverse the pan from front to back about halfway through, continuing until the tuiles are rimmed with ½ inch of brown. Remove from the oven and let firm up for about 20 seconds. Then while the cookies are pliable, lift up with a wide spatula and drape them over lightly greased rolling pins or empty wine bottles. (If the last cookies firm up too much while the first are being shaped, slip the pan back into the oven to soften them.) Once firmed up, transfer them to racks until thoroughly cooled.

Yield: Makes about twenty-five 4-inch tuiles

Storage: Store these, airtight, with the tuiles stacked. Store in a cool spot but not refrigerated. They will keep for several days. They can be frozen, airtight, for up to 1 month.

1 cup (2 sticks) cool and firm
   unsalted butter, cut into
   chunks
¾ cup (packed) dark brown sugar or
   pure maple sugar granules
2 teaspoons vanilla extract
¼ teaspoon salt
2 cups unbleached all-purpose
   white flour
1½ tablespoons turbinado
   (granular brown) sugar or other
   coarse granulated sugar for
   garnish, optional

Tip

The same basic recipe may also
be used to prepare a chamomile
or lavender shortbread. See the
variation.

BROWN SUGAR (OR MAPLE) PETTICOAT TAILS SHORTBREAD

It's long, slow baking that brings out the butter flavor of this simple, irresistible shortbread. A second baking after the round is cut into wedges helps lightly brown and crisp the individual pieces all over so they are crisp-firm to the bite.

This version is equally good readied with brown sugar or maple sugar; the latter, of course, will give it an American twist. The fan-like "petticoat tails" shape of the cookies is traditional; some historians think the term references the bell-hoop skirts of early English court ladies. Another (less fanciful!) theory is that "petticoat tails" is merely a corruption of the French words *petite galettes*, or "little cakes." The petticoat tails taste lovely, regardless.

Baking Preliminaries: Position a rack in the middle of the oven; preheat to 300°F. Set out a 9- to 10-inch springform pan or 10- to 11-inch pie plate. (If using a pie plate, line it with foil that overhangs 2 inches all around.) Set out a large ungreased baking sheet.

Processor mixing: **Combine the butter, brown sugar, vanilla, and salt in a food processor. Process in on/off pulses until the butter is cut in and the mixture is crumbly. Add the flour. Process in pulses just until the ingredients are evenly blended and no pieces of butter are visible.**

Alternative mixer method: **Let the butter soften slightly. In a large bowl, with a mixer on medium speed, beat the butter, brown sugar, vanilla, and salt on medium speed just until well blended, scraping down the bowl as needed. On low speed, beat in the flour just until evenly incorporated; don't overbeat. If the mixer motor labors, stir in the last of the flour with a large spoon.**

Turn out the dough onto wax paper. Press it into a smooth mass with your hands. If the dough is crumbly, work in up to 3 teaspoons water until it holds together. Press it evenly into the bottom of the springform pan or pie plate. Smooth the dough surface by laying a sheet of wax paper over the top, then smoothing out and pressing down with your fingertips. Using the tines of a fork or the dowel-like part of a wooden spoon handle, press decorative indentations into the dough edge all the way around. With a table knife, carefully score (avoid cutting the pan bottom) the dough into quarters, then score each quarter into 4 or 5 wedges. If desired, garnish the top with a sprinkling of coarse sugar; pat it down.

Bake (middle rack) for 45 to 55 minutes or until the shortbread is fragrant and tinged with brown. Let the pan cool for 10 to 15 minutes on a wire rack. Carefully remove the springform sides and slide the shortbread off the bottom onto a cutting board. (Or very carefully lift out the shortbread from the pie plate using the foil.) Using a large knife, cut through the dough at the scored marks to yield 16 (or 20) wedges. Using a wide spatula, place the wedges, slightly separated, onto the baking sheet. Bake for 10 to 15 minutes longer, until lightly browned all over. Using a wide spatula, gently transfer the wedges to a wire rack. Let stand until completely cooled.

Yield: Makes 16 or 20 petticoat tails (wedges)

Storage: Store these, airtight, at room temperature for up to 3 weeks.

Variation: Chamomile or Lavender Petticoat Tails Shortbread Prepare exactly as directed except substitute $\frac{2}{3}$ cup granulated sugar for the brown sugar. Use the alternative mixer method to combine the ingredients. Beat in 3 tablespoons pure chamomile tea (removed from their tea bags) or $2\frac{1}{2}$ tablespoons very finely pulverized dried lavender along with the butter and granulated sugar. Reduce the flour to 2 cups minus 2 tablespoons. Proceed exactly as directed.

OTHER SHORTBREAD SHAPING OPTIONS

1. For slightly easier shaping with a more professional look, bake the shortbread in a 10- to 11-inch fluted tart pan with a removable bottom. Finish the dough edges by pushing it into the indentations in the pan; be sure the dough edge is evenly thick all the way around. In this case, the edges don't need to be decorated with a fork or wooden spoon.
2. Bake the shortbread in a ceramic shortbread mold designed for the purpose. Follow the directions that come with the mold. Gently tip the baked shortbread out onto a cutting board after it has cooled in the mold for 10 to 15 minutes, then cut it into pieces following the lines imprinted on the shortbread bottom. Return the cookies to the oven for crisping following the recipe directions.

1 cup (2 sticks) unsalted butter, slightly softened and cut into chunks
1 cup powdered sugar, plus ⅓ to ½ cup more for coating cookies
2 large egg yolks, at room temperature
2½ teaspoons vanilla extract
1 tablespoon finely grated orange zest (orange part of the peel)
¼ teaspoon ground cinnamon
⅛ teaspoon salt
2⅔ cups unbleached all-purpose white flour, plus more if needed

Tip

If you have homemade vanilla powdered sugar (page 327), by all means use it to garnish the cookies in place of the plain powdered sugar called for in the ingredients list.

POLVORONES DE MARANJAS (ORANGE DUSTIES)

Many people are familiar with Mexican wedding cookies, the small tender shortbread balls rolled in powdered sugar. These are similar in style, except that they are flavored with orange zest and a touch of cinnamon, a lovely, aromatic combination. They are often served at Christmastime, when oranges are in season in Mexico.

Take care handling these when they are warm; they are quite fragile.

Baking Preliminaries: Position a rack in the upper third of the oven; preheat the oven to 350°F. Lightly grease several large baking sheets or coat with nonstick spray.

In a large mixer bowl with the mixer on medium speed, beat together the butter and sugar until the mixture is lightened in color and well blended. Beat in the egg yolks, vanilla, zest, cinnamon, and salt until well blended and smooth. Beat in half the flour. Stir or beat in the remaining flour until thoroughly incorporated and smooth. If the dough is very soft, work in up to 2 tablespoons more flour to stiffen it slightly; if crumbly, work in a teaspoon or two of water.

Working on baking parchment or wax paper, divide the dough into quarters. Then divide each quarter into 12 equal portions and roll into balls. Space about 2 inches apart on the baking sheets.

Bake (upper rack) for 16 to 20 minutes or until they are barely brown at the edges. About halfway through baking, rotate the pans from front to back to promote even browning.

Let the cookies cool on the baking sheets for 5 minutes; they are too tender to move when hot. Gently transfer to wire racks; let stand until cooled completely. Working with a few cookies at a time, roll them in powdered sugar (or Vanilla Powdered Sugar, page 327) until evenly coated.

Yield: Makes forty-eight 2¼-inch cookies

Storage: Store these, airtight, for up to 1 week. They can be frozen, airtight, for up 1½ months.

2 cups blanched slivered almonds
1¼ cup granulated sugar
¼ teaspoon almond extract or
  vanilla extract
⅛ teaspoon salt
  ¼ to ⅓ cup egg whites (2 or 3
  large egg whites), at room
  temperature
  About 40 whole, blanched
  almonds for garnish, optional

Cookie Jar Wisdom
Don't cry over spilled
milk unless you drop your
cookies, too.

TOASTED ALMOND MACAROONS

The enticing nutty flavor and slight crunch of toasted almonds comes through clearly in these simple yet extremely appealing macaroons. They are a great solution when you need a gluten-free sweet that doesn't compromise at all on texture or taste; everybody just loves them! Note that because the egg whites aren't beaten, these are more substantial and less fluffy than meringue-based macaroons. (And easier to make, as well!)

Baking Preliminaries: Position a rack in the middle of the oven; preheat to 350°F. Line several large baking sheets with baking parchment.

Spread the almonds in a small roasting pan or rimmed baking sheet. Bake, stirring every 3 or 4 minutes, until fragrant and lightly colored, 7 to 9 minutes. Set aside until cooled. Reset the oven to 375°F.

Combine the sugar, extract, and salt in a processor. Process until well blended. Add the toasted almonds. Process just until they are very finely chopped and the mixture is not quite completely smooth. Immediately add ¼ cup egg whites, pulsing just until evenly incorporated. If the mixture is too dry and crumbly to hold together, a bit at a time add in more egg white until a slightly sticky dough forms. Turn it out onto a nonstick spray–coated sheet of parchment or wax paper.

With well-greased hands, pull off dough portions and shape into 1-inch balls. Space them about 2 inches apart on the baking sheets. If desired, press a whole blanched almond into the center of each ball. Or simply press down the tops just slightly.

Bake (middle rack) one sheet at a time for 13 to 16 minutes or until the macaroons are lightly browned at the edges and the centers are almost firm when pressed. Let the pans cool on wire racks to firm up for about 3 minutes. Transfer to cooling racks using a wide spatula. Cool thoroughly.

Yield: Makes thirty-five to forty 2-inch cookies

Storage: Store these, airtight for up to 1 week. They can be frozen, airtight, for up to 1 month.

⅔ cup granulated sugar

2 tablespoons chopped fresh
sage leaves (stems removed)

Grated zest (orange part of the
peel) from 1 large orange

1 teaspoon baking powder

¼ teaspoon salt

2 cups unbleached all-purpose
white flour, divided

¾ cup (1½ sticks) very cold unsalted
butter, cut into chunks

1 large egg, at room temperature
and beaten with a fork

1½ cups dried sweetened
cranberries, coarsely chopped
if very large

Orange-scented sugar (page
333) or ¼ cup chopped
pistachios for garnish, optional

Tip

Use only *fresh* sage, which is most
readily available in supermarkets
around Thanksgiving (when folks are
preparing their turkeys). This works
out nicely, as the cookies are perfect
for the holidays. If you frequent
farmers' markets, or you garden,
fresh sage can be had during the
entire growing season; the cookies
are worth making then, too.

CRANBERRY, ORANGE, AND SAGE COOKIES

I was a little skeptical about using sage in cookies at first. But I'd been extremely pleased with the lavender and rosemary in several recipes, and the fresh sage from one of my tester's gardens looked so gorgeous, I just had to try it.

The results were not merely good, but awesome! The combination of cranberries, orange, and sage smells and tastes spectacular, and as a bonus, the cookies are quite attractive. The complex, unusual citrus-herb taste definitely complements the cranberries, which contribute their usual color and zip.

Baking Preliminaries: Position a rack in the middle of the oven; preheat to 350°F. Lightly grease several baking sheets or coat with nonstick spray.

Combine the sugar, sage, orange zest, baking powder, and salt in a food processor. Process for 1 to 2 minutes or until the sage is chopped into very fine flecks. Add half the flour, stirring it in with a spoon until partially incorporated. Sprinkle the butter over the mixture. Process just until only fine bits of butter are visible. Drizzle the egg over the dough. Incorporate using about fifteen 1-second pulses, stopping and stirring to lift and fold in the dough on the bottom several times.

As soon as the dough begins to come together, turn it out onto a large sheet of wax paper or baking parchment. Sprinkle over and knead in the remaining flour and the cranberries just until the dough is thoroughly mixed. (If it is very soft, wrap the paper around it and refrigerate for about 10 minutes until firmer and easier to handle.)

Divide the dough into quarters. Divide each quarter into 8 equal balls, spacing about 2½ inches apart on the baking sheets. Pat down with a greased palm until just flattened. If desired, sprinkle the tops with orange-scented sugar (or pistachios, if preferred); pat down to imbed.

Bake (middle rack) one sheet at a time 10 to 12 minutes or until the cookies are lightly browned at the edges and the centers are almost firm with pressed. Let the pans cool on wire racks to firm up for 3 minutes. Transfer the cookies to racks using a wide spatula. Let cool.

Yield: Makes thirty-two 2¾-inch cookies

Storage: Store these, airtight, for up to 1 week. They can be frozen, airtight, for up to 1 month.

Fairly Easy
One-pot, one-spoon mixing.
Hand shaped into balls,
flattened with a glass.

- 1 15-ounce can pumpkin
     (not seasoned pie filling)
- 10 tablespoons (1¼ sticks) unsalted
      butter, cut into chunks
- 1¾ cups granulated sugar, plus
      ¼ cup for garnish
- 1½ teaspoons baking powder
- 1 tablespoon ground cinnamon,
     plus 1 teaspoon for garnish
- 1 teaspoon ground allspice
- ½ teaspoon ground cloves
     Generous ¾ teaspoon salt
- 1 large egg, at room temperature
- 2½ cups unbleached all-purpose
      white flour, plus more if
      needed

Tip

If you have a drinking glass with a 2½-inch diameter bottom, use it as a guide to press the balls of dough out to just the right size.

Tip

Some of the excess liquid is squeezed from the pumpkin puree before it is used. (You'll be amazed at how much can be removed!) This makes it possible to use a lot of pumpkin without causing the cookies to become too cakey or soggy. The result: extra "pumpkiny" flavor and goodness.

PUMPKIN SOFTIES

The same unmistakable come-hither aroma and taste that have made pumpkin pie a classic will be your reward for baking these. Due to the abundance of pumpkin in the recipe, they are soft, fragrant, and exceedingly homey. While delightful as is, they may be tucked around the marshmallow vanilla filling on page 320, for whoopie-pie-like treats.

Baking Preliminaries: Position a rack in the middle of the oven; preheat to 350°F. Grease several baking sheets or coat with nonstick spray.

Line a colander with a triple thickness of sturdy paper towels. Put the pumpkin into the colander. Cover with 3 more layers of towels. Pat down the towels. Let the pumpkin stand in the sink to drain.

In a large saucepan over medium heat, melt the butter until runny, stirring, then immediately remove the pan from the heat. Stir in 1¾ cups sugar, then the baking powder, 1 tablespoon cinnamon, the allspice, cloves, and salt until the mixture is very well blended.

Press down very hard on the towels and pumpkin and squeeze out as much liquid as possible; if the towels start to tear, replace them with fresh ones and continue until the pumpkin seems fairly dry and compact. Vigorously stir the pumpkin into the butter mixture until completely smooth and well blended. Vigorously stir in the egg. Stir in the flour until evenly incorporated. If the dough is too soft to shape, stir in up to 3 tablespoons more flour and let stand.

Stir together the ¼ cup sugar and 1 teaspoon cinnamon for garnishing in a small shallow bowl. Scoop up dough portions and shape into generous 1¼-inch balls with well-greased hands. Space them about 3 inches apart on the baking sheets. Grease the bottom of a wide-bottomed drinking glass. Dip the glass into the garnishing sugar, then flatten the balls until 2½ inches in diameter. Dip the glass in sugar before flattening each cookie; wipe off any buildup and re-grease it as necessary.

Bake (middle rack) one sheet at a time for 9 to 12 minutes or until the cookies are barely tinged with brown and feel almost firm when pressed in the center; be careful not to overbake. Let the sheets stand on a wire rack until the cookies firm up, about 2 minutes. Using a wide spatula, transfer the cookies to the racks. Let cool completely.

Yield: Makes thirty to thirty-five 3-inch cookies

Storage: Store these, airtight, for up to 1 week. They can be frozen, airtight, for 3 to 4 weeks.

1 cup (2 sticks) unsalted butter, slightly softened
1 cup packed light brown sugar
⅔ cup granulated sugar
2 large eggs, at room temperature
½ cup light or dark molasses
1 tablespoon peeled and finely grated fresh gingerroot
½ teaspoon baking powder
2 teaspoons ground ginger
½ tablespoon ground cinnamon, Saigon cinnamon preferred
1¼ teaspoons ground cloves
½ teaspoon salt
4 cups unbleached all-purpose white flour

Glaze

1 cup powdered sugar, sifted after measuring
1 tablespoon unsalted butter, cut into bits

Tip

The best way to keep fresh gingerroot is in a glass jar or bottle covered in a little white wine or sherry and refrigerated. The acidity and cool temperature will preserve it for up to 3 months. Simply pat it dry and peel before using.

GLAZED DOUBLE-GINGER MOLASSES MONSTER COOKIES

I suppose the reason more baked goods don't call for fresh gingerroot is that it's not usually a kitchen staple. But its taste is so fresh, clean, and pungent—especially when combined with molasses—that it's worth keeping around just to make these. I've never come across a molasses-spice cookie fan who didn't like them—not only for their zesty flavor and aroma, but also because of their toothsome texture and inviting look. Even though they are large, I can never eat just one!

Baking Preliminaries: Position a rack in the middle of the oven; preheat to 350°F. Grease several large baking sheets or coat with nonstick spray.

In a large mixer bowl, beat the butter and brown and granulated sugars until light and fluffy. Add the eggs, then the molasses, gingerroot, baking powder, ginger, cinnamon, cloves, and salt and beat until smoothly incorporated. Gradually beat in the flour until the dough is smooth and well blended. If the dough is crumbly, work in up to 3 teaspoons water until it holds together. Let stand for 10 minutes, if needed, to firm up slightly.

Divide the dough in half. Then shape each half into 12 balls. Space them about 3½ inches apart on the baking sheets. With a palm, press the balls down until evenly thick and 3 inches in diameter.

Bake (middle rack) for 10 to 15 minutes or until the cookies are browned on top and just beginning to firm up when tapped in the center; be careful not to overbake. Remove the pans from the oven. Let the cookies firm up for several minutes. Using a wide-bladed spatula, transfer the cookies to racks and let cool completely.

For the glaze: In a 1-quart saucepan, stir together the powdered sugar, butter, and 3½ tablespoons water until blended. Bring to a boil, stirring, over medium-high heat. Boil just until smooth and translucent, 30 to 45 seconds. Stir to recombine the glaze, then use immediately while still hot; it may become grainy or thick if allowed to cool.

Using a pastry brush (or a paper towel) dipped into the glaze, brush evenly over the cookies until all are glazed. Thin glaze with drops of water if needed. Let stand until the glaze sets, at least 30 minutes. It may become sugary and flaky like doughnut glaze; this is normal.

Yield: Makes twenty-four 4-inch cookies

Storage: Store these, airtight, for up to 1 week. They can be frozen for up to 1½ months.

ROLLED COOKIES }

Most people immediately think of old-fashioned, cutout sugar cookies and gingerbread boys when rolled cookies are mentioned, and these standards ought to be in every baker's repertoire. But, as this chapter proves, rolled cookies can take a great variety of shapes and forms and yield many enticing, less traditional results.

Consider the effect achieved with a single, understated cutter form like a scalloped round, symmetrical flower petal, fluted oval, or ruffle-edged square, for example: The simple lines of geometric cutters effectively create drama and an aura of sophistication that appropriately show off cookies like the Chocolate, Grapefruit, and Tarragon Wafers. In contrast, a jumble of holiday shapes lends an air of informality and good cheer and perfectly introduces more down-to-earth treats like Good and Easy Rolled Sugar Cookies.

Don't take this to mean that sugar cookies, gingerbreads, and other old favorites can't be given the more dramatic single-cutter treatment, though. A whole batch of one heart, flower petal, snowflake, shamrock, gingerbread man, or teddy bear shape decorated identically or in coordinating themed colors can be absolutely spectacular. (Maybe I should fess up here to being a fairly compulsive cutter collector: I own literally hundreds!)

You may be surprised to see that some cookies in the chapter don't require cutters at all. The Easy Apricot-Walnut Rugelach (and several variations) involve rolling out the dough into large rounds, then cutting each round, pizza-style, into wedges. These are then brushed with filling and rolled up into little bite-size pinwheels. The Rolled Almond Shortbread-Fingers call for quickly cutting a large square of rolled-out dough into finger-like rectangles. The final cookies have a nicely finished look that's extremely simple to achieve.

By its very nature, rolling out dough involves more effort than dropping or hand shaping, but the method I've used for decades and highly recommend makes rolling and cutting much, much easier than it used to be. It also almost completely eliminates countertop cleanup because the dough is rolled out between sheets of baking parchment or wax paper.

This technique has several other huge advantages over the old-fashioned method of rolling out on a floured surface: The dough doesn't become dry and blotchy from absorbing excess flour. Plus, whenever the dough becomes warm and difficult to work with, it (and the underlying paper) can be slid onto a tray and refrigerated until firmed up again. Chilled dough not only cuts much more neatly, but the cookies can also be lifted from the paper to baking sheets without being stretched out of shape. The end result: cutout cookies that are tender and buttery rather than tough and floury tasting and shapes that look as crisp and clean as those prepared by professional bakers. If at any point dough sticks to cutters and cookies are difficult to slide out onto the baking sheet, dip the cutters into flour, tapping off the excess, before cutting out each cookie.

Keep in mind that cookies are more likely to get done at the same time if they are all the same thickness, so try to roll out the dough evenly thick all over. The best approach is to keep rolling out in every direction starting from the dough center; this helps keep the edges from becoming too thin. However, if you find that some cookies are thicker than others, it's possible to compensate by placing the thicker ones around the outside of the baking sheet and the thinner ones in the interior. More heat reaches the ones around the outside, which will cause them to bake a little faster. If you're using cutters of different sizes, place the larger cookies around the outside for the same reason.

Easy
One-bowl mixing.
Easy to handle,
versatlie dough.

GOOD AND EASY ROLLED SUGAR COOKIES

These are very good, middle-of-the-road, all-occasion sugar cookies; I've made them for several years. The dough is easy to mix, roll, and cut out, and the cookies are pleasingly tender-crisp. They taste pleasantly buttery and faintly sweet, yet aren't overly rich or too sugary. They are satisfying served plain or sprinkled with nonpareils or decorating sugar, but they will stand up to whatever elaborate decorations, glazes, and icings you might desire. (See the Frostings, Fillings & Finishing Touches chapter for the various options.) Note that the recipe makes a fairly generous batch of dough.

Like the other rolled cookies in the book, these are readied between sheets of baking parchment. (If parchment is unavailable, wax paper will do.) This method not only minimizes cleanup but also ensures that the cookies don't become over-floured and tough. For more details on making the most of this technique, see the chapter introduction on page 111.

1½ cups (3 sticks) unsalted butter, slightly softened
1⅔ cups granulated sugar
1 teaspoon baking powder
½ teaspoon salt
2 large eggs, at room temperature
1 tablespoon vanilla extract
¼ teaspoon almond extract or lemon extract, optional
4¼ cups unbleached all-purpose white flour, plus more if needed
Purchased or homemade sprinkles, colored sugar, or glaze, icing, or royal frosting as desired

Preliminaries: Set out six large sheets of baking parchment and a large tray or baking sheet.

In a bowl with a mixer on medium speed, beat together the butter, sugar, baking powder, and salt until very light and fluffy. Beat in the eggs, vanilla, and almond extract (if using) until very well blended and smooth; scrape down the bowl as needed.

On low speed, gradually beat in about half of the flour. Beat or stir the remaining flour into the butter mixture to form a smooth, slightly stiff dough. If it is very soft, beat or stir in up to 4 tablespoons more flour to stiffen it slightly. If too dry to hold together, stir or beat in a little water a teaspoon at a time until it comes together smoothly. Let the dough stand for 5 to 10 minutes to firm up a bit more.

Divide the dough into thirds. Roll out each portion a scant ¼ inch thick between sheets of baking parchment or wax paper; check the underside and smooth out any wrinkles. Stack the rolled portions (paper still attached) on a baking sheet. Refrigerate for about 45 minutes or until cold and firm. Or freeze for about 25 minutes to speed chilling. (Alternatively, don't roll out; wrap the portions airtight. Freeze for up to 2 months. Thaw in the refrigerator. Then roll out between parchment sheets; chill as directed above; then proceed with the directions below.)

Baking Preliminaries: Position a rack in the middle of the oven; preheat to 350°F. Generously grease several large baking sheets or coat with nonstick spray.

Working with one portion at a time and leaving the remainder chilled,

gently peel away one sheet of paper, then pat it back into place. (This will make it easier to lift cookies from the paper later.) Peel off and discard the second sheet. Using assorted 2½-inch to 3-inch cutters (or as desired), cut out the cookies. If at any point the dough softens too much to handle easily, transfer the paper and cookies to a tray or baking sheet and refrigerate until firm again.

Using a spatula, carefully transfer the cookies from the paper, spacing about 1¼ inches apart on the baking sheets. Re-roll any dough scraps; re-chill the dough. Continue cutting out the cookies until all dough is used; if it becomes too warm to handle, refrigerate briefly before continuing. If desired, add sprinkles or decorating sugars (except for natural berry decorating sugar, which should be added near the end of baking to prevent it from fading).

Bake (middle rack) one sheet at a time for 8 to 11 minutes or until the cookies are faintly colored on top and slightly darker at the edges. Rotate the pan about halfway through baking if necessary to ensure even browning. Transfer the pan to a cooling rack; let the cookies firm up for several minutes. Using a wide spatula, transfer the cookies to wire racks. Let cool thoroughly. Then add any glaze or icing desired following the specific directions provided in their recipes.

Yield: Makes forty to fifty 2¾- to 3¼-inch cookies (depending on the cutters used)

Storage: Store these, airtight, for up to 2 weeks. They can be frozen, airtight, for up to 2 months.

Tip

Always place the larger or thicker cookies around the perimeter of the baking sheets and the smaller or thinner ones on the interior. This helps ensure that they all get done at the same time, as those on the outside are exposed to a little more heat and thus bake a little faster. (This tip works not only for sugar cookies and brown sugar alfajores (at right) but for any other kind of cookie.)

Tip

Dough may stick in cutters with more intricate designs such as those used to form the daisy cookies pictured at right. In this case, dip the cutter into flour (tapping off the excess) before cutting out each cookie.

2⅓ cups unbleached all-purpose
white flour, plus more if
needed

⅓ cup powdered sugar, plus more
for garnish

¼ teaspoon salt

1 cup (2 sticks) very cold unsalted
butter, cut into chunks

3 tablespoons well-chilled heavy
cream, plus more if needed

2½ teaspoons vanilla extract

1 batch berry buttercream
(page 326), cocoa or cocoa-
berry buttercream (page 324),
citrus buttercream (page 328),
or coffee buttercream (page
321), or other flavor variations

DELICATE VANILLA-CREAM SANDWICH COOKIES

"Delicate" seems the best way to describe these: They are exceedingly tender, rich yet light, and subtly flavored. They are also barely sweet and a pale cream color, which makes them perfect for creating a whole array of sublime-tasting, elegant-looking little buttercream cookie sandwiches. I like to tuck them around any of the various berry buttercreams (page 326), the cocoa or cocoa-berry buttercream (page 324), or quick citrus buttercreams (pages 328–329). (They taste fine with the vanilla buttercream on page 321, too, they just won't be as colorful.) In fact, if you're enchanted with the rainbow flavors and colors of French macarons but want easier-to-prepare cookies, several batches of these filled with different buttercream flavors and shades will serve the purpose beautifully.

The sandwiches are best served within a day or two of assembly, although the cookies can be made up to 1½ months ahead and frozen until needed.

Preliminaries: Set out six large sheets of baking parchment (or wax paper) and a large tray or rimmed sheet.

In a food processor, process the flour, ⅓ cup powdered sugar, and salt until blended. Sprinkle the butter over the mixture. Process until no bits of butter are visible; the dough should not be clumping or coming together yet.

Combine the cream and vanilla. Drizzle the mixture over the dough. Incorporate it using ten to fifteen 1-second pulses. Stop and stir to lift the mixture and incorporate the crumbs on the bottom. Check the dough consistency by pinching it between the fingers; if it is too dry to hold together, add up to 1 tablespoon more cream. Incorporate the cream using 4 or 5 more pulses; for the most tender cookies, don't over-process. If it is very soft, sprinkle over 1 tablespoon more flour, but don't work it in.

Remove the blade and turn out the dough onto the paper. If necessary, gently knead it just until evenly blended and cohesive. If it is very soft, wrap the paper around it and refrigerate for about 10 minutes, until firmed up slightly; if it is dry and crumbly, gradually knead in up to 1 tablespoon more cream. If, after chilling, the dough is still soft, lightly knead in 1 tablespoon more flour.

Divide the dough into thirds. Roll out each portion a scant ¼-inch thick between sheets of baking parchment. Check the undersides and smooth out any wrinkles. Stack the dough portions (paper attached) on the tray. Freeze for at least 30 minutes and up to 24 hours, if desired.

This dough is much easier to handle when well chilled. If it starts to warm and soften, instead of struggling, just return it to the freezer until firm again. Also, chill a baking sheet in advance and lay the rolled out layer on it while cutting out the cookies to keep the dough cool.

Cookie Jar Wisdom
Broken cookies have no calories. Cookie crumbs have even fewer.

Baking Preliminaries: Position a rack in the middle of the oven; preheat to 375°F. Lightly grease several large baking sheets or coat with nonstick spray.

Working with one dough portion and keeping the others frozen, peel off one sheet of paper, then pat it back into place. Invert the dough, then peel off and discard the second sheet. Using a 2¼-inch (or similar) small round or scalloped cutter, cut out the cookies. Using a spatula, transfer to the baking sheets, spacing about 2 inches apart. If the dough becomes too soft to work with, return it to the freezer until firm, then continue. Repeat the process with the other portions. Gather any scraps; press together and re-roll; chill; then cut out until all the dough is used.

Bake (middle rack) one sheet at a time for 7 to 11 minutes or until the cookies feel set when pressed in the center and the tops are just barely beginning to tinge at the edges. Let the pans cool on wire racks until the cookies firm up, about 3 minutes, then gently transfer them to racks using a spatula. Cool thoroughly before preparing the sandwiches.

For the sandwiches: Ready the preferred buttercream(s) as directed. Spread enough filling to yield a ¼-to ⅓-inch-thick layer on the undersides of half the cookies. Cover with similarly sized wafers, top side up, gently pressing down until the filling spreads almost to the edges. Put some additional powdered sugar in a fine-mesh sieve and dust the wafer tops until lightly coated. Or, if a berry or cocoa buttercream was used, very lightly sift the appropriate berry decorating powder or sugar (pages 336–337) or light dusting of cocoa over the cookie tops.

Yield: Makes about thirty 2½-inch sandwiches, or 60 wafers

Storage: Store these, airtight, for up to 1 week. They can be frozen, airtight, for up to 1 month.

Easy
Short ingredient list.
Elegant yet easy.

3 sticks (1½ cups) unsalted butter, cool but slightly softened and cut into chunks
¾ cup powdered sugar, plus more for garnish, if needed
2 teaspoons vanilla extract
¼ teaspoon almond, lemon, raspberry, or Flowers of Sicily extract
Scant ½ teaspoon salt
2¾ cups plus 2 tablespoons unbleached all-purpose white flour, plus more if needed
Assorted buttercream frostings (pages 321–332)

Tip

The recipe calls for a 1½- to 2-inch round cutter. If you don't have one this small, use a shot glass, liqueur glass, or perhaps a discarded spice or condiment bottle top or a metal cap or a small, thin jar lid.

VANILLA SHORTBREAD BUTTONS

I created these super-buttery, melt-in-the-mouth rounds as a way to showcase the assorted buttercreams in the book. Since the shortbreads are button-size, not very sweet, and sturdy enough to hold up when decorated, they make perfect platforms for a colorful little swirl or piped rosette of frosting on top. They can also be turned into luscious little sandwich cookies by tucking buttercream between two buttons and dusting the tops with powdered sugar. The resulting treats, are, of course, ideal for special occasions.

Berry, citrus, chocolate, and herb-scented buttercreams are all spectacular with the buttons, and I like to decorate them with at least two different flavors for an eye-catching presentation. Besides incorporating vanilla into the dough, you can add another extract to tailor the cookies to the particular buttercream(s) used. (The Flowers of Sicily extract suggested here has a highly aromatic almond, vanilla, and orange flavor; see page 18 for more information.)

It's possible to take the recipe even a step further by incorporating some finely ground dried lavender or chamomile blooms, following the variation at the end of the recipe. (The fine bits of herbs won't affect dough appearance but can add great flavor interest.) Both these herbs complement any of the citrus buttercreams; the lavender is also a wonderful complement to the berry buttercreams. Be sure to use herbs harvested specifically for culinary use, not just for crafting projects.

Preliminaries: Set out four large sheets of baking parchment and a large tray or rimmed sheet.

In a large bowl with a mixer on medium speed, beat the butter, powdered sugar, vanilla, almond extract, and salt. Raise the speed to high and beat for 2 to 3 minutes, until very light in color and texture, scraping down the bowl as needed. On low speed, beat in half the flour. Beat or stir in the remaining flour until evenly incorporated, scraping down the sides. Let stand for 10 minutes so the dough can firm up slightly. If it is still very soft, beat in up to 4 tablespoons more flour to stiffen it just slightly.

Divide the dough in half. Roll each portion out into a ⅓-inch-thick layer between sheets of baking parchment or wax paper. Check the undersides and smooth out any wrinkles. Stack the dough portions (paper attached) on the baking sheet. Refrigerate for about 30 minutes, until firm enough to neatly cut out, or freeze for at least 15 minutes and up to 24 hours, if desired. (Let frozen dough warm up and soften slightly before using.)

Baking Preliminaries: Position a rack in the middle of the oven; preheat to 325°F. Lightly grease several large baking sheets or line with baking parchment.

Working with one dough portion at a time, peel off one sheet of paper, then pat it back into place. Invert the dough, then peel off and discard the second sheet. Using a 1½- to 2-inch (or similar) small round cutter, cut out the wafers. Using a spatula, transfer them to a baking sheet, spacing about 1½ inches apart. If the dough softens too much to handle, return it to the freezer until firm, then continue. Repeat the process with the other portion.

Bake (middle rack) one sheet at a time for 12 to 16 minutes or until the cookies are just firm in the centers and tinged at the edges. Let the pans cool until the cookies firm up, about 3 minutes, then transfer them to racks using a spatula. Cool thoroughly before topping or filling with buttercream frosting.

To decorate with the buttercream(s): Put little dollops of the desired buttercream(s) on the cookie tops, then swirl it slightly decoratively with the tip of a knife until the cookie top is mostly covered. Or spoon the mixture into a pastry bag fitted with a ½-inch-diameter open star tip. Pipe generous rosettes onto the tops by squeezing and rotating the tip at the same time; the tops should be mostly covered. Let stand until the buttercream sets, at least 45 minutes and up to 1½ hours, if desired.

To make sandwich cookies: Place enough buttercream on the undersides of half the buttons to yield a ¼-inch-thick layer. Top with the remaining buttons, pressing down until the filling extends to the edges. Garnish the sandwich tops with a light sifting of powdered sugar.

Yield: Makes fifty to sixty 2-inch mini shortbreads, or 25 to 30 sandwiches

Storage: Store these, airtight and in one layer, at room temperature for up to 10 days. They can be frozen, airtight, for up to 1½ months; serve at room temperature.

Variation: Lavender or Chamomile Shortbread Buttons Grind 2 tablespoons dried lavender or chamomile blooms in a food processor with a generous ¾ cup powdered sugar until the flowers are almost powder-fine; stop and stir to redistribute the contents several times. Sift the infused powdered sugar through a very fine-mesh sieve into the butter called for in the recipe until the infused sugar passes through; stop sifting before any large herb particles pass through the sieve and discard them. Proceed exactly as directed in the recipe.

½ cup plus 2 tablespoons
   granulated sugar
1 tablespoon freshly grated
   lemon zest (yellow part of the
   peel)
⅛ teaspoon salt
2 tablespoons finely chopped
   fresh rosemary needles (no
   coarse stems)
½ teaspoon lemon extract or vanilla
   extract
2¼ cups unbleached all-purpose
   white flour
1 cup (2 sticks) very cold unsalted
   butter, cut into chunks
1½ tablespoons fresh orange juice,
   plus more if needed

ROSEMARY-LEMON WAFERS

If you've only used rosemary in savory recipes, you'll be surprised at how enticing it is in these rich, tender wafers. It's more delicate and mellow than you might expect; the pungent piney quality is muted and the herbal notes seem floral and sweet, though still refreshing. Most people aren't able to identify the flavor as rosemary; they just notice that there is "something special" and pleasing going on in these treats.

Note that the recipe requires fresh rosemary; don't try to substitute dried, as the needles are too tough and dry to incorporate smoothly. Also, the 2 tablespoons of fresh rosemary called for may seem like a lot, but is actually just the right amount.

Preliminaries: Set out six large sheets of baking parchment and a baking sheet.

In a food processor, process the sugar, lemon zest, and salt for several minutes, until the sugar is pale yellow. Add the rosemary and extract and continue processing just until the rosemary is very finely pulverized. Set 2 tablespoons of the sugar mixture aside to use as a garnish. Add the flour to the processor, stirring it in with a spoon until partially incorporated.

Sprinkle the butter over the mixture. Process just until no bits of butter are visible; the dough should not be clumping or coming together. Drizzle the orange juice over the top. Incorporate using ten to fifteen 1-second pulses, stopping and stirring to lift and fold in the mixture on the bottom as necessary. Check the dough consistency by pinching it between the fingers; if it is too dry to hold together, add up to 1 tablespoon more juice, incorporating it using 4 or 5 more pulses; for the most tender wafers, don't over-process.

Turn out the dough onto a sheet of wax paper. Gently knead the dough just until evenly blended and cohesive. If it is very soft, wrap the paper around it and refrigerate for about 10 minutes, until firmed up slightly; if it is dry and crumbly, gradually knead in a little cold water until cohesive.

Divide the dough into thirds. Roll out each portion to a generous ⅛ inch thick between sheets of baking parchment. Check the undersides and smooth out any wrinkles. Stack the dough portions (paper attached) on the baking sheet. Freeze for at least 20 minutes and up to 24 hours, if desired. Let completely frozen dough warm up just slightly before using.

Baking Preliminaries: Position a rack in the middle of the oven; preheat to 350°F. Grease several large baking sheets or coat with nonstick spray.

Working with one dough portion and keeping the others frozen, peel off one sheet of paper, then pat it back into place. Invert the dough, then peel off and discard the second sheet. Using a 2½- to 2¾- inch (or similar) round or scalloped cutter, cut out the wafers. Using a spatula, place about 2 inches apart on the baking sheets. Sprinkle a little of the reserved rosemary-sugar mixture over the cookie tops, patting down slightly to imbed. If the dough becomes too soft to work with, return it to the freezer to firm up, then continue. Repeat the process with the other portions. Combine the dough scraps and continue rolling, chilling, and cutting out until it is all used.

Bake (middle rack) one sheet at a time for 8 to 11 minutes or until the wafers are just faintly rimmed with brown; watch carefully, as they brown rapidly near the end of baking. Let the pans cool on wire racks until the wafers firm up, about 3 minutes, then gently transfer them to racks using a wide spatula. Cool thoroughly before serving.

Yield: Makes about thirty-five 2¾-inch wafers

Storage: Store these, airtight, for up to 1 week. They can be frozen, airtight, for up to 1½ months.

Tip

The recipe calls for working with the dough while partially frozen because it is easier to handle that way. If it warms up, it will soften, in which case simply stop and chill it again before continuing. It will stay cold longer if you place it on an extra chilled baking sheet during the cutting out process.

ROLLED ALMOND SHORTBREAD FINGERS

Like most rolled cookies in the book, these are prepared by rolling the dough between sheets of baking parchment. But the shaping method is unusual and involves cutting a large square of dough into long, thin (finger-like) rectangles instead of into individual cookies using cutters.

Then, the dough (still in one whole, intact layer including the scraps around the edges) goes into the oven and bakes until partially done. After cooling, the fingers are gently separated, then returned to the oven and baked all the way through, which further accentuates their crisp, toothsome texture. The almond extract and toasted almonds on top lend them a satisfying nutty taste and crunch.

If desired, you can also add some spice to the dough. The resulting fingers will be very reminiscent of the Dutch Jan Hagel cookies. See the variation at the end.

1¼ cups (2½ sticks) unsalted butter, slightly softened
½ cup granulated sugar
1 teaspoon vanilla extract
¾ teaspoon almond extract
Scant ¼ teaspoon salt
2¾ cups unbleached all-purpose white flour, plus more if needed
1 large egg, beaten with a fork, for garnish
1 cup finely chopped blanched or unblanched slivered almonds for garnish
¼ cup coarse crystal sugar for garnish (use 3 tablespoons granulated sugar if unavailable)

Preliminaries: Set out four large sheets of baking parchment and a baking sheet.

In a large mixer bowl with the mixer on low speed, beat together the butter, sugar, vanilla, almond extract, and salt until blended. Raise the speed to high; beat until very well blended and lightened in color, about 2 minutes. Working on low speed, beat in about half the flour just until thoroughly incorporated. Beat or stir in the remaining flour until smoothly incorporated. If the dough is crumbly, gradually work in up to 3 teaspoons water; if very soft, work in up to 2 tablespoons flour. Let stand for 5 minutes to firm up slightly.

Divide the dough in half. Roll each portion between sheets of baking parchment into an evenly thick 10½-inch square. Cut and patch as necessary to form the squares. Check the underside and smooth out any wrinkles. Stack the rolled portions (paper still attached) on the baking sheet. Refrigerate for about 30 minutes or until cold and firm. (Or freeze for about 15 minutes to speed chilling.)

Baking Preliminaries: Position a rack in the middle of the oven; preheat to 325°F. Grease several baking sheets or coat with nonstick spray.

Working with one portion at a time, gently peel away one sheet of paper, then pat it back into place. (This makes it easier to lift the cookies from the paper later.) Peel off the second layer. Brush the portions lightly but evenly with the egg. Immediately sprinkle half the almonds and half the crystal sugar evenly over each layer. Pat the sheet of paper down on the surface to imbed the toppings slightly, then remove the paper again.

Using a large sharp knife or pizza wheel, trim the dough perimeter all around to form a tidy square, leaving the uneven edges in place on the parchment. Then cut the area inside the squares crosswise into fourths in one direction and into eighths or ninths in the other. (If at any point the dough softens too much to cut easily, transfer the paper and dough to a baking sheet and refrigerate until firm again.) Slide each sheet of dough and parchment onto a baking sheet.

Bake (middle rack) one sheet at a time for 10 to 15 minutes or until the dough is just barely firm in the center and the scraps around the edges are beginning to brown. Carefully retrace the cut originally made in the dough. Set the dough aside until cool enough to handle, then gently separate the individual fingers.

Return them to the baking sheet, placing any underdone ones around the perimeter and the more done ones in the center. Continue baking until barely tinged on top and lightly browned at the edges, 9 to 13 minutes. Transfer the pans to wire racks. Let stand until completely cooled.

Yield: Makes sixty to seventy $1\frac{1}{3}$ by $2\frac{3}{4}$-inch fingers

Storage: Store these, airtight, for up to 10 days. They can be frozen, airtight, for up to 2 months.

Variation: Spiced Almond Fingers Add $1\frac{1}{4}$ teaspoons ground cinnamon and $\frac{1}{4}$ teaspoon ground allspice along with the almond extract. Proceed exactly as directed.

Fairly Easy
Food processor or
mixer mixing.
Decadence with ease.

1 cup (2 sticks) cool and firm
  unsalted butter, cut into
  chunks
⅔ cup (packed) light or dark
  brown sugar
1 large egg, at room temperature
1 tablespoon whole or low-fat
  milk
2 teaspoons vanilla extract
  Generous ¼ teaspoon salt
2 cups plus 2 tablespoons
  unbleached all-purpose white
  flour, plus more if needed
⅔ cup finely ground white or
  yellow cornmeal
1 batch Chocolate Dulce de
  Leche (page 315)

Tip

If cornmeal in cookies doesn't appeal
to you, check out the coconut
alfajores on page 100.

BROWN SUGAR ALFAJORES

The people of Argentina, Chile, Uruguay, and Peru are all fond of alfajores—simple shortbread sandwiches with a gooey milk caramel filling tucked inside. This particular version is unusual in that it calls for dark brown sugar and a bit of cornmeal. It imparts a mild, sweet corn taste and adds a slight crunchiness that contrasts nicely with the creamy filling.

Although these sandwich cookies can be paired with a traditional caramel-flavored filling, they are particularly nice with the chocolate version, pictured. The resulting sandwiches are less sweet, and the filling provides more noticeable visual contrast to the shortbread. The classic homemade dulce de leche recipe is on page 323; store-bought will also do fine.

Preliminaries: Set out six large sheets of baking parchment or wax paper and a baking sheet.

Combine the butter, brown sugar, egg, milk, vanilla, and salt in a food processor. Process in on/off pulses until the mixture is evenly blended; stop and scrape down the sides as needed. Add the flour. Process in pulses just until the mixture comes together into a dough. (Alternatively, soften the butter slightly. Combine it with the brown sugar, egg, milk, vanilla, and salt in a large bowl. Beat with a heavy-duty mixer on medium speed, until well blended and smooth. Add the flour; beat on low speed until evenly incorporated, scraping down the sides as needed.)

Turn out the dough onto a sheet of wax paper. Sprinkle over the cornmeal. Knead it in with the hands until the dough is well blended. If it is dry and crumbly, work in a little water until it holds together; if it is very soft, work in a tablespoon or two more flour.

Divide the dough into thirds. Place each portion between large sheets of baking parchment. Roll out the portions a scant ¼ inch thick; check the underside of the dough and smooth out any wrinkles that form. Stack the rolled portions (sheet still attached) on a baking sheet. Refrigerate for 20 to 25 minutes, until cold and firm. (Or freeze for about 15 minutes.)

Baking Preliminaries: Position a rack in the middle of the oven; preheat to 350°F. Grease several large baking sheets or coat with nonstick spray.

Working with one portion at a time, gently peel away one sheet of paper, then pat it back into place. (This will make it easier to lift the cookies from the sheet later.) Peel off and discard the second layer. Using a 2- to 2¼-inch plain round cutter, cut out the cookies. (If at any point the dough softens too much to handle easily, transfer the paper and cookies

to a baking sheet and refrigerate until firm again.)

Using a spatula, carefully transfer the cookies from the paper, spacing about 1¼ inches apart on the baking sheets. Re-roll any dough scraps. Continue cutting out the cookies until all dough is used; refrigerate as necessary if it becomes too soft to handle.

Bake (middle rack) one sheet at a time for 11 to 15 minutes or until the cookies are tinged with brown at the edges and just barely firm when pressed in the center top. Transfer the pan to a cooling rack. Let the cookies stand to firm up for 5 minutes; they are too tender to handle when still very warm. Transfer to wire racks using a wide-bladed spatula. Let stand until thoroughly cooled.

For the sandwiches: Ready the chocolate dulce de leche as directed. Spread enough on the underside of a cookie to yield a ¼- to ⅓-inch-thick layer of filling for a finished sandwich. Cover the filling with another similar-size cookie, underside down. Gently press down until the filling squeezes out just to the edges. Repeat until all the sandwiches are assembled. They may be served immediately or made several days ahead.

Yield: Makes twenty to twenty-five 2¼- to 2½-inch cookie sandwiches

Storage: Store these, airtight and refrigerated, for up to 1 week. They can be frozen, airtight, for up to 3 weeks. Serve the cookies at room temperature.

Tip

This dough softens as it warms up, so for easy handling return it to the refrigerator several times while rolling and cutting out the cookies. You can also chill several extra baking pans or trays and lay the sheets of dough on them while you work. Always proceed like this when your kitchen is warm.

Tip

If the cornmeal used is coarse, after measuring out what's called for, grind it for several minutes in a food processor. For an even finer consistency, sift it through a fine-mesh sieve to remove any larger bits.

Easy
Food processor mixing.
Sophisticated yet simple.

1 cup 55 to 70 percent cacao
    semisweet or bittersweet
    chocolate morsels
½ cup good-quality unsweetened
    Dutch-process cocoa powder
¼ teaspoon baking powder
¼ teaspoon salt
2¼ cups unbleached all-purpose
    white flour, divided, plus more
    if needed
1 cup powdered sugar
1 cup (2 sticks) very cold unsalted
    butter, cut into chunks
    Assorted buttercreams for
    cookie sandwiches, optional

Tip

Remember that to make sandwich
cookies that pair up exactly, the
shape used has to be symmetrical,
or half of the cookies must be
turned over so their undersides are
facing up as they go on the sheets
and are baked. Then the undersides
of the two kinds will match up as the
cookies are sandwiched together.
(This may sound confusing, but if
you try to put the undersides of
non-symmetrical cookies together,
you'll see why this step is necessary!)

CHOCOLATE-COCOA WAFERS (OR COCOA SANDWICHES)

These are lovely served as is with coffee or tea, or lightly garnished with the chocolate drizzle on page 314. The wafers may be tucked around a ganache filling (page 318) or one of several different chocolate or berry buttercream fillings (page 324 and page 326) to create chichi sandwich cookies. It's also possible to vary the recipe slightly and turn out cocoa-mint or cocoa-lavender wafers. See the instructions for these options at the end of the recipe.

For Valentine's Day I often cut out the wafers using heart-shaped cutters and turn them into sandwiches with rose or lavender buttercream (page 330). To heighten the drama, I use tiny heart-shaped or plain round mini cutters to form a center opening so the pink or lavender-colored buttercream peeks through. (Well-scrubbed thimbles and some pen caps and small plain pastry piping tubes can serve as makeshift mini cutters for forming cutaways, too.) Other pretty cutaway sandwich cookie options: shamrocks, five- or six-pointed stars, snowflakes, and symmetrical flowers, as well as non-seasonal rounds, squares, and ovals.

Preliminaries: Set out six large sheets of baking parchment and a baking sheet.

In a food processor, process the chocolate morsels, cocoa powder, baking powder, and salt until the morsels are ground powder-fine. Add 1¼ cups flour and the sugar and process until evenly incorporated. Sprinkle the butter over the mixture. Process in pulses until no bits of butter are visible; the dough should be beginning to clump and come together.

Turn out the dough onto a large sheet of wax paper. Sprinkle over the remaining 1 cup flour and knead it in with the hands until evenly incorporated. Let stand to firm up for 5 minutes. If the dough still seems too soft to roll out, work in up to 2 tablespoons more flour to firm it slightly.

Divide the dough into thirds. Roll each portion out into a generous ¼-inch evenly thick layer between sheets of baking parchment or wax paper. Check the undersides and smooth out any wrinkles. Stack the dough portions (paper attached) on the baking sheet. Refrigerate until very firm, at least 1 hour. Or freeze for at least 25 minutes and up to 24 hours, if desired.

Baking Preliminaries: Position a rack in the middle of the oven; preheat to 350°F. Lightly grease several large baking sheets or line with baking parchment.

Working with one dough portion and keeping the others well chilled, peel off one sheet of paper, then pat it back into place. Invert the dough, then peel off and discard the second sheet. Using a 2¼-inch (or similar) small round, scalloped, or other desired cutter (or assorted cutters, if preferred), cut out the wafers. If planning to make sandwich cookies with cutaways, cut out the centers from half the cookies.

Using a spatula, transfer the cookies to a baking sheet, spacing about 1½ inches apart; arrange all the cutaway cookies in the center of the sheet, as otherwise they will bake faster and be done before the cookie "bottoms." If the dough softens too much to handle as you work, return it to the freezer until firm, then continue. Repeat the process with the other portions.

Bake (middle rack) one sheet at a time for 7 to 9 minutes or until the wafers are just firm when pressed in the centers. Let the pans cool until the wafers firm up slightly, then transfer them to racks using a spatula. Cool thoroughly before garnishing or serving. If garnishing with the chocolate drizzle (page 314), ready it and decorate as desired. If using it to decorate the tops of sandwich cookies with cutaways, garnish the tops before placing them on the sandwiches.

For the sandwiches: Ready the preferred buttercream(s) as directed. Spread enough filling on the undersides of half the cookies to yield a ¼-inch-thick layer. Cover with similar-size wafers, top side up, gently pressing down until the filling spreads almost to the edges (and peeks out the cutaways if the cookies have them).

Yield: Makes sixty to seventy 2½-inch wafers, or 30 to 35 sandwiches

Storage: Store these, airtight for up to 1 week. They can be frozen, airtight, for up to 1 month.

Variation: Chocolate-Cocoa-Mint Wafers

Add ½ teaspoon peppermint or spearmint extract along with the butter. If desired, substitute mint-flavored chocolate morsels for regular semisweet chocolate morsels. For a festive garnish, as the wafers come from the oven, sprinkle their tops with a pinch of finely crushed peppermint or spearmint hard candies or candy cane bits. Return to the oven for 1 minute so the heat can partially melt the candy bits. Then cool as directed in the original recipe. These wafers can be sandwiched around the mint buttercream on page 332.

Variation: Chocolate-Cocoa-Lavender Wafers

Grind 1 tablespoon dried lavender blooms with 1 tablespoon powdered sugar in a food processor until very fine. Stir the mixture through a fine-mesh sieve back into the processor. Add the chocolate and other ingredients called for and proceed exactly as directed. The wafers are, of course, delightful decorated with lavender sugar and/or sandwiched around the lavender buttercream on page 330.

Fairly Complicated
Food processor mixing.
Sophisticated flavor combo.

CHOCOLATE, GRAPEFRUIT, AND TARRAGON WAFERS (OR SANDWICH COOKIES)

If you have been looking for both chichi *and* unusual, stop now and make these elegant chocolate, grapefruit, and tarragon wafers! I borrowed the idea for this addictive and unique combination from my talented chocolatier friend Michael Recchiuti, who features it in one of his luscious, *très chic* truffles. I've maximized the impact of the haunting herb-citrus pairing by using it on top of as well as in the wafers. With each bite, you both inhale its fragrance and revel in its flavor. (For a little scientific discussion of how smelling enhances tasting, see page 187.)

Another key to intensifying the flavor is incorporating some candied grapefruit peel. Yes, this ingredient can be hard to come by unless you have access to a high-end confectionery or gourmet shop, so feel free to substitute the best purchased candied orange peel you can find. The resulting cookies will still be delectable, just not quite as novel.

While the wafers are delightful by themselves, you can use a tarragon-grapefruit-cocoa buttercream to turn them into drop-dead decadent little sandwich cookies. The wafers are prepared exactly the same either way. Just tuck them around the buttercream on page 325 for the *non plus* ultra experience.

Preliminaries: Set out four large sheets of baking parchment and a baking sheet.

In a small microwave-safe bowl, melt the chocolate in a microwave oven on 100 percent power for 30 seconds. Continue microwaving on 50 percent power, stopping and stirring at 30-second intervals, until just mostly melted. (Alternatively, in a medium heavy saucepan warm the chocolate over lowest heat, stirring constantly, until mostly melted. Immediately remove from the heat.) Stir until completely melted.

In a food processor, process the tarragon, zests, and sugar until the tarragon is finely ground and the sugar is brightly colored, 1 to 2 minutes. Remove 2 tablespoons sugar mixture and set aside to use as a garnish. Add the chocolate, cocoa powder, baking powder, and salt to the processor; pulse until evenly incorporated. Add the butter; process until the mixture is well blended. Add the egg and grapefruit or orange peel and process until the peel is finely chopped. Sprinkle over a generous half of the flour, pulsing until mostly incorporated.

Put half of the remaining flour on a sheet of wax paper. Turn out the dough onto it. Sprinkle over the remaining flour. Work the flour into the dough with your hands until evenly incorporated. If the dough is soft

Ingredients

3½ ounces 60 to 70 percent cacao bittersweet or semisweet chocolate, broken up or coarsely chopped

1½ tablespoons dried tarragon leaves

1 tablespoon grated grapefruit zest (yellow part of the peel)

1¼ teaspoons grated lemon zest (yellow part of the peel)

¾ cup granulated sugar

¼ cup unsweetened Dutch-process cocoa powder, sifted after measuring, if lumpy

¼ teaspoon baking powder

⅛ teaspoon salt

⅔ cup (1 stick plus 2⅔ tablespoons) unsalted butter, slightly softened but still cool, cut into chunks

1 large egg, at room temperature

⅓ cup diced candied grapefruit peel (or substitute good quality candied orange peel, if necessary)

2 cups unbleached all-purpose white flour, plus more if needed

Be sure the egg is at room temperature and the butter is not too cold; it should be cool and just beginning to soften. Cold ingredients can cause the melted chocolate to set up into hard bits rather than blending smoothly into the dough.

and wet, knead in several more tablespoons flour; if dry and crumbly, knead in a teaspoon or two of water.

Divide the dough in half. Roll out each portion $\frac{1}{4}$ inch thick between large sheets of baking parchment or wax paper. Check the underside of the dough and smooth out any wrinkles. Stack the portions (paper still attached) on the baking sheet. Refrigerate for about 45 minutes until cold and firm. (Or freeze for about 20 minutes.)

Baking Preliminaries: Position a rack in the middle of the oven; preheat to 350°F. Lightly grease several baking sheets or coat with nonstick spray.

Working with one portion at a time, gently peel away one sheet of paper, then pat it back into place. (This will make it easier to lift cookies from the paper later.) Peel off and discard the second layer. Using a $2\frac{1}{2}$- to $2\frac{3}{4}$-inch fluted round, oval, or scalloped cutter (or as desired), cut out the cookies. (If at any point the dough softens too much to handle easily, transfer the paper and cookies to a baking sheet and refrigerate until firm again.)

Using a spatula, place the cookies about $1\frac{1}{4}$ inches apart on the baking sheets. Add a generous pinch of the reserved sugar-herb-zest mixture to the tops of the cookies, pressing down to imbed. Re-roll any dough scraps. Continue cutting out the cookies until all the dough is used; refrigerate it as necessary if it becomes too soft to handle.

Bake (middle rack) one sheet at a time for 7 to 10 minutes or until the cookies are just barely firm when pressed in the center top. (They will puff up slightly, then flatten, as they bake.) Remove from the oven, and let the cookies stand to firm up for 3 or 4 minutes; they are too tender to handle when still very warm. Transfer to wire racks using a wide-bladed spatula. Let stand until thoroughly cooled.

Serve the cookies as is, or ready the Tarragon-Grapefruit-Cocoa Buttercream (page 325), and use it to create sandwich cookies following the directions with the buttercream recipe. Or create sandwich cookies by tucking them around Chocolate Ganache Filling (page 318).

Yield: Makes fifty to sixty $2\frac{3}{4}$- to 3-inch cookies, or 25 to 30 sandwiches

Storage: Store these, airtight, for up to 10 days. They can be frozen, airtight for up to $1\frac{1}{2}$ months.

DOUBLE-CHOCOLATE AND HAZELNUT THINS

These dark, wafer-like thins have the shape and light, crisp texture of crackers, but are definitely as rich tasting and satisfying as most cookies. The chocolate and hazelnut flavor is full-bodied, partly because both cocoa powder and finely chopped chocolate are incorporated into the dough, and also because the hazelnuts are well toasted during baking. A little coffee powder and almond extract heighten the flavor.

The rolling-out method is different from that used for most cookies in the chapter: A whole sheet of dough is rolled out thinly, garnished with the nuts, then placed in the oven. After the dough sets (but is not completely baked through), it is then separated into cookies by cutting it lengthwise and crosswise into a grid. The resulting rectangles are then separated and returned to the oven to finish baking. (This method is also used with great results in a number of cracker-like cookies in the Semisweet Crisps, Savory Cocktail Cookies & Crackers chapters.)

¾ cup granulated sugar
5 tablespoons unsweetened
    Dutch-process cocoa powder,
    sifted after measuring, if lumpy
¼ teaspoon salt
½ cup (1 stick) unsalted butter, very
    soft but not melted
2 teaspoons vanilla extract
1 teaspoon instant coffee
    granules dissolved in
    ½ tablespoon warm water
½ teaspoon almond extract
1 cup unbleached all-purpose
    white flour, plus more if
    needed
½ cup chopped 50 to 65 percent
    cacao semisweet or bittersweet
    chocolate
1 cup chopped hulled hazelnuts*

Baking Preliminaries: Position a rack in the middle of the oven; preheat to 350°F. Set out a large baking sheet.

In a large bowl, stir together the sugar, cocoa powder, and salt until well blended. Vigorously stir in the butter, vanilla, coffee mixture, and almond extract until very well blended and smooth. Stir in the flour and chocolate just until evenly incorporated throughout. Let the dough stand to firm up for 10 minutes. If it is still soft, stir in a little more flour to firm it up slightly.

Turn out the dough onto a 15-inch-long sheet of parchment; shape into a rough 5 by 6-inch rectangle. Top with a second parchment sheet. Roll out into a thin 12 by 14-inch evenly thick rectangle; the shape doesn't need to be perfect. Sprinkle the nuts evenly over the dough. Replace the top sheet, then roll over the dough to imbed the nuts. Remove and discard the top sheet. Slide the dough (bottom parchment still attached) onto the baking sheet.

Bake (middle rack) for 15 to 18 minutes or until the dough is lightly browned at the edges and set but still slightly soft in the center. Remove from the oven; slide the parchment and dough onto a large cutting board. Using a large sharp knife or pizza wheel, trim off and discard the edges all around to form a tidy rectangle. Then cut the dough lengthwise into sixths and crosswise into eighths to form the thins.

Return the cookies, slightly separated, to a parchment-lined baking sheet, placing any underdone ones around the edges and more done ones in the middle. Lower the oven to 325°F. Bake for 8 to 12 minutes longer or until the thins are slightly tinged all over and firm when pressed in the center. Thoroughly cool on wire racks before packing for storage.

Yield: Makes forty-eight 1½-by 2-inch thins.

Storage: Store these, airtight, for up to 10 days. They can be frozen, airtight, for up to 1 month.

* **To toast and hull hazelnuts:** Preheat the oven to 325°F. Spread the whole unhulled hazelnuts on a rimmed baking pan and toast, stirring every 3 or 4 minutes, for 14 to 18 minutes or until the hulls loosen and the nuts are nicely browned; be careful not to burn. Set aside until cool enough to handle. Rub the nuts between your hands or in a clean kitchen towel, loosening and discarding the hull. It's all right if some small bits remain. Cool the nuts thoroughly before using them.

MOCHA MOLE ROLLED SHORTBREADS

Three forms of chocolate—ground, morsel-size bits, and cocoa powder—mingle with a hit of espresso and kick of cayenne, cinnamon, and allspice in these richly flavored, quietly handsome rounds. The complex chocolate, spice, and coffee blend is quite captivating, even for those palates usually too timid to enjoy "exotic" dishes like the Mexican moles that inspired these cookies. They have a tender-crisp, very substantial texture, too.

The food processor, which is required for this recipe, makes short work of the prepping tasks, including chopping and finely grinding the chocolate, blending together the other dry ingredients, and quickly cutting in the butter.

8   ounces 60 to 70 percent cacao semisweet or bittersweet chocolate, coarsely chopped
1   cup granulated sugar
5   tablespoons unsweetened natural (non-alkalized) cocoa powder
1¾   teaspoons ground cinnamon
¾   teaspoon ground allspice or ¼ teaspoon ground cloves, or use both
    Generous ¼ to ½ teaspoon ground cayenne pepper, to taste
¼   teaspoon salt
2⅓   cups unbleached all-purpose white flour, divided
1   cup (2 sticks) unsalted butter, cool but slightly soft and cut into chunks
1   tablespoon instant espresso powder dissolved in 1½ tablespoons water

Preliminaries: Set out four large sheets of baking parchment or wax paper and a baking sheet.

In a food processor, chop the chocolate into morsel-size pieces. Measure out 1 cup pieces and reserve. Add the sugar, cocoa powder, cinnamon, allspice, pepper, salt, and 1⅓ cups flour to the remaining chocolate in the processor. Process until the chocolate is very finely ground and the ingredients are well blended. Sprinkle the butter over the mixture. Process until no bits of it are visible; stop and stir well to redistribute contents once or twice. Sprinkle the espresso mixture over the top. Pulse until it is just evenly incorporated and the mixture starts to come together; stop and stir to redistribute the ingredients if necessary.

Carefully remove the processor blade. Turn the mixture out onto a large sheet of wax paper. Sprinkle over the reserved chocolate pieces and about half the remaining 1 cup flour. Knead the mixture with your hands, gradually adding the rest of the flour until the mixture is evenly blended. Gradually work in up to 1 tablespoon cold water if the mixture is too dry to form a smooth, cohesive dough.

Divide the dough in half. Roll out each portion ⅓ inch thick between sheets of baking parchment or wax paper, smoothing out any wrinkles on the underside. Stack the portions (paper still attached) on a tray or baking sheet. Refrigerate the dough for at least 30 minutes, until it is cold and firm (or speed chilling by freezing the dough for 20 minutes). Or refrigerate up to 24 hours, then let warm up just slightly before using.

Baking Preliminaries: Position a rack in the middle of the oven; preheat to 325°F. Line several large baking sheets with baking parchment.

Cut out the shortbreads using a 2- to 2½-inch scalloped or plain round cutter (or as desired), spacing about 2 inches apart on the baking sheets.

Bake (middle rack) one sheet at a time for 9 to 12 minutes, or just until the cookies are almost firm when pressed in the center. Transfer to a wire rack and let stand until cooled completely.

Yield: Makes about sixty $2\frac{1}{4}$- to $2\frac{3}{4}$-inch cookies

Storage: Store these airtight and at room temperature for up to 10 days. They can be frozen, airtight, for up to $1\frac{1}{2}$ months; let come to room temperature before serving.

Tip

If you add the minimum $\frac{1}{4}$ teaspoon of cayenne pepper, the cookies will just be slightly spicy, in the way very gingery ginger cookies are. Add $\frac{1}{2}$ teaspoon and they will have a noticeable afterburn that adventurous tasters find addictive but that sometimes unsettles fans of bland. Add even more cayenne at your own risk!

Tip

I really like these plain, but you could dress them up with some accenting squiggles of Glossy Chocolate Drizzle (page 314), if desired.

Fairly Easy
Updated classic.
Versatile recipe:
choice of three
fillings.

¾ cup (1½ sticks) unsalted butter, slightly softened and cut into chunks

6 ounces (two 3-ounce packages) cream cheese, slightly softened and cut into chunks

½ cup powdered sugar
Generous ¼ teaspoon baking soda

⅛ teaspoon salt

2 cups unbleached all-purpose white flour, plus more if needed

Filling

Very generous 1 cup coarsely chopped walnuts
Very generous 1 cup apricot preserves

¼ teaspoon ground cinnamon

Garnish

1 large egg beaten with 1 tablespoon whole or low-fat milk for garnish
A generous 2 tablespoons granulated sugar for garnish

EASY APRICOT-WALNUT RUGELACH (OR TRIO OF RUGELACH)

As is true of many rugelach doughs, this one features cream cheese and is barely sweet. It nicely complements the quick, very tempting apricot-walnut filling provided here, but is equally good with the raspberry-pecan or spiced raisin-nut fillings presented in the variations at the end. Or, turn out a batch of two or all three fillings for a very colorful as well as delectable assortment.

Preliminaries: Set out six large sheets of baking parchment and a baking sheet.

In a large bowl, combine the butter, cream cheese, sugar, baking soda, and salt. Beat on medium speed until very well blended and smooth. On low speed, beat in half the flour until evenly incorporated. Beat or stir in the remaining flour until evenly incorporated.

Divide the dough into three equal portions. Roll each portion out into a thin, 12-inch-diameter round between sheets of baking parchment; the dough doesn't have to be perfectly round. Check the underside and smooth out any wrinkles.

Stack the rounds (paper attached) on the tray or sheet. Refrigerate for at least 45 minutes or until cold and firm, and for up to 2 days, if desired.

For the filling: In a food processor, process the walnuts, preserves, and cinnamon just until any large pieces of nuts and apricot are chopped fairly fine and the mixture has spreading consistency. (Alternatively, chop the walnuts with a large knife. Chop any large pieces of apricot fine. Stir together the walnuts, apricots, and cinnamon.) The filling may be made up to 2 days ahead, covered, and set aside in a nonreactive container at room temperature.

Baking Preliminaries: Position a rack in the middle of the oven; preheat to 350°F. Line several baking sheets with baking parchment.

Working with one dough round at a time and keeping the others chilled until needed, remove the top sheet of parchment. Using a third of the filling (no need to measure), spread it evenly to within ¼ inch of the edge; the filling layer will be thin. Using a pizza cutter or large sharp knife, cut the round into quarters, then eighths, then sixteenths.

While the dough is still cool and slightly firm, working from the outside edge inward, roll up each wedge into a pinwheel. Space the rugelach about 2 inches apart on the baking sheets. Lightly but evenly brush the tops with the egg wash, then generously sprinkle with the granulated sugar. Repeat the process with the two remaining rounds.

Bake (middle rack) one sheet at a time for 17 to 23 minutes or until the rugelach are nicely browned all over; don't underbake. Let the pans cool on wire racks until the rugelach firm up, about 3 minutes. Then transfer them to racks using a wide spatula. Thoroughly cool on wire racks before packing for storage.

Yield: Makes forty-eight 2½-inch-wide rugelach

Storage: Store these, airtight, for up to 1 week. They can be frozen, airtight, for up to 1 month.

Variation: Raspberry-Pecan Rugelach Replace the walnuts and apricot preserves called for in the original recipe with a very generous 1 cup each pecans and seedless raspberry preserves. Otherwise, prepare the filling and then the rugelach exactly as directed.

Variation: Raisin-Walnut Rugelach For the filling, use a generous ½ cup each raisins and walnuts, and 1 cup apricot preserves, plus ¼ teaspoon ground cinnamon. Otherwise, prepare the filling and then the rugelach exactly as directed.

1 cup (2 sticks) unsalted butter,
   slightly softened
1¼ cups granulated sugar
1 tablespoon ground ginger
1 tablespoon ground cinnamon
1 teaspoon ground cloves
1 teaspoon baking powder
   Scant ½ teaspoon salt
1 cup molasses
1 large egg, at room temperature
4¼ cups unbleached all-purpose
   white flour, plus a little more
   if needed
   Cinnamon red hot candies
   and snipped raisins for
   garnishing gingerbread
   people, optional
   Glaze, icing, drizzle or royal
   frosting for garnishing cookies,
   optional

NICE 'N' SPICY ROLLED GINGERBREAD COOKIES

In my humble opinion, classic gingerbread cookies should be full of fragrance and spice and enlivened with molasses. Namby-pamby and pale are not what I expect or want, and I think most folks who grew up enjoying baking or eating gingerbread boys and other rolled gingerbread shapes feel the same way. That said, these aren't overly dark, austere, or bitter like some old-fashioned ginger cookies; in fact, the spice blend gives them sweetness and ample butter adds just a hint of richness.

Happily, this dough is simple both to make and to handle. Use it for gingerbread people, plain rounds, or other cutout cookie shapes. They can be decorated with currants, bits of raisins, or cinnamon Red Hots for eyes or buttons before baking or with drizzled or piped icing or glaze after baking, if desired. You can also use them to ready stained glass accented cookies (as shown here) following the recipe on page 294.

Note that it's possible to obtain various cookie textures just by adjusting the dough thickness and baking time. For slightly soft cookies, roll the dough ⅓ inch thick. Then, underbake slightly; remove the cookies from the oven when the edges just begin to brown. For chewy-crisp cookies, roll the dough ¼ inch thick and bake until the tops *just start* to tinge. Watch carefully, and immediately remove them from the oven—that is, unless you like them crunchy-brittle instead.

Preliminaries: Set out four large sheets of baking parchment and a baking sheet.

In a very large nonreactive saucepan, melt the butter over medium heat just until melted and runny, stirring. Immediately remove from the heat. Vigorously stir in the sugar, ginger, cinnamon, cloves, baking powder, and salt until thoroughly and smoothly incorporated. Vigorously stir in the molasses, then the egg until evenly incorporated. Stir in 4¼ cups flour until evenly incorporated.

Refrigerate the dough until cooled to room temperature, 30 to 40 minutes; it will stiffen considerably. (If inadvertently left until cold and stiff, let it warm up until soft enough to handle again.) If the dough is still soft when at room temperature, add in several more tablespoons of flour until just slightly firmer but not at all dry or stiff; it's easiest to knead it in with your hands.

Divide the dough in half. Roll out the portions ¼ inch to ⅓ inch thick between large sheets of baking parchment or wax paper, checking the

underside and smoothing out any wrinkles. Stack the rolled portions (paper still attached) on a baking sheet. Refrigerate for at least 30 minutes, until cool and firm, or for up to 24 hours, if desired. (Allow dough that has been refrigerated longer than 1 hour to warm up slightly if it is too cold to cut out.)

Baking Preliminaries: Position a rack in the middle of the oven; preheat to 350°F. Line several baking sheets with baking parchment or coat them with nonstick spray.

Working with one dough portion at a time, gently peel away, then lightly pat one sheet of paper back into place. (This will make it easier to lift the cookies from the paper after they are cut out.) Peel off and discard the second layer.

Using 5- to 6-inch cutters for large gingerbread people or bears, or assorted 2- to 3-inch cutters in desired shapes, cut out the cookies. (If the dough becomes soft and difficult to handle, transfer the paper and cookies to a tray or baking sheet and briefly refrigerate again.) Using a spatula, transfer the cookies to the baking sheets, spacing $2\frac{1}{2}$ inches apart. Re-roll any dough scraps. Continue cutting out cookies until all the dough is used; refrigerate it if necessary to firm it up. If desired, firmly press cinnamon Red Hots and chopped raisins into the cookies for buttons and eyes before baking.

Bake (middle rack) one sheet at a time for 6 to 9 minutes for small and medium cookies and 8 to 12 minutes for 5- to 6-inch gingerbread people. For slightly soft cookies, bake until not quite firm in the center and just barely darker at the edges; for crisper ones, bake just until lightly tinged all over, then immediately remove from the oven. Let stand for 3 to 4 minutes to firm up. Then, using a wide spatula, transfer to wire racks and let cool completely. The

cookies may be decorated with Traditional Powdered Sugar Icing (page 302), or Easy Powdered Sugar Drizzle (page 304), Royal Frosting (page 313), or Glossy Chocolate Drizzle (page 314), if desired.

Yield: Makes twenty to twenty-five 6-inch gingerbread people, or 50 to 60 assorted $2\frac{1}{2}$- to 3-inch cookies

Storage: Store these, airtight, for up to 2 weeks. They can be frozen, airtight, for up to 2 months.

Fairly Easy
One-pot, one-spoon mixing.
Shaping by cutting dough
into a grid.

Glaze

1½ cups powdered sugar, sifted after measuring, if lumpy

2 tablespoons kirsch (clear cherry brandy) or fresh orange juice, if preferred

¼ teaspoon vanilla extract

Dough

⅔ cup clover honey or other mild honey

⅔ cup granulated sugar

¼ cup corn oil or other flavorless vegetable oil

2½ tablespoons kirsch (clear cherry brandy) or fresh orange juice, if preferred

2¾ teaspoons ground cinnamon

¼ teaspoon ground cloves

¼ teaspoon baking soda

1 tablespoon finely grated orange zest (orange part of the peel)

1 cup finely chopped blanched slivered almonds

2½ cups unbleached all-purpose white flour

Tip

The dough will be stiff, so use a pressing action and bear down firmly when rolling it out.

BASEL HONEY-SPICE WAFERS (BASEL LECKERLI)

Crunchy-chewy, spicy, and addictive, these rectangular wafers are topped with a translucent sugar glaze. While the original cookies date back centuries (and are still made in the Swiss city of Basel), my recipe is updated for improved taste and texture.

Baking Preliminaries: Place two racks in the center third of the oven and preheat to 350°F. Set out two large baking sheets.

In a small saucepan, stir together the powdered sugar, kirsch, vanilla, and 1 teaspoon warm water until blended. Set aside.

In a large heavy sauce pan over medium heat, stir together the honey, sugar, oil, and kirsch. Heat, stirring, until the sugar dissolves and the mixture begins to boil at the edges. Remove from heat and stir in the cinnamon, cloves, baking soda, orange zest, and almonds until blended. Stirring vigorously, gradually add the flour; the dough will stiffen.

Divide the dough in half. Roll each portion between parchment sheets into a 9 by 13-inch rectangle. Patch the dough if necessary to yield a rectangle. Peel off and discard the top sheet. Transfer the dough and bottom sheet to the baking sheets. Prick the dough lightly with a fork.

Bake both pans in the center third of the oven; switch their positions halfway through baking for even browning. Bake for 13 to 16 minutes or until just slightly darker on the edges; avoid overbaking, or the cookies will become too hard. Set aside.

Immediately bring the glaze just to a boil, stirring. Boil, stirring, until smooth, and translucent, about 30 seconds. Pour it over the dough tops and quickly spread it using a pastry brush or spatula. Lift each rectangle to a cutting board and cut away the uneven edges using a large sharp knife. Then, cut the rectangles into fourths lengthwise and eighths crosswise. Let stand until the glaze sets, 30 to 40 minutes.

Yield: Makes fifty to sixty 1½ by 2-inch rectangular wafers

Storage: Store these, airtight, for up to 3 weeks. They can be frozen, airtight, for up to 2 months.

BROWNIES & BARS }

The beauty of brownies and other bar cookies is that you get very attractive, individual treats without having to do *any* cookie shaping. Bars come in a wide variety of styles and flavors, too: The Cream of Coconut Ripple Bars and Easiest-Ever Dulce de Leche Bars, for example, are rich, homey, and chewy-gooey. The Simple Shortbread Bars and Honey-Oat Bars with Chocolate–Peanut Butter Glaze are satisfyingly firm and on the crunchy side.

Without exception, the brownies in this chapter fall into the moist, sumptuous, even chewy-gooey category (read that as not cakey!). But you still get to choose from a variety of styles—like straightforward classic fudge, or gussied-up mocha–cream cheese swirl, or sophisticated raspberry-bittersweet.

You'll see that each recipe includes cutting instructions and provides the associated yield. The yield information is based on what seems a reasonable, normal portion size, considering the richness, thickness, and character of that particular bar. But feel free to re-size the bars to suit your own taste or purposes—for

example, cut them smaller to stretch the number of servings or create a daintier look, or larger to provide more substantial, dessert-size portions.

Do follow the guidelines on prepping pans and cooling or chilling after baking, as this can greatly affect how easy bars are to cut and remove from their pans. In many cases instructions call for lining the baking pan with aluminum foil. You may find it helpful to turn the pan upside down and smooth and shape the foil around the bottom to approximate the size needed. The next step is to gently slide the formed foil off and turn the pan upright again. Finally, the foil is pushed down into the pan and further shaped to conform to the interior.

The foil lining often makes it possible to lift out the whole slab and, working on a cutting board, trim off the uneven edges and neatly cut the slab into bars. Besides the assortment of bars here, check out the No-Bake Cookies chapter, beginning on page 248, for some plain to fancy bars that can be turned out without turning on the oven.

½ cup (1 stick) unsalted butter, cut into chunks

2 cups (about 11 ounces) coarsely chopped bittersweet 55 to 65 percent cacao chocolate, divided

½ cup good-quality unsweetened natural (non-alkalized) cocoa powder or Dutch-process cocoa powder, sifted after measuring, if lumpy
Scant 1 cup granulated sugar

¼ teaspoon salt

3 large eggs, at room temperature

¼ cup very finely chopped freeze-dried raspberries (or 2½ tablespoons finely ground and sieved freeze-dried raspberries, if preferred)

¼ cup seedless raspberry preserves

½ teaspoon raspberry extract

1 cup unbleached all-purpose white flour
Chocolate Ganache Glaze (page 318) or Pure Satin Chocolate Icing (page 316), optional

Tip
These are lovely as is, but to-die-for gilded with chocolate icing or ganache.

RASPBERRY–BITTERSWEET CHOCOLATE CHUNK BROWNIES

I tried teaming up raspberries and chocolate in brownie recipes several times in the past, but they weren't nearly as fruity or fudgy as these beauties. They are dark, as rich as candy, and burst with berry and chocolate flavor.

Baking Preliminaries: Position a rack in the middle of the oven; preheat to 350°F. Line an 8-inch square baking pan with aluminum foil; let the foil slightly overhang on the two opposite sides. Grease the foil or coat with nonstick spray.

In a large microwave-safe bowl with the microwave on medium power, melt the butter and 1 cup chopped chocolate, stopping and stirring every 30 seconds, until the chocolate mostly melts. Stir until completely melted.

Vigorously stir the cocoa, sugar, and salt into the chocolate mixture until smoothly incorporated, free of lumps, and cooled to warm. Vigorously stir in the eggs, then the chopped raspberries, raspberry preserves, and raspberry extract. Stir in the flour until the batter is smooth and shiny. Lightly fold in the remaining 1 cup chopped chocolate. Put the batter in the pan, spreading evenly to the edges.

Bake (middle rack) for 20 to 25 minutes or until the edges are just pulling away from the pan sides and a toothpick inserted in the center comes out clean except for the bottom ¾ inch, which should still look moist and gooey.

Transfer to a wire rack until cooled to room temperature. Ready the icing or ganache as directed in the recipe, if desired. You will need only half of the icing; reserve the other half for another purpose. If topping with ganache, use the whole amount. Immediately spread out evenly over the brownie top. Refrigerate the brownie slab for at least 45 minutes so it will cut more neatly. Using the overhanging foil as handles, lift the slab onto a cutting board. Peel off and discard the foil. Using a large sharp knife, cut the brownie crosswise and lengthwise into quarters to yield 16 bars; or cut as desired. Use a damp paper towel to wipe the blade of buildup between cuts. Let the brownies warm up slightly before serving them.

Yield: Makes sixteen 2¼-inch squares

Storage: Store these, airtight, for 2 or 3 days. They can be frozen, airtight, for up to 1 month.

10 tablespoons (1¼ sticks) unsalted
    butter, cut into chunks
3   ounces unsweetened chocolate,
    coarsely broken or chopped
1½ cups granulated sugar
¼   cup good-quality unsweetened
    natural (non-alkalized) cocoa
    powder or Dutch-process
    cocoa powder, sifted after
    measuring, if lumpy
¼   teaspoon salt
3   large eggs, at room temperature
¾   cup unbleached all-purpose
    white flour

Tip

If you're one who finds the toppings, swirls, and chichi flavors of many of today's brownies just too much, these simple, classic bars will deliver the straightforward fudgy goodness you crave.

CLASSIC FUDGE BROWNIES

The first *real* chocolate brownies turned up in a 1906 Fannie Farmer cookbook, and, like these, they called for unsweetened chocolate. (I stress the word "real" because some dark-colored molasses drop cookies with the name "brownies" appeared before that.) The first brownie bars were not quite as chocolaty or as thick as these, but the basic formula was the same.

It's no wonder the original recipe caught on and endured: It was a winner needing at most minimal tweaking, which is what was done here.

Baking Preliminaries: Position a rack in the middle of the oven; preheat to 350°F. Line an 8-inch square baking pan with aluminum foil, allowing it to overhang on two opposite sides. Coat the foil with nonstick spray.

In a large microwave-safe bowl with the microwave on 50-percent power, melt the butter and chocolate, stopping and stirring at 30-second intervals, just until mostly melted. (Alternatively, in a large heavy saucepan, heat the butter and chocolate over lowest heat, stirring, until mostly melted. Immediately remove from the heat.) Stir until the butter and chocolate are completely melted and smooth.

Vigorously stir the sugar, cocoa, and salt into the chocolate mixture until smoothly incorporated and free of lumps. Let cool until just warm to the touch. Then, vigorously stir in the eggs and 2 tablespoons water until well blended and the sugar dissolves. Stir in the flour until the batter is smooth and shiny. Turn it out into the pan, spreading evenly to the edges.

Bake (middle rack) for 20 to 25 minutes or until the edges are just pulling away from the pan sides and a toothpick inserted in the center comes out clean except for the bottom ½ inch, which should still look moist and gooey.

Transfer the pan to a wire rack until cooled. Refrigerate the brownie slab at least 45 minutes to facilitate cutting. Using the overhanging foil as handles, lift the slab out of the pan onto a cutting board. Peel off and discard the foil. Using a large sharp knife, trim off and discard the edges all around, if desired. Cut the slab lengthwise and crosswise into fourths (or as desired). Using a damp paper towel, wipe the blade of any buildup between cuts.

Yield: Makes sixteen 2-inch squares

Storage: Store these, airtight, for 2 or 3 days. They can be frozen, airtight, for up to 1 month.

6 tablespoons unsalted butter, cut into chunks

4 ounces semisweet or bittersweet chocolate, coarsely broken or chopped

¼ cup finely crushed peppermint pinwheel hard candies, plus 1 tablespoon more for garnish, if desired

⅔ cup granulated sugar

2½ tablespoons unsweetened natural (non-alkalized) cocoa powder or Dutch-process cocoa powder sifted after measuring, if lumpy

2 large eggs, at room temperature

¼ teaspoon peppermint extract 3 or 4 drops oil of peppermint, optional

¼ teaspoon salt

⅔ cup unbleached all-purpose white flour

½ cup (3½ ounces) chopped semisweet or bittersweet chocolate

Tip

The easiest way to crush the peppermint candies is to put the unwrapped pieces in a triple layer of sturdy plastic bags or between two plastic chopping mats and pound them with a kitchen mallet or the back of a heavy spoon. They need to be in ⅛-inch or smaller bits.

PEPPERMINT-FUDGE BROWNIES

People love the entertaining culinary lore behind recipes, so I wish I could tell you that this one resulted when a resourceful baker ran out of nuts and threw some crushed peppermint candies into her brownie batter. And that the spontaneous act opened up a new, exciting chapter of brownie history. But the truth is that I just like chocolate and peppermint together and wanted to come up with an appealing holiday twist on the classic brownie, which, as it turns out, was a very tasty idea!

Note that if you happen to have oil of peppermint on hand, a few drops will definitely add extra pep to the minty–fudgy flavor.

Baking Preliminaries: Position rack in the middle of the oven; preheat to 350°F. Line an 8-inch square baking pan with aluminum foil, allowing it to overhang on two opposite sides. Coat the foil with nonstick spray.

Melt the butter in a heavy medium saucepan over very low heat, stirring occasionally, until fluid. Add the chocolate and crushed candy and stir constantly until completely melted and smoothly incorporated. Immediately remove from the heat; stir in the sugar and cocoa powder until evenly incorporated. Set aside until cooled to barely warm (if the mixture is too warm, it will cook the eggs).

Whisk the eggs, extract, oil of peppermint (if using), and salt into the cooled chocolate mixture until very smooth and glossy. Stir the flour into the mixture just until well blended. Turn out the batter into the foil-lined pan, spreading into an even layer, then smoothing out the top.

Bake, middle rack, until a toothpick inserted in the center comes out clean, 24 to 28 minutes; if the pick comes out with wet batter clinging to it, continue several minutes longer, then check again. Continue checking until just barely baked through. Immediately sprinkle some fine peppermint shards over top, if desired. Bake 1 minute longer, then let the pan cool on the rack.

For easiest cutting, refrigerate the brownies until chilled and firm. Lift them to a cutting board using the foil. Gently peel off and discard the foil. Trim off the edges all the way around, then cut into quarters in both directions to make 16 brownies. (Or cut as desired.)

Yield: Makes sixteen 2-inch squares.

Storage: Store these, airtight, for 2 or 3 days. They can be frozen, airtight, for up to 1 month.

½ cup (1 stick) unsalted butter, cut
   into chunks
3 ounces unsweetened chocolate,
   coarsely broken or chopped
1½ cups granulated sugar
¼ teaspoon salt
2 large eggs plus 1 large yolk
   (reserve the white for the
   cream cheese mixture)
⅔ cup unbleached all-purpose
   white flour

**Mocha–Cream Cheese Swirl
Mixture**

One 8-ounce package cream
   cheese, slightly softened
1 large egg white (left over from
   chocolate batter preparation)
   combined with 2 teaspoons
   instant coffee granules
¼ cup granulated sugar
½ tablespoon unsweetened
   natural (non-alkalized) cocoa
   powder or Dutch-process
   cocoa powder
1 teaspoon vanilla extract

Tip

I suppose I don't really need to
mention that these are rich and best
served in small portions. . . .

MOCHA–CREAM CHEESE SWIRL BROWNIES

These are decadent in the way cream cheese swirl brownies always are, but in my humble opinion they are even tastier than most due to the mocha flavor. Though not visually dramatic, the chocolate-coffee blend balances out the flavor of the dark brownie dough particularly nicely.

Baking Preliminaries: Position a rack in the middle of the oven; preheat to 350°F. Line an 9-inch square baking pan with aluminum foil, allowing it to overhang two opposite sides. Coat the foil with nonstick spray.

In a large microwave-safe bowl with the microwave on high power, melt the butter and chocolate for 1 minute, stopping and stirring at the 30-second interval. Microwave on 50 percent power, stopping and stirring every 20 seconds, until completely melted. (Alternatively, in a large saucepan over medium-low heat, melt the butter and chocolate, stirring. Immediately remove from the heat.) Let cool slightly.

Vigorously stir the sugar and salt into the chocolate mixture until evenly incorporated and free of lumps. Vigorously stir in the eggs and yolk, then the flour, until the batter is very well blended. Turn out about two-thirds of the batter into the pan, spreading to the edges.

For the swirl mixture: In a food processor, combine the cream cheese, egg white–coffee mixture, sugar, cocoa, and vanilla. Process until smooth, scraping down the bowl sides as needed. Evenly drop spoonfuls of the cream cheese mixture over the chocolate batter. Drop spoonfuls of the remaining chocolate batter over the top. Holding a table knife, vertically run it through the batter to form decorative swirls.

Bake (middle rack) for 35 to 40 minutes or until the cream cheese areas are tinged and a toothpick inserted in the center comes out clean except for the bottom ½ inch, which should still look moist.

Transfer to a wire rack until cooled. Refrigerate the brownie slab for about 45 minutes so it will cut more neatly. Using the overhanging foil as handles, lift the brownie slab onto a cutting board. Peel off and discard the foil. Cut the slab into quarters in both directions using a large sharp knife. Using a damp paper towel, wipe the blade of any buildup between cuts. Let the brownies warm up slightly before serving them.

Yield: Makes sixteen 2¼-inch squares

Storage: Store these, airtight, for 2 or 3 days. They can be frozen, airtight, for up to 1 month.

ONE-BOWL CHOCOLATE, ESPRESSO, AND WHITE CHOCOLATE CHUNK BROWNIES

I don't call for white chocolate in too many baked goods. It often seems overly sweet and bland to me and disappears into the dough, never to be noticed again! But occasionally it can be wonderful; and this is one of those times.

For one thing, the brownie batter is dark and bittersweet, so it contrasts beautifully with the light color, sweetness, and creamy-mildness of the white chocolate. For another, these are espresso brownies, and the espresso-chocolate blend has the same sort of unexplainable but undeniable affinity for white chocolate that coffee has for cream. Finally, the white chocolate is not melted but appears as succulent, satisfying, eye-catching chunks. So, even if you, too, are normally ho-hum about white chocolate, you may want to try these. Not only is the flavor sumptuous, but they are also moist and fudge-like. And—happily—they are easy to make.

¾ cup (1½ sticks) unsalted butter, cut into chunks

3½ ounces unsweetened chocolate, broken up or very coarsely chopped

2½ ounces 65 to 75 percent cacao bittersweet chocolate, broken up or very coarsely chopped

1⅔ cups granulated sugar
Generous ¼ teaspoon salt

4 large eggs, at room temperature

2 teaspoons vanilla extract

1 tablespoon instant espresso powder dissolved in 2 tablespoons hot water

¾ cup unbleached all-purpose white flour

8 to 10 ounces very coarsely chopped good-quality white chocolate

Baking Preliminaries: Position a rack in the middle of the oven; preheat to 350°F. Line a 9-inch square baking pan with aluminum foil, letting the foil slightly overhang on the two opposing sides. Grease the foil or coat with nonstick spray.

In a large microwave-safe bowl with the microwave on medium power, melt the butter and chocolates, stopping and stirring at 30-second intervals, until just barely melted. (Alternatively, stirring constantly, melt the butter and chocolates in a large heavy saucepan over lowest heat until mostly melted. Immediately remove from the heat.) Stir until the chocolate completely melts.

Vigorously stir the sugar and salt into the chocolate mixture until smoothly incorporated, and cooled to warm. Vigorously stir in the eggs, one at a time, then the vanilla and the espresso mixture. Stir until the sugar completely dissolves and the mixture is smooth and shiny. Stir in the flour just until the batter is evenly blended and smooth. Turn out about half the batter into the pan, spreading to the edges.

Sprinkle about a third of the white chocolate chunks over the top. Spoon and spread the remaining batter over the chocolate to cover it. Sprinkle the remaining white chocolate evenly over the top, rapping the pan, then patting down to imbed the pieces just slightly.

Bake (middle rack) for 25 to 35 minutes or until the edges are just pulling away from the pan sides and a toothpick inserted in the center comes out clean except for the bottom ¾ inch, which should still look moist and gooey. While the brownies bake, fill a large shallow pan

$\frac{1}{2}$-inch deep with ice cubes and water. Remove the brownie pan from the oven and place it in the ice water to stop the cooking. Let stand until completely cooled, 30 to 45 minutes.

Refrigerate the brownie slab for about 45 minutes so it will cut neatly. Using the overhanging foil as handles, transfer the slab to a cutting board. Carefully peel off and discard the foil. Cut away and discard the dry edges using a large sharp knife. Then cut the brownie slab lengthwise and crosswise into quarters to form bars; using a damp paper towel, wipe the blade of any buildup between cuts.

Yield: Makes sixteen $2\frac{1}{4}$-inch squares

Storage: Store these, airtight, for 2 or 3 days. They can be frozen, airtight, for up to 1 month.

1 batch Simple Shortbread Bars dough (page 166)
1½ cups (6 ounces) chopped pecans, divided
1½ cups lightly packed sweetened flaked or shredded coconut
¾ cup (1½ sticks) unsalted butter, slightly softened and cut into chunks
⅔ cup packed light or dark brown sugar
¼ cup light corn syrup
¼ teaspoon salt
2 teaspoons vanilla extract

Tip
There is nothing German about German chocolate cake. It was named for the particular blend of chocolate originally called for, which in turn was named for its creator, a Mr. German.

PRALINE-PECAN-COCONUT BARS

The topping for these delectable yet easy bars tastes a bit like the filling for German chocolate cake, but instead of being soft and moist, it's wonderfully crispy-crunchy. Made using the Simple Shortbread Bars recipe (page 166), the bottom layer is barely sweet and buttery, and pairs with the decadent topping perfectly. Expect these to disappear fast—even those who aren't normally coconut fans usually love them.

I like to cut these small to create very petite servings, but feel free to cut them "regular" bar size if preferred.

Baking Preliminaries: Position a rack in the middle of the oven; preheat to 325°F. Line a 9 by 13-inch baking pan with a long sheet of foil, smoothing it into the pan and allowing the excess to overhang the narrow ends.

Prepare the shortbread dough exactly as directed. Press the dough into the pan to form a smooth, evenly thick layer. Parbake (middle rack) for 18 to 23 minutes or until lightly tinged and just slightly darker at the edges.

Combine the pecans, coconut, butter, brown sugar, corn syrup, and salt in a medium heavy saucepan. Stirring constantly, bring the mixture to a full boil over medium heat. Start timing and boil for 2 minutes. Remove from the heat. Stir in the vanilla.

Pour the mixture evenly over the still warm parbaked dough. Bake (middle rack) for 25 to 30 minutes longer or until the top is bubbly, golden brown, and just slightly darker at the edges.

Transfer to a wire rack. Let stand until completely cooled. Using the foil as handles, lift the slab from the pan to a cutting board. Cutting through the foil, cut the slab in half crosswise. Gently invert each half and peel off the foil. Turn the portions upright and cut each half into quarters crosswise and lengthwise (or as desired) using a large sharp knife. Trim off and discard the edges, if desired.

Yield: Makes thirty-two 1½ by 2⅛-inch bars

Storage: Store these, airtight, for up to 2 weeks. They can be frozen, airtight, for up to 2 months.

6 tablespoons (¾ stick) unsalted
    butter, cut into chunks
2 ounces unsweetened chocolate,
    coarsely chopped or broken up
¾ cup granulated sugar
¼ teaspoon baking soda
¼ teaspoon salt
1 cup cream of coconut, divided
2 large eggs, at room temperature
¾ cup plus 2 tablespoons
    unbleached all-purpose white
    flour
½ cup chopped almonds, optional
¼ teaspoon almond extract
1 cup shredded or flaked
    sweetened coconut
    Chocolate Ganache Glaze (page
    318), optional

CREAM OF COCONUT RIPPLE BARS

These are designed for coconut lovers, or maybe for those who swoon for coconut and chocolate together. As you'd guess from the name, these are enhanced with lots of succulent ripples and streaks of cream of coconut and coconut shreds. They lean in the direction of brownies but are moister and lighter in texture. While it's entirely optional, for an over-the-top treatment, garnish them with the Chocolate Ganache Glaze on page 318.

Baking Preliminaries: Position a rack in the middle of the oven; preheat to 350°F. Grease a 9-inch square baking pan or coat with nonstick spray.

In a large saucepan, heat the butter and chocolate over low heat, stirring, until they are mostly melted. Remove from the heat, stirring until the chocolate melts. Stir in the sugar, baking soda, and salt until the sugar dissolves. Vigorously stir ¼ cup cream of coconut, and then the eggs, into the chocolate mixture. Stir the flour into the chocolate mixture just until the batter is evenly blended. Turn out the batter into the pan, spreading it evenly to the edges.

In a small bowl, stir together the remaining ¾ cup cream of coconut, the almonds (if desired), almond extract, and coconut. Drop by 12 heaping tablespoons onto the batter, spacing them evenly. Using the tip of a table knife held vertically, swirl the coconut mixture into the batter to create a rippled and streaked effect. The two should be fairly well intermingled.

Bake (middle rack) for 25 to 30 minutes or until the center top springs back when lightly pressed and a toothpick inserted in the center comes out clean. Transfer the pan to a wire rack. Let cool till warm, about 30 minutes.

If glazing the bars, pour the warm ganache glaze over them when they are barely warm. Immediately spread it with an offset spatula to even the surface. Let stand until it cools and sets before serving.

Yield: Makes sixteen 2⅛-inch squares.

Storage: Store these, airtight at room temperature, for 3 or 4 days. They can be frozen, airtight, for up to 1½ months.

DULCE DE LECHE SWIRL CONGO BARS

Rich and mellow, congo bars are always good, but when you add in little swirls of milk caramel they are even moister, chewier, and more decadent than usual. If you haven't used the popular Latin American milk caramel product dulce de leche before, this recipe is a great way to try it: The unique caramel taste pairs beautifully with the nuts, brown sugar, and chocolate morsels in the bars.

Dulce de leche can now be found in many supermarkets, often near the condensed milk or in the international foods section. You can also make it at home using my no-fuss recipe on page 323.

¾ cup (1½ sticks) unsalted butter, cut into chunks

1½ cups packed light brown sugar

1½ teaspoons baking powder

½ teaspoon salt

2 teaspoons vanilla extract

3 large eggs, at room temperature

2 cups unbleached all-purpose white flour

1 cup chopped walnuts or pecans

1 cup (6 ounces) semisweet chocolate morsels

1 generous cup purchased or homemade (page 323) dulce de leche

Baking Preliminaries: Position a rack in the middle of the oven; preheat to 350°F. Generously grease a 9 by 13-inch baking pan or coat with nonstick spray.

In a large saucepan, melt the butter over medium heat, stirring, until mostly melted and runny. Stir until completely melted and free of lumps, then set aside until cooled to warm. Stir in the sugar, baking powder, salt, and vanilla until well blended. One at a time, vigorously stir in the eggs. Stir in the flour just until evenly incorporated. Fold in the nuts and chocolate morsels until evenly distributed.

Spread a generous half of the mixture evenly in the pan. Put evenly spaced heaping tablespoonfuls of the dulce de leche over the batter. Then drop spoonfuls of the remaining batter over the top. Using a table knife held vertically, swirl the two together to produce a slightly rippled effect; don't blend them too much.

Bake (middle rack) for 25 to 30 minutes, until nicely browned on top and a toothpick inserted in the center comes out clean. Cool completely on a wire rack before cutting. Cut lengthwise into thirds and crosswise into sixths (or as desired).

Yield: Makes eighteen 2 by 3-inch bars.

Storage: Store these, covered, for 2 or 3 days. They can be frozen, airtight, for up to 1 month.

8 ounces 50 to 70 percent cacao
   semisweet chocolate, coarsely
   chopped
3 ounces milk chocolate, coarsely
   chopped
⅔ cup heavy (whipping) cream
2 cups finely broken-up (⅛-inch
   to ¼-inch pieces) honey
   graham crackers
4 cups mini marshmallows,
   divided
1 cup sweetened dried
   cranberries, optional
½ cup chopped walnuts or pecans,
   optional

Tip
Add the optional cranberries and
nuts for a dessert with a winter
holiday look and taste.

ALMOST NO-BAKE S'MORES BARS

Like s'mores, these bars feature graham crackers, marshmallows, and chocolate. Only here, they are mixed together and pressed into a baking pan. Then, a layer of mini marshmallows goes on top and the bars are slipped into the oven just until they brown and partly melt. In warm weather, these are a great dessert for a deck or swimming party.

Baking Preliminaries: Line a 9-inch square broiler-proof baking pan with aluminum foil, allowing the foil to overhang slightly on two opposing ends. Preheat the oven to 500°F (or to broiling temperature).

In a food processor, combine the chocolates and process until fairly fine. Put the cream in a 2-cup glass measure. Microwave the mixture on high power for 1 minute; stop and stir. Continue microwaving on high, watching closely and stopping when the cream boils, usually in 20 to 30 seconds. (Alternatively, heat the cream to boiling in a heavy saucepan over medium-high heat, stirring occasionally.)

Pour the hot cream over the chocolate in the processor (or add the chocolate to the cream in the saucepan); do not stir. Let stand, without stirring, for 5 minutes so the heat softens the chocolate. Process or stir until completely smooth, stopping and scraping down the bowl as needed.

Turn out the chocolate mixture into a large bowl. Fold the broken-up graham cracker pieces, then 1¾ cups marshmallows, and the cranberries and nuts (if using) into the chocolate mixture until evenly incorporated. Spread the mixture in the baking pan, smoothing and patting down evenly. Neatly and attractively arrange the remaining 2¼ cups marshmallows over the filling top, spacing them close together and pressing down slightly to imbed.

Slide the pan onto the rack just under the broiler and broil for 1 to 1½ minutes, until the marshmallows just begin to brown; watch carefully, as they may scorch quickly. Rotate the pan if necessary for even browning and remove it as soon as the top is tinged. Let cool slightly, then refrigerate for at least 1 hour, until cooled and set, before serving. Lift the slab out of the pan onto a cutting board using the foil as handles. Peel off the foil. Cut the slab into fourths in both directions using a large sharp knife (wipe it clean as necessary); or cut as desired.

Yield: Makes sixteen 2⅛-inch squares

Storage: Store these, airtight at cool room temperature, for up to 1 week. They can be frozen, airtight, for up to 10 days. Thaw before serving.

ALMOND–BITTERSWEET CHOCOLATE CHUNK BARS

I often turn to this recipe when I need bars that seem a bit fancy but are in fact completely foolproof and simple. The secret to the pronounced, very appealing almond flavor is almond paste. Sliced almonds on top add both visual appeal and texture.

A gourmet-quality dark chocolate likewise contributes to the sophisticated feel of these bars. Chunks with a 60 to 70 percent cacao content will taste boldly bittersweet but not off-putting when tucked into the not-too-sweet dough. (Don't use chocolate with a cacao percentage of higher than about 72 percent, as the pieces may melt and spread too much during baking.) The secret to the toothsomeness of these bars is in the double baking. First the dough is spread in a flat pan, then baked till it is sturdy enough to cut into small bars. These go back in the oven and are baked until firm and crisp.

½ cup (1 stick) unsalted butter, softened and cut into chunks
1 7- to 8-ounce package or can almond paste, cut or spooned into chunks
5 tablespoons granulated sugar
¼ teaspoon baking powder
¼ teaspoon salt
2 large eggs, at room temperature and beaten with a fork
1½ cups unbleached all-purpose white flour
2 cups gourmet-quality morsel-size chunks 60 to 70 percent cacao semisweet or bittersweet chocolate
1 cup blanched or unblanched sliced almonds

Tip
Either of the brands of almond paste that come in cans or tubes will do fine in this recipe.

Baking Preliminaries: Position a rack in the middle of the oven; preheat to 350°F. Line a 9 by 13-inch baking pan with heavy-duty foil, allowing it to overhang on the two narrow ends slightly. Grease the foil or coat with nonstick spray.

In a large bowl with a mixer on medium speed, beat the butter, almond paste, sugar, baking powder, and salt until well blended. Reserve 2 tablespoons egg for glazing the top; beat the rest of the egg into the mixture until thoroughly incorporated. On low speed, beat in the flour just until the mixture begins to mass. (If the mixer motor labors, stir in the last of the flour with a large spoon.) Stir in the chocolate chunks until evenly incorporated.

Press the dough into the baking pan. Lay a sheet of wax paper over the top and press and smooth out to even the surface; discard the sheet. Brush the top evenly with the reserved egg mixture. Evenly sprinkle the almonds over the surface. Pat down lightly.

Bake (middle rack) for 20 to 25 minutes, until the bars are lightly browned all over and slightly darker at the edges.

Transfer to a wire rack. Let stand until cooled completely; the dough will be crumbly while warm. Using the foil as handles, transfer the bars to a cutting board. If desired, trim off the dry edges all around. Cut the bars lengthwise and crosswise into sixths using a large sharp knife.

Yield: Makes thirty-six 1½ by 2⅛-inch bars

Storage: Store these, covered and at room temperature, for up to 1 week. They can be frozen, airtight, for up to 2 months; thaw before serving.

Base

- ½ cup (1 stick) unsalted butter, slightly softened and cut into chunks
- ¼ cup granulated pure maple sugar or granulated sugar
- 2 tablespoons pure maple syrup, dark amber preferred
- ¼ teaspoon baking powder
- ¼ teaspoon salt
- 1 large egg, at room temperature
- 1⅔ cups unbleached all-purpose white flour

Topping

- 6 tablespoons (¾ stick) unsalted butter, cut into chunks
- 2½ tablespoons each granulated pure maple sugar and granulated sugar (or use 5 tablespoons granulated sugar, if necessary)
- ½ cup pure maple syrup, dark amber preferred
- 3 tablespoons light or dark corn syrup
  Scant ¼ teaspoon salt
- 1⅔ cups coarsely chopped pecans or walnuts, chopped moderately fine

MAPLE-NUT BARS

Some years back, I spent an exciting four days during the March sugaring season traveling all over Vermont to steep myself in the maple culture. It seemed that wherever I went the sweet, woodsy smell of maple syrup enveloped me: It furled up from the bubbling pot as the Harold Howrigan family in Fairfield, Vermont, took me into their kitchen and showed me how to boil down syrup for maple candy and maple on snow. It swirled in moist clouds from the evaporator chugging away at the Morse Farm Sugarworks sugarhouse in Montpelier. And it perfumed the air at the Butternut Mountain Farms bottling plant in Johnson, where a steady stream of glinting amber-filled jugs paraded past us and boxes of maple products stretched to the ceiling.

Not surprisingly, David Marvin, owner of Butternut Mountain Farms, was highly enthusiastic about my plan to create some sweet treats that called for maple syrup. "And the more you use, the better they'll be," he said with a laugh.

Which brings me to these bars. They are slightly crisp and sticky, with a not-too-sweet maple shortbread crust studded with a succulent, crunchy maple-nut topping. Though they are a bit more trouble than many recipes in the book, they are much easier than the little maple tassies that inspired them. They taste and smell like the steam that hovered during the Vermont sugaring season—subtle, natural, and haunting, with none of the all-too-familiar cloying artificial notes of imitation maple extract. Maple most often seems to be paired with walnuts, but I love these bars just as much with pecans, so take your pick!

Baking Preliminaries: Position a rack in the middle of the oven; preheat to 350°F. Line a 9 by 13-inch baking pan with heavy-duty foil, allowing it to overhang the two narrow ends slightly. Grease the foil or coat with nonstick spray.

For the base: In a large bowl with a mixer on medium speed, beat the butter, sugar, maple syrup, baking powder, and salt until well blended. Beat in the egg until the mixture is thoroughly incorporated; don't worry if the mixture looks separated. On low speed, beat in the flour just until the mixture begins to mass. (If the mixer motor labors, stir in the last of the flour with a large spoon.) If the dough is crumbly, stir in up to 3 teaspoons of water until it holds together.

Press the dough into the baking pan. Lay a sheet of wax paper over the top and press and smooth out to even the surface; discard the paper.

Bake (middle rack) for 20 to 25 minutes or until the shortbread is lightly browned at the edges. Set aside.

For the topping: In a 2-quart, heavy, nonreactive saucepan, melt the butter over medium-high heat. Thoroughly stir in the sugars, maple syrup, corn syrup, and salt. When the mixture begins to boil at the edges, adjust the heat so it boils briskly. Boil, uncovered, for $2\frac{1}{2}$ minutes or until the mixture forms large glassy bubbles and boils down just slightly. Stop and check the consistency; if the syrup is still very runny, boil for another 30 to 45 seconds to thicken it slightly.

Pour the syrup over the par-baked shortbread, spreading it out until the dough is evenly coated. Sprinkle the nuts evenly over the top, then shake the pan to even the layer. Lay a sheet of foil over the nuts and pat down lightly to imbed them slightly. Discard the foil.

Bake (middle rack) for 17 to 22 minutes or until the filling darkens just slightly and the entire surface is bubbly. Transfer to a wire rack. Let stand until cooled to warm; don't touch during cooling, as the syrup will be hot.

When the bars have cooled to warm, cut them crosswise into sixths and lengthwise into quarters using a large sharp knife; try not to cut through the foil and don't lift them, as they will still be crumbly. Let the bars cool and firm up completely, then lift them out, peeling them off the foil as necessary.

Yield: Makes twenty-four $2\frac{1}{8}$ by $2\frac{1}{4}$-inch bars

Storage: Store these, covered and at room temperature, for up to 1 week. They can be frozen, airtight, for 2 months; thaw completely before serving.

6 tablespoons (¾ stick)
    unsalted butter
6 tablespoons whole milk or half-
    and-half
¼ cup clover honey or orange
    blossom honey
1⅓ cups powdered sugar, sifted after
    measuring
¾ cup unbleached all-purpose
    white flour
1½ cups chopped unblanched
    almonds
1½ cups chopped blanched
    hulled hazelnuts
⅔ cup finely diced dried pineapple
    rings or diced candied orange
    peel
    Very finely grated zest of 2 large
    oranges (orange part of the
    peel)
    Chocolate Ganache Glaze (page
    318) or Glossy Chocolate
    Drizzle (page 314)

Tip
Dried pineapple can stand in for the
candied orange peel traditionally
called for in Florentines; it's often
more economical and easier to find.
And it lends extra chew. Usually
dried pineapple rings are stocked
with other dried fruit. Dice them
by hand.

FLORENTINE BARS

I've always adored the chewy-brittle, candy-like character and sophisticated orange-nut flavor of Florentines. I never made the cookies often, though, because they were time-consuming. Which is why I decided to come up with bars that tasted similar but could be readied a bit more easily.

Normally, either the tops of classic Florentines are drizzled with chocolate or the bottoms are coated with a layer of it. Here, ganache gets smoothed over the top or it is quickly garnished with glossy chocolate drizzle.

Baking Preliminaries: Position a rack in the middle of the oven; preheat the oven to 350°F. Line a 9 by 13-inch pan with aluminum foil, overlapping the narrow ends. Be careful not to puncture the foil. Generously grease or spray the foil with nonstick spray.

Combine the butter, milk, honey, and sugar in a medium saucepan. Bring to a boil, stirring, over medium heat and continue to boil the mixture, stirring, for 30 seconds. Remove the saucepan from the heat. Sift the flour over the boiled mixture. Stir until smooth. Thoroughly stir in the chopped nuts, diced pineapple, and orange zest. Pour the batter into the prepared pan, smoothing and spreading out to the edges.

Bake (middle rack) for 18 to 23 minutes or until a rich golden brown; rotate the pan from front to back halfway through the baking to ensure even browning. Watch carefully at the end of baking, as the top may brown very rapidly. Remove from the oven and let stand for 15 minutes. Using the foil as handles, lift the slab out of the pan onto a cooling rack. Cool for about 30 minutes or until barely warm. Peel off the foil. Working on a cutting board and using a large sharp knife, trim off the edges all the way around, if desired.

Prepare the ganache or drizzle as directed. Spread an even layer of warm ganache over the entire top or attractively drizzle the drizzle over it. Let stand on the cutting board until the chocolate sets, about 1 hour. Using a large sharp knife, cut the bars lengthwise into fourths and crosswise into sixths. Then, if desired, cut diagonally across the squares to yield small triangle-shaped Florentines.

Yield: Makes forty-eight 2-inch triangle-shaped Florentines

Storage: Store these, airtight, in a single layer at cool room temperature for up to 1 week. They can be frozen, airtight, for up to 2 months.

½ cup (1 stick) unsalted butter,
   melted
1¾ cups graham cracker crumbs
1 6-ounce package (1 cup)
   semisweet chocolate morsels
1 cup (4½ ounces) chopped
   pecans or walnuts
1 cup (5½ ounces) dried cherries
   (or substitute sweetened dried
   cranberries)
1 14-ounce can sweetened
   condensed milk
1 large egg, at room temperature
2½ teaspoons vanilla extract and/or
   ½ teaspoon almond extract

Tip

While it is certainly more convenient
to rely on ready-to-use graham
cracker crumbs in the recipe, if you
have a food processor, consider
breaking up whole crackers and
grinding them into crumbs yourself.
They taste a lot fresher.

OOEY-GOOEY CHOCOLATE CHIP–CHERRY (OR CRANBERRY) BARS

These bars are a variation on Hello Dollies, aka Six-Layer Bars. Dried cherries or cranberries replace the coconut often used, and the recipe also calls for an egg. The resulting treats are more colorful and toothsome, less sweet, and less crumbly than the originals. If you like, add a little almond extract to bring out the taste of the cherries.

Turn to this recipe when you need a tempting homemade treat in a hurry—the bars can be mixed up and in the oven in less than 10 minutes. They're perfect for a bake sale, potluck, holiday gift, or family picnic. The nuts add both flavor and crunch but may be left out if you like. If you wish, you can even omit the dried cherries or cranberries, or replace them with a cup of flaked coconut.

Baking Preliminaries: Position a rack in the middle of the oven; preheat to 350°F. Generously grease a 9 by 13-inch baking pan or coat with nonstick spray.

In a medium bowl, stir together the butter and graham cracker crumbs until blended. Spread the mixture evenly in the baking pan; press down firmly to form a crust.

Sprinkle the chocolate morsels, nuts, and dried cherries over the crust. Wipe out the bowl used for the graham cracker mixture, then with a fork, beat together the condensed milk, egg, and vanilla in it. Spoon the condensed milk mixture evenly over the top.

Bake (middle rack) for 25 to 30 minutes, until tinged with brown and just slightly darker at the edges. Transfer to a wire rack; let cool. For easiest cutting, firm up in the refrigerator for 15 to 20 minutes. Then cut crosswise into sixths and lengthwise into fourths (or as desired) using a large sharp knife.

Yield: Makes twenty-four 2⅛-inch squares

Storage: Store these, airtight, for up to 1 week. They can be frozen, airtight, for up to 2 months.

Quick bowl-and-spoon mixing.
Gluten-free (if using
certified gluten-free oats,
chocolate, and nut butter).

½ cup (1 stick) unsalted butter,
    slightly softened
⅔ cup clover honey or other mild
    honey
¼ teaspoon salt
3¼ cups old-fashioned rolled oats
    or quick-cooking (not instant)
    oats
1 cup flaked or shredded
    sweetened coconut
1⅓ cups (8 ounces) semisweet
    chocolate morsels
⅓ cup smooth peanut butter, or
    almond butter, at room
    temperature
¾ cup chopped salted peanuts or
    chopped slivered almonds

HONEY-OAT BARS WITH CHOCOLATE–PEANUT BUTTER GLAZE (OR CHOCOLATE–ALMOND BUTTER GLAZE)

These are reminiscent of granola bars, only they are topped with a fairly decadent chocolate–peanut butter glaze and sprinkled with peanuts. Or, if you prefer, make the recipe using almond butter and almonds for a completely different taste and look.

Baking Preliminaries: Position a rack in the middle of the oven; preheat to 350°F. Line a 9 by 13-inch flat baking dish with aluminum foil, overhanging the narrow sides. Generously coat the foil with nonstick spray.

In a large heavy saucepan, combine the butter, honey, and salt over medium-high heat, stirring, until the butter melts and the mixture just begins to boil at the edges. Start timing and gently boil, stirring, for 2 minutes. Remove from the heat. Stir in the oats and coconut until evenly incorporated. Turn out the oat mixture into the baking pan, spreading it out evenly. Firmly press down into an even layer with greased hands.

Bake (middle rack) for 14 to 18 minutes or until the layer is golden all over and almost firm when pressed in the center top. Let cool on a wire rack for 10 minutes.

In a small, deep microwave-safe bowl, microwave the chocolate morsels on 50 percent power, stopping and stirring every 30 seconds, until mostly melted. Stirring occasionally, let the residual heat complete the melting.

Vigorously stir the peanut butter into the chocolate until smoothly incorporated. Spread the chocolate–peanut butter mixture over the still-slightly warm oat layer, smoothing and spreading it evenly to the edges. Immediately sprinkle the peanuts evenly over the chocolate. Refrigerate until the bars just firm up, 25 to 30 minutes. (Or to speed chilling, freeze for 15 minutes.) Using the foil, lift the slab onto a cutting board. Using a large sharp knife, trim off and discard the edges all the way around. Cut the slab crosswise into sixths and lengthwise into fourths (or as desired). Gently peel the bars off the foil.

Yield: Makes twenty-four 2 by 2¼-inch bars

Storage: Store these, airtight at cool room temperature or refrigerated, for up to 1 week. Or freeze for up to 2 months; warm up slightly before serving.

Streusel

1¼ cups unbleached all-purpose
white flour
1 cup old-fashioned rolled oats
Generous ¾ cup granulated
sugar
½ teaspoon ground cinnamon
¼ teaspoon baking powder
¼ teaspoon salt
10 tablespoons (1¼ sticks) unsalted
butter, melted
½ cup coarsely chopped pecans,
optional

Filling

1 cup fresh raspberries (or
partially thawed frozen berries),
coarsely chopped
1 cup finely chopped dried apples
⅔ cup seedless raspberry jam

Tip

If you have seeded raspberry jam
instead of seedless preserves, simply
heat the jam until fluid, then stir and
strain it through a fine-mesh sieve
to remove the seeds. The sieved
amount needs to measure ⅔ cup.

RASPBERRY-APPLE STREUSEL BARS

The crumbly streusel mixture in these attractive, homespun bars does
double-duty: Some is pressed into the pan bottom to create the crust. The
rest is strewn over a raspberry-apple filling and forms an effortless crumb
topping.

Don't think that because the filling is simple (only three ingredients) it can't
be really good. It makes the bars delightfully chewy and, thanks to the trio
of fresh raspberries, seedless raspberry jam, and dried apples, gives them an
intensely fruity taste.

Baking Preliminaries: Position a rack in the upper third of the oven;
preheat oven to 350°F. Generously spray a 7 by 11-inch (or a 9-inch
square) baking pan with nonstick spray.

For the streusel: In a large bowl, thoroughly stir together the flour, oats,
sugar, cinnamon, baking powder, and salt. Add the butter, stirring until
the mixture is well blended and crumbly. Firmly press a scant two-thirds
(no need to measure) of the streusel into the baking dish, forming a
packed, even layer. Stir the nuts (if using) into the remaining streusel; set
aside for topping. Par-bake the crust in the upper third of the oven for
12 minutes; the layer will not be browned.

For the filling: Meanwhile, combine the berries, apples, and jam in a
medium saucepan. Stirring constantly, bring to a full boil over medium-
high heat. Boil, stirring, for 2 minutes or until just beginning to thicken
but not burned. Remove from the heat. Evenly spread the mixture over
the crust. Sprinkle the remaining streusel evenly over the filling. Pat
down lightly.

Readjust the rack to the middle of the oven. Bake (middle rack) for 25
to 30 minutes or until the top is lightly browned all over. Transfer the pan
to a wire rack. Let cool to warm. If desired, trim off and discard any overly
brown edges all the way around using a large sharp knife. Cut the bars
crosswise into sixths and lengthwise into thirds (or cut as desired). Let
cool completely before serving.

Yield: Makes eighteen 1¾ by 2¾-inch bars

Storage: Store these, covered and at room temperature, for up to 1 week.
Or freeze, airtight, for up to 2 months; thaw before serving.

13 tablespoons (scant 1⅔ sticks)
     cool and firm unsalted butter,
     cut into chunks
½ cup granulated sugar, plus 1 to
     2 tablespoons more for
     optional garnish
1½ teaspoons vanilla extract
     Scant ½ teaspoon salt
2 cups unbleached all-purpose
     white flour

SIMPLE SHORTBREAD (OR CHOCOLATE-ICED SIMPLE SHORTBREAD) BARS

Buttery tasting and not too sweet, this unfussy shortbread can stand alone or serve as a base for a number of bars in this book. Among the easiest (and yummiest) uses is just to fully bake the shortbread, then top it with Chocolate Ganache Glaze (page 318), or the Satin Chocolate Icing (page 316).

A number of recipes in the book—the Easiest-Ever Dulce de Leche Bars (page 168), Gone to Heaven Gooey Caramel-Nut Bars (page 170), and Pucker Up Lemon Bars (page 169), for example—also call for using this shortbread as the base for a filling. Usually, it is partially baked first; follow the specific instructions in each recipe. In most cases, the dough goes into a 9 by 13-inch pan, but you can use only half the dough for an 8-inch square pan, if needed. (Then, freeze the remaining half to use in another batch of bars later, or just turn it into plain shortbread by pressing it into a second 8-inch pan, sprinkling the top with a little sugar, and baking it as is.)

Note that you can prepare this very versatile dough using a food processor or mixer, or by hand.

Baking Preliminaries: To prepare simple shortbread bars, position a rack in the middle of the oven; preheat to 350°F. Line a 9 by 13-inch baking pan with aluminum foil, allowing it to overhang on the 9-inch sides slightly. Lightly grease the foil or coat with nonstick spray. (If using the dough as a bottom crust for layered bars, after making the dough proceed as directed in the individual recipes.)

Food processor method: Combine the butter, sugar, vanilla, and salt in a food processor. Process in on/off pulses until the mixture is just evenly blended. Add about two-thirds of the flour (no need to measure). Process in pulses just until the ingredients begin to mass together; stop and scrape the sides and bottom of the bowl as needed. Turn out the mixture onto a sheet of parchment. Sprinkle over the remaining flour, then knead it in with your hands until evenly incorporated.

Mixer method: Let the butter warm up until just slightly soft. In a large bowl with a mixer on medium speed, beat the butter, sugar, vanilla, and salt just until evenly blended, scraping down the bowl as needed. On low speed, beat in the flour just until the mixture forms a mass. (If the mixer motor labors, stir in the last of the flour with a large spoon; or gradually knead it in with your hands.)

Hand method: Let the butter warm up until just barely soft. In a large bowl using a large spoon, vigorously stir together the butter, sugar, vanilla, and salt until evenly blended. Gradually stir in the flour until incorporated and the mixture forms a mass; or gradually knead it in with your hands.

If the dough prepared by any of the methods is too crumbly to hold together, gradually work in up to 4 teaspoons water until it holds together smoothly. Press and pat the dough into the pan until evenly thick all over. (Laying a sheet of wax paper over the surface may make it easier to smooth out the dough.) If planning to serve the shortbread as is, garnish the top by evenly sprinkling over a little sugar. Bake (middle rack) for 23 to 28 minutes or until the shortbread is nicely browned all over, slightly darker at the edges, and just firm when pressed in the center. Transfer the pan to a wire rack to cool to firm up slightly and cool to warm.

If serving the shortbread as is, if desired, trim off and discard the uneven edges all the way around using a sharp knife while still warm (it becomes much harder to cut when cool). Then cut lengthwise into fifths and crosswise into sixths (or as desired) to form bars, but let them stand and firm up until cooled before removing them from the pan.

If topping with the Chocolate Ganache Glaze or Satin Chocolate Icing, spread it evenly thick over the entire top while the slab is still just slightly warm. Let stand until the ganache or icing sets, about 1 hour, then chill before cutting into bars. Lift the slab to a cutting board and after cutting, peel them from the foil.

Yield: Makes one 9 by 13-inch pan of shortbread or shortbread crust, or two 8-inch square or 7 by 9-inch shortbread crusts; or thirty 2- by 1¾-inch bars

Storage: Store the bars, airtight, for up to 10 days. Refrigerate the dough, covered, in the baking pan or wrapped in plastic for up to 3 days. The bars or crust can be frozen, airtight, for up to 1½ months.

MAKE-AHEAD OPTIONS: CHOOSE THE OPTION THAT BEST FITS YOUR SCHEDULE.

1. Prepare the dough well in advance—up to 1½ months ahead, if desired. Wrap it in plastic; then tuck it into an airtight freezer bag. (Be sure to label and date the bag.) Let the dough thaw completely in the refrigerator, at least 3 hours, before using.

2. Prepare the dough, wrap it airtight in plastic, then refrigerate for up to 3 days. Remove the dough from the refrigerator and let soften slightly. Then press it into the baking pan and bake while you make the topping or filling.

3. Ready the dough, pat it into the baking pan specified in the bar recipe you're using, then cover and refrigerate it for up to 3 days. Transfer to the oven and bake the crust (if directed to) while preparing the filling or topping.

1 batch Simple Shortbread Bars
dough (page 166)

Filling

2 14-ounce cans sweetened
condensed milk
1 tablespoon vanilla extract
⅛ teaspoon almond extract or
coconut extract
⅛ teaspoon salt
1½ cups shredded or flaked
sweetened coconut

Tip
Be sure to use sweetened
condensed milk, not evaporated
milk, which is too thin and won't
work.

TIME-TRIMMER OPTION
It's definitely best to start with
a homemade shortbread crust
for this recipe, but if you're really
pressed for time and don't mind
a little extra sweetness, use a 16-
to 18-ounce package of
refrigerated sugar cookie dough
for the base. Shape and bake
it just as for the dough in the
Super-Easy Cheesecake Bars
(page 277).

EASIEST-EVER DULCE DE LECHE BARS
This recipe showcases the distinctive creamy-sweet taste of homemade milk caramel, or *dulce de leche* (literally translated as "sweetness of milk"), along with toasted coconut. Also called "cajeta" or "manjar," milk caramel is a much-loved ingredient in Central and South American desserts and frequently turns up in the popular filled cookies called alfajores (see page 100 or page 126 for recipes).

Normally, the boiled-down milk-sugar mixture is time-consuming to prepare, which is why cooks frequently settle for the canned or bottled store-bought dulce de leche (often found in Latin American markets). The following recipe takes advantage of a simple fuss-free method—condensed milk cooks down into caramel right while the bars bake. Near the end of baking, the top is garnished with shredded coconut, which adds an appealing flavor counterpoint, plus color and crunch. If you enjoy traditional alfajores, you'll adore this greatly simplified bar cookie version.

Baking Preliminaries: Position a rack in the middle of the oven; preheat to 350°F. Line a 9 by 13-inch baking pan with heavy-duty aluminum foil, letting the foil slightly overhang on the narrow sides. Lightly grease the foil or coat with nonstick spray.

If the shortbread dough has not been prepared ahead, ready it; press it evenly into the foil-lined baking pan. Bake for 20 to 25 minutes, until the shortbread is tinged with brown and just slightly darker at the edges. Reset the oven to 325°F.

For the filling: In a medium bowl, thoroughly stir together the sweetened condensed milk, vanilla, almond extract, and salt. Evenly pour the mixture over the crust. Cover the pan tightly with foil. Bake (middle rack) for 40 to 45 minutes or until the filling is the color of caramel candies. Sprinkle the coconut evenly over the top. Bake, uncovered, for 10 to 15 minutes longer, until the coconut is nicely browned and crisp.

Transfer to a wire rack; let cool completely. Using the foil as handles, lift the slab to a cutting board. Carefully peel off and discard the foil. Cut away the overbaked edges using a large sharp knife. Cut the slab crosswise into sixths and lengthwise into quarters.

Yield: Makes twenty-four 2⅛ by 2¼-inch bars

Storage: Store these, covered and refrigerated, for up to 1 week. They can be frozen, airtight, for up to 1 month. Cut and serve at room temperature.

1 batch Simple Shortbread Bars
    dough (page 166)
1½ cups granulated sugar
5 tablespoons cornstarch
4 large eggs, at room temperature
¾ cup fresh lemon juice (from
    about 3 large lemons)
1½ tablespoons finely grated lemon
    zest (yellow part of the peel)
    About ¼ cup powdered sugar
    for garnish

Tip
When a recipe calls for grated
lemon (or other citrus) zest, be sure
to remove only the outer colored
layer of the peel—the white pith
underneath is bitter. And if you
haven't already switched to a
Microplane grater, consider trying
one. It's by far the most efficient tool
for the job.

Cookie Jar Wisdom
Cookie-fucius says: When
life gives you lemons, make
lemon bars.

PUCKER UP LEMON BARS

Lemon bars are always a hit, and with this recipe you can not only make delectable ones, but make them fairly quickly as well. As with most good lemon bars, the key to these is the filling—the layer is generous and it tastes intensely citrusy and tart.

During several testings I used bottled lemon juice to see if it made an acceptable time-trimming substitute for just-squeezed. It doesn't have the same clean taste and zip, but when combined with the tablespoon of fresh lemon zest, it's passable (but nothing more). Fresh zest is *absolutely essential* for the bracing citrus flavor and aroma, though, so it really makes sense to make use of the fresh juice from those leftover, bald-looking zested lemons and skip the bottled juice.

Baking Preliminaries: Position a rack in the middle of the oven; preheat to 350°F. Grease a 9 by 13-inch baking pan or coat with nonstick spray. Ready the shortbread dough as directed, if it is not already prepared. Press and pat the dough into the pan until evenly thick all over.

Bake (middle rack) for 20 to 25 minutes, until nicely browned all over and just slightly darker at the edges. (The dough may be baked ahead, cooled, covered, then set aside for up to 48 hours, if desired.)

Reset the oven to 325°F. In a large bowl, thoroughly whisk together the sugar and cornstarch. Whisk in the eggs, lemon juice, and zest until the eggs are smoothly incorporated. Pour the mixture over the par-baked crust. Return to the oven and bake until the filling is barely firm in the center when the pan is jiggled, 15 to 20 minutes.

Transfer to a wire rack. Let cool; then refrigerate to facilitate cutting. Garnish by generously sifting powdered sugar over the top just before serving. Cut crosswise into eighths and lengthwise into quarters (or as desired) using a large sharp knife.

Yield: Makes thirty-two 1½ by 2⅛-inch bars

Storage: Store these, covered and in the refrigerator, for up to 1 week. They can be frozen in an airtight plastic or other nonreactive container for up to 1 month. Serve at room temperature.

Fairly Complicated
Shortbread make-ahead
convenience.
Shortbread base
shaped by pressing
dough into the pan.

GONE TO HEAVEN GOOEY CARAMEL-NUT BARS (OR GOOEY SALTED CARAMEL-NUT BARS)

Shortbread on the bottom, luscious homemade caramel with nuts in the middle, and if desired, a chocolate ganache on top—how could these bars not be heavenly? Plus, if you're one of the many people who loves the taste of coarse crystal salt with caramel, you've got the option of adding that, too. (Personally, I prefer the taste of the salt sprinkled *directly* on the caramel, not garnishing the chocolate top, so I suggest that in the recipe.)

Admittedly, making the caramel takes a little more time than unwrapping and tossing in little store-bought squares. But the homemade is so *superior* that it's more than worth the effort. (And the following method makes it fairly easy, too.)

For bars reminiscent of turtle candies, use pecans in the recipe; for ones reminiscent of Snickers, use peanuts. Either way, tasters will swoon when they bite into these!

1 batch Simple Shortbread Bars dough (page 166)

Caramel-Nut Topping

1⅓ cups heavy (whipping) cream
1½ cups packed light brown sugar
⅔ cup dark corn syrup
2 tablespoons unsalted butter, soft but not melted
¼ teaspoon salt
2 teaspoons vanilla extract
1½ cups coarsely chopped pecans or peanuts
½ teaspoon pure coarse-crystal sea salt, such as fleur de sel, optional
1 recipe Chocolate Ganache Glaze (page 318), optional

Make-Ahead Option: For convenience, make and shape the shortbread layer up to 3 days ahead. Then just pull it from the refrigerator at baking time. Or thaw frozen shortbread dough, then press it in the pan and bake it while you cook the caramel filling.

Baking Preliminaries: Position a rack in the middle of the oven; preheat to 350°F. Line a 9 by 13-inch baking pan with aluminum foil, letting it overhang the narrow ends. Be careful not to puncture the foil. Lightly coat the foil with nonstick spray.

If the shortbread dough has not been made ahead, ready it; press the dough evenly into the baking pan. If necessary, lay a sheet of wax paper over the top and press and smooth the dough into an even layer. Bake (middle rack) for 20 to 25 minutes or until the shortbread is lightly browned and slightly darker at the edges.

For the topping: While the crust bakes, thoroughly stir together the cream, sugar, corn syrup, butter, and salt in a heavy, nonreactive 4-quart saucepan. Bring the mixture to a full, rolling boil over high heat, stirring. Adjust the heat so the mixture boils briskly. Immediately start timing, and boil, uncovered, frequently gently stirring and scraping the pan bottom with a wooden spoon, for 6 minutes, watching carefully; the caramel will thicken and darken just slightly. If it starts to darken a lot before the 6 minutes are up, immediately remove it from the heat and stir for 1 minute longer.

Tip ⌇

Don't skimp on the size of the
caramel pot; in a small one the
cream-sugar mixture might bubble
up and go over the pan sides.

Tip ⌇

Be sure the bars have cooled to
barely warm before adding the
ganache as too much heat can mar
its consistency.

Gently stir the vanilla and nuts into the caramel until smoothly
incorporated. Evenly pour the caramel over the still-warm crust; don't
scrape out the pan bottom, as this can cause graininess. Spread out the
caramel evenly with a greased long-bladed metal spatula. Tightly cover
the pan with foil.

Bake for 25 minutes covered. Uncover and bake for 6 to 12 minutes
longer or until the caramel is slightly darker and bubbly all over. If
desired, sprinkle the caramel evenly with the sea salt. Transfer to a wire
rack; let cool till barely warm.

For glazing the bars, if desired: Prepare the ganache as directed. When
it is well blended and smooth, immediately pour it over the barely warm
caramel layer, spreading evenly to the edges. If sea salt was not sprinkled
over the caramel layer, sprinkle it over the chocolate, if desired. Let the
bars stand until completely cooled. Refrigerate 15 minutes to facilitate
cutting.

Using the overhanging foil as handles, lift the slab onto a cutting
board. Cut away and discard any overbaked edges from the slab using a
large sharp knife. Cut it crosswise and lengthwise into sixths. Serve the
bars at room temperature.

Yield: Makes thirty-six 1½ by 2⅛-inch bars

Storage: Store these in a single layer, airtight and at room temperature,
for up to 1 week. They can be frozen, airtight, for up to 2 months; thaw
completely before serving.

CARAMEL CUES

Use a very large, heavy, flat-bottomed saucepan or pot. It contains the
mixture when it boils up the sides and evenly distributes the heat so
the bottom doesn't scorch. Keep gently but continuously stirring and
scraping the pan bottom so the caramel is redistributed as it cooks.
But stir gently—vigorous mixing encourages graininess. Also in the
interest of avoiding graininess, don't scrape out the last of the partly
cooked caramel from the cooking pot; the scraping action encourages
grittiness, too.

SLICE & BAKE COOKIES }

For the home baker who loves to offer guests a little something fresh from the oven along with that cup of coffee or tea, a log of slice-and-bake cookie dough stashed in the freezer is a wonderful thing!

In fact, the homemade logs offer the same convenience as store-bought refrigerator case doughs—they just taste infinitely better due to the freshness and quality of the ingredients, often including an abundance of butter. Actually, slice-and-bakes often have a higher proportion of butter than even many other homemade cookies; the thorough chilling keeps them easy to handle and prevents excess spreading during baking even when they're super rich.

The homemade slice-and-bake logs also come in many more interesting flavors than purchased logs: In this chapter you'll find everything from chocolate and nut to cranberry, spice, coconut, brown sugar, citrus, and more. And their looks and textures are also more varied than you might expect due to different amounts of spreading, browning, and occasionally garnishing details.

One handy technique I recommend for every slice-and-bake recipe is using discarded paper towel, plastic wrap, or even cut-down wrapping paper tubes to keep the logs of dough round during chilling and firming. Simply slit the tubes lengthwise as they're emptied, then stack them together and save them until needed. If the log is too fat for one tube to enclose it, just slip two tubes around it, one on each side so they overlap.

Not only do the tubes serve as handy shaping sleeves, but they also provide a very convenient place to add a cookie name and date and even the baking temperature and time for the slices. (Trust me, it's best not to skip the labeling in hopes of remembering; you may end up with logs of both unknown flavor and uncertain freshness!) If a garnish is to be added later, put it in a zip-top plastic bag and tuck it in the tube, too. Finish by closing the tube with tape or rubber bands, slipping the logs into a heavy plastic bag, and refrigerating or freezing them until needed.

Since homemade doughs aren't loaded with preservatives, hold them in the refrigerator for no more than 3 days. Wrapped airtight, they can be satisfactorily frozen for several months.

Several especially convenient recipes—the Chocolate-Almond Crisps and Toasted Pecan–Brown Sugar Crisps—feature doughs that don't freeze too hard, so they can pulled directly from the freezer and sliced after only 5 or 10 minutes on the countertop. The best way to thaw other logs is to transfer them back to the refrigerator the day before baking. If you're not the plan-ahead type or have an unexpected need for fresh cookies, place the log out at room temperature; just keep checking until it's soft enough to cut through neatly. If it thaws completely it won't slice attractively, and thawing time can vary greatly depending on how cold your freezer is. (Remedy overly soft dough by popping it back in the refrigerator or freezer again briefly.)

If you absolutely must speed up countertop thawing, place the unwrapped log on a microwave-safe plate and microwave on 10 percent power, stopping to rotate the log every 30 seconds, for up to 3 minutes. Then, simply return the log to the counter, cover it, *and wait. Don't try to completely thaw logs in the microwave oven*, as it heats unevenly and can create hot, melted spots throughout the dough.

8   ounces coarsely chopped
    (½-inch pieces) 60 to 70
    percent cacao bittersweet
    (not unsweetened) chocolate,
    divided
½   cup packed light or dark brown
    sugar
2½ tablespoons gourmet-quality
    ground coffee, dark roast
    preferred
1½ teaspoons instant espresso
    powder
    Generous ¼ teaspoon salt
1   cup (2 sticks) cool and firm
    unsalted butter, cut into ½-inch
    chunks
½   cup powdered sugar
2   teaspoons vanilla extract
2   cups unbleached all-purpose
    white flour, plus more if
    needed

Tip
While it's not necessary, you can
dress up the crisps by lightly
accenting them with Glossy
Chocolate Drizzle (page 314).

GO WITH JOE CHOCOLATE CHUNK–ESPRESSO CRISPS

Understated, yet chic and sophisticated, these delectable shortbread rounds demand a companion cup of joe. Quickly slice and bake some to go with a carafe of your best brew, and watch even the most discriminating java fans swoon. Packed in a decorative jar, the crisps make a thoughtful gift for a coffee lover, too, especially when paired with a pound or two of gourmet roast beans.

In a food processor, chop half the chocolate into ⅛-inch bits (mini morsel size); remove from the processor and set aside on wax paper. Combine the brown sugar, ground coffee, espresso, and salt in the processor. Process for 2 minutes or until powder-fine; don't under-process. Stir the mixture through a very fine-mesh sieve back into the processor bowl, discarding any bits that aren't powder-fine. Add the remaining chocolate; process until finely ground. Add the butter, powdered sugar, and vanilla. Continue processing in pulses until the butter is cut in evenly. Add half the flour. Pulse until the ingredients are evenly blended and no butter bits are visible.

Turn out the dough onto a sheet of wax paper. Gradually knead in the remaining flour and reserved chopped chocolate until evenly incorporated. If the dough is very soft, work in up to 2 tablespoons more flour.

Divide the dough in half. Shape each portion into a scant 12-inch-long, evenly thick log on a sheet of plastic wrap. Roll up the logs in the plastic; twist the ends to prevent unrolling. For uniformly round cookies, slip each log into a paper towel tube (or a wrapping paper tube cut into two tubes) that has been slit lengthwise, securing each tube with tape or rubber bands. Chill the logs for 30 to 40 minutes or until slightly firm, or for up to 48 hours, if preferred. (Let the chilled dough warm up slightly before using.) The logs can also be wrapped airtight and frozen for up to 2 months; let thaw in the refrigerator before using.

Baking Preliminaries: Position a rack in the middle of the oven; preheat to 325°F. Line several large baking sheets with baking parchment. Using a sharp knife, cut the dough crosswise into ¼-inch-thick rounds. For round slices, rotate the log a quarter turn after each cut. (If the chocolate bits cause the slices to break apart, just press them back together with your fingers.) Space cookies about 1½ inches apart on the baking sheets.

Tip
If you like the combination of chocolate, espresso, and cardamom—I love it!—try the variation at the end of the recipe.

Tube Trick
For dough logs that stay completely round during chilling, slide each log into an empty paper towel tube that's slit lengthwise. Use rubber bands or tape to secure the tube around the logs. This technique is handy for any kind of slice and bake cookie.

Bake (middle rack) one pan at a time for 14 to 18 minutes or until just firm when pressed in the center top. Transfer the pan to a wire rack. Let cool completely; the cookies are too tender to handle while warm.

Yield: Makes about forty-five 2-inch cookies

Storage: Store these, airtight, for up to 3 weeks. They can be frozen, airtight, for up to 1½ months.

Variation: Chocolate-Espresso-Cardamom Crisps Add 1 to 1½ teaspoons ground cardamom to the processor when the brown sugar is added.

WHO'S JOE?

One well-circulated explanation of why we call coffee "joe" is that Josephus Daniels, an early twentieth-century Secretary of the Navy, decided to abolish the officers' wine mess. After that, the strongest drink aboard Navy ships was coffee, eventually referred to as "joe" to reflect Daniel's act. But the real story is probably less colorful. "Joe" may be slang for the island of Java, once a key source of the world's coffee. Or perhaps it references the popularity of coffee with the ordinary man, a regular Joe, or lower-ranking military man, a GI Joe.

¾ cup granulated sugar

¼ cup unsweetened Dutch-
process cocoa powder, sifted
after measuring, if lumpy

¼ teaspoon salt

½ cup (1 stick) unsalted butter, very
soft but not melted

2 teaspoons vanilla extract

½ teaspoon almond extract

1 cup unbleached all-purpose
white flour

½ cup finely chopped semisweet
chocolate

1 cup chopped blanched or
unblanched almonds, plus
½ cup for garnish

Tip

This and other recipes in the chapter
call for placing the dough log in a
discarded paper towel tube prior
to chilling. This keeps the log from
flattening on one side during
storage.

CHOCOLATE-ALMOND CRISPS

Simple, not too sweet, and spotlighting the classic chocolate-almond flavor pairing, these crisp, thinnish rounds lean in the direction of sophisticated but won't put off those who prefer homey. The dough thaws fairly quickly, so is especially convenient when you need to pull a log from the freezer and ready cookies promptly.

In a large bowl, stir together the sugar, cocoa powder, and salt until blended. Vigorously stir in the butter, 2 tablespoons water, vanilla, and almond extract until very well blended and smooth. Stir in the flour, chocolate, and 1 cup almonds just until evenly incorporated. If the dough is crumbly, work in up to 4 teaspoons water; if soft, work in up to 2 tablespoons flour.

Turn the dough out onto a long sheet of wax paper or baking parchment. Using oiled hands, form the dough into a scant 12-inch-long, evenly thick log. Smooth out the middle, so it isn't thicker. Firmly roll up the log in plastic wrap, twisting the ends to secure it. Place the dough log in a cardboard tube that has been slit open down its length. Secure it with rubber bands or tape. Place in a freezer bag, along with the remaining ½ cup almonds. Freeze, at least 1 hour and up to 2 months. Let thaw on the countertop (or thaw overnight in the refrigerator) for 10 to 15 minutes, or until just soft enough to cut through, before slicing.

Baking Preliminaries: Position a rack in the middle of the oven; preheat to 350°F. Grease several large baking sheets or coat with nonstick spray.

Cut the log crosswise into ⅛-inch-thick cookies, spacing about 2 inches apart on the sheets. For round slices, rotate the log a quarter turn after each cut. Sprinkle the cookie tops with a few almonds, patting down slightly.

Bake (middle rack) one sheet at a time for 7 to 10 minutes or until the cookies are just firm at the edges but still slightly soft in the center. Let the cookies stand on the pans to firm up about 3 minutes, then transfer them to racks using a wide spatula. Thoroughly cool before storing.

Yield: Makes forty-five to fifty-five 2-inch crisps

Storage: Store these, airtight, for up to 1 week. They can be frozen, airtight, for up to 1 month.

1½ cups chopped pecans
½ cup (1 stick) unsalted butter,
     softened
¾ cup plus 2 tablespoons packed
     light brown sugar
½ teaspoon baking soda
     Generous ½ teaspoon salt
1 large egg, at room temperature
7 tablespoons corn oil or other
     flavorless vegetable oil
2 teaspoons vanilla extract
2⅓ cups unbleached all-purpose
     white flour

Tip

Note that because the dough contains oil as well as butter, the logs don't become as hard during chilling as most slice-and-bakes. So, they are sliceable right out of the refrigerator and only a few minutes after being removed from the freezer. This makes them especially convenient when you need to retrieve a log and bake on short notice.

TOASTED PECAN–BROWN SUGAR CRISPS

I'm a big fan of pecan cookies—especially ones like these, which feature an abundance of toasted pecans and brown sugar. Both the toasting and the sugar bring out sweetness and nuttiness, so though the cookies seem pretty straightforward, they are quite special taste-wise. These have a homey, nut-studded appearance, plus a pleasing meltaway texture; paradoxically, they are both crunchy and tender when you bite into them.

Preheat the oven to 300°F. Spread the pecans in a large baking dish or small roasting pan and toast in the oven for 12 to 15 minutes, stirring every 3 or 4 minutes, until fragrant and lightly toasted all over. Let cool.

In a large bowl with a mixer on medium speed, beat the butter, brown sugar, baking soda, and salt until fluffy and smooth, about 2 minutes. On low speed, beat in the egg, oil, and vanilla, then half the flour until evenly incorporated. Stir in the remaining flour and half the cooled pecans; reserve the remaining nuts for a garnish. Cover and refrigerate the dough for at least 1½ to 2 hours or until firm enough to shape.

Divide the dough in half. Lay each portion on a long sheet of plastic wrap and shape into a smooth 2 by 9-inch log. Press and pat the remaining pecans into the sides of the logs. Roll up the logs in the plastic, twisting the ends to secure. Slip each log into a discarded paper towel tube that has been slit lengthwise. Secure the tubes with tape or rubber bands. Refrigerate for at least 4 hours or until firm enough to slice, or place the logs in a plastic bag and refrigerate for up to 1 week. (Or freeze for up to 2 months, then thaw on the countertop 5 to 10 minutes.)

Baking Preliminaries: Position a rack in the middle of the oven; preheat to 375°F. Grease several large baking sheets or coat with nonstick spray.

Working with one chilled log at a time and using a large sharp knife, cut crosswise into scant ¼-inch-thick slices; rotate the log one quarter turn after each slice to help keep it round. Space the cookies 1½ inches apart on the sheets.

Bake (middle rack) one pan at a time for 8 to 11 minutes or until golden all over and slightly darker around the edges. Let the pan stand 2 minutes. Then transfer the cookies to racks; let cool completely.

Yield: Makes fifty-five to sixty-five 2½-inch cookies

Storage: Store these, airtight, for up to 10 days. They can be frozen, airtight, for up to 2 months.

Easy
Quick processor mixing.
Touch of elegance, with ease.

CHOCOLATE-HAZELNUT SABLÉS

I became captivated with the classic sweets combination of hazelnut and dark chocolate years ago while living in Europe. Coming from a family of solidly mainstream American country cooks and home bakers, I'd never been treated to hazelnut and bittersweet chocolate confections growing up, so this sophisticated duo immediately caught my attention. With assorted chocolate-hazelnut tortes, tarts, bonbons, and cookies calling from nearly every Konditerei or patisserie, I was soon utterly smitten. And I still am.

During my time overseas, I made a point of learning how to turn out some of the more doable of the pastry shop hazelnut-chocolate offerings. This sablé, a sandy-textured French shortbread, is a prime example; it's easy to make and actually looks fairly plain, yet it seems just as decadent as many of the really grand Old World café treats often served. The simple rounds are rich, tender-crisp, and slightly under-sweet, with the bittersweetness and nuttiness balancing each other beautifully.

While these sablés are very good as is, if you enjoy the pairing of chocolate and orange, zip them up by incorporating a little orange zest.

1   cup whole hazelnuts, toasted, hulled, and very coarsely chopped*
1   cup granulated sugar
2   teaspoons instant espresso powder dissolved in 1½ tablespoons warm water
½   teaspoon finely grated orange zest, optional
1   cup (5 ounces) 60 to 70 percent cacao bittersweet chocolate, coarsely chopped
6   tablespoons good-quality unsweetened Dutch-process cocoa powder
½   teaspoon baking powder
¼   teaspoon salt
1⅔ cups unbleached all-purpose white flour, divided
1   cup (2 sticks) cool and slightly firm unsalted butter, cut into chunks

In a food processor, process the hazelnuts, sugar, espresso mixture, and orange zest (if using) until the nuts are very finely ground but not oily. Add the chocolate, cocoa powder, baking powder, and salt. Process until the chocolate is very finely ground. Add about half the flour; process until evenly incorporated. Sprinkle the butter over the mixture. Pulse until the butter is cut in and no bits of it remain visible.

Turn out the mixture onto a large sheet of wax paper. Gradually knead in the remaining flour until evenly incorporated. If the dough is crumbly, work in up to 4 teaspoons water until it holds together; if very soft, work in up to 2 tablespoons flour.

Divide the dough in half. Shape each portion into an 11-inch-long, evenly thick log. Stretch out from the center so it isn't thicker. Roll up each log in plastic wrap, twisting the ends to keep them from unrolling. For uniformly round cookies, slip the logs into empty paper towel tubes (or a wrapping paper tube cut into two tubes) that have been slit lengthwise. Close the tubes with rubber bands or tape. Refrigerate the logs until completely firm, at least 2 hours (or speed up chilling by freezing for 1 hour). Use immediately, or transfer to a freezer bag and freeze for up to 2 months.

Baking Preliminaries: If the dough is frozen, let stand at room temperature for 15 minutes or until just thawed enough to slice. Position

Tip

For a dressier look, garnish these with the chocolate drizzle, page 314, after the sables are cool.

a rack in the middle of the oven; preheat to 350°F. Line several large baking sheets with baking parchment.

Using a large serrated knife or a chef's knife, cut the logs crosswise into generous ¼-inch-thick slices; rotate the dough log slightly after each cut to help maintain a round shape. Space the sablés about 2 inches apart on the sheets; if they are slightly crumbly pat the cookies back together with your fingertips.

Bake (middle rack) one sheet at a time for 9 to 12 minutes, just until the rounds are beginning to feel firm when pressed at the edges; be careful not to overbake. Transfer to a wire rack and let stand until cooled.

Yield: Makes about fifty-five 2½-inch cookies

Storage: Store these, airtight and at room temperature, for up to 1 week. They can be frozen, airtight, for up to 2 months.

* To toast and hull hazelnuts: Preheat the oven to 325°F. Spread the whole unhulled hazelnuts on a rimmed baking pan and toast, stirring every 3 or 4 minutes, for 14 to 18 minutes or until the hulls loosen and the nuts are nicely browned; be careful not to burn. Set aside until cool enough to handle. Rub the nuts between your hands or in a clean kitchen towel, loosening and discarding the hull. It's all right if some small bits remain. Cool the nuts thoroughly before using them.

CRANBERRY (OR DATE) PINWHEELS

A lightly spiced fruit filling and mild, barely sweet cream cheese dough give these convenient slice-and-bake cookies a pleasing chewiness and enticing taste. The cookies are also eye-catching, with the dark fruit and light dough swirls contrasting one another nicely. The dough is sturdier than many, to facilitate the rolling up process.

I'm a big fan of dates, so I prefer them in these, but, honestly, the cranberry filling is equally good. The cranberry pinwheels are more festive looking, so are a fine choice for holiday baking.

Tube Trick: Slit open two discarded 12-inch cardboard paper towel tubes (or a wrapping paper tube cut into two 12-inch tubes) until open down their entire length. Set aside for shaping the logs of dough.

For the filling: In a food processor, combine the cranberries (or dates), raisins, honey, marmalade, cinnamon, zest, and 2 tablespoons orange juice. Process until chopped fairly fine, stopping and stirring once or twice, about 1 minute. If the mixture seems dry, add about 1 tablespoon more orange juice. (The filling may be refrigerated in a nonreactive container for up to 4 days; let come to room temperature and stir before using.)

For the dough: In a large bowl using a mixer, beat the butter, cream cheese, sugar, cinnamon, salt, and baking powder until light and fluffy. Beat in the flour; if the motor labors, stir in the last of it by hand. If the dough seems too dry to roll out, mix in a teaspoon or two of water; if too soft and wet, mix in a little more flour.

Divide the dough in half. Roll out each portion between sheets of baking parchment or wax paper into a 9-inch square. (If it seems too soft to handle, refrigerate for about 10 minutes to firm it slightly.) Trim and patch the dough if needed to make it fairly square.

Peel off the top sheet from the dough layers, then pat the paper back into place. Turn over, and peel off and discard the second sheets. Divide the filling equally between the two squares, evenly spreading it to within ¼-inch of the edges all around.

Working from one side and using the paper to lift up the dough, roll up each square into a tight pinwheel log. Working from the center of each log, pull out until evenly thick and about 10½ inches long. Wrap each log in plastic wrap; twist the ends to secure each log. Tuck each log into a

Filling

2¼ cups (about 7 ounces) sweetened dried cranberries or pitted chopped dates
¾ cup golden raisins, rinsed under hot water and thoroughly drained
¼ cup clover honey or other mild honey
¼ cup orange marmalade
1¼ teaspoons ground cinnamon Finely grated zest (orange part of the peel) of 1 large orange
2 tablespoons fresh orange juice, plus more if needed

Dough

¾ cup plus 1 tablespoon unsalted butter, softened slightly
6 ounces (two 3-ounce packages) cream cheese, softened slightly
5 tablespoons granulated sugar
¾ teaspoon ground cinnamon
½ teaspoon salt
¼ teaspoon baking powder
2 cups unbleached all-purpose white flour

cardboard tube. Secure them with tape or rubber bands. Freeze the logs until firm enough to slice neatly, at least 1 hour. Or insert in freezer bags and freeze for up to 1 month, if desired.

Baking Preliminaries: Position a rack in the middle of the oven; preheat to 350°F. Set out two large baking sheets. Line with baking parchment.

Let the log(s) thaw on the countertop for at least 10 minutes or until just soft enough to cut through before slicing. On a cutting board, slice crosswise into generous ¼-inch-thick slices; rotate the log(s) a quarter turn after each slice to keep it from flattening on one side. (If a log is too hard to slice, let it warm up for a few minutes, then try again.) Space the slices about 1½ inches apart on the baking sheets.

Bake (middle rack) one sheet at a time for 12 to 14 minutes or until the dough is just tinged and almost firm when pressed in the center. Set aside to firm up slightly. Transfer to racks and let stand until cooled thoroughly, then pack airtight.

Yield: Makes about seventy 2-inch cookies

Storage: Store these, airtight, for up to 10 days. They can be frozen, airtight, for up to 2 months.

CRANBERRY-ORANGE-SPICE SHORTBREAD SLICES

Orange and cardamom always seem to bring out the best in one another, and both of them enhance the cranberries in these zesty shortbread rounds. Wonderfully fragrant, crisp, and colorful, they are great with tea, for Thanksgiving and Christmas, or when you just want fruit and spice shortbread cookies that are a bit out of the ordinary.

The recipe calls for frozen (thawed) orange juice concentrate, which will lend the most intense orange flavor, but if you don't happen to have it on hand, fresh orange juice can be substituted.

½ cup granulated sugar
1 tablespoon orange zest (orange part of the peel)
1 teaspoon ground cardamom
1 teaspoon finely minced peeled fresh gingerroot
⅛ teaspoon salt
1 cup sweetened dried cranberries
¼ cup homemade or good-quality purchased chopped candied orange peel, optional
2¼ cups unbleached all-purpose white flour, divided, plus more if needed
1 cup (2 sticks) very cold unsalted butter, cut into pats
Generous 2 tablespoons frozen (thawed) orange juice concentrate (or substitute fresh orange juice), plus more if needed

Tube Trick: Slit open two discarded 12-inch cardboard towel roll tubes (or a wrapping paper tube cut into two 9-inch-long tubes) until open down their entire length. Set aside for shaping the logs of dough.

In a food processor, process the sugar, zest, cardamom, ginger, and salt until the sugar is colored and very fragrant, about 1½ minutes. Add the cranberries and candied peel (if using), pulsing until chopped moderately fine. Using a spoon, stir in about half the flour, scraping up the bottom to blend the mixture evenly. Sprinkle the butter over the mixture. Process in pulses just until no bits of butter are visible. Drizzle the orange juice concentrate over the top. Incorporate using ten to fifteen 1-second pulses just until partly incorporated and the mixture just starts to come together.

Turn out the dough onto a large sheet of wax paper. Slowly knead in the remaining flour until just evenly blended and cohesive. If it is slightly dry or crumbly, gradually knead in a teaspoon or two more orange juice concentrate until cohesive; if soft, sprinkle over a tablespoon or so of flour and knead in until slightly firmer.

Divide the dough in half. On sheets of plastic wrap, shape each portion into a 9-inch-long, evenly thick log. (Stretch each out from the center slightly so it is not thicker in the middle.) Roll up each log in plastic wrap, smoothing the dough as you work. Twist the ends of the plastic to keep it from unrolling. Slip each log into a discarded paper tube. Secure the tube with tape or rubber bands.

Freeze until firm, at least 1 hour and up to 2 months, if desired. If the frozen dough is hard, let it warm up and soften just slightly before using.

Baking Preliminaries: Position a rack in the middle of the oven; preheat to 350°F. Line several baking sheets with baking parchment or lightly spray with nonstick spray.

To dress these up for holidays, garnish the baked and cooled rounds with thin zigzags of Quick Powdered Sugar Drizzle (page 304). Or to make a huge splash, garnish the center tops of the cookies with a swirl (or piped rosette) of Orange or Fresh Ginger-Orange Buttercream (page 328); the pairing is spectacular.

Working with one dough portion and keeping the other chilled, slice crosswise into scant ¼-inch-thick slices. To help keep the log round, rotate it a quarter turn after each slice. Space about 1½ inches apart on the baking sheets. If the dough becomes too soft to work with, return it to the freezer until firmed up, then continue. Repeat the process with the second portion.

Bake (middle rack) one sheet at a time for 5 minutes. Rotate the sheet from front to back and bake for 3 to 5 minutes more or until the cookies are just faintly rimmed with brown; watch carefully, as they brown rapidly near the end of baking. Let the pans cool on wire racks until the cookies firm up, about 3 minutes, then gently transfer them to racks using a wide spatula and cool completely.

Yield: Makes fifty-five to sixty 2¾- to 3-inch slices

Storage: Store these, airtight, for up to 1 week. They can be frozen, airtight, for up to 2 months.

Fairly Easy
One-bowl mixing.
Convenient
make-ahead recipe.
Unusual spice cookie flavor.

1 tablespoon ground cinnamon

1¼ teaspoons ground cloves

1¼ teaspoons ground ginger

1 teaspoon ground cardamom

1 teaspoon ground nutmeg

¾ cup (1½ sticks) unsalted butter, slightly softened

⅓ cup light or dark corn syrup

¾ cup granulated sugar, plus 2 tablespoons for garnish

¼ teaspoon baking soda

1 large egg, at room temperature

1 tablespoon finely grated lemon zest (yellow part of the peel)

3 cups unbleached all-purpose white flour

NOT YOUR NANA'S SPICE THINS

Perhaps I need to start by saying that I have nothing against anybody's Nana's classic gingersnaps or molasses-spice cookies! I love those kinds of spice cookies and have included several recipes in the book; see pages 89 and 109 for some options. However, *these* spice thins are another sort altogether and will suit if you're interested in spicing up your cookie life (and perfuming your kitchen) with a little something different.

First off, these thin, crisp rounds contain no molasses, so they aren't dark or "gingersnappy" looking. Second, the usual cast of spice characters—cinnamon, ginger, and so on—is supplemented with generous hits of cardamom and lemon zest. The end result is a cookie with a light, fresh, unique spice taste, which my hubby—the most avid gingerbread and spice cookie aficionado I know—just loves.

Thoroughly stir together the cinnamon, cloves, ginger, cardamom, and nutmeg in a small cup. In a large mixer bowl with the mixer on medium speed, beat the butter, corn syrup, ¾ cup sugar, and baking soda until lightened and smooth. Reserve 2 teaspoons of the spice blend for garnish, then add the remainder to the butter mixture. Add the egg and lemon zest to the butter mixture. Beat until well blended, scraping down the bowl as needed. Beat in about half the flour until evenly incorporated. Stir or beat in the remaining flour; the dough will be fairly stiff. (If overly stiff and dry, work in a few drops of water.)

Divide the dough in half. On wax paper, shape each portion into an 11-inch-long, evenly thick log. Stretch each out from the center slightly if thicker in the middle. Thoroughly stir 2 tablespoons granulated sugar into the reserved spice mixture. Sprinkle each of the logs with half the spice-sugar mixture, turning them until lightly coated all over. Roll up each log in plastic wrap, smoothing the dough as you work. Twist the ends of the plastic to secure it. For nicely rounded wafers, slip each log into a discarded paper towel tube (or a wrapping paper tube cut into two tubes) that has been slit lengthwise, then secure with tape or rubber bands.

Freeze the dough for 30 to 40 minutes or until it is very firm but not too hard to cut. Or insert in freezer bags and freeze for up to 2 months. Let thoroughly frozen logs soften at room temperature for about 20 minutes before using.

Baking Preliminaries: Position a rack in the middle of the oven; preheat to 350°F. Line several large baking sheets with baking parchment.

Cut each partially thawed log into scant ¼-inch-thick slices using a very sharp knife. To help keep the log round, rotate it a quarter turn after each cut. Space the cookies about 2 inches apart on the baking sheets.

Bake (middle rack) one sheet at a time for 9 to 12 minutes, just until the cookies are beginning to feel firm when pressed in the center; be very careful not to overbake. Transfer to a wire rack and let stand until cooled completely.

Yield: Makes sixty to seventy 2¼- to 2½-inch wafers

Storage: Store these, airtight and at room temperature, for up to 10 days. They can be frozen, airtight, for up to 1½ months; let come to room temperature before serving.

6   tablespoons fresh lime juice or
    good-quality bottled Key lime
    juice
¾   cup granulated sugar
3   tablespoons grated lime zest
    (green part of the peel)
1   cup (2 sticks) unsalted butter,
    slightly softened but still cool,
    cut into chunks
¾   cup powdered sugar
    Scant ½ teaspoon baking soda
¼   teaspoon salt
1   teaspoon lemon extract
2⅓ cups unbleached all-purpose
    white flour

Tip

I prefer not to add any food color
when making the lime zest–infused
sugar for recipes, but if you want a
brighter color, you can incorporate
a drop of green food dye when
processing the sugar and zest.

Tip

Be sure to grate only the colored
part of the lime skin when zesting—
the white pith underneath is bitter.

LIME LIGHTS

I've often found that lime cookies aren't as pungent and intensely "limey" as
I'd like. So in this recipe I experimented and incorporated a couple of unusual
but simple steps to intensify the tantalizing citrusy taste and tang.

To heighten the puckery quality without producing soggy cookies, I boil
down lime juice to concentrate its sour power. To increase the lime aroma
and flavor, I call for processing the zest together with sugar (which brings out
its aromatic volatile oils), then use the lime-infused sugar both in the cookies
and on top of them. This means that every time someone takes a bite, these
cookies deliver a fabulous one-two sensory punch—tartness to the taste
buds and a hit of pure, pungent lime fragrance to the nose. As a nice bonus,
they also possess an amazing light, crisp texture. And they are shaped to
(vaguely) look like lime half-slices.

The flavor-boosting techniques used here work so well that I've used
them in a number of other citrus cookies and citrus-herb cookies in the
book, including Chocolate, Grapefruit, and Tarragon Wafers (page 131) and
Rosemary-Lemon Wafers (page 121). They are effective primarily because
many of the key taste components of citrus, herbs, and some spices
are actually enjoyed through our sense of smell, not our sense of taste.
(Specifically, this is because their volatile oils aren't water soluble and, thus,
can't be detected by the tastebuds, only by the aroma sensors in the nose.)

In a 2-cup glass measure, heat the lime juice in a microwave oven on
high power until it boils and reduces to 2 tablespoons. (Alternatively,
in a small nonreactive saucepan over medium-low heat, gently simmer
the lime juice until reduced to 2 tablespoons; be careful not to burn the
juice.) Let cool.

In a food processor, combine the granulated sugar and lime zest.
Process for 1 to 2 minutes, scraping down the bowl as needed, until
the mixture is green and the zest is finely ground. Remove ¼ cup sugar
and spread it out on a piece of baking parchment to dry and use later
as a garnish. Add the butter, powdered sugar, baking soda, salt, lemon
extract, and cooled lime juice to the sugar in the processor. Process in
on/off pulses until the mixture is well blended and lightened; scrape
the bowl and bottom as needed. Sprinkle 1⅓ cups flour over the butter
mixture. Process in on/off pulses until evenly incorporated.

Turn out the dough onto a long sheet of baking parchment or wax
paper. Gradually knead in the remaining flour with your hands until
evenly incorporated. Shape the dough into an 11-inch-long, evenly thick

log; it will be fairly thick. (Stretch out from the middle if needed to make it evenly thick.) Roll up in plastic wrap, twisting the ends to keep it from unrolling. Put the log in a discarded 12-inch cardboard paper towel tube that has been slit lengthwise; or to more fully encase the log, use two discarded tubes, one around one side, the second around the other. Secure the tube(s) with rubber bands or tape. Freeze, airtight, until firm, at least 1½ hours and up to 1 month.

Baking Preliminaries: Position a rack in the middle of the oven; preheat to 350°F. Line several large baking sheets with baking parchment or coat with nonstick spray.

When the log has warmed up a few minutes at room temperature and is just soft enough to slice, cut crosswise into ¼-inch-thick slices using a large sharp knife. To help keep the log round, rotate it a quarter turn after each slice. Immediately cut the rounds into half-slices, and space about 2 inches apart on the baking sheets. Sprinkle heavily with the lime-scented sugar.

Bake (middle rack) one pan at a time for 11 to 14 minutes or until almost firm when pressed in the center top and tinged with brown at the edges. Transfer the pan to a cooling rack; let stand until cooled to warm. Using a spatula, gently transfer the cookies to wire racks. Let cool completely.

Yield: Makes about fifty 2½-inch cookies

Storage: Store these, airtight, for up to 1 week. They can be frozen, airtight, for up to 1½ months.

Tip

Be sure to grate only the colored part of the lime peel when zesting—the white pith underneath is bitter.

Tip

If you are using the log of dough promptly, simply spread the lime sugar reserved for garnishing on a baking parchment–lined pan and let it air-dry while the dough chills firmly enough for slicing and baking. Otherwise, place the pan in an oven that has been turned on for 1 minute, then turned off again, until the sugar is thoroughly dry, at least 30 minutes. Then crush out any lumps (by hand or using a processor) and pack it in a small, airtight plastic bag. Tuck the bag in the cardboard tube along with the dough, to be right there when you later need it.

Easy
Quick one-bowl mixing.
Short ingredient list.

1 cup (2 sticks) unsalted butter,
    slightly softened and cut into
    chunks
⅔ cup packed dark brown sugar
2 teaspoons vanilla extract
    Scant ½ teaspoon salt
¼ cup crushed butterscotch hard
    candies
2 cups unbleached all-purpose
    white flour, plus more if
    needed

Tip

The readily available golden-colored
butterscotch hard candy disks
are what you need for this recipe.
One way to crush them is to put
the unwrapped rounds in a triple
thickness of plastic bags, then pound
them with a kitchen mallet or the
back of a heavy metal spoon. Even
better, if you have a large plastic
cutting mat, lay the unwrapped
candies in the center of a cutting
board; top with the mat; then whack
away. The shards should be pounded
into ⅛-inch or finer pieces.

BROWN SUGAR–BUTTERSCOTCH SLICE-AND-BAKES

This is a very straightforward and simple recipe, yet the results are
remarkably good. Just the generous amount of butter and dark brown sugar
would likely be enough to satisfy, but the sweet, crunchy little shards of
butterscotch candy in the dough make these homey-looking rounds extra
special. They are tender, mild, and at the top of my comfort food list.

In a large bowl with a mixer on medium speed, vigorously beat together
the butter, brown sugar, vanilla, and salt for about 3 minutes, until
lightened in color, smooth, and fluffy. Beat in the crushed candy, then
beat or stir in the flour just until evenly incorporated. Let stand to firm up
for 5 minutes. If very soft work in up to 2 tablespoons more flour.

Divide the dough in half, placing each portion on a long sheet of
plastic wrap. With well-greased hands, shape each portion into a
10-inch-long, evenly thick log. Roll up the logs in the plastic, smoothing
and shaping until evenly thick. Twist the ends of the plastic wrap so
the rolls will stay closed. For slices that stay round, slide each log into
a discarded paper towel tube slit open lengthwise. Use tape or rubber
bands to close the tubes. Freeze the dough logs for at least 45 minutes
or until firm enough to slice neatly but not frozen and hard. (Or insert
into freezer bags and freeze for up to 2 months.) Let the frozen logs thaw
in the refrigerator overnight or on the countertop for about 20 minutes
before using.

Baking Preliminaries: Place a rack in the middle of the oven; preheat
to 350°F. Set out several large baking sheets. Line them with baking
parchment.

Working with one log at a time and keeping the other one chilled, slice
crosswise into ⅓-inch-thick slices, turning the log a quarter turn after
each cut to help keep the log round. Space the slices about 2½ inches
apart on the baking sheets.

Bake (middle rack) one sheet at a time for 12 to 16 minutes or until
the slices are lightly tinged at the edges and firm when pressed in the
middle. Transfer the baking sheets to wire racks; let stand until the
cookies firm up, about 10 minutes. Using a wide spatula, transfer the
cookies to wire racks. Let cool.

Yield: Makes about forty 2-inch slices

Storage: Store these, airtight, for up to 1 week. They can be frozen,
airtight, for up to 1 month.

1¾ cups flaked or shredded
sweetened coconut, plus
about ⅓ cup for garnish

1 cup (2 sticks) unsalted butter,
slightly softened and cut into
chunks

1 cup minus 2 tablespoons
granulated sugar

½ teaspoon almond extract

¼ teaspoon real coconut extract,
if available

¼ teaspoon baking soda
Scant ½ teaspoon salt

⅓ cup almond flour (also called
almond meal; or substitute
blanched almond slices
ground powder-fine in a food
processor)

1¾ cups unbleached all-purpose
white flour, plus more if
needed

TOASTED COCONUT SLICES

As pastry chefs will tell you, toasting coconut before folding it into a dough is perhaps the best way to bring out its flavor and aroma in baked goods. Here, I call for toasting coconut shreds or flakes thoroughly—until they are the same golden brown shade as graham crackers. This step involves baking slowly and frequently stirring so that the coconut toasts evenly and deeply instead of burning in a few spots and remaining underdone in most. Admittedly this process is a touch tedious, but it pays huge taste dividends and also gives the cookie dough an appealing faint tawny-toast color. To further heighten flavor, the recipe calls for both a little almond flour and almond extract. Somehow, these just seem to boost the "coconuttiness"; they don't give the cookies a pronounced almond taste.

These simple shortbread rounds are rustically handsome and have a unique light, tender-crisp texture. They certainly don't need any additional adornment, but you can dress them up with the Glossy Chocolate Drizzle (page 314), if desired.

Baking Preliminaries: Position a rack in the middle of the oven; preheat to 300°F.

Spread 1¾ cups coconut on a large tray or baking sheet. Toast in the oven, stirring every 3 minutes to redistribute the contents, until evenly toasted and the color of graham crackers all over, usually 12 to 15 minutes. Cool slightly. In a food processor, process the toasted coconut until it is ground almost to a flour consistency; stop and scrape it up from the bottom several times.

In a large bowl with a mixer on medium speed, beat together the butter, sugar, almond extract, coconut extract, baking soda, and salt until very well blended and fluffy, about 2 minutes. On low speed, beat in the ground coconut and almond flour, then half the flour, until evenly incorporated, stopping and scraping down the bowl several times. Stir or beat in the last of the flour until evenly incorporated. If the dough is crumbly, work in up to 3 teaspoons water until it holds together; if very soft, work in up to 2 tablespoons flour.

Let the dough stand for 5 minutes to firm up slightly. If it is too soft to shape into logs, stir in up to 2 tablespoons more flour to stiffen it slightly. Divide the dough in half. Place each half on a long sheet of plastic wrap and shape into evenly thick 9-inch-long logs. Stretch out from the center so they aren't thicker in the middle. Roll them up in the plastic wrap, twisting the ends to secure them. Slip each log into a discarded paper towel tube (or a wrapping paper tube cut into two tubes) that has been slit lengthwise. Divide the untoasted coconut between two small plastic bags and tuck them into the ends of the tubes so they will be there with the dough when needed. Secure the tubes with tape or rubber bands.

Refrigerate for at least 2 hours, until firm enough to slice, or place in a plastic bag and refrigerate for up to 48 hours. Let warm up at room temperature for a few minutes or until just softened enough to slice. (Or insert in freezer bags and freeze the logs for up to 2 months; place in the refrigerator to thaw overnight before using.)

Baking Preliminaries: Position a rack in the middle of the oven; preheat to 375°F. Grease several large baking sheets or coat with nonstick spray.

Working with one chilled log at a time and using a large sharp knife, cut crosswise into scant $\frac{1}{4}$-inch-thick slices; rotate the log a quarter turn after each slice to help keep the log round. Space the cookies about 2 inches apart on the sheets. Generously garnish the tops of the rounds with the shreds or flakes of untoasted coconut, patting them down to imbed slightly.

Bake (middle rack) one sheet at a time for 8 to 12 minutes or until the cookies are just nicely browned, darker at the edges and barely firm in the center top. Let the pans cool on wire racks until the cookies firm up, about 3 minutes, then transfer them to racks using a wide spatula. Thoroughly cool on racks before packing them for storage.

Yield: Makes about sixty $2\frac{1}{2}$-inch rounds

Storage: Store these, airtight, for up to 1 week. They can be frozen, airtight, for up to 1 month.

BISCOTTI }

Once upon a time, biscotti were found primarily in Italian baking repertoires and were mostly flavored with anise, almonds, pine nuts, or lemon. But over the past several decades, as the whole world has discovered the charms of these toothsome, double-baked slices, they have become decidedly more multicultural and decadent. Today they come in enough flavors to make a traditional Italian baker's head spin!

Of course, it all depends on where you're buying them, but modestly, I'll tell you I think these biscotti are all significantly better than most of the ones in typical coffee bars. They don't cost $2 or so apiece, either!

One ingredient that now turns up regularly and to great effect in biscotti (thanks, perhaps, to chichi cafés) is chocolate. The chapter contains four different chocolate choices—"plain," spiced, chocolate-almond, and a fun German-inspired faux "brown bread" that blends chocolate and anise seeds and looks remarkably like, yes, dark bread slices! The recipe even comes with a faux "butter" icing that is spread on the "bread" to complete the entertaining visual effect.

Other biscotti I'm particularly taken with include a gingerbread-scented version shared by a friend of mine, and a colorful American-inspired cranberry-ginger. The most aromatic and unusual offering is my Lavender-Lemon Biscotti. Trust me on the lavender—it's captivating, not strange.

One problem home bakers occasionally confront with biscotti is the tendency of the slices to break or crumble during cutting. You can usually remedy this by chilling the par-baked loaves in the refrigerator or in the freezer (briefly) before slicing them. Although recipes provide the appropriate instructions, if the loaves *still* seem too crumbly, just chill them further and try again. In some cases, a large chef's knife works well, but a large serrated knife is usually the best choice for very cold, firm loaves, especially ones studded with nuts or brittle chocolate bits.

By the way, it is normal for many of the biscotti here to crack on top a bit as they bake, so don't be alarmed about this. They are leavened loaves, after all, and the fissures just indicate that they have expanded during baking.

Generous 1 cup granulated
   sugar
¾ cup good-quality unsweetened
   natural (non-alkalized) cocoa
   powder or Dutch-process
   cocoa powder, sifted after
   measuring, if lumpy
⅔ cup very finely chopped good-
   quality 55 to 75 percent cacao
   semisweet or bittersweet
   chocolate
1 teaspoon baking powder
¼ teaspoon salt
3 large eggs, at room temperature
1 teaspoon instant espresso
   powder dissolved in 1
   tablespoon water
½ teaspoon vanilla extract
½ teaspoon almond extract
1⅔ cups unbleached all-purpose
   white flour
1½ cups whole blanched or
   unblanched almonds or whole
   hazelnuts (or a combination),
   toasted and cooled

MY FAVORITE CHOCOLATE BISCOTTI

Crunchy-crisp, chocolaty, and loaded with whole almonds or hazelnuts or both (my preference), these attractive slices are great with a steaming cup of coffee. While they are terrific as is, for a quick decorative touch, I accent them with squiggles or zigzag lines of the Glossy Chocolate Drizzle on page 314 or dip one end of each slice into the Ganache Glaze on page 318.

Baking Preliminaries: Position a rack in the middle of the oven; preheat to 350°F. Lightly grease two 5 by 9-inch loaf pans or line a very large baking sheet with baking parchment.

In a large bowl, stir or beat together the sugar, cocoa, chocolate, baking powder, and salt until well blended. Vigorously stir or beat in the eggs one at a time, then the espresso mixture and extracts until thoroughly incorporated. Stir in the flour and nuts until thoroughly and evenly incorporated; or if preferred, knead them in with your hands. If the dough is crumbly, work in up to 4 teaspoons water; if extremely soft, work in up to 2 tablespoons flour.

Let the dough stand for 5 to 10 minutes; it will firm up and become less sticky.

Divide the dough in half. Put each half in a loaf pan. With lightly oiled hands, press and flatten the dough until it covers the pan bottom in an evenly thick layer. (Alternatively, working on a large parchment-lined baking sheet, shape and flatten each half into a 3 by 8-inch log; keep them well separated.)

Bake (middle rack) for 30 to 35 minutes, until a toothpick inserted into the center of the loaves comes out clean. Set the pans (or sheet) aside until cooled. Refrigerate the loaves until very well chilled, at least 1½ hours. On a cutting board, cut each loaf on a slight diagonal into ¼- to ⅓-inch-thick slices using a large serrated knife or large, sharp chef's knife. Lay the slices flat, slightly separated, on a very large parchment-lined baking sheet. Meanwhile, reheat the oven to 325°F.

Bake the slices until slightly darker at the edges, 10 to 13 minutes. Turn off the oven; let the biscotti stand in the oven for 10 minutes longer. Remove them from the oven. Let cool on the baking sheet until firmed up and cool; then cool completely on wire racks.

If adding the chocolate drizzle, line up the slices, slightly separated, on a wire rack over paper to catch drips. Drizzle fine lines back and forth over the slices, as desired. Let them stand until the glaze sets, at least 30 to 40 minutes. If adding the ganache, dip one end of each slice into the ganache glaze until about a 2-inch length of each slice is coated. Follow

the detailed dipping instructions provided in the ganache recipe on page 318.

Yield: Makes thirty-five to forty 4- to 6-inch-long biscotti

Storage: Store these, airtight, for up to 10 days. They can be frozen, airtight, for up to 2 months.

Tip

The easiest, quickest way to shape the dough portions is to press them into two 5 by 9-inch loaf pans. But if you don't have pans this size, just shape each portion into a log as directed in the alternative instructions.

Tip

Chocolate biscotti have a tendency to crumble and break during slicing unless the dough is well chilled first. If they are difficult to slice even after being refrigerated, tuck them in the freezer for about 30 minutes to chill them even further. And definitely slice them using a large, sharp serrated knife.

Easy
Unusual and sophisticated
but easy.
Subtle, complex flavor.

5 tablespoons unsalted butter, melted and slightly cooled

¾ cup granulated sugar

1 large egg plus 2 large egg yolks
Generous 1 tablespoon finely grated orange zest (orange part of the peel)

1 teaspoon finely minced peeled fresh gingeroot, optional

1 teaspoon baking powder

¼ teaspoon salt

¾ teaspoon Flowers of Sicily extract, or substitute ¾ teaspoon each vanilla extract, almond extract, and lemon extract

2⅔ cups unbleached all-purpose white flour, plus more if needed

1 cup coarsely chopped slivered almonds or pistachio nuts, or a combination

⅓ cup finely chopped candied orange peel

⅓ cup fresh orange juice, plus more if needed

ORANGE-NUT BISCOTTI

These nut-studded biscotti aren't flashy, but they have a gentle, not-too-sweet orange taste and satisfying texture that give them a lot of staying power. Their aroma is faintly floral, especially if the enticing Italian extract Flowers of Sicily is added. (Ordering information for the extract is on page 19.) Not to worry, though—the biscotti will be appealing even if you must substitute the extracts suggested. Try these with tea, or perhaps juice or milk.

Baking Preliminaries: Position a rack in the middle of the oven; preheat to 350°F. Line a large baking sheet with baking parchment.

In a large bowl, stir together the butter and sugar until blended. Vigorously stir in the egg and yolks, zest, ginger (if using), baking powder, salt, and extract(s) until well blended. Stir in the flour, nuts, candied peel, and ⅓ cup orange juice until smoothly incorporated. If the mixture is at all dry or crumbly, stir in another tablespoon or two of orange juice. If the dough is sticky or soft, let stand to firm up for 5 minutes. Then work in up to 3 tablespoons more flour to stiffen it slightly.

Divide the dough in half. With lightly oiled hands and working on the parchment-lined baking sheet, shape each half into a 3 by 10-inch, evenly thick loaf. Space the loaves as far apart as possible.

Bake (middle rack) for 25 to 30 minutes, until a toothpick inserted in the center comes out clean. Set aside until completely cooled, at least 45 minutes. On a cutting board, cut each loaf on a slight diagonal into ¼-inch-thick slices using a large serrated knife or large sharp chef's knife. Lay the slices flat, slightly separated, on parchment-lined baking sheets. Meanwhile, reheat the oven to 325°F.

Bake the slices until toasted and faintly tinged with brown, about 10 minutes. Gently turn over; toast until faintly tinged with brown, about 10 minutes more. Transfer biscotti to wire racks. Let cool completely.

Yield: Makes about thirty-five 5-inch biscotti

Storage: Store these, airtight, for up to 2 weeks. They can be frozen, airtight, for up to 2 months.

¼ cup (½ stick) unsalted butter, softened slightly

1 cup granulated sugar

1½ teaspoons anise seeds, lightly crushed with a mortar and pestle or coarsely chopped in a food processor or coffee mill

½ teaspoon ground cinnamon

¼ teaspoon ground cloves

¼ teaspoon salt

3 large eggs, at room temperature

⅔ cup good-quality unsweetened natural (non-alkalized) cocoa powder or Dutch-process cocoa powder, sifted after measuring, if lumpy

2 teaspoons baking powder Finely grated zest (orange part of the peel) of 1 large orange

¾ teaspoon anise extract, or substitute ¼ teaspoon almond extract

2½ cups unbleached all-purpose white flour

1½ cups chopped walnuts or chopped pistachios, or a combination

SPICED CHOCOLATE BISCOTTI

Just reading through the ingredients is reminding me of how appealing these are! Unless I immediately pack them up and give them away, I keep going back and nibbling until the jar is empty. In fact, I've gotten up twice while writing this and have the telltale crumbs on my desk to prove it!

Part of the appeal comes from the texture—these are pleasantly crunchy but are not tooth breakers requiring dunking. They also seem light, low-key, and not too sweet or rich, so I don't feel guilty or like I'm bolted to my chair after eating a few.

The most memorable part is the tantalizing yet subtle flavor—cocoa intermingled with a good deal of anise, and smaller amounts of cinnamon, cloves, and orange. Even if you're not a fan of anise—I'm usually not—I think you'll like it here. It just blends in and lends an indefinable something extra that really heightens the overall appeal.

Baking Preliminaries: Position a rack in the middle of the oven; preheat to 350°F. Line a large baking sheet with baking parchment.

In a large bowl with an electric mixer on medium speed, beat the butter with the sugar, anise seeds, cinnamon, cloves, and salt until light and fluffy, about 2 minutes. Beat in the eggs one at a time, then the cocoa, baking powder, zest, and extract, scraping down the bowl as needed. On low, then medium, speed, beat in a generous half of the flour. Vigorously stir in the remaining flour and the nuts until evenly incorporated; or, if desired, work them in with well-greased hands. If the dough is crumbly, work in up to 4 teaspoons water; if very soft, work in up to 2 tablespoons flour. If necessary, let the dough stand for 5 minutes to firm up a bit more.

Divide the dough in half. Working on the parchment-lined baking sheet, shape and flatten each half into a 4 by 10-inch rectangle; keep them well separated.

Bake (middle rack) for 30 to 35 minutes, until a toothpick inserted in the center comes out clean. Set aside until cool. Then refrigerate until well chilled. On a cutting board, cut each loaf on a slight diagonal into ¼-inch-thick slices using a large serrated knife or a large, sharp chef's knife. (If the slices seem crumbly or hard to cut, chill further by putting the loaves in the freezer a few minutes.) Place the slices, lying flat and slightly separated, on a very large parchment-lined sheet. Meanwhile, reheat the oven to 325°F.

Bake the slices until faintly tinged with brown, 12 to 14 minutes. Turn off the oven; let the biscotti stand in the oven to toast for 10 minutes longer. Remove from the oven. Let cool on the baking sheet until firmed up and cool; then cool completely on wire racks.

Tip

The recipe calls for crushing the anise seed to bring out its flavor. The best tool for this is a mortar and pestle. Another option is coarsely grinding the seeds in a food processor or mini chopper with a little of the sugar for about 30 seconds or in a spice grinder for about 15 seconds.

Cookie Jar Wisdom
Cookie-fucious says: May your life be long and your cookie jar full.

DOUBLE-ALMOND DOUBLE-CHOCOLATE BISCOTTI

I'm fond of many kinds of biscotti, but I adore these. The combination of almonds and almond paste, plus cocoa powder and chocolate morsels, gives the slices a rich, gratifying chocolate-almond flavor and delightful munchable texture. If you, too, like almond and chocolate together, you'll likely enjoy these.

These really don't need any embellishment, but for a slightly dressier look, feel free to garnish them with Glossy Chocolate Drizzle (page 314).

1½ cups blanched slivered almonds

1 7-ounce package or one 8-ounce can almond paste, cut or spooned into chunks

½ cup good-quality unsweetened natural (non-alkalized) cocoa powder or Dutch-process cocoa powder

¼ cup (½ stick) unsalted butter, melted

¾ cup plus 2 tablespoons granulated sugar

1 teaspoon baking powder

¼ teaspoon salt

3 large egg whites, at room temperature

1 teaspoon vanilla extract or almond extract

1½ cups unbleached all-purpose white flour, divided

1 cup 50 to 65 percent cacao semisweet or bittersweet chocolate morsels

1 batch Glossy Chocolate Drizzle (page 314) for garnish, optional

Baking Preliminaries: Position a rack in the middle of the oven; preheat to 325°F. Set out a long sheet of wax paper. Line a very large baking sheet with baking parchment.

Spread the almonds on a small rimmed baking sheet. Toast (middle rack) for 6 to 10 minutes, stirring to redistribute every 3 minutes, until fragrant and barely tinged with brown. Let cool.

Meanwhile, in a large bowl with a mixer on medium speed, beat together the almond paste, cocoa powder, butter, sugar, baking powder, and salt until very well blended. Gradually add the egg whites and extract, beating until evenly incorporated, scraping down the sides as necessary.

Stir in 1 cup flour, the thoroughly cooled almonds, and chocolate morsels. Stir in the remaining flour, then knead the dough until the ingredients are evenly incorporated. If the dough is crumbly, work in up to 4 teaspoons water; if very soft, work in up to 2 tablespoons flour. If the dough is very sticky, let stand for about 10 minutes, until firmed up slightly.

Divide the dough in half. With lightly greased hands, shape each half into a 2 by 11-inch, evenly thick loaf on the parchment-lined baking sheet, spacing as far apart as possible. Flatten each loaf just slightly.

Bake (middle rack) for 35 to 40 minutes, until a toothpick inserted in the center comes out clean. Set aside until cooled. Put the loaves on a tray or sheet and refrigerate until chilled, at least 1 hour; this makes slicing easier.

On a cutting board, cut each loaf on a slight diagonal into generous ¼-inch-thick slices using a large serrated knife or large, sharp chef's knife. Lay the slices flat, slightly separated, on a parchment-lined baking sheet. Meanwhile, reheat the oven to 300°F.

Bake until lightly toasted, 12 to 15 minutes. Turn off the oven; toast for about 10 minutes more. Transfer the pan to a cooling rack. Let the biscotti stand until cooled completely before serving or garnishing with the optional chocolate drizzle.

If using the drizzle, line up the biscotti, slightly separated, on a rack set over paper to catch drips. Pipe very fine zigzag lines back and forth crosswise over the slices (or decorate as desired). Let stand until the drizzle sets, at least 30 to 40 minutes.

Yield: Makes thirty-five to forty $3\frac{1}{2}$- to 5-inch biscotti

Storage: Store these, airtight and at room temperature, for up to 2 weeks. They can be frozen, airtight, for up to 2 months.

1   cup (about 5½ ounces)
    whole, lightly toasted and
    hulled hazelnuts*
1   cup (about 6 ounces) chopped
    60 to 70 percent cacao
    chocolate
¼   cup unsweetened natural (non-
    alkalized) cocoa powder or
    Dutch-process cocoa powder
2¾ cups unbleached all-purpose
    white flour, divided, plus more
    if needed
¼   cup (½ stick) unsalted butter,
    slightly softened
1   cup granulated sugar
    Finely grated zest (orange part
    of the peel) of 2 large oranges
1   tablespoon whole anise seeds
    or fennel seeds, divided
2   teaspoons baking powder
¼   teaspoon salt
3   large eggs, at room temperature
    and beaten with a fork, divided

GERMAN "BROWN BREAD" SLICES ("BUTTERED" OR "PLAIN")

Garnished with anise seeds, dark with cocoa and chocolate, and "buttered" with a light orange icing, these *trompe l'oeil* treats actually do look very much like the German black bread slices they are supposed to mimic. I got the idea for the recipe from a German cookbook I bought when I lived in Europe many years ago. It featured some very realistic-looking *Falsches Swartzbrot Platzchen*, or "fake black bread cookies," although they didn't include the faux butter icing and so weren't quite as realistic as these.

These really are a lot of fun and very flavorful. Normally, children might find the flavor combination too sophisticated, but the playfulness and novelty usually win them over. Although the slices can be iced in advance or even left plain if preferred, kids absolutely love it when you serve a crock of "butter" along with the cookies and let everybody smear it on their own "bread." (Grown-ups try not to show it, but they seem to enjoy the activity, too!)

Baking Preliminaries: Position a rack in the middle of the oven; preheat to 325°F. Line a very large baking sheet with baking parchment.

Chop the nuts in a food processor until fairly finely ground. Transfer to a large bowl. Process the chocolate and cocoa until the chocolate is finely ground. Stir the chocolate mixture and a generous half of the flour (no need to measure) into the ground nuts.

In the processor, combine the butter, sugar, orange zest, half the anise seeds, the baking powder, and salt until well blended. Add in all but 2 tablespoons eggs to the processor; reserve the 2 tablespoons egg to garnish the loaves. Process the butter mixture until well blended, stopping and scraping down the bowl sides as needed. Stir the mixture into the nut-flour mixture. Vigorously stir the remaining flour into the dough just until evenly incorporated.

If the dough is too soft or sticky to handle, let it stand for 5 to 10 minutes to firm up slightly; if still too soft, knead in a little more flour. If the dough is too crumbly to hold together, knead in a little water. With greased hands, divide the dough in half.

Working on parchment, shape each half into a 3 by 8-inch domed loaf; they should look more or less like loaves of dark bread. Space the loaves on the parchment-lined baking sheet as far apart as possible. Using a pastry brush (or a paper towel), lightly but evenly brush the loaves with the remaining egg mixture. Immediately sprinkle them with the remaining anise seeds.

Bake (middle rack) for 35 to 40 minutes or until a toothpick inserted in the center comes out clean; it's normal for the loaves to crack a bit. Set them aside until cooled, then refrigerate until well chilled. On a

Faux Butter Icing

2½ tablespoons unsalted butter, just slightly softened

2 cups powdered sugar, plus more if needed

1½ to 3 tablespoons frozen (thawed) orange juice concentrate, or substitute plain orange juice

Tip ⌐

The icing calls for frozen (thawed) orange juice concentrate, which will lend it a realistic butter yellow color. You can use plain orange juice instead; the "butter" will just be a little pale and the flavor less pronounced.

Tip ⌐

Things will go much faster in this (and any other) recipe if you use hazelnuts that are already hulled and ready to use. Occasionally, they're available at gourmet stores such as Whole Foods and Trader Joe's, but they can be purchased online as well. I usually buy in quantity; they keep well packed airtight in the freezer.

cutting board, cut each loaf crosswise into ¼-inch-thick slices using a large serrated knife or large, sharp chef's knife. Lay the slices flat, slightly separated, on a parchment-lined baking sheet. If you wish to easily reassemble the slices after baking to form and serve in a "loaf" as shown in the photograph, lay them on the parchment in the order sliced. (Use two sheets, if necessary.) Meanwhile reheat the oven to 325°F.

Bake the slices (middle rack) until toasted and just slightly darker but not at all burned, 15 to 18 minutes. Turn off the oven and let the slices stand in it until cooled completely, at least 45 minutes.

For the icing: In a medium bowl, beat together the butter, powdered sugar, and 1 tablespoon orange juice concentrate until very smooth. As needed, beat in more juice concentrate to create a stiff, just spreadable consistency. Or, if the icing is too fluid, add enough additional powdered sugar to stiffen it. Use immediately by roughly spreading it over thoroughly cooled cookie slices. Or serve it along with them and let diners "butter" their own bread. It can be made ahead, covered, and refrigerated in a nonreactive container for up to 1 week. Let come to cool room temperature before using.

Yield: Makes thirty-five to forty 4- to 5-inch slices

Storage: Store these, airtight, for up to 10 days. They can be frozen, airtight, for up to 2 months.

* To toast and hull hazelnuts: Preheat the oven to 325°F. Spread the whole unhulled hazelnuts on a rimmed baking pan and toast, stirring every 3 or 4 minutes, for 14 to 18 minutes or until the hulls loosen and the nuts are nicely browned; be careful not to burn. Set aside until cool enough to handle. Rub the nuts between your hands or in a clean kitchen towel, loosening and discarding the hull. It's all right if some small bits remain. Cool the nuts thoroughly before using them.

5 tablespoons unsalted butter, melted and cooled slightly
¾ cup plus 2 tablespoons packed light brown sugar
2¾ teaspoons ground cinnamon
2¾ teaspoons ground ginger
½ teaspoon ground cloves
2 teaspoons baking powder
Scant ½ teaspoon salt
2 large eggs, at room temperature
¼ cup molasses
2¾ cups unbleached all-purpose white flour
1 cup chopped macadamia or pistachio nuts, or a combination, optional
About 5 tablespoons turbinado sugar or other coarse crystal sugar (omit if planning to ice the biscotti)
1 batch Traditional Powdered Sugar Icing (page 302), optional

Tip

For a quick finish, roll the loaves in coarse sugar before baking. Or top the slices with powdered sugar icing after baking for a pretty "snowy" look.

GINGER-SPICE BISCOTTI

Easy, yet extremely appealing and attractive, these gingerbread-scented biscotti make a memorable holiday gift. They'll also fill your house with a heady spice scent as they bake. The recipe was shared with me by a friend and fellow food writer, Connie Hay, who says it's one of her favorites. It's won me over, too.

Baking Preliminaries: Position a rack in the middle of the oven; preheat to 375°F. Line a large baking sheet with baking parchment.

In a large bowl, vigorously stir together (or beat using a mixer) the butter, brown sugar, cinnamon, ginger, cloves, baking powder, and salt until well blended. Vigorously stir or beat in the eggs and molasses until smoothly incorporated. Stir in 2 cups flour and the nuts (if using), then work in the remainder of the flour by kneading until evenly incorporated. If the dough is sticky, let stand to firm for 5 to 10 minutes.

Divide the dough in half. With lightly oiled hands, shape each half into a 2½ by 9-inch, evenly thick loaf on a sheet of baking parchment. If not planning to ice the biscotti, evenly roll each loaf in 2 tablespoons crystal sugar. Transfer the loaves to the parchment-lined baking sheet, spacing as far apart as possible. Flatten each into a 3 by 10-inch rectangle. Sprinkle each top with about ½ tablespoon more coarse sugar, pressing down to imbed slightly.

Bake (middle rack) for 25 to 30 minutes or until a toothpick tested in the center comes out clean. Set aside until cooled, at least 1 hour. On a cutting board, cut each loaf on a slight diagonal into ¼-inch-thick slices using a large serrated knife or large sharp chef's knife. Lay the slices flat, slightly separated, on a parchment-lined baking sheet. Meanwhile, reheat the oven to 325°F.

Bake the slices until toasted and faintly tinged with brown, 15 to 20 minutes. Turn off the oven; toast 10 minutes more. Remove the biscotti to wire racks. Let cool completely.

To ice with powdered sugar glaze (if the crystal sugar garnish was omitted): Ready the glaze, adjusting the consistency so it is spreadable but not too runny. Using a table knife, spread one side of each slice with a thin, even layer of glaze. Let the biscotti stand, glaze side up, until completely set, at least 1 hour.

Yield: Makes thirty-five 4- to 5-inch biscotti

Storage: Store these, airtight, for up to 2 weeks. They can be frozen, airtight, for up to 2 months.

1½ cups blanched slivered almonds

1 7-ounce package or one
   8-ounce can almond paste, cut
   or spooned into chunks

½ cup (1 stick) unsalted butter,
   slightly softened and cut into
   chunks

6 tablespoons granulated sugar

1 teaspoon baking powder

¼ teaspoon salt

4 large egg whites, at room
   temperature

1 teaspoon vanilla extract or
   almond extract

2 cups unbleached all-purpose
   white flour, plus more if
   needed

Tip

Tuck biscotti into a stylish
apothecary for a thoughful gift.

BEST ALMOND BISCOTTI

I like classic almond biscotti, but recently I updated my repertoire and now prefer ones that include almond paste along with almonds. The flavor is fuller and the slices are more fragrant.

The only drawback is that almond paste does make the dough a little more difficult to handle: It's stickier, so you need to oil your hands before shaping the loaves. And be sure to chill the partly baked loaves very thoroughly before attempting to slice them.

Baking Preliminaries: Position a rack in the middle of the oven; preheat to 325°F. Set out a long sheet of baking parchment or wax paper. Set out a small rimmed baking sheet. Line a very large baking sheet with baking parchment.

Spread the almonds on the rimmed baking sheet. Toast (middle rack) for 10 to 15 minutes, stirring to redistribute every 3 or 4 minutes, until fragrant and lightly tinged with brown. Set aside until cooled.

Meanwhile, combine the almond paste, butter, sugar, baking powder, and salt in a food processor. Process in pulses until very well blended. Gradually add the egg whites and extract, processing until evenly incorporated; stop and scrape down the bowl sides as needed. (Alternatively in a large bowl, with a mixer on medium speed, beat the almond paste, butter, sugar, baking powder, and salt until very well blended, scraping down the bowl as needed. Gradually beat in the egg whites and extract until thoroughly incorporated.)

Add 1 cup flour, processing in pulses (or beating) until evenly incorporated. Scrape out the dough onto the paper. Sprinkle over the remaining 1 cup flour and the cooled toasted almonds. Gently knead the dough until the flour and almonds are evenly incorporated throughout. If the dough is very soft, let it stand for 10 to 15 minutes, until firmed up slightly and easier to handle. If necessary, work in up to 3 tablespoons more flour to stiffen the dough a bit more.

Divide the dough in half. With lightly oiled hands, on the parchment-lined baking sheet shape and flatten each half into a 3½ by 10-inch, evenly thick loaf, spacing them as far apart as possible.

Reduce the heat to 300°F. Bake (middle rack) for 25 to 30 minutes or until a toothpick inserted in the center comes out clean. Set aside until cool, then refrigerate until thoroughly chilled. On a cutting board, cut each loaf on a slight diagonal into ¼-inch-thick slices using a large, serrated knife or large, sharp chef's knife. If they are still a bit crumbly and difficult to slice, chill them further by freezing them a few minutes. Lay the slices flat, just barely separated, on a parchment-lined baking sheet. Meanwhile reset the oven to 300°F.

Bake the slices until toasted and golden brown, about 10 minutes. Gently turn over; toast until golden, about 10 minutes more. Remove from the oven; let cool slightly. Transfer the biscotti to wire racks. Cool completely.

Yield: Makes thirty-five to forty 3- to 5-inch biscotti

Storage: Store these, airtight, for up to 10 days. They can be frozen, airtight, for up to 2 months.

Cookie Jar Wisdom
A balanced diet is a cookie in each hand.

¾ cup granulated sugar
5   tablespoons unsalted butter,
     melted and cooled
     Finely grated zest (orange part
     of the peel) of 1 large orange
2½ teaspoons ground ginger
1   teaspoon baking powder
1¼ teaspoons ground cardamom,
     or substitute ground allspice if
     unavailable
¾ teaspoon lemon extract or ½
     teaspoon Flowers of Sicily
     extract
½ teaspoon salt
3   large eggs, at room temperature
1½ cups sweetened dried
     cranberries
½ cup finely chopped crystallized
     ginger
1   cup coarsely chopped
     pistachios, or a combination of
     pistachios and almonds
2½ cups unbleached all-purpose
     white flour, plus more if
     needed
     Quick Powdered Sugar Drizzle
     (page 304), optional

CRANBERRY-GINGER-SPICE BISCOTTI

I tend to think of this as a holiday recipe because the biscotti are studded with colorful bits of cranberries crystallized ginger, and pistachios. Plus, they have a spicy scent that calls to mind traditional Christmas baking. They are zingy, chewy-crisp, and appealing on a holiday buffet.

Baking Preliminaries: Position a rack in the middle of the oven; preheat to 350°F. Line a very large baking sheet with baking parchment.

In a large bowl, stir or beat together the sugar, butter, orange zest, ground ginger, baking powder, cardamom, extract, and salt until very well blended. One at a time, vigorously stir or beat in the eggs, then the cranberries, crystallized ginger, and nuts until thoroughly incorporated. Gradually stir in the flour until well blended; if desired, work in the last of it with your hands. If the dough is crumbly, work in up to 4 teaspoons water; if very soft, work in up to 2 tablespoons flour. If necessary, let the dough stand for 5 minutes to firm up slightly.

Divide the dough in half. Working on the parchment-lined baking sheet with greased hands, shape and smooth each half into a 2 by 12-inch, evenly thick loaf, spacing as far apart as possible.

Bake (middle rack) for 25 to 30 minutes, until a toothpick tested in the center comes out clean. Set aside until cooled, then refrigerate until well chilled to facilitate easier cutting. On a cutting board, cut each loaf on a slight diagonal into generous ¼-inch-thick slices using a large serrated knife or large sharp chef's knife. Lay the slices flat, slightly separated, on a parchment-lined baking sheet. Meanwhile, reheat the oven to 325°F.

Bake the slices until lightly toasted, 10 to 15 minutes. Turn over; toast for 7 to 12 minutes longer, till just barely tinged, watching closely to avoid over-browning. Remove from the oven; let cool completely.

If a garnish is desired, line up the slices, slightly separated, on wire racks set over paper to catch drips. Ready the drizzle on page 304. Place it in a pastry bag fitted with a fine writing tip, or in a paper piping cone, or in a small plastic bag with one corner snipped off to yield a small opening. Squeeze out, drizzling or zigzagging very fine lines attractively over the slices as desired. Let the biscotti stand until the drizzle completely sets, at least 45 minutes.

Yield: Makes thirty-five to forty 3- by 4- inch slices

Storage: Store these, airtight and at room temperature, for up to 10 days. They can be frozen, airtight, for up to 2 months.

5 tablespoons unsalted butter,
   melted and cooled slightly
¾ cup granulated sugar
2 large eggs, at room temperature
¼ cup fresh orange juice, plus more
   as needed
2 teaspoons grated lemon zest
   (yellow part of the peel)
2 teaspoons grated orange zest
   (orange part of the peel)
2 teaspoons finely crushed or
   coarsely ground fennel seeds
1 teaspoon baking powder
   Generous ¼ teaspoon salt
1⅔ cups unbleached all-purpose
   white flour, plus more if
   needed
1 cup whole wheat flour
1¼ cups diced Calimyrna figs
¾ cup coarsely chopped pistachios

Tip

The whole wheat flour in the recipe
enhances the flavor, color, and aura
of wholesomeness and, along with
the figs, boosts fiber content. But if
you don't have it on hand, you can
use all white flour with good results.

SICILIAN-STYLE FIG, FENNEL SEED, AND PISTACHIO BISCOTTI

Anise, which has a licorice taste, turns up often in traditional Italian biscotti, but, for some reason, fennel, which also has licorice notes, appears much less often. I hope this will change, however, as fennel seeds have a more complex, interesting, and subtle character than anise, especially when baked along with figs, pistachio nuts, and citrus zest. The combination seemed very Mediterranean when I first tried it, and I've since been told it's Sicilian.

These biscotti are just slightly crisp and have a rustic, unfussy look. The bits of fig here and there are like little sensory gifts, adding not only visual appeal but also fruity taste, chewiness, crunchy seeds, and sweetness every time you come upon them.

Baking Preliminaries: Position a rack in the middle of the oven; preheat to 350°F. Line a large baking sheet with baking parchment.

In a large mixer bowl with a mixer on medium speed, beat together the butter and sugar until blended. One at a time, beat in the eggs, then ¼ cup orange juice, the citrus zests, fennel seeds, baking powder, and salt until well blended. Beat or stir in the flours, then the figs and nuts, until smoothly incorporated; if desired, finish the last of the mixing by kneading. If the mixture is dry or crumbly, stir in another tablespoon or two of orange juice; if sticky or soft, let it stand for 5 minutes. Then, if necessary, work in up to 3 tablespoons more flour.

Divide the dough in half. With lightly greased hands and working on the parchment-lined baking sheet, shape each half into a 2 by 11-inch, evenly thick loaf. Space the loaves as far apart as possible on the sheet.

Bake (middle rack) for 25 to 30 minutes, until a toothpick inserted in the center comes out clean. Set aside until cooled, about 30 minutes. On a cutting board, cut each loaf on a slight diagonal into ⅓-inch-thick slices using a large serrated knife or large sharp chef's knife. Lay the slices flat and just slightly separated on parchment-lined baking sheets. Meanwhile, reheat the oven to 325°F.

Bake the slices until toasted and faintly tinged with brown, 12 to 15 minutes. Gently turn over; toast until faintly tinged with brown, 10 to 12 minutes more. Transfer the biscotti to wire racks. Let cool completely.

Yield: Makes about thirty-five 5-inch biscotti

Storage: Store these, airtight, for up to 2 weeks. They can be frozen, airtight, for up to 2 months.

2¼ cups unbleached all-purpose white flour, plus more if needed

⅔ cup granulated sugar

1 tablespoon finely grated orange zest (orange part of the peel)

½ teaspoon saffron threads

¼ teaspoon ground cardamom

¼ teaspoon ground coriander

5 tablespoons unsalted butter, melted and cooled to barely warm

2 large eggs plus 1 large egg yolk (reserve the extra white for glazing the loaves), at room temperature

1½ teaspoons baking powder

2½ teaspoons vanilla extract
   Scant ½ teaspoon salt

2 tablespoons orange-scented decorating sugar (page 333) or store-bought orange sanding sugar or plain crystal sugar for garnish

SAFFRON-ORANGE-SPICE BISCOTTI

The distinctive aroma, taste, and golden color of saffron combined with orange and hints of cardamom and coriander give these slices their unique, slightly exotic appeal. The flavor seems vaguely Persian or Indian, though, of course, biscotti aren't typical fare in either cuisine. These are also somewhat richer, more tender, and more refined looking than most of the other biscotti in the book. I especially like them with a dish of sliced mangos or mango sorbet.

Baking Preliminaries: Position a rack in the middle of the oven; preheat to 350°F. Line a very large baking sheet with baking parchment.

Put the flour in a large bowl. In a food processor, process the sugar, zest, saffron, cardamom, and coriander until the sugar is colored and the saffron is chopped into fine flecks, 2 to 3 minutes. Add the butter, eggs and yolk, baking powder, vanilla, and salt. Process until evenly incorporated, stopping and scraping down the bowl if needed.

Pour the egg mixture over the flour. Stir just until thoroughly incorporated; if desired, work in the last of the flour with lightly greased hands. If the dough is soft and sticky, work in up to 3 more tablespoons flour; if crumbly, work in up to 1 teaspoon water.

Divide the dough in half. Working on the parchment-lined baking sheet with greased hands, shape each half into a 2 by 12-inch evenly thick loaf; space the loaves as far apart as possible. Pat down each loaf to flatten slightly. Evenly brush each loaf with some of the reserved egg white. Sprinkle each loaf lightly but evenly with the garnishing sugar.

Bake (middle rack) for 25 to 30 minutes, until a toothpick tested in the center comes out clean. Set aside until cooled to barely warm, at least 30 minutes. On a cutting board, cut each loaf on a slight diagonal into ¼-inch-thick slices using a large serrated knife or large sharp chef's knife. Lay the slices flat, slightly separated, on a parchment-lined baking sheet. Meanwhile, reheat the oven to 325°F.

Bake the slices until toasted and faintly tinged with brown, 10 to 12 minutes. Turn off the oven; toast for 10 minutes more. Transfer the biscotti to wire racks. Let cool completely.

Yield: Makes thirty-five to forty 3- to 4-inch biscotti

Storage: Store these, airtight and at room temperature, for up to 10 days. They can be frozen, airtight, for up to 2 months.

2 large eggs, at room temperature
½ cup clover honey or other mild
   honey
2 teaspoons vanilla extract or
   ¾ teaspoon almond extract
1 teaspoon baking powder
   Generous ½ teaspoon salt
⅔ cup whole wheat flour
¾ cup toasted and salted whole
   almonds
¾ cup toasted and salted whole
   cashews
¾ cup toasted and salted whole
   pistachios
⅔ cup unbleached all-purpose
   white flour, plus more if
   needed
   2 to 3 tablespoons turbinado
   sugar, pearl sugar, or other
   plain coarse crystal sugar for
   garnish

HONEY-NUT BISCOTTI

"Natural" is the first word that comes to mind to describe these chunky, crunchy, honey-sweetened biscotti. They contain no fat and very little sugar and are just loaded with nuts. They also include some whole wheat flour, which improves them nutritionally and gives them a hearty (but not health-foody) taste. Enjoy them as a snack, with tea, or in place of the typical trail mix treat.

Baking Preliminaries: Position a rack in the middle of the oven; preheat to 325°F. Coat two 5 by 9-inch loaf pans with nonstick spray.

In a large bowl, beat the eggs with a fork. Set aside 1½ tablespoons egg, covered, to use as a glaze. Stir the honey, vanilla, baking powder, salt, and whole wheat flour into the remaining egg mixture until well blended. Stir in the nuts, then the white flour, working in the last of the flour with well-oiled hands. If the dough is crumbly, work in up to 4 teaspoons water. If the dough is very soft, work in up to 3 tablespoons more white flour to stiffen it slightly.

Divide the dough between the two pans. Lay a piece of wax paper over the dough, then press down to spread the dough over the bottom and form a very compact, evenly thick layer. Using a pastry brush (or paper towel), evenly brush each layer with the reserved egg mixture. Immediately sprinkle the tops with the coarse sugar, dividing it between them.

Bake (middle rack) for 25 to 30 minutes, until golden brown. Set aside until cooled to barely warm. On a cutting board, cut each loaf on a sharp diagonal into long ¼-inch-thick slices using a large serrated knife or large sharp chef's knife. Lay the slices flat, slightly separated, on a large parchment-lined baking sheet. Meanwhile, reheat the oven to 325°F.

Bake the slices until toasted and faintly tinged with brown, about 10 minutes. Turn them over. Bake for 5 minutes or until just barely tinged on the second side. Transfer the biscotti to wire racks. Let cool completely.

Yield: Makes thirty-five to forty 4- to 5½-inch biscotti

Storage: Store these, airtight, for up to 10 days. They can be frozen, airtight, for up to 2 months.

2¼ cups unbleached all-purpose white flour, plus more if needed
¾ cup granulated sugar
1 tablespoon grated lemon zest (yellow part of the peel)
3 tablespoons chopped fresh lavender flower heads (no stems) or 1½ tablespoons dried lavender
5 tablespoons unsalted butter, melted
1½ teaspoons baking powder
   Scant ½ teaspoon salt
2 large eggs
1½ tablespoons fresh lemon juice
2 teaspoons vanilla extract
   About 2 tablespoons homemade lavender sugar (page 338) or purple or crystal sanding sugar combined with 1 teaspoon finely pulverized dried lavender blooms, if available

Tip

If using purchased dried lavender, be sure it is labeled as suitable for culinary use. Health food stores, gourmet boutiques and the internet are good sources.

LAVENDER-LEMON BISCOTTI

If this is the first time you've seen lavender called for in a baked good and are a wee bit skeptical, let me assure you these light, not-too-sweet biscotti have great charm. Their taste and aroma are elusive but enticing, and their texture is reminiscent of very crisp and compelling sugar cookies. Nobody ever guesses that the mystery flavor is lavender and most people find it quite pleasing. Fresh lavender flower heads are definitely the best choice for this recipe, if you don't have them, dried lavender will work fine.

Baking Preliminaries: Position a rack in the middle of the oven; preheat to 350°F. Line a very large baking sheet with baking parchment.

Put the flour in a large bowl. In a food processor, process the sugar, lemon zest, and lavender until very finely ground, 2 to 3 minutes. Add the butter, baking powder, and salt. Process until evenly incorporated. Add the eggs, lemon juice, and vanilla. Process until blended, stopping and scraping down the bowl as needed.

Gradually stir the egg mixture into the flour just until thoroughly incorporated. If the dough is crumbly, work in up to 4 teaspoons water; if sticky, let it stand to firm for 10 minutes. Then work in up to 3 tablespoons more flour, if necessary.

Divide the dough in half. With lightly oiled hands and working on the parchment-lined baking sheet, shape each half into a 2½ by 10-inch, evenly thick loaf; space the loaves as far apart as possible. Sprinkle each top lightly but evenly with the decorating sugar, pressing down all over to imbed.

Bake (middle rack) for 25 to 30 minutes, until a toothpick tested in the center comes out clean. Let loaves cool completely, at least 1 hour. On a cutting board, cut each loaf on a slight diagonal into ¼-inch-thick slices using a large serrated knife or large sharp chef's knife. Lay the slices flat, slightly separated, on a parchment-lined baking sheet. Meanwhile, reheat the oven to 325°F.

Bake the slices until toasted and just tinged with brown, 14 to 16 minutes. Turn off the oven; toast for 10 minutes more. Transfer the biscotti to racks and cool.

Yield: Makes thirty-five to forty 4- to 5-inch biscotti

Storage: Store these, airtight and at room temperature, for up to 10 days. They can be frozen, airtight, for up to 2 months.

SEMISWEET CRISPS, SAVORY COCKTAIL COOKIES & CRACKERS }

The idea of nibbles that fall somewhere between classic crackers and cookies isn't new: think cheese straws and animal crackers, for example. Still, the trend toward crossover treats combining characteristics of both cookies and crackers didn't take hold until pretty recently. It's exciting, because it opens up many intriguing opportunities for fresh, unexpected cookie sensory experiences and even totally new kinds of cookies.

For example, some of the recipes in this chapter, like the chocolate chip crisps and peanut butter crisps, are lighter, munchier, more cracker-like versions of classic cookies. These two serve up the familiar appealing flavor of the originals but are a bit less sweet and much thinner. Formed by rolling out dough on a grid (like many crackers) and cutting it into little squares, they also look like crackers. Besides moving beyond the same old, same old, these provide a terrific new option for those yearning for favorite tastes but wanting or needing slightly more healthful, lower-calorie treats.

Other selections here go in an entirely different direction, retaining a familiar shortbread or butter cookie appearance and texture but swapping the sweetness for savory elements and producing wonderful cocktail or hors d'oeuvres cookies. Several especially tempting choices in this category—the blue and cheddar cheese sandwich cookies stuffed with cranberry and fig conserve and the Herbed Chèvre Nuggets—take the old cheese straws concept and breathe new life into it. Both of these serve up more sophisticated flavors and are garnished with colorful coarse salt or seeds (which mimic the look of traditional sweet cookie sprinkles) for a more interesting look.

The Oil-Cured Black Olive and Black Pepper Biscotti and Savory Sun-Dried Tomato & Tapenade Cocktail Rugelach are also cocktail cookies, but not in cheese straws–style. In fact, they are made exactly the same way as classic biscotti and rugelach, but they just replace the usual sweet components with savory ones. (Tip: If the idea of savory biscotti and rugelach seems too nouvelle to you, feel free to call them "rusks" and "roll-ups.")

You'll find plenty of other tempting selections in the chapter that don't fit neatly into the old cookie or cracker mold. I hope you'll be tempted to try them, too.

2 cups unbleached all-purpose
   white flour
7 tablespoons packed dark brown
   sugar
1½ teaspoons baking powder
   Scant ½ teaspoon salt
⅓ cup corn oil or other flavorless
   vegetable oil
2 teaspoons vanilla extract
   combined with ½ cup room
   temperature water
1 cup (6 ounces) semisweet
   chocolate morsels, chopped
   fairly fine
½ teaspoon each coarse crystal salt
   and crystal sugar combined

Tip

The crisps are a fine solution when
you crave the classic chocolate
chip flavor but either want or need
a satisfying but somewhat diet-
friendly snack.

SWEET & CRUNCHY CHOCOLATE CHIP CRISPS

If there were any doubt that the lines between cookies and crackers are blurring, this recipe should dispel it. These are as thin and crunchy-crisp as the most munchable crackers, yet they most definitely taste like not-too-sweet chocolate chip cookies.

Baking Preliminaries: Position a rack in the middle of the oven; preheat to 350°F. Set out two large baking sheets; four large sheets of baking parchment; and very large rimmed pan lined with parchment.

In a large bowl, stir together the flour, brown sugar, baking powder, and salt until well blended; mash out any sugar lumps with the back of the spoon. Whisk together the oil and vanilla-water mixture, then immediately stir it and the morsels into the flour mixture until incorporated. If the dough is crumbly, gradually stir in enough more water so that it holds together when pinched between fingertips. If it is very soft, stir in up to 2 tablespoons flour.

Divide the dough in half. Roll out each portion between sheets of baking parchment into a (thin) 12-inch square. Cut and patch to make the sides fairly even. Peel off the top parchment sheets. Sprinkle each top evenly with one-quarter of the salt-sugar mixture. Lay the parchment back on the dough, then roll with the rolling pin to imbed the mixture. Turn over the dough; peel off the top sheets. Repeat the garnishing steps on the second sides. Remove the top sheets of parchment.

Using a pizza cutter, pastry wheel, or large knife, cut each dough sheet lengthwise and crosswise into 8 equal strips to form a grid (with uneven edges all around). Slide the paper and dough (leave the edges in place) onto baking sheets. Bake (middle rack) one pan at a time for 15 to 18 minutes or until the dough is set but not firm in the center; set aside. Reset the oven to 225°F.

When the crisps are cool enough to handle, discard the scraps. Separate the squares and spread them on the parchment-lined pan. Return the pan to the oven for 20 minutes; gently stir to redistribute the crisps halfway through. Turn off the oven; let the crisps stand in the oven for 20 to 30 minutes longer. Remove them from the oven; let stand until completely cooled.

Yield: Makes about one hundred twenty-five 1½-inch crisps

Storage: Store these, airtight, for up to 2 weeks or freeze up to 2 months.

1⅓ cups unbleached all-purpose
     white flour
⅔ cup whole wheat flour
6½ tablespoons packed light or
     dark brown sugar
1½ teaspoons baking powder
½ teaspoon salt
¼ cup peanut oil or other flavorless
     low-saturated-fat vegetable oil
¾ cup smooth or chunky peanut
     butter
2 tablespoons molasses
4 tablespoons turbinado sugar or
     other plain coarse crystal sugar
     for garnish
1 cup finely chopped, roasted,
     salted peanuts for garnish

Tip

The recipe is designed for
"mainstream" palates, but, if you
wish, you can trim back the salt
and sugar slightly and increase the
whole wheat flour a bit, too. Cutting
back on the peanuts will reduce the
fat but also the protein, and it's the
protein that makes them a more
substantial, hunger-curbing snack.

SWEET & SALTY PEANUT CRISPS

These crisps are really a cross between cookies and crackers—though slightly sweet, they are thin and rectangular like crackers, and, crunchy-crisp.

Baking Preliminaries: Position a rack in the middle of the oven; preheat to 350°F. Set out two large baking sheets; four long sheets of baking parchment; and a very large rimmed pan lined with parchment.

In a large bowl, stir together the white and whole wheat flours, the brown sugar, baking powder, and salt until well blended; mash out any sugar lumps with the back of the spoon. Whisk together the oil, peanut butter, molasses, and a scant ⅔ cup warm water in a small deep bowl until very well blended and smooth. Immediately stir the mixture into the flour mixture until evenly incorporated. If the dough is dry, stir in enough more water until the mixture holds together when pinched between fingertips. If very soft, work in up to 3 tablespoons more flour to stiffen it slightly.

Divide the dough in half. Roll out each portion between sheets of baking parchment into a (thin) 12-inch square. If necessary, cut and patch it to make the sides fairly even. Peel off the top sheets of parchment. Sprinkle each layer evenly with 1 tablespoon coarse sugar and one-quarter of the peanuts. Lay the parchment back on the dough, then roll with the pin to imbed the garnishes. Turn over the dough, peel off the top sheets, repeat the steps on the second sides. Discard the top sheets of parchment.

Using a pizza cutter or a large knife, cut each sheet of dough lengthwise and crosswise into 9 or 10 equal strips to form a grid of squares (with uneven edges all around). Slide the paper and dough (leave the scraps in place) onto the baking sheets.

Bake (middle rack) one pan at a time for 15 to 18 minutes or until the dough sheets are set but still not firm in the center. Set aside to cool. Reset the oven to 225°F.

When the crisps are cool enough to handle, discard the edges and scraps (or nibble on them!). Separate the squares; spread them on the rimmed pan. Toast (middle rack) for 20 minutes; gently stir to redistribute halfway through. Turn off the oven; let the crisps stand in the oven for 20 to 30 minutes more. Then remove them from the oven and let stand until completely cooled.

Yield: Makes about one hundred 1½-inch crisps

Storage: Store these, airtight and at room temperature, for up to 2 weeks. They can be frozen, airtight, for up to 2 months.

Sweet & Crunchy Chocolate Chip Crisps (page 218) and Sweet & Salty Peanut Crisps (opposite).

¾ cup unbleached all-purpose
white flour
⅓ cup whole wheat flour
½ teaspoon salt
⅛ teaspoon ground white pepper
or black pepper
¼ cup (½ stick) unsalted butter,
softened slightly and cut into
chunks
4 ounces Stilton cheese,
crumbled or coarsely chopped,
or substitute Roquefort, if
necessary
2 tablespoons dry white wine or
water, plus more if needed
¼ cup chopped dried apricots
¼ cup sweetened dried cranberries
1½ cups chopped walnuts, toasted*,
plus ½ cup chopped
(untoasted) walnuts for garnish

Tip
The flecks of color from the apricots
and cranberries make these very
attractive. They are nice with
cocktails, even better with wine.

Tip
Since these are slice-and-bakes,
the dough can be made ahead,
then readied when you need some
memorable munchies.

FRUITED STILTON-WALNUT COCKTAIL COOKIES

Stilton, walnuts, and fruit are often paired, and these rich, slightly crisp cookies underscore why the combination is a classic: The sharp edge of the cheese; the nutty, mellow taste and crunch of the walnuts; and the sweet-tartness of the fruit balance one another beautifully.

In a food processor, combine the flours, salt, pepper, butter, and cheese. Process in pulses until the ingredients are well blended and the mixture is crumbly. Drizzle the wine over the flour mixture; pulse just until the dough begins to come together and mass. If necessary, add a little more wine, pulsing until the dough holds together smoothly. Turn it out onto a large sheet of wax paper.

With greased hands, work the fruit and 1½ cup walnuts into the dough until evenly incorporated. Divide it in half. Place each on a long sheet of plastic wrap. Roll each portion into a 2 by 8-inch evenly thick log; use the plastic wrap to aid in forming the logs. Stretch out the logs until evenly thick.

Sprinkle each log with ¼ cup walnuts, turning to coat all over. Press down to embed the nuts. Twist the ends of the plastic wrap to keep the logs from unrolling. Slit two discarded paper towel tubes lengthwise and slip the logs into them. Secure the tubes with tape. Freeze for at least 1 hour or until very firm. (Or freeze the logs airtight for up to 3 months; thaw slightly before using.)

Baking Preliminaries: Position a rack in the middle of the oven; preheat to 375°F. Grease several large baking sheets or line with baking parchment.

Using a sharp knife and working with one chilled log at time, slice crosswise into ¼-inch-thick rounds. To keep the log round, rotate it a quarter turn after each slice. Space about 1½ inches apart on the baking sheets. Bake for 8 to 10 minutes, until golden all over and just slightly darker at the edges. Cool for 5 minutes; then transfer to a wire rack. Let cool thoroughly.

Yield: Makes about fifty 2-inch slices

Storage: Store these, airtight, at room temperature for up to 1 week. They can be frozen, airtight, for up to 1 month.

*To toast the walnuts: Place in a preheated 325°F oven, stirring frequently until fragrant and tinged, about 10 minutes.

4 ounces chèvre cheese, slightly softened and cut into chunks

¾ cup (1½ sticks) unsalted butter, slightly softened and cut into chunks

1½ teaspoons granulated sugar

1 large egg, at room temperature and beaten with a fork

2 tablespoons finely chopped fresh chives or 1 tablespoon dried chives, plus more for garnish

1 tablespoon dried tarragon leaves or 2½ tablespoons finely chopped fresh tarragon leaves (stems removed)

½ teaspoon coarsely and freshly ground black pepper, plus more for garnish

½ teaspoon baking powder

1⅓ cups unbleached all-purpose white flour, plus more if needed

Tip

The dough omits salt because chèvre is often fairly salty. But if the brand you're using isn't on the salty side (take a taste to see), add ¼ teaspoon of salt (or more to taste) to the dough to bring up its flavor.

HERBED CHÈVRE NUGGETS

Rich, succulent, and savory, these have the consistency of slightly soft, very tender, buttery cookies. The combination of the chèvre and tarragon gives them an elegant flavor that I associate with classic French cuisine, partly because tarragon turns up fairly frequently in French dishes. (And maybe partly because *chèvre* means "goat" in French!)

These little nuggets are excellent served in place of traditional cheese straws—you might offer them as table hors d'oeuvres or to replace crackers or bread normally served with a bisque or cream soup.

Baking Preliminaries: Position a rack in the middle of the oven; preheat to 350°F. Generously grease several large baking sheets or coat with nonstick spray.

In a large bowl with a mixer on medium speed, beat the chèvre, butter, and sugar until very light and well blended, about 1½ minutes, scraping down the sides as needed. Add 1½ tablespoons egg; reserve the remainder for garnishing the nuggets. Add the chives, tarragon, pepper, and baking powder, then beat until well blended.

Gradually beat or stir in the flour until evenly incorporated. If the dough is too soft and sticky to shape with the hands, stir in a tablespoon or two more flour to stiffen it slightly. If necessary, let stand to firm up for 5 minutes.

On a long sheet of wax paper, divide the dough into quarters. With well-greased hands, shape each into a 10-inch-long, evenly thick rope. Cut each rope into 10 equal segments.

Space the nuggets about 2 inches apart on the baking sheets. Using a pastry brush (or a paper towel), lightly but evenly brush the tops with the remaining egg. Immediately top with a pinch of chives and grind a little black pepper over them.

Bake (middle rack) one pan at a time for 17 to 20 minutes or until the nuggets are tinged with brown all over and slightly darker at the edges. Transfer the pan to a cooling rack and let stand for 2 minutes. Using a wide spatula, transfer the nuggets to racks. Let cool until warm, then serve immediately. Alternatively, serve at room temperature, or reheat before serving until warm in a 300°F oven for about 10 minutes.

Yield: Makes forty 1½-inch nuggets

Storage: Store these, airtight, for up to 2 weeks. They can be frozen, airtight, for up to 2 months. Serve warm.

2 cups unbleached all-purpose
   white flour
¼ cup finely chopped fresh chives
1 teaspoon baking powder
½ teaspoon onion salt
½ cup (1 stick) corn oil margarine or
   other vegetable oil stick
   margarine, melted (do not use
   soft or tub-style)
1 teaspoon red, pink, or white
   coarse sea salt or coarse kosher
   salt

Tip

The original recipe was designed to
be kosher, so it calls for margarine—
which happens to work just fine and
means the crackers are also vegan. I
suppose you could substitute butter,
if desired.

Tip

The ingredient that really makes the
difference is fresh chives. Yes, you
could substitute 2 tablespoons of
freeze-dried chopped chives, but
it's better just to wait until the fresh
ones are available!

CHIVE AND ONION CRACKERS WITH SEA SALT

Considering how simple this recipe looks, you might be tempted to pass
it by. That was my reaction when a writer friend, Cronshi Englander, shared
the original version with me. But I was wrong! The resulting crispy, munchy
crackers are so much tastier than store-bought, yet they are easy, fuss-free,
and economical to make. Plus it's comforting knowing exactly what's in the
baked goods I serve. These turned me into a regular cracker baker and might
turn you into one, too!

Baking Preliminaries: Position a rack in the middle of the oven; preheat
to 350°F. Set out two very large baking sheets and four 16-inch-long
sheets of baking parchment.

In a large bowl, stir together the flour, chives, baking powder, and
onion salt until well blended. Vigorously stir in the margarine until very
well blended and smooth. Then stir in 5 tablespoons water, plus more as
needed to make the dough hold together when pinched between the
fingertips.

Divide the dough in half. Roll out each portion between baking
parchment into a 10 by 15-inch, evenly thick rectangle; the layers will be
very thin. If necessary, cut and patch to make the sides fairly even.
Peel off and discard the top sheets of parchment. Sprinkle the tops
evenly with the sea salt. Pat down all over to imbed it. Using a pizza
cutter or knife, cut each rectangle lengthwise into 4 strips and crosswise
into 8 strips to yield 32 whole wafers with scraps all around the edges.
Transfer the paper and dough (leave scraps in place) to the baking
sheets.

Bake (middle rack) one pan at a time for 13 to 15 minutes or until the
dough sheet is set but still not firm in the center. Set the pans aside until
the crackers are cool. Meanwhile, reset the oven to 275°F.

Remove and discard the scraps (or nibble on them!). Separate the
crackers, spacing slightly separated, with the underdone ones around
the outside, the more done ones in the center. Return the pan to the
oven and toast the crackers for 15 to 20 minutes, until just beginning to
be tinged with brown. Let the pan stand on a wire rack until the crackers
are cooled thoroughly, then pack them airtight.

Yield: Makes sixty-four 1¾ by 2⅓-inch crackers

Storage: Store these, airtight, for up to 10 days. They can be frozen,
airtight, for up to 1 month.

1 cup unbleached all-purpose white flour

1 cup yellow cornmeal, stone ground and not degerminated preferred

½ teaspoon onion salt or garlic salt
Generous ¼ teaspoon ground chipotle pepper or ground cayenne pepper

¼ cup corn oil or olive oil

¾ cup lightly packed shredded or grated extra-sharp cheddar cheese

1 teaspoon red, pink, or white sea salt or poppy or sesame seeds for garnish, or a combination of salt and seeds.

Tip

Some cheddars are quite salty, so taste the dough before adding the coarse salt garnish. If necessary, use half coarse salt and half seeds, or omit the salt and garnish entirely with poppy or sesame seeds.

SNAPPY CHEDDAR-CORN SNACKERS

Yes, these are reminiscent of the commercial cheese crackers out there, but they are much zippier from the chipotle and cayenne pepper and much fresher tasting. Plus, since they contain a bit of cornmeal, they are a better source of fiber and nutrients and have a more interesting texture. (The snackers are shown in a bowl on page 227).

Baking Preliminaries: Position a rack in the middle of the oven; preheat to 350°F. Set out two large baking sheets and four large sheets of baking parchment.

In a large bowl, stir together the flour, cornmeal, onion salt, and pepper until well blended. Vigorously stir in the oil and cheese until very well blended and smooth. Stir in ½ cup water, or enough more so that the dough holds together when pinched between the fingertips.

Divide the dough in half. Roll out each portion between sheets of baking parchment into a 10 by 15-inch, evenly thick rectangle; the dough will be very thin. As needed, cut and patch so dough sides are fairly even.

Peel off and discard the top sheets of parchment. Sprinkle half the coarse salt or seeds evenly over each sheet of dough. Press down lightly all over to imbed them. Using a pizza cutter or a large knife, cut each sheet lengthwise into 4 strips and crosswise into 8 strips; this will yield 32 whole wafers, plus scraps all around the edges. Transfer the parchment and dough (including the scraps) to the baking sheets.

Bake (middle rack) one sheet at a time for 15 to 18 minutes or until the dough is set but still not firm in the center. Set the pans aside until the wafers are cool enough to handle. Remove and discard the scraps. (I save them for nibbling!) Separate the crackers, spacing, slightly separated, with the more done ones in the center and the underdone ones around the outside.

Lower the oven to 300°F. Return the pan to the oven and toast the crackers for 10 to 15 minutes, until just beginning to tinge with brown. Place the pan on a wire rack and let the crackers cool thoroughly before packing airtight.

Yield: Makes sixty-four 1¾ by 2⅓-inch crackers

Storage: Store these, airtight, for up to 1 week. They can be frozen, airtight, for up to 1 month.

Easy
Easy, food processor filling.
Gourmet look
and taste.
Convenient make-ahead
recipe.

CRANBERRY & FIG CONSERVE–STUFFED BLUE & CHEDDAR CHEESE COCKTAIL SANDWICH COOKIES

Expect oohs and ahs and a quickly emptied platter when you serve these unusual semi-savory sandwich cookies; they are eye-catching, irresistibly tasty, and lend a gourmet touch to any occasion. The slightly tangy, fruity filling pairs perfectly with the slightly tender cheese-flavored cookies. Plus its bright color is pretty on a plate. Serve these at a brunch or elegant lunch, with drinks, or accompanying a vegetarian menu. (I keep fresh frozen cranberries in the freezer so I can make these year-round.)

To ready the sandwiches, you'll need a batch of the wafers on page 228. Then make the cranberry and fig conserve and complete the sandwiches as directed below. They can be readied completely in advance and frozen, or assembled up to two days ahead and stored airtight at room temperature.

1 cup trimmed and coarsely
   chopped dried Calimyrna figs
1 cup chopped fresh (or frozen,
   thawed) cranberries
¼ cup clover honey or other mild
   honey
1 batch Blue & Cheddar Cheese
   Wafers with Sea Salt (page 228),
   previously baked and ready
   to use

In a food processor, process the figs and cranberries until the fruits are finely chopped but not pureed. Stir the mixture together with the honey and 3 tablespoons water in a medium, heavy, nonreactive saucepan. Cook over medium heat, stirring, until the mixture just comes to a boil. Cook, stirring, for 1 minute, then set aside until cooled. (The conserve may be covered and refrigerated in a nonreactive container for up to 1 week; let return to room temperature before using.)

Arrange half the wafers underside up. Stir the conserves, adding in a few teaspoons of warm water until spreadable if the mixture seems dry or crumbly. Center about a teaspoon of conserve on each wafer, then top with another wafer (top side visible), pressing down till the preserves just spread out to the edges.

Serve immediately or store, airtight, until ready to serve; they will soften some but will still be good. They may be made ahead and frozen; serve at room temperature.

Yield: Makes about thirty 2-inch sandwich cookies

Storage: Store these, airtight, for up to 2 days. They can be frozen, airtight, for up to 1 month.

The crackers shown in the background of this picture are Snappy Cheddar-Corn Snackers (page 225)

Easy
Easy food
processor mixing.
Gourmet yet easy.
Make ahead recipe.

1   tablespoon granulated sugar
4   ounces blue cheese, slightly
     softened and cut into chunks
2   ounces sharp cheddar cheese,
     cut into small pieces
½   cup (1 stick) unsalted butter,
     slightly softened and cut into
     chunks
1   large egg
½   teaspoon baking powder
1½ cups unbleached all-purpose
     white flour, plus more if
     needed
     Red, pink, or white coarse-
     crystal sea salt for garnish,
     or substitute poppy or sesame
     seeds, if the dough is salty

Tip

Tuck pairs of these wafers around
a simple fig-cranberry conserve to
produce the stunning little cocktail
sandwiches on page 226.

BLUE & CHEDDAR CHEESE WAFERS WITH SEA SALT (OR SEEDS)

These rich, tender cheese rounds are another great example of how the line between cookies and crackers is now blurring. They definitely have the consistency of rich, buttery cookies, yet they are salty and savory, not sweet. They are great for serving with cocktails.

In a food processor, process the sugar, blue cheese, cheddar, butter, egg, and baking powder until very well blended, about 1½ minutes, stopping and scraping down the sides as needed. Add 1 cup flour, pulsing 10 to 12 times until partially incorporated.

Turn out the mixture onto wax paper. Fully knead in the remaining flour. If the dough is very soft, knead in up to 3 tablespoons more flour; if still soft, let it firm up for 5 minutes.

Divide the dough in half. On wax paper, using greased hands, shape each half into a 9-inch-long, evenly thick log. Stretch it out until evenly thick. Roll up each log in plastic wrap, twisting the ends to close. For nicely rounded wafers, slip each log into a paper towel tube that has been slit lengthwise. Secure the tube with rubber bands.

Freeze the dough logs for at least 45 minutes or until just firm enough to cut neatly. Or pack in freezer bags and freeze for up to 3 months. Let frozen logs soften at room temperature for about 15 minutes before slicing.

Baking Preliminaries: Position a rack in the middle of the oven; preheat to 350°F. Line several large baking sheets with baking parchment.

Cut each partially thawed log crosswise into ¼-inch-thick slices using a very sharp knife. Turn the log a quarter turn after each slice to keep it round. Space the wafers about 1½ inches apart on the baking sheets. Garnish the wafer tops with a few grains of coarse salt, patting down lightly.

Bake (middle rack) one pan at a time for 11 to 15 minutes or until the wafers are lightly browned at the edges. Place the pans on cooling racks; let stand for 2 minutes. Using a wide spatula, gently transfer the wafers to racks. Let cool completely.

Yield: Makes sixty to seventy 2-inch wafers

Storage: Store these, airtight, for up to 10 days. They can be frozen, airtight, for up to 2 months.

2 cups unbleached all-purpose
   white flour
¼ teaspoon baking powder
2 teaspoons ground paprika
   Scant 1 teaspoon garlic salt
1 teaspoon dried thyme leaves
1 teaspoon dried oregano leaves
¼ teaspoon ground cayenne
   pepper
¼ teaspoon ground black pepper
⅓ cup good-quality olive oil
½ teaspoon red or white coarse
   crystal sea salt or kosher salt

CAJUN PEPPER STICKS

These attractive nibbles are very long and thin (like some breadsticks), with a cracker-like consistency and a definite pepper kick. They look particularly appetizing served standing upright in a short, wide-mouthed cocktail glass or small jar.

The herb-spice blend is very similar to the one used in blackened fish seasoning, so they have that familiar appealing Cajun-style aroma and taste. The sticks are great with beer or cocktails, as well as with very flavorful soups. Other pluses: They are easy, fairly low-fat, vegan, and quite economical.

Baking Preliminaries: Position a rack in the middle of the oven; preheat to 350°F. Set out two large baking sheets and four sheets of baking parchment.

In a large bowl, stir together the flour and baking powder. In a small bowl, stir together the paprika, garlic salt, thyme leaves, oregano leaves, cayenne pepper, and black pepper. Reserve 2 teaspoons spice mixture for garnish. Stir the remainder into the flour mixture. Thoroughly stir the oil and ¼ cup water into the flour mixture until blended; if desired, finish the mixing by kneading with well-oiled hands.

Divide the dough in half. Roll out each portion between sheets of baking parchment into a 10-inch evenly thick square; the layers will be thin. If necessary, cut and patch the squares to make the sides fairly even. Peel off the top layer of parchment. Sprinkle ½ teaspoon reserved spice blend and ⅛ teaspoon salt crystals evenly over one portion of dough. Replace the parchment, then roll the pin back and forth to embed the seasonings. Invert the dough and peel off the second sheet. Sprinkle evenly with ½ teaspoon spice blend and ⅛ teaspoon coarse crystal salt. Press down the seasonings by rolling over the sheet, then discard the sheet. Repeat the procedure with the second dough portion.

Using a pizza cutter or a large chef's knife, trim off the edges to make the portions perfectly square, but leave the trimmings in place. Then cut each portion into long, ¼-inch-wide sticks; try not to dislodge the sticks or cut through the paper. Transfer the paper and dough to baking sheets.

Bake (middle rack) one pan at a time for 13 to 15 minutes or until the dough is set but still not firm in the center. Set the pans aside until the sticks are cool and firm enough to handle. Meanwhile, reset the oven to 300°F.

Gently separate the sticks, discarding the trimmings (or save them for nibbling). Return the sticks to the pan, slightly separated; place any underdone sticks around the outside and more done ones in the center. Return the pan to the oven and toast for 10 to 15 minutes, until they just begin to be tinged with brown. Let the pan stand on a wire rack until the sticks are cooled thoroughly, then pack them airtight.

Yield: Makes about 80 thin, 9½-inch-long sticks

Storage: Store these, airtight, for up to 10 days. They can be frozen, airtight in a sturdy container, for up to 1½ months.

Fairly Easy
Quick one-bowl mixing.
Convenient make-ahead.

3 large eggs, at room temperature
3½ tablespoons snipped or chopped
    fresh chives
3 tablespoons finely chopped
    fresh rosemary (coarse stems
    removed)
1 teaspoon baking powder
½ teaspoon onion salt or garlic salt
½ teaspoon very coarsely ground
    or crushed black peppercorns
    or gourmet (green, black,
    pink, and so forth) peppercorn
    blend
1 cup white whole wheat flour or
    regular whole wheat flour
½ cup chopped and well-drained
    oil-cured black olives
1½ cups unbleached all-purpose
    white flour
½ cup pistachios or slivered
    almonds, or a combination,
    optional
    About ½ teaspoon paprika or
    smoked paprika for garnish

Tip
Be sure to use oil-cured black olives:
The more common brine-cured
olives have a higher moisture
content, and the resulting biscotti
will not come out crisp.

OIL-CURED BLACK OLIVE AND BLACK PEPPER BISCOTTI

These biscotti have a savory-salty taste and pleasant crunchiness that make them perfect munchies for serving with cocktails, wine, or beer. The olive and rosemary flavor combination also means they pair well with an Italian-style meal; I like to serve them in place of grissini or other breadsticks. The nuts add a little crunch and visual interest, but they may be omitted if you can't eat nuts.

Baking Preliminaries: Position a rack in the middle of the oven; preheat to 375°F. Line a large baking sheet with parchment paper.

In a large bowl, whisk together the eggs, chives, rosemary, baking powder, onion salt, and pepper until well blended. Add the whole wheat flour, ½ cup water, and olives, stirring until smoothly incorporated. Stir in the white flour and nuts (if using) until evenly incorporated. If desired, work in the last of the flour with your hands. If the dough is crumbly, work in up to 4 teaspoons water as needed; if it is very soft, work in up to 2 tablespoons more flour. Divide the dough in half.

Working on the parchment-lined sheet, with lightly oiled hands, shape each half into a 3 by 9-inch, evenly thick loaf; space them as far apart as possible. Flatten them slightly. Sprinkle each lightly with paprika. Bake (middle rack) for 25 to 30 minutes until the tops spring back when pressed in the thickest part. Set aside until cooled to warm, about 30 minutes. On a cutting board, cut each loaf on a sharp diagonal into long, ¼-inch-thick slices using a large serrated knife or large sharp chef's knife. Lay the slices flat on a parchment-lined baking sheet. Meanwhile, reheat the oven to 325°F.

Bake the slices until toasted and faintly tinged with brown, 18 to 20 minutes. Turn off the oven and let the biscotti toast and dry out for 10 to 15 minutes more. Transfer the biscotti to wire racks. Let cool completely.

Yield: Makes thirty-five to forty 4- to 6-inch biscotti

Storage: Store these, airtight and at room temperature, for up to 1 week. They can be frozen, airtight, for up to 1½ months.

Variation: Oil-Cured Black Olive, Tomato, and Black Pepper Biscotti
Add ½ teaspoon paprika along with the peppercorns. Mix in 2 tablespoons very well-drained, finely chopped oil-packed sun-dried tomatoes when the olives are added. Proceed as directed.

½ cup (1 stick) unsalted butter,
   slightly softened but still cool,
   cut into chunks

1 3-ounce package cream
   cheese, cool and cut into
   chunks

¼ teaspoon baking soda

¼ teaspoon onion salt

¼ teaspoon smoked paprika or
   regular paprika

¼ cup well-drained and chopped
   oil-packed sun-dried tomatoes

1¾ cups unbleached all-purpose
   white flour, plus more if
   needed

¾ cup coarsely chopped pitted
   Kalamata olives, rinsed,
   drained, and patted dry

3 tablespoons chopped fresh
   chives or finely chopped
   scallions

3 tablespoons extra-virgin olive oil

1 large egg beaten with 1 tablespoon milk for garnish
   About 2 teaspoons poppy seeds
   or black sesame seeds for
   garnish

SAVORY SUN-DRIED TOMATO & TAPENADE COCKTAIL RUGELACH

The idea of creating a savory instead of the usual sweet rugelach may seem over the top at first, but these roll-ups turn out to be attractive, wonderfully savory, and satisfying as appetizers, snacks, and accompaniments for soups. The sun-dried tomatoes and paprika give the easy-to-handle dough a distinctive terra-cotta hue, and the black olives in the tapenade filling lend both rich, hearty flavor and eye-catching contrasting color. These cocktail rugelach can be made well ahead and so are great for entertaining.

These go together fairly quickly, but if you're in a huge hurry, substitute a purchased tapenade. You'll need about 1 cup. Or, substitute a good-quality store-bought sun-dried tomato and green olive bruschetta spread in place of the tapenade.

Preliminaries: Set out a large tray or baking sheet. Set out four squares of baking parchment.

In a food processor, process the butter, cream cheese, baking soda, onion salt, and paprika until well blended. Add the tomatoes; pulse until they are evenly incorporated and finely chopped. Sprinkle over 1 cup flour; pulse until evenly incorporated, scraping down the bowl if necessary. Sprinkle half the remaining flour onto a sheet of wax paper. Turn out the dough onto the paper, then knead in the remaining flour just enough to form a smooth dough. If it is dry, work in up to 3 or 4 teaspoons water until it holds together; if too soft, work in up to 2 tablespoons more flour.

Divide the dough in half. Roll each portion out into a 12-inch-diameter round between sheets of baking parchment; the dough doesn't have to be perfectly round. Check the underside and smooth out any wrinkles. Lay the dough (paper attached) on the tray or sheet. Refrigerate until cool and firm, at least 20 minutes or (covered) up to 24 hours, if desired.

In a clean food processor, process the olives, chives, and olive oil until the olives are coarsely pureed. The tapenade may be readied up to 3 days ahead, covered, and refrigerated in a nonreactive container, if desired. Let warm to room temperature before using.

Baking Preliminaries: Position a rack in the middle of the oven; preheat to 350°F. Line two large baking sheets with baking parchment.

Working with one dough round at a time, peel off the top sheet of parchment, then pat it back into place. Turn over the dough; peel off and discard the second sheet. Using half the filling (no need to measure),

If you don't need to go vegetarian
and want even more substantial
appetizers, simply sprinkle ¼ cup
finely crumbled bacon or diced lean
cooked ham over the tapenade
on each round before cutting and
rolling up the rugelach. Don't use
very salty ham, as tapenade is
usually already fairly salty.

Tip

For a picture showing how these
and other rugelach are formed, see
page 138.

spread it evenly to within ¼ inch of the edge; the layer will be very thin.
Using a pizza cutter or large sharp knife, cut the round into quarters,
then eighths, then sixteenths.

While the dough is still cool and slightly firm, working from the outside
edge, roll up each wedge as though preparing a crescent roll. Space the
rugelach, with ends underneath to prevent unrolling, about 2 inches
apart on the baking sheets. Lightly but evenly brush the tops with the
egg wash, then sprinkle each with a pinch of seeds. Repeat the process
with the remaining round.

Bake (middle rack) one sheet at a time for 18 to 22 minutes or until
the rugelach are well browned; don't underbake. Let the pans cool on
wire racks until the rugelach firm up, about 3 minutes. Then transfer
them to racks using a wide spatula. Serve warm or at room temperature.
Thoroughly cool on wire racks before packing for storage.

Yield: Makes thirty-two 2¾-inch-long rugelach

Storage: Store these, airtight, for up to 2 days; the rugelach tend to lose
their crispness upon longer standing. They can be frozen, airtight, for up
to 1 month. They are best rewarmed in a 300°F oven before serving.

COOKIES-IN-JARS MIXES & BARS-IN-JARS MIXES }

Several decades ago, someone gave me my first container of bars-in-jars mix. The look of the ingredients neatly layered in the pretty glass apothecary jar was striking and reminded me of sand art creations. I also loved the convenience of dumping the contents into a bowl and making bars merely by stirring in some butter and an egg. In essence, the jars were just handsomely packaged convenience mixes—except that the ingredients were fresh and fine quality and the resulting goodies tasted homemade. (I often keep a jar handy so I can quickly make a treat for my own family.)

I've been creating my own bars-in-jars and cookies-in-jars recipes and giving them out ever since. They make thoughtful, eagerly received presents for all sorts of occasions. The jars of mix are siimple to assemble, so young children can help. Older kids can make their own personal kitchen gifts (and may be quite proud of this accomplishment!). If the ingredients are bought in bulk and presented in recycled jars, they are budget friendly. Note that the recipes in this chapter all require either 1-quart or 1-liter jars—32-ounce mayo and spaghetti

sauce jars are perfect, as are leftover 1-quart canning jars. And remember that you'll need to furnish a recipe or sheet providing the mixing and baking directions along with every jar.

Of course, it's possible to purchase decorative storage canisters to further enhance your bars-in-jars gifts. Wide-mouth containers can even serve as a cookie jar once the goodies are made. But if you want to go this route, be sure to shop well in advance of the holidays, as most suitable containers get snapped up long before the fall baking season begins.

For some reason, most of the mix recipes in circulation are for comfort-food cookies—like the chocolate chip drops, cowboy cookies, and brownies in this chapter. But you'll see the repertoire here also includes some less familiar offerings such as the Spiced Apple-Oatmeal Cookies-in-a-Jar Mix or the even more unusual Cherry-Berry Biscotti-in-a-Jar Mix and Mocha-Hazelnut Biscotti-in-a-Jar Mix, which are much more sophisticated and better suited to a recipient with gourmet tastes.

1⅔ cups unbleached all-purpose
   white flour
1 teaspoon baking powder
½ teaspoon salt
⅔ cup granulated sugar
⅓ cup packed light or dark brown
   sugar
1¼ cups (about 7½ ounces)
   semisweet chocolate morsels

CHOCOLATE CHIP DROP COOKIES-IN-A-JAR MIX

Here is the classic chocolate chip cookie presented in layered gift mix form. A jar makes a thoughtful present for a friend, relative, or special teacher, but it can also serve as an emergency kit when you want a quick treat for yourself or must quickly whip up a pan of bake-and-take sweets.

Preliminaries: Set out a clear 1-quart or 1-liter jar, and its lid. Set out a square of heavy-duty aluminum foil to use as a funnel. (Or, use a funnel.) Center the flour, baking powder, and salt on the foil. Stir until well blended. Using the foil as a funnel, add the mixture to the jar. Rap it on the counter to even the layer.

Thoroughly stir together the granulated and brown sugars on the foil; don't worry if they aren't completely smooth. Add to the jar; lightly press down the layer using a rubber spatula. Wipe down the jar sides, if necessary. Add the chocolate morsels, pressing them down. If shipping the jar, firmly stuff the top with crumpled wax paper. Secure the lid. Attach the recipe instructions to the jar.

Yield: Makes 1 quart of mix, enough for about twenty-five 2½-inch cookies

Storage: Keep mix 1 month, unrefrigerated, 2 months refrigerated.

Instructions to provide with the jar:
CHOCOLATE CHIP DROP COOKIES

¾ cup (1½ sticks) unsalted butter,
   very soft but not melted
1 large egg, beaten with 1
   tablespoon water
2½ teaspoons vanilla extract
1 1-quart jar Mix

Preheat the oven to 350°F. Grease several baking sheets. In a large bowl using a large spoon or a mixer, stir or beat the butter until lightened in color and fluffy. Vigorously stir or beat in the egg-water mixture and vanilla until evenly incorporated. Thoroughly stir in the the contents. Using a heaping soupspoon, drop the dough into 1½-inch mounds, spacing about 2½ inches apart on sheets.

Bake (middle rack) for 7 to 10 minutes or until nicely browned and barely firm when pressed in the center tops; don't overbake. Let the pans cool 5 minutes, then thoroughly cool cookies on racks.

Yield: Makes about twenty-five 2½-inch cookies

Storage: Store these, airtight, for up to 4 days. Or freeze, airtight, for up to 1 month.

Easy
Great kitchen gift mix.
Extra-easy one-
bowl brownies.

- 1 cup unbleached all-purpose white flour
- ½ cup unsweetened natural (non-alkalized) cocoa powder or Dutch-process cocoa powder
- 1 cup granulated sugar
- ¼ teaspoon baking soda
- ¼ teaspoon salt
- 1½ cups (9 ounces) semisweet or bittersweet chocolate morsels, divided

- ½ cup (1 stick) unsalted butter, very soft but not melted
  One 1-quart jar Mix
- 3 large eggs lightly beaten with 2 tablespoons cold water

FUDGY CHOCOLATE CHIP BROWNIE BARS-IN-A-JAR MIX

Jars of brownie mix are fun to make up and easy enough that older kids can do it on their own and younger ones can help.

Preliminaries: Have ready a clear glass, 1-quart or 1-liter jar, and its lid. Set out a square of heavy-duty aluminum foil to use as a funnel. (Or use a funnel.)

Put the flour on the foil. Using the foil as a funnel, put the flour in the jar. Rap the jar to even the layer. In a food processor, process the cocoa powder, sugar, baking soda, salt, and ¾ cup chocolate morsels until the morsels are finely chopped. Put the cocoa mixture on the foil, then add to the jar. Rap it again. Add the remaining chocolate morsels to the jar, pressing down. If shipping the jar, firmly stuff the top with crumpled wax paper. Secure the lid. Attach a card with the recipe instructions to the jar.

Yield: Makes 1 quart of mix, enough for 16 brownies

Storage: Keep mix 1½ months, unrefrigerated, 3 months refrigerated.

Instructions to provide with the jar:
FUDGY BROWNIE BARS

Preheat the oven to 350°F. Line an 8-inch square pan with nonstick foil, letting it overhang two sides. Vigorously stir the butter and the jar of mix together until evenly incorporated; the mixture will be dry. Thoroughly stir in the egg-water mixture until very well blended. Turn it out into the pan, smoothing out until evenly thick.

Bake (middle rack) for 25 to 35 minutes or until a toothpick inserted in the center comes out clean. Let cool, then refrigerate until firm. Using the overhanging foil, transfer the brownie slab to a cutting board. Peel off the foil. Cut the slab into 16 squares using a sharp knife; trim off and discard the edges, if desired.

Yield: Makes 16 squares

Storage: Store these, airtight and at room temperature, for up to 3 days. Or freeze, airtight, for up to 2 months.

Attractive gift kit.
Easy, economical,
versatile recipe.

SPICED APPLE-OATMEAL COOKIES-IN-A-JAR MIX

If you want or need to prepare a gift jar that doesn't contain chocolate, this homespun, spiced apple-oatmeal cookie mix is a great choice. The cookies are highly aromatic, moist, and satisfying, and also quietly handsome.

The recipe seems particularly appropriate for autumn occasions, but this can be turned into a holiday cookie mix gift simply by using a cranberry-apple blend instead of all apples. This, of course, looks more colorful in a jar and yields more festive looking cookies.

Be sure to chop the dried apples finely—once they hydrate, they will be larger than you expect.

1   cup plus 2 tablespoons
     unbleached all-purpose white
     flour
1   cup granulated sugar
1½ teaspoons ground cinnamon
¾   teaspoon ground allspice or
     ½ teaspoon ground nutmeg
½   teaspoon baking soda
¼   teaspoon salt
1½ cups old-fashioned rolled oats
⅔   cup finely chopped dried apples

Preliminaries: Have ready a clear 1-quart or 1-liter jar, and its lid. Set out a square of suitable heavy-duty aluminum foil to use as a funnel. (If you have a funnel substitute that!)

Put the flour on the foil. Using the foil as a funnel, put the flour in the jar. Rap the jar on the counter. On the same sheet, thoroughly stir together the sugar, cinnamon, allspice, baking soda, and salt. Using the foil, add the sugar mixture to the jar. Rap the jar. Add the rolled oats, rapping, then pressing down firmly, to compact the layer. Put the dried apples (and cranberries) in a small plastic bag; close it tightly. Tuck the bag in the top of the jar; don't mash down the apples. Secure the lid. Attach a card with the cookie baking instructions to the jar.

Yield: Makes 1 quart of mix, enough for about 30 cookies

Storage: Keep 2 months, unrefrigerated, 4 months refrigerated.

Instructions to provide with the jar:
SPICED APPLE-OATMEAL COOKIES

1   1-quart jar Mix
½   cup (1 stick) unsalted butter,
     soft but not melted
1   large egg, at room
     temperature

Depending on the amount of moisture in the dried fruit (this can vary), the cookies may spread a good bit or not very much—but they are yummy either way.

Preheat the oven to 350°F. Grease several baking sheets or coat with nonstick spray. Vigorously stir the fruit from the mix into the butter, then stir in the egg. Let stand for 5 minutes, so the fruit can plump up from the moisture. Vigorously stir in the entire jar of mix. If the mixture is dry and crumbly, thoroughly stir in up to 2 tablespoons water. Using a heaping 1-tablespoon measuring spoon, drop the dough onto the

Cookie Jar Wisdom
Baking cookies every day won't keep anyone away—in fact, they'll come running.

sheets, spacing 2½ inches apart.

Bake (middle rack) one pan at a time for 10 to 12 minutes or until barely firm on top and browned at the edges. Let stand on the pans for 3 minutes, then transfer the cookies to wire racks. Let cool.

Yield: Makes about 30 cookies

Storage: Store these, airtight, for 2 to 3 days. Or freeze, airtight, for up to 2 months.

Variation: Apple-Cranberry-Oatmeal Cookies In-A-Jar Use ⅓ cup each finely chopped dried apples and chopped dried sweetened cranberries. Proceed exactly as directed.

1¼ cups unbleached all-purpose
white flour
Scant ¼ teaspoon baking soda
¼ teaspoon salt
⅔ cup minus 1 tablespoon
granulated sugar
¼ cup packed light brown sugar
Generous ¾ cup old-fashioned
rolled oats
¼ cup coarsely chopped Heath bars
or ready-to-use Heath bar
crunch
1 cup (6 ounces) semisweet
chocolate morsels

½ cup plus 2 tablespoons
(1¼ sticks) unsalted butter, soft
but not melted
1 1-quart jar Mix
1 large egg beaten with
1½ tablespoons water

COWBOY COOKIES-IN-A-JAR MIX

I have searched and searched, but I haven't found any explanation for the name "cowboy cookies," although it's a good bet cowboys (and most everybody else!) will like these rich, chewy-crisp rounds. What I have determined is that cookies with this name usually include chocolate chips, and rolled oats, and, sometimes, nuts.

Preliminaries: Have ready a clear glass 1-quart or 1-liter jar, and its lid. Set out a square of heavy-duty aluminum foil to use as a funnel. (Or use a funnel.)

Put the flour, baking soda, and salt on the foil. Use the foil as a funnel to pour the flour mixture into the jar. Rap the jar on the counter to even the layer. On the same sheet of foil, thoroughly stir together the granulated and brown sugars, don't worry if they aren't completely blended. Add the sugar mixture to the jar. Rap the jar. Stir together the oats and chopped Heath bars on the foil. Add to the jar, pressing down to even the layer. Add the chocolate morsels, pressing down so they fit.

If shipping the jar, stuff the top with crumpled wax paper. Secure the lid. Attach the recipe card to the jar.

Yield: Makes 1 quart of mix, enough for about twenty-five 3-inch cookies

Storage: Keep 2 months, unrefrigerated, 4 months refrigerated.

Instructions to provide with the jar:
COWBOY COOKIES

Preheat the oven to 350°F. Grease several baking sheets or coat with nonstick spray. Stir the butter and the jar of mix together vigorously until well blended. Vigorously stir in the egg-water mixture until evenly incorporated. Let the dough stand for about 5 minutes. Using a heaping measuring tablespoon, drop dough into 1½-inch mounds; space about 2½ inches apart.

Bake (middle rack) one pan at a time for 7 to 10 minutes or until barely firm on top, tinged with brown, and darker at the edges. Let stand on the pans for 3 minutes, then transfer to wire racks. Cool completely.

Yield: Makes about twenty-five 3-inch cookies

Storage: Store these, airtight, for 2 to 3 days. Or freeze, airtight, for up to 2 months.

Cowboy Cookies in a Jar

1 cup unbleached all-purpose
   white flour
½ teaspoon baking powder
¼ teaspoon salt
¾ cup granulated sugar
1 tablespoon unsweetened
   natural (non-alkalized) cocoa
   powder or Dutch-process
   cocoa powder, sifted after
   measuring, if lumpy
1 cup semisweet chocolate
   morsels, plus ½ cup more for
   garnish
⅔ cup chopped pecans or
   walnuts, or substitute white
   chocolate morsels

1 1-quart jar Mix
½ cup (1 stick) unsalted butter,
   very soft but not melted
1 large egg, at room
   temperature

CHOCOLATE-GLAZED CHOCOLATE CHIP BARS-IN-A-JAR MIX

This mix recipe yields a quick batch of yummy chocolate–chocolate chip bars that are topped with a pure chocolate glaze. Give the jar of mix as a gift, or keep it to make up your own quick treat.

Preliminaries: Have ready a clear 1-quart or 1-liter jar, and its lid. Set out a square of heavy-duty aluminum foil to use as a funnel. (Or use a funnel.)

Thoroughly stir together the flour, baking powder, and salt on the foil. Pour the mixture into the jar. Rap the jar on the counter. On the same sheet, thoroughly stir together the sugar and cocoa powder. Add the sugar mixture to the jar. Rap the jar several times. Wipe down the jar sides, if necessary. Continue layering, adding 1 cup chocolate morsels, then the nuts, rapping the jar after each. Put the remaining ½ cup chocolate morsels in a small plastic bag. Label the bag: "Glaze—to add after baking." Tuck the bag in the top. Secure the lid. Attach a card with the recipe instructions to the jar.

Yield: Makes 1 quart of mix, enough for sixteen 2-inch bars

Storage: Keep mix 1½ months, unrefrigerated, 3 months refrigerated.

Instructions to provide with the jar:
CHOCOLATE-GLAZED CHOCOLATE CHIP BARS

Preheat the oven to 350°F. Grease a 7 by 11-inch (or 9-inch square) baking pan. Remove the small bag of chocolate morsels, set aside to use for the glaze. Using a large spoon, vigorously stir together the butter, egg, and the jar of mix until thoroughly blended.

Spread the mixture evenly in the baking pan. Bake (middle rack) for 20 to 25 minutes, until barely firm on top and a toothpick inserted in the center comes out clean. Set aside and let cool for 5 minutes. Then sprinkle the remaining chocolate morsels over the top. Let stand to melt, 2 to 3 minutes, then spread them out using a table knife; they won't completely cover the surface. Cool well before cutting.

Yield: Makes sixteen 2-inch bars

Storage: Store, covered, up to 3 days. Or freeze, airtight, for 3 weeks.

Easy
Chic, sophisticated
cookie mix gift.
Special, fuss-free
gourmet biscotti.

1½ cups unbleached all-purpose
   white flour
½ teaspoon baking powder
   Scant ½ teaspoon salt
   Generous ½ cup granulated
   sugar
¼ teaspoon ground cinnamon
1 cup coarsely chopped slivered
   almonds
1 cup coarsely chopped
   sweetened dried cherries
⅔ cup coarsely chopped freeze-
   dried raspberries

1 large egg, plus 2 large egg
   whites
2 tablespoons corn oil, canola
   oil, or other flavorless
   vegetable oil
1¼ teaspoons vanilla extract
½ teaspoon almond extract or
   lemon extract, optional
1 1-quart jar Mix

CHERRY-BERRY BISCOTTI-IN-A-JAR MIX

This is a twist on the typical "bars-in-jars" gift recipes featuring ingredients that conveniently bake up into bars or drop cookies. Instead of yielding homey sweets, this mix produces biscotti and appeals to more sophisticated tastes.

A jar of this mix makes a festive, thoughtful gift for a gourmet and is quite doable for even the baker new to making biscotti. Note that the recipe calls for freeze-dried raspberries—the Just Raspberries brand (from the Just Tomatoes Etc! company) is the best known and has excellent flavor. It is available at some supermarkets and many gourmet and health food stores.

Preliminaries: Set out a clear glass, 1-quart or 1-liter jar, and its lid. Set out a square of heavy-duty aluminum foil to use as a funnel. (Or use a funnel.)

Center the flour, baking powder, and salt on the foil. Thoroughly stir together. Using the foil as a funnel, pour into the jar. Rap, the jar on the counter. Thoroughly stir together the sugar and cinnamon on the foil. Add to the jar; then rap it to even the layer. Wipe down the jar sides, if necessary. Add the almonds, cherries, then the raspberries, to the jar. Rap the jar to even the surface. If the jar will be shipped, firmly stuff the top with crumpled wax paper. Secure the lid. Attach a recipe tag or card to the jar.

Yield: Makes 1 quart of mix, enough for 25 to 30 biscotti

Storage: Keep mix 1 month, unrefrigerated, 2 months refrigerated.

Instructions to provide with the jar:
CHERRY-BERRY BISCOTTI

This mix makes biscotti that are not too sweet and are just slightly crispy-crunchy, with enticing bursts of cherry, raspberry, and almond flavor throughout. Great with coffee or tea.

Preheat the oven to 350°F. Line two 4½ by 9-inch (or similar) loaf pans with foil. Grease the foil. In a large bowl, beat together the egg and whites, oil, vanilla, and extracts. Gradually stir in all the jar ingredients until well blended. Divide the dough in half; smooth each half evenly into a loaf pan using a lightly greased rubber spatula or table knife. (If only one pan is available, bake one pan at a time.)

Bake (middle rack) for 25 to 30 minutes or until golden on top and just firm when pressed in the center top. Set the pans aside until cool; then refrigerate until well chilled to make cutting easier.

Reset the oven to 325°F. Remove the biscotti loaves from the pans; transfer to a cutting board. Cut crosswise into ¼- to ⅓-inch-thick slices using a large serrated knife or chef's knife.

Lay the slices, slightly separated, on foil-lined baking sheets. Bake until nicely toasted and golden, 8 to 12 minutes; the slices will brown quickly at the end, so watch carefully. Turn over; repeat the toasting on the second side for 6 to 10 minutes. Cool the slices completely on wire racks.

Yield: Makes 25 to 30 slices

Storage: Store these, airtight and at room temperature, for up to 2 weeks. Or freeze, airtight, for up to 2 months.

Tip

The recipe calls for completing the baking in two 4 by 8-inch loaf pans. If you think the recipient might not have these, you could supply two foil pans along with the jar of gift mix.

Extra Easy
Unusual gourmet gift mix.
Bowl-and-spoon mixing.
Dough shaped instantly
in a loaf pan.

1¼ cups unbleached all-purpose
white flour

¾ cup plus 1 tablespoon granulated
sugar

3½ tablespoons unsweetened
cocoa powder, Dutch-process
preferred

1½ tablespoons instant espresso
powder

¾ teaspoon baking powder
Generous ¼ teaspoon salt

1 cup (6 ounces) semisweet
chocolate morsels or chopped
semisweet chocolate

1 cup whole hulled hazelnuts
(or whole unblanched
almonds), toasted* and
thoroughly cooled

Nifty Gifty Tip
An attractive decorator jar can do
double duty to store the mix, then
the biscotti. You'll need a 1-quart or
1-liter jar—both hold about 4 cups
of water. Since the dough is shaped
and par-baked in two loaf pans,
consider providing disposable foil
loaf pans with the gift mix.

MOCHA-HAZELNUT (OR ALMOND) BISCOTTI-IN-A-JAR MIX

This recipe is different from most layered gift mixes in that it yields elegant biscotti instead of simple bars or drop cookies. The mocha-almond flavor will appeal to those who like sophisticated flavors and not-too-sweet, crunchy textures. Remarkably, even if the recipient is an inexperienced baker, the finished slices will look just as appealing as fancy store-bought—and will probably taste much better!

Preliminaries: Have ready a clear glass, transparent plastic, or other attractive 1-quart or 1-liter jar, along with its lid. Set out a square of heavy-duty aluminum foil to use as a funnel. (If you have a funnel, substitute that!)

Center the flour on the foil. Using the foil as a funnel, pour the flour into the jar. Rap the jar on the counter to even the layer. In a food processor, process the sugar, cocoa powder, espresso powder, baking powder, salt, and chocolate morsels until the morsels are ground powder-fine; don't under-process. Add the mixture to the jar; rap it again. Add the hazelnuts. Rap the jar, then press them down. If shipping the jar, firmly stuff any empty space at the top with crumpled wax paper. Secure the lid. Attach a tag or card with the recipe instructions to the jar.

Yield: Makes 1 quart of mix, enough for 25 to 30 biscotti

Storage: Keep 1 month, unrefrigerated, or 2 months refrigerated.

* To toast whole hulled hazelnuts or whole unblanched almonds, spread the nuts on a medium rimmed baking sheet. Toast in a preheated 325°F oven, stirring every 3 minutes, for about 10 minutes; the nuts should be fragrant and tinged with brown. If only unhulled hazelnuts are available, after the nuts are cool enough to handle, rub them between the fingers or in a clean kitchen towel to loosen and discard as many of the bits of hull as possible.

Instructions to provide with the jar mix:
MOCHA-HAZELNUT (OR ALMOND) BISCOTTI

No need to visit a chichi coffee bar or café to enjoy great biscotti. These crunchy, nutty gourmet slices are easy to make yet are quite delectable!

3 large eggs, at room
   temperature
2 tablespoons corn oil or other
   flavorless vegetable oil
1 teaspoon vanilla extract,
   optional
1 1-quart jar Mix

Preheat the oven to 300°F. Line two 5 by 9-inch (or similar) loaf pans with foil; or use two disposable foil loaf pans. Spray with nonstick spray. In a large bowl, beat together the eggs, oil, and vanilla (if using) with a fork. Vigorously stir in the jar of mix until evenly incorporated; the mixture will be stiff. Divide the dough in half; press each half evenly into a loaf pan using a greased rubber spatula.

Bake (middle rack) for 45 to 50 minutes or until fragrant and firm when pressed in the center top. Let stand until the loaves are cool. Then refrigerate until well chilled; this makes slicing easier.

Set the oven to 300°F. Gently remove the loaves from the pans; transfer to a cutting board. Cut crosswise on a diagonal into ¼-inch-thick slices using a large serrated knife or chef's knife. Lay the slices, slightly separated, on a large baking parchment–lined baking sheet. Bake (middle rack) for about 12 minutes, until nicely toasted and crisp. Turn over and bake for about 10 minutes longer; the slices may begin to scorch if overbaked, so watch carefully at the end. Let the slices cool completely on wire racks.

Yield: Makes 25 to 30 slices

Storage: Store these, airtight and at room temperature, for up to 2 weeks. Or freeze, airtight, for up to 2 months.

NO-BAKE COOKIES }

No-bake cookies are a great choice when you need cookies in a hurry. Or you don't want to heat up the kitchen by turning on the oven. Or you don't *have* an oven!

Most recipes do call for heating or melting using a stovetop or a microwave oven, but mixing usually involves simply stirring ingredients together. "Doughs" are then dropped, hand shaped into balls, or pressed into a pan to form quick bar cookies. Since the risks of burning oneself during baking are eliminated, these recipes are particularly appropriate for making with young children.

Typically, no-bake cookies include ready-to-eat cereals or crumbled wafers or graham crackers to replace the usual flour. Since they normally lack eggs, no-bakes also require a binder like melted chocolate or peanut butter (or other nut spread) to hold everything together. A good example is the Quick Indoor S'mores Bars, an easy treat calling for folding together graham cracker pieces with melted chocolate, marshmallows, and chocolate morsels.

Many other no-bakes tend toward the unsophisticated, but they can make the right audience absolutely swoon.

Folks who grew up enjoying good old Rice Krispies marshmallow treats (including me!) go crazy over the Chocolate-Marshmallow Crispies Drops and Peanut Butter–Marshmallow Crispies Drops. These have the same sort of chewy-crispy character as the original squares, but they're more succulent because the proportion of gooey stuff is a little higher and the drops are studded with partly melted mini marshmallows. (Be forewarned: These are sweet and almost candy-like.)

Another comfortable, home-style selection is the Chocolate-Honey Streusel Bars. These are vaguely reminiscent of granola bars, but are slightly softer and much more sumptuous due to a gooey chocolate–peanut butter or chocolate–almond butter layer tucked in the middle.

But not all no-bakes in the chapter are designed to appeal to the child in us. The Nanaimo Truffle Bars and Chocolate-Glazed Cherry-Almond Chocolate Bars are elegant, and tempting enough to satisfy your favorite food snob (who will likely never guess these were easy to make).

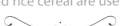
CHOCOLATE-MARSHMALLOW CRISPIES DROPS

True, these drops aren't sophisticated (some might even call them lowbrow), but kids won't be the only ones who'll keep sneaking back for more! One reason is the chewy-crispy texture; it's like that of the old-fashioned rice cereal–marshmallow squares, only gooier and more succulent. And, the chocolate and whole mini marshmallows studding the drops help sweeten the deal!

These go together in just a few minutes; are easy enough for young "bakers" to either make themselves or help ready; and are an ideal treat for a community event or family outing. Though no baking is actually involved, the recipe is a good way to introduce very small children to basic cookie-making skills, including following directions, measuring and mixing ingredients, and dropping cookie portions.

¼ cup (½ stick) unsalted butter, cut into chunks
2 cups (one 10- to 11-ounce bag) semisweet chocolate morsels, divided
5 cups mini marshmallows, divided
1 teaspoon vanilla extract
3½ cups crisp rice cereal

Tip

For cookies with more protein and crunch, feel free to fold in 1 cup of chopped walnuts or pecans along with the rice cereal. If readied with gluten-free chocolate, marshmallows, and crisp rice cereal, crispies drops are fine for those with gluten allergies.

Preliminaries: Line two medium baking sheets with aluminum foil. Grease or coat with nonstick spray coating.

In a large heavy pot over low heat, warm the butter until completely melted. Add 1½ cups morsels and 4 cups marshmallows, and heat, stirring constantly, until mostly melted. Remove from the burner. Add the vanilla and continue stirring until completely melted. Vigorously stir in the cereal and remaining 1 cup marshmallows until well blended; the marshmallows should not completely melt. Stir in the remaining ½ cup chocolate morsels just until incorporated; don't overmix, as this causes them to melt too much.

Immediately drop the dough by measuring tablespoons onto the sheets, spacing about 2 inches apart. Let stand until cool and firmed up, at least 30 minutes. (Or speed the setting by refrigerating for about 20 minutes.)

Yield: Makes about twenty-five 2-inch drops

Storage: Store these, covered and at cool room temperature, for up to 1 week. They can be frozen, airtight, for up to 2 months; thaw before serving.

Extra Easy
Quick food processor mixing.
Updated classic.
Short ingredient list.

2 cups coarsely crushed or
   broken-up vanilla wafers
1⅔ cups chopped pecans, divided
½ cup (2½ ounces) semisweet
   chocolate morsels
½ cup powdered sugar
2 tablespoons light or dark corn
   syrup
¼ cup light or dark rum

RUM BALLS

These popular boozy no-bakes have been around for decades, and there's a reason why—they're both easy and good. (Even those who normally have more sophisticated tastes often go for these.)

This updated version takes advantage of the food processor, so the "dough" can be mixed together in about a minute. The balls are best when allowed to mellow at least overnight and are even better after a couple of days, so plan to make them ahead.

Preliminaries: Line a tray or rimmed baing sheet with wax paper or baking parchment.

In a food processor, process the wafers and 1 cup pecans until finely ground. Remove a generous ⅓ cup; place in a shallow bowl to use for garnish. Add the chocolate morsels and powdered sugar to the processor; process until the chocolate is finely chopped. With the motor running, add the corn syrup and rum through the feed tube; process just thoroughly blended. Sprinkle over the remaining ⅔ cup pecans, then pulse a few times to incorporate, but don't chop them fine. Let the mixture stand for about 10 minutes to firm up slightly.

Turn out the mixture onto a greased sheet of parchment. Shape portions of the mixture using greased hands into 1-inch balls. Roll the balls in the reserved crumb mixture until coated all over. Place, slightly separated, on the tray. Let the cookies mellow, covered, for at least 12 hours before serving.

Yield: Makes about twenty-five 1-inch balls

Storage: Store these, airtight and at room temperature, for 3 or 4 days; refrigerate for up to 2 weeks. They can be frozen, airtight, for up to 1 month.

Extra Easy
One-bowl mixing.
Drop-from-a-spoon shaping.
Gluten-free (if gluten-free
marshmallows, cereal, and
peanut butter are used).

¼ cup (½ stick) unsalted butter, cut into chunks

4 cups mini marshmallows, divided

⅓ cup smooth or chunky peanut butter

3½ cups crisp rice cereal (or plain gluten-free granola)

⅔ cup chopped peanuts

1 teaspoon vanilla extract

Tip
It's easy to make these gluten-free. Just use gluten-free rice cereal, marshmallows, and peanut butter.

Cookie Jar Wisdom
Mean Cookie Math: Asking three kids to divide two-and-a-half cookies.

PEANUT BUTTER–MARSHMALLOW CRISPIES DROPS

Yes, these easy peanut butter and peanuts drop cookies are a variation on the classic marshmallow–rice cereal bars theme. While I designed these primarily for kids, every grown-up who has tried them sheepishly comes back for more. They bring back fond memories for all those who made and scarfed down rice cereal bars as children.

Middle-schoolers and older kids will have fun making these on their own and younger children will be able to help with preparations.

Preliminaries: Line two large baking sheets with aluminum foil. Grease the foil or coat with nonstick spray.

In a medium microwave-safe bowl, microwave the butter and 3 cups marshmallows on 50 percent power, stopping and stirring every 30 seconds, until they completely melt. Vigorously stir in the peanut butter until smoothly incorporated. Stir in the cereal, peanuts, vanilla, and the remaining 1 cup marshmallows until well mixed.

Immediately drop heaping measuring tablespoons of dough onto the prepared baking sheets, spacing about 2 inches apart. Let stand until firm, about 30 minutes, or refrigerate until just slightly firm, about 15 minutes.

Yield: Makes about twenty-five 2-inch drops

Storage: Store these, covered and at cool room temperature, for up to 1 week. They can be frozen, airtight, for up to 2 months; thaw before serving.

CHOCOLATE-CRUNCH CLUSTERS

In truth, these are more like candies than cookies. But they are a snap to make, everyone likes them, and they provide something vegans and those with gluten allergies can enjoy when everybody else is munching on the usual array of forbidden cookies. Note that you must make sure to use gluten-free chocolate and cereal for a gluten-free version, so check labels carefully. (See the end of the recipe for a sugar-free version.)

Be sure to heat the chocolate exactly as directed below, as the method, called "quick tempering," ensures that it will set up properly. Melting and cooling it down in the specified way keeps the natural fat (cocoa butter) from rising and causing surface blotches or streaking. It also keeps the chocolate in the desired chemical state so it will set up hard and glossy. It's important to use chocolate that is smooth and glossy (not left over or discolored) when you begin, as it "seeds" the batch with the right type of crystals. And make sure you refrigerate the clusters as soon as you drop them all; this helps them quickly set up as they should.

1 cup very coarsely chopped
     salted nuts (your choice) or
     peanuts
1 cup regular or gluten-free crisp
     rice cereal or 1 cup fine-
     textured granola or gluten-free
     granola
8 ounces bittersweet or
     semisweet chocolate, divided
1 tablespoon corn oil or canola oil
     oil (do not substitute butter)

Preliminaries: Line a large rimmed tray or baking sheet with aluminum foil; try not to wrinkle the foil. Refrigerate the nuts and cereal until chilled, at least 30 minutes and up to 1 hour.

Break up or coarsely chop the chocolate. In a medium microwave-safe bowl, microwave a generous half of the chopped chocolate and the oil on 100 percent power for 1 minute. Stop and stir. Continue microwaving on 50 percent power, stopping and stirring every 30 seconds, until the chocolate is mostly melted. Stir in the remaining chocolate.

Stir until all the chunks melt and the mixture is almost cool to the touch. It's best to let the residual heat gradually melt all the pieces, so be patient and just keep stirring. Don't microwave further unless absolutely necessary to melt all the pieces, and then only for 10 or 15 seconds on 50 percent power.

As soon as all the pieces are melted, stir in the chilled nuts and cereal. Immediately drop small spoonfuls onto the foil, spacing about 1 inch apart. Stir the mixture frequently to prevent it from setting. If it does set, return to the microwave and microwave on 50 percent power for about 10 seconds, then stir well.

Transfer the tray to the refrigerator. Refrigerate for 20 to 30 minutes or until the chocolate completely sets. Peel the clusters from the foil. Store at very cool room temperature or refrigerated. Let the clusters return to cool room temperature before serving.

Yield: Makes about eighteen 1¼-inch clusters

Storage: Store these, airtight and at cool room temperature or refrigerated, for up to 10 days. Or freeze for up to 2 months. Let warm up before serving.

Variation: Sugar-Free Chocolate-Crunch Clusters Substitute sugar-free bittersweet chocolate for the regular chocolate. Proceed exactly as directed.

2 cups coarsely crushed or
    broken-up vanilla wafers
1⅔ cups chopped walnuts
3 tablespoons unsweetened
    natural (non-alkalized) cocoa
    powder or Dutch-process
    cocoa powder
½ teaspoon finely grated orange
    zest (orange part of the peel),
    optional
½ cup (2 ounces) bittersweet
    chocolate morsels
⅔ cup powdered sugar
3 tablespoons light or dark corn
    syrup
3 tablespoons good-quality
    brandy

{ **Cookie Jar Wisdom**
A cookie is love that goes
straight from hand to mouth
to heart.

CHOCOLATE-BRANDY BALLS

This recipe takes the good old rum ball idea and gives it a little spin. The cookies look a bit like chocolate truffles and feature bittersweet chocolate, walnuts, and a slug of brandy instead of rum. If you like the slightly sophisticated combination of chocolate and orange, add the optional orange zest, too.

Preliminaries: Line a tray or rimmed baking sheet with wax paper or baking parchment.

In a food processor, process the wafers, walnuts, cocoa powder, and orange zest (if using) until finely ground. Remove a generous ⅓ cup; reserve in a shallow bowl for garnish. Add the chocolate morsels and powdered sugar to the processor; process until the chocolate is finely chopped. With the motor running, add the corn syrup and brandy through the feed tube, continuing to process until the ingredients are just thoroughly blended. Let the mixture stand for about 10 minutes to firm up slightly.

Turn out the mixture onto a greased sheet of baking parchment. Shape portions of the mixture using greased hands into 1-inch balls. Roll the balls in the reserved crumb mixture until coated all over. Space, slightly separated, on the tray. Let the cookies mellow, covered, at least overnight before serving.

Yield: Makes about twenty-five 1-inch cookies

Storage: Store these, airtight and at room temperature, for 3 or 4 days; refrigerate for up to 2 weeks. They can be frozen, airtight, for up to 1 month.

2½ cups semisweet chocolate
morsels

½ teaspoon instant coffee granules
or instant espresso powder

1 tablespoon kirsch (clear cherry
brandy), or substitute fresh
orange juice

¼ teaspoon almond extract

3 tablespoons unsalted butter,
softened to room temperature
and cut into small pieces

2½ cups broken-up (⅛- to ¼-inch
pieces) dark chocolate wafers

1 cup coarsely chopped slivered
almonds

½ cup chopped white chocolate
pieces (from cut-up bars)

1 cup coarsely chopped dried
cherries

CHOCOLATE-GLAZED CHERRY-ALMOND CHOCOLATE BARS

These gourmet no-bake bars are super chocolaty and heavily studded with cherries, almonds, and white chocolate chunks—a combination that's quite delectable and attractive. If you always thought that no-bakes had to be prosaic, this recipe should change your mind.

Preliminaries: Line a 9-inch square baking pan with foil, allowing it to overhang on two opposing sides. Evenly spray the foil with nonstick spray.

In a large bowl, drizzle ⅔ cup boiling water over the chocolate morsels and coffee granules; let stand, without stirring, for a few minutes so the morsels can soften. Then slowly stir until the chocolate completely melts and the mixture is well blended and smooth. Stir in the kirsch, almond extract, and butter until melted. Remove ¾ cup of the chocolate mixture and reserve for the glaze.

Stir the chocolate cookie pieces, almonds, white chocolate, and cherries into the large bowl of chocolate. Turn out the mixture into the pan, spreading out and pressing down very firmly all over using a greased rubber spatula. Pour the glaze over the top, spreading out evenly. Rap and shake the pan to even the glaze further. Let stand until cooled completely, at least 1 hour. Cover and refrigerate until well chilled and firm, at least 1½ hours, and up to several days if desired.

Using the foil as handles, transfer the slab to a cutting board. Peel off the foil. Using a large knife dipped in hot water and wiped clean between cuts, cut crosswise and lengthwise into fourths or fifths. Let the bars warm up for a few minutes before serving; however, they will become overly soft if left unrefrigerated for long periods.

Yield: Makes sixteen 2¼-inch or twenty-five 1½-inch squares

Storage: Store these, covered and refrigerated, for up to 1 week. They can be frozen, airtight, for up to 2 months. Let partially thaw before serving.

NANAIMO TRUFFLE BARS

Nanaimo is a scenic coastal town on Vancouver Island, in British Columbia, but it is probably most famous with Canadians for some widely popular no-bake bars that supposedly originated there. The following recipe is adapted from one shared with me by Canadian chocolate expert Pam Williams, from a cookbook of her truffle recipes. It's one of the best, and certainly the most elegant, no-bake bar recipes I know.

The bottom layer of these rich, candy-like treats features a nut-, graham cracker–, and coconut-enriched chocolate ganache. The top is the same smooth, glossy ganache used solo and simply spread over the top to form a very inviting, succulent glaze.

These are best cut small and served much as you would truffles or other confections. I like to present the squares individually in mini cupcake papers or fluted paper candy cups, but they look fine just placed on a serving plate. No one will ever guess that they are easy to make. Plus, they are extremely convenient because they can be prepared well ahead and kept refrigerated.

10 ounces 50 to 65 percent cacao bittersweet or semisweet chocolate, coarsely chopped
⅔ cup heavy (whipping) cream
2 tablespoons light corn syrup
2 tablespoons cognac or good brandy, or substitute fresh orange juice
2 teaspoons vanilla extract
1 cup chopped walnuts or toasted, hulled, and chopped hazelnuts
1⅓ cups fine graham cracker crumbs, plus extra for garnish, optional
¾ cup flaked sweetened coconut

Preliminaries: Line an 8-inch square pan with aluminum foil, letting it overhang two opposing sides. Lightly spray the foil with nonstick spray.

In a large microwave-safe bowl, microwave the chocolate on high power for 1 minute, then stir well. Microwave on 50 percent power, stopping and stirring at 30-second intervals, until the chocolate is mostly melted. Combine the cream, corn syrup, cognac, and vanilla in a 2-cup measure (or microwave-safe bowl). Microwave on high power for about 1 minute or until steaming hot; watch carefully to avoid a boil-over. Stir well.

Pour the hot cream mixture over the chocolate without stirring; let stand for 2 minutes so the chocolate can soften. Gently whisk the cream mixture into the chocolate until smoothly incorporated; at first it will look separated, but keep whisking and it will gradually come together. Remove and set aside a generous ½ cup of the chocolate ganache in a 1-cup microwave-safe glass measure to use as the glaze.

Stir the walnuts, graham cracker crumbs, and coconut into the remaining chocolate ganache until well blended. Let cool until barely warm. Turn out the filling into the prepared pan. Refrigerate, uncovered, until it is firm on top, at least 1 hour. Lay a sheet of wax paper over the top and press down firmly to compact and smooth the filling layer.

Pour the reserved ganache glaze over the filling. (If it is too thick to flow readily, microwave it on 50 percent power for 30 seconds, then stir until fluid. Repeat the microwaving for a few more seconds, if necessary.) Tip

the pan from side to side and rap it on the counter several times to even the glaze surface. If garnish is desired, lightly sprinkle the top with some fine graham cracker crumbs. Let the bars stand at room temperature for at least 1 hour so the ganache can absorb some moisture and thicken slightly. Cover and refrigerate until cooled completely, at least 2 hours, and up to several days if desired, before cutting.

Lift the slab from the pan using the foil as handles. Gently peel off the foil and place the slab on a cutting board. Using a large sharp knife, trim off and discard the edges. The bars are very rich, so cut the slab into thirds in one direction and into eighths in the other for small, narrow bars; or into sixths in both directions for mini squares; or as desired. Let the bars warm up just slightly before serving.

Yield: Makes twenty-four 1 by $2\frac{2}{3}$-inch small bars or thirty-six $1\frac{1}{3}$-inch square mini bars

Storage: Store these, airtight and at cool room temperature or refrigerated, for up to 1 week; let refrigerated bars warm up slightly before serving. They can be frozen, airtight, for up to 2 months.

½ cup unsalted butter, cut into
   chunks
¼ cup clover honey or other mild
   honey
¼ cup packed light brown sugar
¼ teaspoon salt
2 teaspoons vanilla extract
2½ cups old-fashioned rolled oats
1½ cups semisweet chocolate
   morsels, divided
½ cup almond butter or peanut
   butter
½ cup coarsely chopped slivered
   almonds or peanuts, optional

CHOCOLATE-HONEY STREUSEL BARS (TWO WAYS)

Think gussied-up granola bars and you'll be on the right track with these: They have that crumbly, nubby granola look, but they are a little moister and richer and decidedly more decadent due to a chocolate layer slipped in the middle.

The same basic recipe can be used for two completely different effects: For a distinctive, kid-pleasing flavor, incorporate peanut butter and chopped peanuts. For a more subtle and sophisticated taste (or for those with peanut allergies), use almond butter and slivered almonds.

Preliminaries: Line a 9-inch square baking pan with aluminum foil, letting it overhang two opposing sides. Lightly spray the foil with nonstick spray.

In a medium microwave-safe bowl, microwave the butter on 50 percent power until mostly melted, about 1 minute. Stir well. Thoroughly stir the honey, sugar, salt, vanilla, then the oats, into the butter until evenly blended. Let cool slightly. Spread about two-thirds of the oat mixture in the baking pan, pressing into a compact, evenly thick layer. Reserve the remaining crumbs for the topping.

In a medium microwave-safe bowl, microwave 1 cup of the chocolate morsels and the almond butter or peanut butter on 50 percent power for 1 minute. Stir well, then microwave on 50 percent power, stopping and stirring every 30 seconds, until the chocolate mostly melts. Stir until the chocolate melts, then fold in the almonds (or peanuts), then the remaining morsels.

Spread the mixture evenly over the streusel layer. Sprinkle the remaining streusel over the top. Pat down to imbed slightly. Refrigerate until firm, at least 1 hour, before cutting crosswise and lengthwise into fourths.

Yield: Makes sixteen 2⅛-inch square bars

Storage: Store these, covered and at room temperature, for up to 1 week. They can be frozen, airtight, for up to 2 months; thaw completely before serving.

3 cups milk chocolate or
semisweet chocolate morsels,
or a combination, divided
1 teaspoon instant coffee
granules, optional
¼ cup (½ stick) unsalted butter
(don't substitute margarine),
softened and cut into small
pieces
2 cups broken-up (⅛- to ¼-inch
pieces) graham crackers
2½ cups mini marshmallows

QUICK INDOOR S'MORES BARS

These feature the typical s'mores ingredients (plus chocolate chips for crunch!), chopped up and served in a quick, convenient bar cookie form. Classic s'mores recipes usually call for milk chocolate, but if you prefer a more bittersweet taste, use semisweet chocolate morsels or a combination of the two. Note that the coffee called for doesn't lend a coffee taste—it just heightens the chocolate flavor. But you can leave it out, if desired.

These make an appealing bake-and-take treat for a school event or family outing. Older middle school kids and teens can prepare them on their own.

Preliminaries: Line an 8-inch square baking pan with aluminum foil, allowing it to overhang on two opposing sides. Evenly spray the foil with nonstick spray.

Combine 2½ cups chocolate morsels and the coffee granules (if using) in a large bowl. Drizzle ⅔ cup boiling water over the top; let stand, without stirring, for a few minutes so the morsels can soften. Then slowly stir until the chocolate completely melts and the mixture is well blended. Stir in the butter until melted. Remove ¾ cup of the chocolate mixture and reserve for the glaze.

Stir the graham cracker pieces and marshmallows into the large bowl of chocolate. Chop the remaining ½ cup chocolate morsels into ⅛-inch bits (larger pieces are too hard to eat when chilled); then fold into the mixture. Turn out the mixture into the pan, spreading out and pressing down very firmly using a greased rubber spatula. Pour the glaze over the pan surface, spreading out evenly. Rap and shake the pan to even the glaze further. Let stand until cooled. Cover and refrigerate until well chilled and firm, at least 1½ hours.

Using the foil as handles, transfer the s'mores square to a cutting board. Peel off the foil. Using a large knife dipped in hot water and wiped clean between cuts, cut the square crosswise and lengthwise into quarters. Let warm up for a few minutes before serving; however, they will become overly soft if allowed to stand at room temperature for long periods.

Yield: Makes sixteen 2⅓-inch squares

Storage: Store these, airtight and refrigerated, for up to 1 week. They can be frozen, airtight, for up to 2 months. Let come at least to cool room temperature before serving.

2½ cups semisweet chocolate
    morsels
¾ teaspoon instant espresso
    powder or instant coffee
    granules
1 teaspoon raspberry extract
2 tablespoons unsalted butter
    (don't substitute margarine),
    softened and cut into small
    pieces
2 cups broken-up (⅛- to ¼-inch
    pieces) graham crackers
1 cup slivered almonds or toasted,
    hulled, and coarsely chopped
    hazelnuts, or a combination of
    the two
2 cups mini marshmallows
⅓ cup coarsely chopped freeze-
    dried raspberries, optional

CHOCOLATE-GLAZED RASPBERRY-NUT S'MORES BARS

A chichi variation on the s'mores theme, these simple no-bake bars are dressed up with a chocolate glaze and given a fresh twist. The recipe calls for raspberry extract (now readily available due to the introduction of the McCormick's brand) and includes the option of adding some slivered almonds or chopped hazelnuts and freeze-dried raspberries. The best-known brand of these is called Just Raspberries (from the Just Tomatoes Etc! company) and is sold in many health food stores. They give the bars zip, as well as fuller raspberry flavor, but can be omitted if desired.

Preliminaries: Line an 8-inch square baking pan with aluminum foil, allowing it to overhang on two opposing sides. Evenly spray the foil with nonstick spray.

Combine the chocolate morsels and the espresso powder in a large bowl. Drizzle ⅔ cup boiling water over the top; let stand, without stirring, for a few minutes so the morsels can soften. Then slowly stir until the chocolate completely melts and the mixture is well blended. Stir in the extract. Stir in the butter until melted. Remove ¾ cup of the chocolate mixture and reserve for the glaze.

Stir the graham cracker pieces, nuts, marshmallows, and freeze-dried raspberries (if using) into the large bowl of chocolate. Turn out the mixture into the pan, spreading out and pressing down very firmly using a greased rubber spatula. Pour the glaze over the pan surface, tipping back and forth and shaking the pan to even it. Let stand until thoroughly cooled. Cover and refrigerate until well chilled and firm, at least 1½ hours.

Using the foil as handles, transfer the s'mores square to a cutting board. Peel off the foil. Using a large knife dipped in hot water and wiped clean between cuts, cut the square crosswise and lengthwise into quarters. Let warm up for a few minutes before serving; however, they will become overly soft if allowed to stand at room temperature for long periods.

Yield: Makes sixteen 2⅓-inch squares

Storage: Store these, airtight and refrigerated, for up to 1 week. They can be frozen, airtight, for up to 2 months. Let come at least to cool room temperature before serving.

SEMI-HOMEMADE COOKIES }

This chapter provides some easy ways to jump-start cookie making by taking advantage of commercial refrigerator case doughs and several other convenience products. While I'm not normally a fan of purchased logs simply sliced up and baked (the resulting cookies usually seem too sweet and bland), cleverly doctored doughs can trim time and create "semi-homemade" treats with considerable appeal. Some are even good enough to pass for "from-scratch."

One easy, effective approach is to jazz up store-bought dough with interesting garnishes and flavor enhancers. For example, the Sneakydoodles (semi-homemade snickerdoodles) are rolled in an intensely cinnamony sugar blend prior to baking. The Hazelnut Fancies Sandwich Cookies with Chocolate-Hazelnut Filling are sprinkled with chopped hazelnuts, then after baking are sandwiched around decadent-tasting Nutella chocolate-hazelnut spread. (The resulting cookies are a good example of elegance with ease.)

Other recipes, like the Toasted Coconut–Pecan Dream Bars and Super-Easy Cheesecake Bars, rely on store-bought dough as a base, which is then covered with a good homemade filling. The Shortcut Cranberry Crumb Bars recipe calls for crumbling purchased dough with other ingredients to form a quick streusel, which then serves as both a base and a crumb topping. The Shortcut Cinnamon-Walnut Roll-Ups recipe features rounds of ready-to-use pie dough gussied up with— right, cinnamon and sugar (plus walnuts and a little cream cheese)!

All the recipes in this chapter do require at least some baking. My No-Bake Cookies chapter starts on page 248.

2½ tablespoons granulated sugar
2 to 3 teaspoons ground
    cinnamon, Saigon cinnamon
    preferred, to taste
¾ teaspoon ground nutmeg
1 16- to 18-ounce package
    refrigerator case sugar cookie
    dough
½ tablespoon unsalted butter,
    softened but not melted

Tip

Depending on the brand of dough,
the cookies may spread moderately
or quite a lot. To help ensure that
the cookies won't run together
regardless of the brand, I call for
spacing them far apart on the
baking sheets.

SNEAKYDOODLES

Saving time by jazzing up store-bought basics with some homemade
components is what this recipe and the others in this chapter are all about.
As you might guess, sneakydoodles are just snickerdoodles readied from a
package of refrigerator case sugar cookie dough. The totally simple, no-fuss
step of rolling balls of dough in fresh, good-quality spices works wonders for
cookie flavor and aroma; the "doodles" may even pass for homemade.

Young children enjoy helping with these cookies. Older ones can make
them on their own.

Baking Preliminaries: Position a rack in the upper third of the oven;
preheat to 350°F. Grease several baking sheets or coat with nonstick
spray.

In a small deep bowl, thoroughly stir together the sugar, cinnamon,
and nutmeg. Cut the log of dough in half; return half to the refrigerator.
Then cut the remaining half into 12 equal portions. Put a dab of butter
in your palms, then roll a dough portion into a ball. Drop the ball into
the cinnamon-sugar mixture. Rotate the bowl to lightly coat the ball all
over. Repeat with the remaining portions, spacing about 3 inches apart
on the baking sheets; some brands of dough spread more than others.
Pat down the tops of the balls with your palm until they are flattened just
slightly. Repeat with the second dough half.

Bake (upper rack) one pan at a time for 9 to 13 minutes or until the
cookies are tinged with brown around the edges and just firm in the
center. Transfer the pan to a cooling rack. Let the cookies firm up just
slightly, about 2 minutes. Then, using a wide spatula, transfer them to
racks. Let stand until completely cooled.

Yield: Makes twenty-four 3½-inch cookies

Storage: Store these, airtight, for up to 3 days. They can be frozen,
airtight, for up to 1 month.

Easy
Fast recipe with flair.
Slice-and-bake
convenience.

1 16- to 18-ounce package
 vanilla or sugar cookie
 refrigerator case dough,
 divided

3 tablespoons unsweetened
 natural (non-alkalized) cocoa
 powder or Dutch-process
 cocoa powder

1 teaspoon instant coffee
 granules dissolved in
 1 teaspoon warm water

½ teaspoon almond extract, vanilla
 extract, or orange zest

½ cup semisweet or bittersweet
 chocolate morsels, very finely
 chopped

Tube Trick

Slit the discarded cardboard tube
from a paper towel roll lengthwise.
Slip the pinwheel log into it, then
secure the tube with tape or rubber
bands. This will keep the log from
flattening on one side during
freezing.

CHOCOLATE-VANILLA PINWHEELS

These elegant-looking cookies are fairly easy to make, thanks to the refrigerator case dough used to jump-start the recipe. Half of it is doctored to create a contrasting chocolate portion. The two layers are then stacked and rolled up pin wheel-style, which yields very dramatic slices.

Divide the dough in half. Roll out one half between sheets of baking parchment or wax paper into an 8 by 11-inch evenly thick rectangle. Place on a baking sheet. Refrigerate while preparing the second half.

Break up the second half with the hands until crumbly. Thoroughly mix it in a heavy-duty mixer or bowl with the cocoa powder, coffee mixture, extract, and chopped chocolate. (Or stir, then knead, the dough ingredients with the hands until they are blended.) Roll out the chocolate dough between sheets into an 8 by 11-inch evenly thick rectangle. Refrigerate on a tray until firmed up, about 20 minutes (or speed chilling by freezing for 15 minutes).

Peel off the top sheet from the vanilla dough, then pat the sheet back into place. Turn over; peel off and discard the second sheet. Remove one sheet of parchment from the chocolate dough. Center the dough over the vanilla dough. Press down to bond the layers. Peel off the second sheet.

Working from an 11-inch side and using the paper to lift the dough, roll it into a pinwheel log. Stretch out the middle until evenly thick and about 12 inches long. Roll up the log in plastic wrap, twisting the ends to secure it. Tuck the log in the cardboard tube. Freeze the log until firm enough to slice neatly, 2½ hours, or wrapped airtight up to 1 month, if desired.

Baking Preliminaries: Position a rack in the middle of the oven; preheat oven to 350°F. Set out two large baking sheets.

Unwrap the frozen log. On a cutting board, slice it crosswise into generous ¼-inch-thick slices, rotating the log a quarter turn after each slice to keep it round. (If the log is too hard to slice, let it warm up a few minutes first.) Space the slices about 2½ inches apart on the baking sheets.

Bake (middle rack) one pan at a time for 11 to 15 minutes or until the dough is tinged and almost firm when pressed in the center. Set the pan on a wire rack to cool slightly. Transfer the cookies to racks to let cool.

Yield: Makes about forty-five 2½- to 2¾-inch pinwheels

Storage: Store these, airtight, for up to 3 days. Or freeze for up to 1 month.

Extra Easy

Quick one-bowl mixing.
Clever use of store-
bought dough and filling.

1 16- to 18-ounce package
    refrigerator case vanilla sugar
    cookie dough
    About 1 cup roasted, hulled,
    and chopped hazelnuts
1 teaspoon finely grated orange
    zest (orange part of the peel),
    optional
    A generous 1 cup Nutella
    chocolate-hazelnut spread

Time-Trimmer:

Save time with ready-to-use hulled,
roasted, and chopped hazelnuts.
Gourmet and upscale markets
sometimes stock them and they
can be purchased online. If you can
only find whole, unhulled hazelnuts,
roast them in a 350°F oven for about
10 minutes, stirring occasionally,
to loosen the hulls. Let the nuts
cool, then rub off and discard all
loose bits of hull by rubbing them
using a clean kitchen towel or your
fingertips. (It's fine if some bits of
hull remain.)

HAZELNUT FANCIES SANDWICH COOKIES WITH CHOCOLATE-HAZELNUT FILLING

These are at the very top of my fast-with-flair list. They prove that with a little clever doctoring, refrigerator case dough can yield cookies that will pass for homemade. I've served these without mentioning my shortcut and received both compliments and requests for the recipe.

Here, purchased sugar cookie dough is dressed up with chopped hazelnuts and the ready-to-use chocolate-hazelnut filling, Nutella. (If you're unfamiliar with this spread, it's a wildly popular European convenience product, now usually stocked in American supermarkets near the peanut butter.) For an even more sophisticated taste combination, accent the Nutella with a little freshly grated orange zest.

Baking Preliminaries: Position a rack in the upper third of the oven; preheat to 350°F. Grease several baking sheets or coat with nonstick spray.

Cut the chilled log of dough in half; return half to the refrigerator to stay cold. Cut the remaining portion in half lengthwise. Lay each portion cut side down on a cutting board. With a sharp knife cut the portions crosswise into 12 half slices to yield 24 total half slices. Space the half slices about 2½ inches apart on the baking sheets. Sprinkle the tops generously with the chopped hazelnuts, patting down to imbed. Repeat the process to make 24 more half slices with the second dough half. Bake (upper rack) one pan at a time for 9 to 13 minutes or until the cookies are nicely tinged with brown at the edges. Transfer the pan to a cooling rack, and let stand until the cookies firm up just slightly, about 2 minutes. Using a wide spatula, transfer the cookies to racks. Cool completely.

If desired, in a small deep bowl stir the orange zest into the Nutella until well blended (if an orange flavor is desired). Spread enough Nutella on the underside of half of the cooled cookies to yield a generous ¼-inch-thick layer. Top the filled cookies with a second cookie, nut side up. Press the two together until the filling just squeezes to the edge.

Yield: Makes twenty-four 2½-inch sandwich cookies

Storage: Store these, airtight and refrigerated, for up to 1 week. They can be frozen, airtight, for up to 1 month. Let come to room temperature before serving.

1 16- to 18-ounce package
    (2 rolled-up dough rounds)
    refrigerated pie pastry
⅔ cup granulated sugar
1 tablespoon ground cinnamon
⅔ cup finely chopped walnuts
1 3-ounce package cream
    cheese, softened

Tip

The refrigerator case pie pastry
product needed for this recipe
comes with two handy rounds of
ready-to-use dough rolled up in a
single package. You're not looking
for dough that's sold already fitted
into pie pans!

SHORTCUT CINNAMON-WALNUT ROLL-UPS

Reminiscent of rugelach, these pastry roll-ups *look* time-consuming, but they are quickly made using refrigerated pie dough. You just roll cinnamon-sugar into both sides of purchased ready-to-bake pie pastry rounds. Then simply cut the rounds into wedges and roll these up as you would crescent rolls. The roll-ups are not overly sweet and make a nice addition to a brunch table.

Baking Preliminaries: Position a rack in the upper third of the oven; preheat to 375°F. Line several baking sheets with baking parchment.

Unroll the rounds of pie dough as directed on the package, centering each on a sheet of baking parchment. In a small bowl, stir together the sugar and cinnamon. Sprinkle about one-quarter of cinnamon-sugar and one-quarter of the walnuts evenly over each round. One at a time, top the rounds with a sheet of parchment, then firmly roll back and forth with a rolling pin to imbed the sugar and nuts into the dough. With parchment still in place, turn over the dough rounds so the ungarnished sides are facing up. Then peel off the top sheets of parchment. Spread the cream cheese over the rounds, dividing it equally between them. Sprinkle the remaining sugar mixture and nuts over the rounds, dividing it equally between them. If the dough has warmed and is too soft to handle, slide the bottom parchment layers with the dough rounds onto baking sheets and refrigerate just until firmed up enough to handle.

Working with one round at a time and using a pizza cutter, pastry wheel, or large sharp knife, cut it into quarters, then cut each quarter into fourths to yield 16 wedges (The photo, page 138, shows how this is done). Working from the perimeter, roll up each wedge to form a roll-up. Transfer the roll-ups to baking sheets, with the points underneath to prevent unrolling, spacing about 1½ inches apart on the baking sheets.

Bake (upper rack) one pan at a time for 15 to 20 minutes or until the roll-ups are nicely browned all over. Transfer the pan to a rack. Cool completely.

Yield: Makes thirty-two 2½-inch roll-ups

Storage: Store these, airtight and refrigerated, for up to 1 week. They can be frozen, airtight, for up to 1 month. Let come to room temperature before serving.

1 16- to 18-ounce package
   refrigerator case sugar cookie
   or peanut butter cookie dough,
   at room temperature
½ cup smooth or chunky peanut
   butter
¼ cup unbleached all-purpose
   white flour
   About ½ cup chopped salted
   peanuts, optional
   About ⅓ cup Concord grape
   jelly (or other jelly, if preferred)

PB & J THUMBPRINTS

This is a great "semi-homemade" cookie for kids, as well as for grown-ups who fondly recall the distinctive taste of peanut butter and grape jelly sandwiches from their childhood. Concord grapes are indigenous and unique to North America, and their intense fruity flavor and aroma are highly memorable, so they will instantly bring back the familiar taste of home. Of course, if you prefer to fill the thumbprints with another flavor of jelly, that's fine, too!

Small children can help bake these; older ones can ready them by themselves. I like these garnished with chopped peanuts, but it's fine to omit them if you wish.

Baking Preliminaries: Position a rack in the middle of the oven; preheat to 350°F. Generously grease two large baking sheets or line with baking parchment.

Break up the dough in a large bowl. Stir, beat, or knead in the peanut butter and the flour until evenly incorporated. Divide the dough in quarters, then divide each quarter into 8 equal balls. If desired, press the tops of the balls in chopped peanuts until coated. Space the balls, peanuts facing up, about 2 inches apart on the sheets. Using a knuckle or thumb, make a deep well in the center of each. Put a scant ½ teaspoon grape jelly into each well; don't overfill or the jelly may boil over during baking.

Bake (middle rack) one pan at a time for 10 to 14 minutes or until the cookies are tinged with brown and almost firm at the edges. Transfer the pans to racks; let the cookies firm up for 5 minutes. Transfer the cookies to racks using a wide spatula. Let stand until cooled thoroughly, then pack airtight.

Yield: Makes thirty-two 2½-inch thumbprints

Storage: Store these, airtight, for up to 1 week. They can be frozen, airtight, for up to 2 months.

Store-bought dough base/
homemade topping.
Mixer or food processor
mixing options.

1 16- to 18-ounce package
   refrigerator case sugar cookie
   dough, divided
¾ cup packed light brown sugar
3 large eggs, at room temperature
2 teaspoons vanilla extract
3 cups shredded or flaked
   sweetened coconut, divided
1½ cups chopped pecans, divided

TOASTED COCONUT–PECAN DREAM BARS

Using a package of refrigerator case cookie dough as a bar cookie base, then adding your own filling or topping, is another great way to save time yet produce almost homemade results. Here, the topping is a wonderfully succulent but simple-to-make coconut-pecan blend—it underscores just why these classics are called dream bars! They are so rich and gooey good that nobody ever dreams a little shortcut was taken.

Baking Preliminaries: Position a rack in the middle of the oven; preheat to 350°F. Line a 9 by 13-inch baking pan with aluminum foil, letting it overhang the narrow sides slightly. Coat the foil with nonstick spray.

Set aside 2 tablespoons dough removed from the log. Press the remainder out in the foil-lined pan to cover the bottom in an evenly thick layer. Press a sheet of wax paper onto the dough, then smooth out the surface. Discard the paper.

Bake (middle rack) for 14 to 18 minutes, until tinged with brown at the edges but not completely baked through. Let cool slightly.

Meanwhile, in a mixer or food processor, mix or process the brown sugar and reserved 2 tablespoons dough until blended. Add the eggs and vanilla; beat or process until smoothly incorporated. Stir in about half the coconut and pecans. Pour the filling evenly over the dough. Top with the remaining coconut and pecans.

Bake (middle rack) for 22 to 26 minutes longer or until the filling is bubbly and the coconut is nicely browned.

Set aside on a wire rack. Let cool. To neatly cut the bars, refrigerate until chilled and firm (1 hour or more), then lift out using the foil. Peel off the foil. On a cutting board, cut with a large sharp knife into sixths crosswise and fourths lengthwise (or as desired) to form bars.

Yield: Makes twenty-four 2⅛-inch squares

Storage: Store these, airtight and refrigerated, for up to 1 week. They can be frozen, airtight, for up to 2 months. Serve at room temperature.

Variation: German Chocolate Dream Bars A food processor is required for this version. Add 1 cup semisweet chocolate mini morsels (or regular-size morsels) to the food processor along with the brown sugar and 2 tablespoons dough. Process until the chocolate is very finely ground. Continue exactly as directed.

GRAHAM CRACKER, CHOCOLATE, AND PRALINE BARS

The Reverend Sylvester Graham, a fiery nineteenth-century American diet reformer, believed that very lean, low-sugar, whole grain breads, especially dry, bland ones, were the most nourishing and nutritious. Which is in fact why the plain, mild, fairly wholesome graham cracker is named for him. Dr. Graham would have been appalled with this recipe because it involves cleverly "doctoring" fairly healthful graham crackers to create a quick, utterly decadent treat: A rich, succulent praline mixture gets baked over a cracker base, then chocolate is sprinkled over the top. The resulting thin, rich bars have no redeeming nutritional value but taste really good! In fact, these are one of the tastiest and simplest semi-homemade treats around.

About thirteen 2¼ by 4¼-inch (or similar) graham crackers, broken in half
1 cup (2 sticks) unsalted butter
¾ cup packed light brown sugar
¾ cup chopped pecans or walnuts
½ cup semisweet chocolate morsels, chopped fairly fine

Baking Preliminaries: Position a rack in the middle of the oven; preheat to 325°F. Line a 10 by 15-inch rimmed baking sheet or jelly roll pan with aluminum foil, letting it overhang the narrow ends of the pan slightly. Coat the foil evenly with nonstick spray.

Lay enough graham crackers flat in the pan so they completely cover the pan bottom; cut them to fit as necessary. Bring the butter and sugar to a boil in a large saucepan over medium heat. Gently boil, stirring, for 2 minutes. Pour the hot mixture over the graham cracker layer, then sprinkle the nuts evenly over the top.

Bake (middle rack) for 10 to 14 minutes, until the top is a rich caramel color and bubbly all over. Set the pan on a wire rack and let cool to warm. Sprinkle the chocolate morsels over the top and let cool till barely warm. Using a large sharp knife, cut the sheet lengthwise into fifths and crosswise into sixths to yield 2 by 2½-inch bars. Let cool completely, then lift up the servings and peel them off the foil.

Yield: Makes thirty-two 2 by 2½-inch bars

Storage: Store these, airtight, for up to 1 week. They can be frozen, airtight, for up to 2 months. Let come to room temperature before serving.

2¼ cups fresh (or frozen, thawed)
     whole cranberries, chopped
¾ cup granulated sugar
½ cup orange marmalade (either
     sweet or Seville will do)
1 16- to 18-ounce package
     refrigerator case sugar cookie
     dough
1⅓ cups old-fashioned rolled oats
¼ cup (½ stick) unsalted butter,
     melted
1 teaspoon ground cinnamon
     Powdered sugar for garnish,
     optional

Tip
Speed prep by chopping the
cranberries in a food processor, if
desired.

SHORTCUT CRANBERRY CRUMB BARS

In these full-flavored, handsome bars, store-bought dough is the foundation
for a crumb mixture, which then cleverly serves as both the base and
topping for colorful fruit bars. The dough is doctored with butter and
cinnamon for rich homemade taste and with rolled oats for interesting
texture. A simple, zesty cranberry or apricot filling goes between the two
layers to lend succulence, fruity taste, and chew.

The same basic recipe may be used to ready either the Cranberry Crumb
Bars or the Apricot-Almond Crumb Bars (see the end of the recipe). To serve
a holiday crowd, I sometimes make a pan of each and present the two
together for an impressive yet fuss-free holiday cookie tray. Perhaps because
they contain butter, which refrigerator case doughs normally lack, nobody
ever suspects they are semi-homemade.

Baking Preliminaries: Position a rack in the middle of the oven; preheat
to 350°F. Line a 9 by 13-inch baking pan with aluminum foil, letting the
narrow ends overhang slightly. Coat the foil with nonstick spray.

Combine the berries, sugar, and marmalade in a medium, heavy,
nonreactive saucepan over medium heat. Cook, stirring, until the mixture
comes to a boil. Lower the heat; boil gently for 3 minutes. Set the filling
aside to cool.

Cut or crumble the dough into small chunks. Combine the chunks in
a large bowl with the oats, butter, and cinnamon. With a mixer on low
speed, mix just until the ingredients are well blended but still crumbly.
(Alternatively, combine the ingredients by stirring, then, if necessary,
kneading them with your hands until blended but still crumbly.) Spread
a generous half of the mixture (no need to measure) into the baking dish.
Lay a piece of wax paper on the mixture. Press down firmly all over to
form a compact, evenly thick layer, then discard the paper.

Bake (middle rack) for 13 to 15 minutes or until the dough is just
browned at the edges but not baked through. Let cool and firm up
slightly.

Spread the filling evenly over the dough. Crumble the remainder of the
crumb mixture evenly over the cranberry mixture. Pat down lightly.
Bake (middle rack) for 22 to 26 minutes longer or until the filling is
bubbly and the crumb top is lightly browned.

Set aside on a wire rack. Let cool. To neatly cut the bars, refrigerate
until chilled and firm (1 hour or more), then lift out using the foil. Peel
off the foil. On a cutting board, cut with a large sharp knife into sixths
crosswise and fourths lengthwise (or as desired) to form bars. If desired,

garnish the bars with a dusting of powdered sugar just before serving.

Yield: Makes twenty-four $2\frac{1}{8}$-inch squares

Storage: Store these, airtight and at room temperature, for up to 1 week. They can be frozen, airtight, for up to 2 months. Serve at room temperature.

Variation: Shortcut Apricot-Almond Crumb Bars
Thoroughly stir together 1 cup finely chopped dried apricots and 1 cup apricot preserves in a medium microwave-safe bowl. Microwave, stopping and stirring every 30 seconds, until the preserves soften and the mixture is warm. Let cool slightly, then stir in $\frac{1}{2}$ cup chopped slivered almonds and $\frac{1}{2}$ cup flaked sweetened coconut to complete the filling. Make the streusel and proceed exactly as directed.

Cookie Jar Wisdom
Money talks, but cookies smile and say hello.

1 16- to 18-ounce package
   refrigerator case sugar cookie
   dough
2 8-ounce packages cream
   cheese or Neufchâtel cheese,
   softened
¾ cup granulated sugar
2 large eggs, at room temperature
2 tablespoons fresh lemon juice
1 tablespoon finely grated lemon
   zest (yellow part of the peel)
2½ teaspoons vanilla extract
2 tablespoons graham cracker
   crumbs, vanilla wafer crumbs,
   or gingersnap crumbs, or ¼ cup
   raspberry or red currant jelly,
   melted and then cooled just
   slightly, for garnish

Tip
The quickest way to finish the
bars is to garnish the cheesecake
top after it comes out of the oven
with a sprinkling of cookie or
cracker crumbs. Or, wait until the
pan is well chilled and firm, and
then brush the surface all over
with melted jelly.

SUPER-EASY CHEESECAKE BARS

Here's yet another semi-homemade recipe that uses purchased cookie
dough as the base for bars—in this case for good, effortless, cheesecake
bars. The smooth, flavorful, from-scratch cheesecake filling is whipped
up quickly in a food processor, then poured over the partly baked dough
layer and baked some more. The resulting bars are so much easier than a
completely from-scratch cheesecake, yet are so appealing and attractive,
that they may become a standby.

Baking Preliminaries: Position a rack in the middle of the oven; preheat
to 350°F. Grease a 9 by 13-inch baking pan or coat with nonstick spray.
Crumble the log of dough into the baking pan, then press out to form
an evenly thick layer. Top with a sheet of wax paper; press firmly and
smooth out the layer further. Discard the paper.

Bake (middle rack) for 17 to 22 minutes or until the dough is nicely
browned all over and slightly darker at the edges.

Process the cream cheese and sugar in a food processor until smooth,
scraping down the bowl several times. One at a time, through the feed
tube, add the eggs, the lemon juice, zest, and vanilla, processing until
blended. (Alternatively, in a large bowl using a mixer, thoroughly beat
the cream cheese and sugar until completely smooth. One at a time beat
in the eggs. Beat in the lemon juice, zest, and vanilla.)

Spread the filling mixture evenly over the crust. Rap the pan on the
counter to remove air bubbles. Return the pan to the oven. Bake for 20
to 30 minutes longer or until the cheesecake layer is just barely set when
tapped in the center top.

Set the pan on a wire rack, sprinkle with the crumbs, if desired, and let
cool to room temperature. Refrigerate, covered, for at least 2½ hours or
until chilled and firm, before serving.

To garnish with jelly, if desired, brush it evenly over the cold and firm
cheesecake surface; use a pastry brush for best results. Refrigerate the
pan for a few minutes, until the jelly cools, before cutting and serving the
bars. Cut into quarters lengthwise and crosswise (or as desired).

Yield: Makes sixteen 2¼ by 3¼-inch bars

Storage: Store these, covered in the refrigerator, for up to 1 week. They
can be frozen, covered with plastic wrap then enclosed in a plastic bag,
for up to 1 month; let thaw in the refrigerator. Serve the bars slightly
chilled.

MASTER DOUGH, FANCY COOKIES & DECORATING PROJECTS }

You'll find a grab bag of goodies in this chapter, from a recipe and directions for preparing several piped and pressed cookies to instructions for making and decorating "stained glass" cookies.

One very handy offering here is a master butter dough recipe and directions for turning out six completely different kinds of cookies. With it you can create a handsome, remarkably varied assortment quickly. In fact, the six choices—marbled mocha chip cookies, rolled sugar cookies, fruity cranberry-cinnamon swirls, crunchy almondines, orange cookies, and chocolate-caramel cookies—are so unlike one another that it's doubtful anybody will ever guess they came from a single dough.

I've also included a basic French macaron recipe, as well as directions for producing more than a dozen different flavor variations. These ethereal creations can't, by any stretch of the imagination, be called simple to make, but they are certainly doable and become easier with practice. And remember, they will definitely be delicious even if they come out looking a smidge less than pastry shop perfect.

Easy
Versatile recipe: one dough, six
different cookies.
Convenient make-ahead.
Generous batch.

MASTER BUTTER DOUGH—SIX GREAT COOKIES

Especially handy for holiday baking, this master butter dough recipe goes together quickly and can be used to make six *completely different* cookies. Keep in mind that *one batch of dough* makes a total of at least six dozen cookies in *three unique flavors*. So, for all six kinds, you'll need to make the batch *twice* (which yields 12 dozen cookies). All six kinds presented together will produce a large and quite spectacular holiday array.

For convenience, prepare the dough well ahead, then make the cookies when you need them. Here's the assortment that can be readied with the recipe: Marbled Mocha-Cocoa Chipsters, Cranberry-Cinnamon Swirlies, Rolled Sugar Cookies, Orange (or Apricot or Pineapple) Dabs, Almondines, and Chocolate-Caramel Surprise Cookies. They all look and taste so different from one another that nobody will believe they came from one basic dough!

A major key to the success of this recipe is the ample use of butter—it lends a lush taste and amplifies the other unique flavoring elements in each cookie variety. The butter needs to be warm and soft enough to blend together smoothly when stirred or gently beaten, but it should not be melted and runny. The easiest way to obtain the right consistency is simply to let the butter sit in a bowl in a warm room for about an hour (or a cool room for $1\frac{1}{2}$ to 2 hours).

MASTER BUTTER DOUGH:

Once this basic butter dough is mixed up, divide it into thirds and use it to prepare any *three* of the following six cookies.

2 cups (4 sticks) unsalted butter, slightly softened and cut into chunks
$1\frac{1}{2}$ cups granulated sugar
$2\frac{1}{2}$ tablespoons whole or low-fat milk
1 tablespoon vanilla extract
2 large eggs, at room temperature
2 teaspoons baking powder
1 teaspoon salt
$5\frac{2}{3}$ cups unbleached all-purpose white flour

Mixer method: In a very large bowl, beat the butter on low speed until it is smooth and the consistency of sour cream. On low speed, beat in the sugar, milk, and vanilla until well blended and the sugar dissolves. Beat in the eggs, baking powder, and salt until very evenly incorporated. Gradually beat in the flour; if the motor labors, stir in the last of it just until evenly incorporated.

Mixing by hand: In a very large bowl, vigorously stir the butter until it is smooth and the consistency of sour cream. Stir in the sugar, milk, and vanilla until well blended and the sugar dissolves. Vigorously stir in the eggs, baking powder, and salt until very thoroughly incorporated. Gradually stir in the flour just until evenly incorporated; be sure incorporate the flour in the bottom of the bowl.

If the dough is very soft, mix in up to 4 tablespoons more flour; if crumbly, mix in up to 4 teaspoons water until it holds together. Let the dough stand for 5 minutes to firm up slightly.

Divide the dough into thirds. Use the portions immediately as directed in the individual recipes, or place the portions in airtight plastic bags and refrigerate for up to 48 hours or freeze for up to 2 months. Let the chilled dough portions return to cool room temperature before proceeding. Then prepare each portion using one of the six following recipes.

MARBLED MOCHA-COCOA CHIPSTERS

Have on hand one-third of a batch of the Master Butter Dough (opposite) at cool room temperature and in a large bowl.

3 tablespoons unsweetened natural (non-alkalized) cocoa powder or Dutch-process cocoa powder, sifted after measuring, if lumpy

1 tablespoon granulated sugar

1 teaspoon instant espresso powder or instant coffee granules

1 cup (6 ounces) semisweet or bittersweet chocolate morsels, divided

⅓ batch Master Butter Dough (opposite), at room temperature

Baking Preliminaries: Position a rack in the middle of the oven; preheat to 350°F. Line two large baking sheets with baking parchment.

In a small bowl, stir together the cocoa powder, sugar, espresso granules, and 3½ tablespoons hot water until well blended and smooth. Let cool. Stir or knead the cocoa mixture and ½ cup chocolate morsels into the dough just until partially incorporated; leave attractive mocha swirls and streaks throughout. Let the dough stand to cool and firm for 5 minutes.

Working on wax paper or baking parchment, divide the dough into quarters, then divide each quarter into 6 equal portions. Shape the portions into balls. Dip one side of the balls into the remaining morsels until a few are imbedded. Space the balls, morsel side up, about 2 inches apart on the sheets. Pat down the balls until 2 inches in diameter.

Bake (middle rack) one pan at a time for 8 to 11 minutes or until the cookies are barely firm when pressed in the center tops. Let stand to firm up for 3 minutes, then cool the cookies on wire racks.

Yield: Makes twenty-four 3-inch cookies

Storage: Store these, airtight, for up to 10 days. They can be frozen, airtight, for up to 1 month.

CRANBERRY-CINNAMON SWIRLIES

Have on hand one-third of a batch of the Master Butter Dough (opposite), at room temperature and placed in a large bowl.

Baking Preliminaries: Position a rack in the middle of the oven; preheat to 350°F. Line two large baking sheets with baking parchment or spray with nonstick spray.

1 cup sweetened dried
   cranberries
$\frac{1}{3}$ batch Master Butter Dough
   (page 280)
$2\frac{1}{2}$ tablespoons fresh orange juice or
   water
2 teaspoons ground cinnamon
$\frac{1}{4}$ teaspoon ground cloves
1 teaspoon lemon extract or
   vanilla extract
$\frac{1}{3}$ cup chopped walnuts or
   1 tablespoon granulated sugar
   for garnish

Stir or knead the cranberries into the dough until evenly distributed. In a small bowl, stir together the orange juice, cinnamon, cloves, and extract. Stir or knead the spice mixture into the dough just until partially incorporated; some attractive swirls and streaks should remain. Using a 1½-inch-diameter spring-loaded ice cream scoop or a heaping 1-tablespoon measure, scoop up dough portions; space in even mounds about 2 inches apart on the baking sheets. Lightly pat down the tops. Lightly sprinkle the walnuts over the cookies, then pat down lightly to imbed.

Bake (middle rack) one sheet at a time for 9 to 12 minutes or until lightly tinged with brown at the edges and barely firm when pressed in the center top.

Yield: Makes about twenty-four 2¼-inch cookies

Storage: Store these, airtight, for up to 10 days. They can be frozen, airtight, for up to 1½ months.

ROLLED SUGAR COOKIES
Have on hand one-third of a batch of the Master Butter Dough (page 280). It can be room temperature, or cool yet pliable enough to roll out.

Divide the dough in half. Roll out each half a scant ¼ inch thick between sheets of baking parchment or wax paper. Stack the portions (paper attached) on a tray or baking sheet. Refrigerate for 15 to 25 minutes, until the dough is cold and firm (or speed chilling by freezing for 12 to 15 minutes). (Alternatively, keep the dough refrigerated or frozen for up to 48 hours; let the frozen dough warm up until soft enough to cut out before using.)

$\frac{1}{3}$ batch Master Butter Dough
   (page 280)
$1\frac{1}{2}$ tablespoons granulated sugar,
   homemade vanilla-scented
   granulated sugar (page 327),
   or homemade or purchased
   colored sprinkles for garnish

Baking Preliminaries: Position a rack in the middle of the oven; preheat to 350°F. Line two baking sheets with baking parchment.

Working with one portion and keeping the other chilled, peel away, one sheet of paper, then pat it back into place on the dough. (This will make it easier to lift cookies from the paper later.) Peel off and discard the second paper layer. Using 2- to 2¾-inch cutters, cut out the cookies.

Transfer them to the baking sheets using a wide-bladed spatula, spacing about 1½ inches apart. If the dough softens too much to handle easily, slide the paper and cookies onto a baking sheet and re-chill in the refrigerator or freezer. Repeat preparations with the second dough portion. Gather all the scraps, and repeat the rolling, chilling, and cutting until all the dough is used. Sprinkle the cookie tops with the sugar garnish or sprinkles, if desired.

Bake (middle rack) one sheet at a time for 7 to 11 minutes, or just until the cookies are colored at the edges; rotate the sheet halfway through to ensure even baking. Let the cookies stand to firm up for 2 minutes. Using a thin spatula, transfer the cookies to a cooling rack. Let stand until cooled.

Yield: Makes twenty-five to thirty 2½- to 3-inch sugar cookies

Storage: Store these, airtight, for up to 10 days. They can be frozen, airtight, for up to 1 month.

ORANGE (OR APRICOT OR PINEAPPLE) DABS

Have on hand one-third of a batch of the *Master Butter Dough* (page 280). It should be at cool room temperature and on a large sheet of wax paper.

2½ tablespoons granulated sugar

½ teaspoon finely grated orange zest (orange part of the peel)

¼ teaspoon ground cardamom or ½ teaspoon ground allspice

⅓ batch Master Butter Dough (page 280), at cool room temperature

⅓ to ½ cup orange marmalade or apricot or pineapple jam

Baking Preliminaries: Position a rack in the middle of the oven; preheat to 350°F. Line a very large baking sheet with baking parchment.
In small bowl, stir together the sugar, orange zest, and cardamom until very well blended. Divide the dough in half; then divide each half into 12 equal portions. Shape the portions into balls. Dip the top of each ball into the sugar mixture, then place them dipped side up on the sheet, about 2 inches apart.

Using a knuckle or thumb, press down the center of each ball to make a deep well. Put a generous ¼ teaspoon orange marmalade in each well.

Bake (middle rack) one sheet at a time for 11 to 15 minutes or until the cookies are lightly tinged with brown and the edges are slightly darker. Slide the parchment and cookies onto a flat surface. Let stand until completely cooled.

Yield: Makes twenty-four 2¼-inch cookies

Storage: Store these, airtight, for up to 10 days. They can be frozen, airtight, for up to 1½ months.

ALMONDINES

Have on hand one-third of a batch of the Master Butter Dough (page 280). It should be at cool room temperature and in a large bowl.

1½ tablespoons whole or low-fat milk

1 teaspoon finely grated lemon zest (yellow part of the peel)

1 teaspoon almond extract

¾ cup coarsely chopped slivered almonds, divided

⅓ batch Master Butter Dough (page 280), at room temperature

Baking Preliminaries: Position a rack in the middle of the oven; preheat to 350°F. Line a large baking sheet with baking parchment.

In a small bowl, stir together the milk, lemon zest, almond extract, and ½ cup coarsely chopped almonds. Stir or knead the mixture into the dough until smoothly incorporated. Refrigerate the dough for about 10 minutes or until firmed up slightly. On wax paper, divide the dough into quarters, then divide each quarter into 8 equal balls. Garnish by firmly pressing the top of each ball into a shallow bowl of the remaining ¼ cup coarsely chopped almonds. Space the cookies, nut side up, about 1½ inches apart on the sheet. Pat down the tops just slightly.

Bake (middle rack) one pan at a time for 9 to 13 minutes or until the nuts and dough are lightly tinged with brown. Slide the parchment and cookies onto a flat surface. Let stand until completely cooled.

Yield: Makes thirty-two 2-inch cookies

Storage: Store these, airtight, for up to 10 days. They can be frozen, airtight, for up to 1 month.

CHOCOLATE-CARAMEL SURPRISE COOKIES

To make this recipe, have one-third of a batch of the Master Butter Dough (page 280) on hand and at room temperature.

⅓ batch Master Butter Dough (page 280), at room temperature

24 Rolo candies, Hershey caramel-filled chocolate kisses, Milk Dud candies, or other similar-size milk chocolate–covered caramels

3½ tablespoons clover honey or light or dark corn syrup

A generous ¾ cup finely chopped pecans

Baking Preliminaries: Position a rack in the middle of the oven; preheat to 350°F. Line a very large baking sheet with baking parchment.

On a sheet of wax paper, divide the dough into quarters, then divide each quarter into 6 equal portions. Push a candy into the center of each portion, then shape the dough up around it until the candy is imbedded and the dough forms a ball.

Put the honey in a small shallow bowl. Quickly roll each ball until evenly coated in the honey, then shake off the excess. Immediately roll the ball in the nuts until lightly but evenly coated. Space the cookies about 2 inches apart on the baking sheet.

Bake (middle rack) one pan at a time for 13 to 16 minutes or until the cookies are lightly tinged with brown and feel almost firm when pressed on top. Slide the parchment and cookies onto a flat surface. Let stand until completely cooled.

Yield: Makes twenty-four 2¾-inch cookies

Tip—To Soften Butter Quickly

If you don't have time to set out and soften the butter in advance: Place the butter chunks in a microwave-safe bowl. Microwave on 50 percent or medium power (*never* full power) for 30 seconds. Stir vigorously, then let stand for 1 minute. If the butter is still not soft enough to form a smooth, sour cream consistency when vigorously stirred, microwave it on low power for 20 to 30 seconds longer. Stir well again, then let it stand to soften. To avoid inadvertently melting it, don't microwave any further.

Cookie Jar Wisdom
Cookie-fucious says: Take two, even when they're not small.

6 tablespoons (¾ stick) unsalted butter, softened and cut into chunks

¼ cup corn oil or other flavorless vegetable oil

¾ cup powdered sugar

¼ cup freeze-dried strawberry or raspberry powder (page 336), plus about 1 tablespoon for garnish, optional

½ teaspoon raspberry extract or vanilla extract

1 cup unbleached all-purpose white flour, plus more if needed

1 batch Intensely Strawberry or Raspberry Buttercream (page 326)

Tip

These cookies are designed to be piped using a pastry bag and open star tip, but just in case you don't have them, I've provided alternative hand-shaping directions that produce "buttons" at the end of the recipe.

BEST-EVER FROSTED STRAWBERRY OR RASPBERRY SWIRLS

In the past I always found strawberry or raspberry cookies a bit lacking—even those I created myself! One problem was that artificial berry flavorings tasted, well, artificial. The alternative, incorporating enough berry juice or pulp to lend a berry flavor, had a drawback, too—it produced cakey or soggy cookies.

The solution to both problems turns out to be some recently introduced products: freeze-dried berry powders. These intensely flavored berry essences not only impart appealing natural flavor and aroma to cookies and buttercreams, but they add inviting color, too. At this point the powders are still hard to find except online and in large-quantity packages, but there is a simple alternative. Buy a little package of the plain freeze-dried strawberries and raspberries (stocked in upscale markets and health food stores or available online), then briefly food-process and sieve them to create your own powders; see page 336 for the recipe.

With the powder on hand—you can use strawberry, raspberry, or half of each kind—it's possible to make supremely flavorful cookies and matching frostings that were never doable in the past. These little rounds are not too sweet, wonderfully sandy-crisp, and make a beautiful presentation. Just in case you're wondering, even though the dough has a pretty berry tinge, it will mostly fade away during baking. The berry frostings that top them (page 326) are what provide the beautiful color (plus more fruity flavor and aroma, of course).

Baking Preliminaries: Position a rack in the middle of the oven; preheat to 350°F. Line two large baking sheets with baking parchment.

In a large bowl with a mixer on low, then medium, speed, beat the butter, oil, powdered sugar, strawberry or raspberry powder, and raspberry extract until well blended and smooth. On low speed, beat in the flour just until evenly incorporated. If the mixture is too crumbly or firm to pipe, gradually beat in enough water to yield a soft dough. (Try a test cookie if you aren't sure whether the dough is soft enough to readily pipe.)

Fill the pastry bag no more than half full and close the top. Pipe 1½-inch rosettes, spacing about 2 inches apart on the baking sheets.

Bake (middle rack) one pan at a time for 11 to 13 minutes or until the cookies are just firm on top and barely tinged at the edges.

Transfer the pan to a wire rack. Let the cookies stand until cooled completely, as they are too tender to handle while warm. Ready the matching buttercream as directed, and decorate by piping rosettes

or simply swirling the frosting over the tops of the cookies with a table knife. Garnish by lightly sifting additional berry powder over the top of the buttercream, if desired.

Yield: Makes about thirty-five 2-inch rosettes (or 32 hand-shaped buttons)

Storage: Store these, packed in a single layer in an airtight container at room temperature, for up to 4 days. They can be frozen, airtight, for up to 1 month; let come to room temperature before serving.

Variation: Hand-Shaped Berry Buttons Prepare the dough as directed, except add only enough water so that the dough holds together and can be shaped into balls. Divide the dough in half. Working on wax paper or baking parchment, shape each half into a flat disk. Cut each disk into fourths, then sixteenths. Shape into balls. Space about 2 inches apart on the baking sheets. Proceed exactly as directed in the original recipe.

Fairly Complicated
Gourmet look, gourmet taste.
Versatile recipe: one dough,
multiple flavors.

1 cup powdered sugar

1 cup almond flour, plus more if
   needed

1 teaspoon very finely grated
   lemon or orange zest (colored
   part of the peel), optional
   Pinch of salt

3 large egg whites, scant ½ cup
   aged (see headnote) and at
   room temperature and free of
   yolk, plus more egg white if
   needed, divided

½ teaspoon vanilla or almond
   extract or 1½ teaspoons instant
   espresso powder dissolved in
   1½ teaspoons water

½ cup granulated sugar
   Liquid synthetic or botanically
   based food colors, optional
   Buttercream or Ganache filling
   options—Vanilla, Almond,
   Coffee-Vanilla, Citrus, Ginger-
   Citrus, Cocoa , Chocolate
   Ganache

Tip
Macarons are best if the
"sandwiches" are allowed to mellow
and meld 12 to 18 hours before
serving, so plan accordingly. They
also need to be baked on a dry day.

VANILLA, ALMOND, ESPRESSO, OR CITRUS FRENCH MACARONS

There is no getting around it: These ethereal little French almond meringue sandwiches are a bit of trouble to make—which is why they are mostly turned out by pastry chefs and not home bakers. But they are so incredibly popular these days that, even though they are not as "simply" sensational as most cookies in the book, I had to provide a recipe for them.

If you have the time and pay attention to details, these are not only doable but will probably taste better, maybe even *lots better*, than the average store-bought French macarons. The ones from the high-end Paris patisseries are, of course, not average, but with care, and a little practice yours may even match theirs!

These beauties do involve some advance planning, including separating the egg whites well ahead and letting them "age" in the refrigerator for at least four and preferably six days. While this step takes no skill, it's vital; otherwise the meringue may not puff and set with little raised edges (called "feet") when they bake. The recipe also requires a candy thermometer, piping bag and tip, mixer, and food processor. One bit of good news—they can be made well ahead and even improve upon storage.

To keep things as streamlined as possible, I've created a basic recipe that can be used to make vanilla, almond, espresso, lemon, or orange macarons. Plus, a whole array of additional macaron flavors can be prepared following the variations at the end.

Like most folks, I'm enchanted with the pretty rainbow array of macaron colors, but I much prefer subtle, natural-looking shades over the bright, garish (and to my mind artificial-looking) ones often seen in pastry shops. So, I use a very light hand when adding food coloring so that my lavender macarons come out pale lavender, the raspberry macarons a gentle rose-pink, and the lemon ones a soft yellow. But this is a matter of personal preference, so feel free to create whatever hues you like. Remember as you add in food colors that the shades will become a little more muted once the macarons bake.

One very effective way to heighten visual drama when making French macarons in soft, subtle shades is to add an accent of bolder natural color and aroma after baking. Depending on the macaron flavor, a light dusting of pure, bright raspberry powder, green tea powder, or cocoa powder, or a sprinkling of citrus zest or even edible flower confetti added after the macarons are filled can be the perfect finishing touch (as shown in the photo, page 290).

In the following recipe, add or omit the lemon or orange zest and the

vanilla, or almond extract and espresso powder mixture to produce the macaron flavor desired. Then pair them up with whatever complementary buttercreams you choose, such as the lemon or orange buttercream or ginger-citrus for the citrus macarons; the cocoa buttercream for the almond or espresso macarons, or raspberry or cocoa-berry buttercream for the vanilla macarons. Do experiment with other combinations to suit your own taste.

Preliminaries: Line two large baking sheets with baking parchment. Set out a large pastry bag fitted with a plain ½-inch-diameter tip.

In a food processor, process the powdered sugar, almond flour, zest (if preparing citrus-flavored macarons), and salt until well blended but not oily. Add 2 tablespoons egg whites and the extract (or espresso powder mixture, if making espresso macarons) and pulse several times until incorporated; don't over-process. Turn out the mixture into a large bowl.

In a large, grease-free mixer bowl with the mixer on low speed, then medium speed, beat ¼ cup egg whites until frothy. Use a whisk-shaped beater if available. Raise the speed to medium-high and beat just until they form soft peaks. Turn off the mixer.

In a small heavy saucepan, immediately bring the granulated sugar and 2 tablespoons water to a boil over medium heat, stirring. Wash any sugar from the pan sides with a wet pastry brush. Without further stirring, cook to 238°F on a candy thermometer; if at any point the syrup starts to color, lift and swirl the pan and immediately remove the syrup from the heat. Then stir in ½ teaspoon warm water to stop the cooking.

Start beating the eggs whites again on medium speed, gradually drizzling the hot syrup over them, then food color, if using. (Avoid the bowl sides and beater, as the syrup will stick to them.) Continue

beating on high speed until the whites are glossy and stiffened, adding more food color if necessary to obtain the hue desired. Stir about one-quarter of the meringue into the almond flour mixture until thoroughly incorporated. If it is dry and crumbly, gradually stir in enough more egg whites to yield a smooth, paste-like consistency. Then, thoroughly fold the remainder of the meringue into the almond mixture until very well blended; don't worry about deflating the meringue. If the batter is too stiff to pipe readily or form into rounds on the pan, gently but thoroughly fold in enough more egg whites to moisten it. If it is too soft to hold a shape or runs when piped, fold in enough more almond flour to stiffen it slightly.

Immediately put the batter into the pastry bag, filling no more than two-thirds full. Pipe the batter into generous 1-inch rounds about 1½ inches apart on the baking sheets. Rap the sheets on the counter several times to remove air bubbles and allow the "tails" left on the rounds from piping to flatten out. Then let the macarons stand to firm up for about 30 minutes; a slight crust will form on the top, which helps them hold their shape during baking.

Baking Preliminaries: Position a rack in the middle of the oven; preheat to 350°F.

When the macarons are slightly firm on top, place one pan at a time on the middle rack. Immediately reduce the oven to 325°F; bake for 5 minutes. Reduce the oven to 250°F and bake for 8 to 11 minutes longer or until the macarons are firm inside when lightly pressed in the center top. Slide the macarons and parchment onto a wire rack. Let stand until completely cooled, then gently peel them from the parchment.

At least 8 hours ahead of serving time and preferably longer, form sandwiches by filling pairs of macaroons with a buttercream, the chocolate ganache filling, jam, crème, or other filling of your choice. Spread a $\frac{1}{4}$- to $\frac{1}{3}$-inch-thick layer of filling on the undersides of half the meringues. Top them with similar-size meringue shells, top sides facing up. Press down until the filling squeezes out to the edges. Dust the tops with a coordinating ingredient, such as cocoa over cocoa-filled macarons, or shreds of lime zest over lime macarons, if desired.

Yield: Makes fifteen to eighteen 2-inch French macaron sandwiches

Storage: Store these, airtight and refrigerated, for up to 1 week. They can be frozen, airtight, for up to 1 month. Let come nearly to room temperature before serving.

Variation: Cocoa Macarons Incorporate in the processor along with the powdered sugar and almond flour: $2\frac{1}{2}$ tablespoons unsweetened cocoa powder and process as directed. When adding the egg whites, add $1\frac{1}{2}$ tablespoons water and proceed exactly as directed. Fill the macarons with cocoa buttercream or cocoa-berry buttercream (page 324) or vanilla buttercream (page 321) or raspberry buttercream (page 326) or chocolate ganache filling (page 318). Finish by dusting the tops of filled macarons with a light sifting of cocoa powder, if desired.

Variation: Cocoa-Berry Macarons Incorporate in the processor along with the powdered sugar and almond flour: $1\frac{1}{2}$ tablespoons unsweetened cocoa powder and 2 teaspoons raspberry or strawberry powder and process as directed. Note: Do not be tempted to add extra berry powder; it will ruin the meringue consistency. When adding the egg whites, add $1\frac{1}{2}$ tablespoons water and $\frac{1}{2}$ teaspoon raspberry extract and proceed exactly as directed. Fill with

cocoa or cocoa-berry buttercream (page 324) or raspberry or strawberry buttercream (page 326). Finish by dusting the tops with a light sifting of berry powder, if desired.

Variation: Cocoa-Orange-Spice Macarons Incorporate in the processor along with the powdered sugar and almond flour: 2 tablespoons unsweetened cocoa powder, 1 teaspoon finely grated orange zest, and $\frac{1}{4}$ teaspoon ground cardamom and process as directed. When adding the egg whites, add $1\frac{1}{2}$ tablespoons water and proceed exactly as directed. Fill with cocoa buttercream (page 324), cocoa-cardamom orange buttercream (page 325), or orange buttercream (page 328). Finish by dusting the tops with a light sifting of cocoa powder or garnish with fine shreds of fresh orange zest, if desired.

Variation: Green Tea–Ginger-Lime Macarons Incorporate in the processor along with the powdered sugar and almond flour: 1 tablespoon matcha green tea powder, 1 teaspoon finely grated fresh gingerroot, and 1 teaspoon very finely grated lime zest and process as directed. Tint the meringue mixture green, if desired. Fill with lime-ginger buttercream (page 328). Finish by dusting the tops of the filled macarons with a light sifting of green tea powder, if desired.

Variation: Lavender-Lemon Macarons Grind 1 tablespoon dried lavender and $1\frac{1}{2}$ tablespoons powdered sugar in a processor until mostly powdery (some bits will remain). Stir the mixture through a very fine-mesh sieve until the powdery part and only very fine bits go through; discard the coarse bits remaining in the sieve. Incorporate in the processor along with the powdered sugar and almond flour: the sieved lavender and 1 teaspoon very finely grated lemon zest and process as directed. Tint the meringue mixture lavender (drops of red and blue color) as desired. Fill with lavender buttercream (page 330).

Variation: Raspberry or Very Berry Macarons
Incorporate in the processor along with the powdered sugar and almond flour: 2 teaspoons raspberry or strawberry powder (see page 336 for the recipe) and process as directed. When adding the egg whites, add 2 teaspoons water and 1 teaspoon raspberry extract and proceed exactly as directed. Note: Do not be tempted to add extra berry powder; it will ruin the meringue consistency. Tint the meringue mixture pink or red as desired. Fill with cocoa-berry buttercream (page 324) or raspberry or strawberry buttercream (page 326). Finish by dusting the tops with a light sifting of raspberry or strawberry powder, if desired.

Cookie Jar Wisdom
My Rx: Take two cookies and call me in the morning.

1 batch Good and Easy Rolled
   Sugar Cookie dough (page
   112), or Nice 'n' Spicy Rolled
   Gingerbread Cookie dough
   (page 140), ready for rolling out
   Assorted clear hard candies,
   such as Jolly Ranchers, LifeSav-
   ers, or lollipops, in whatever
   colors are desired
   Small, clean artist's brush for
   brushing away excess candy
   bits

Tip

Unless you are readying light
catcher cookies to be used mostly
for decoration, it's best not to make
the stained glass design elements
too large, as expansive areas of
hard candy can make cookies very
crunchy and unpleasant to eat. Have
on hand mini cookie or aspic cutters,
or the end of a metal pastry piping
tip (or a thimble or small bottle cap)
to cut out the openings to be filled
with the "glass."

Cookie Jar Wisdom
Cookies are the only snack
worth crumbs in the bed.

STAINED GLASS COOKIES

It's fun and easy to make eye-catching "stained glass" or "jewel-studded"
cookies. And if you use the simple method provided here, your creations
will look beautiful every single time. This recipe differs from many in that the
stained glass candy bits are added *after* the cookies are baked. The baked
cookies are simply placed on foil-lined baking sheets and the crushed candy
is inserted into the openings and cutaways. The cookies go back in the oven
just long enough for the hard candy shards to melt and form the smooth
jewel-like insets. The advantage of this approach is that the candy doesn't
boil over, drip, or discolor from too much heat.

Most plain rolled doughs are suitable for making stained glass cookies. The
Good and Easy Rolled Sugar Cookies (page 112) and the Nice 'n' Spicy Rolled
Gingerbread Cookies (page 140) both work well: They are fairly sturdy and
easy to handle, plus the finished cookies hold their cutout shapes nicely.

Once the stained glass components have cooled and hardened, the
cookies can be further decorated with whatever glazed or piped icing
accents are desired.

Roll out the dough between sheets of baking parchment as directed
in the individual recipes. Cut out the cookies using whatever seasonal
cutters you like–hearts for Valentine's Day, pine trees for Christmas,
snowflakes for winter, blossoms for spring, and so forth. Then, using mini
cookie cutters or the end of a metal pastry piping tip (or a thimble or
small bottle cap), cut out small decorative openings and cutaways from
each cookie, as desired.

Bake the cookies following the recipe directions, except reduce the
baking time just slightly. If planning to hang up and display the cookies,
be sure to make a stringing hole in each before you bake. Put small
lengths of toothpicks in the holes to keep them from closing during
baking.

Ready the candies: Put each color of candy in a tightly closed triple layer
of plastic bags or between two plastic chopping mats. Crack or crush the
candies into fairly fine bits using a mallet or heavy metal spoon.

Once the cookies are baked and firm enough to handle, lay them,
slightly separated, on a foil-lined baking sheet; *do not* omit the foil or the
cookies will stick to the pan. Fill the cutaway areas in the cookies with
the crushed clear hard candies. The usual method is to use only one
color per cutaway, but a multicolored or rainbow look can be employed
if desired. Spoon enough candy bits into the cutaways to fill them, but

Tip

The decorating technique shown below right is called marbling. It involves spreading a cookie surface with a fairly fluid icing, then immediately adding a contrasting icing and swirling or drawing it through with a toothpick. With just a little practice the method becomes fairly easy.

don't pile in so much that they overflow. If necessary, use a small, clean artist's paint brush to brush away any shards that drop onto the cookie surface.

Put the cookies back into the oven just long enough for the candy to melt but not boil over, usually about 2 minutes—keep checking, as the time varies considerably depending on the brand of candy. Let the cookies stand on the baking sheet until completely cool again. Do not touch the stained glass parts during cooling, as they will be extremely hot and can cause serious burns. Gently peel the cooled cookies off the foil. Decorate them further as shown, if desired.

Yield: Makes as many stained glass cookies as the batch of selected dough normally yields

Storage: Store these exactly as directed in the individual cookie dough recipe. Stained glass cookie hanging ornaments can be displayed, unwrapped, for up to several weeks; however, they will gradually stale too much to be tasty.

Easy
One-bowl mixing.
Short ingredient list.

1 cup (2 sticks) unsalted butter,
   slightly softened and cut into
   chunks
   Scant 1¼ cups powdered sugar
2 tablespoons whole or low-fat
   milk, plus more if needed
1½ teaspoons vanilla extract or
   ¾ teaspoon almond extract,
   or both
2 large egg yolks, at room
   temperature
¼ teaspoon salt
2⅓ cups unbleached all-purpose
   white flour, plus more if
   needed
   Bits of almond, citrus, or candied
   cherries for garnishing round
   cookies, and sparkling sugar for
   other shapes, optional

Cookie Jar Wisdom
Cookies are made of butter
and love.

PRESSED OR PIPED SPRITZ COOKIES

A good spritz cookie is a nice addition to any dessert tray and any cookie baker's repertoire. Mild, buttery, and elegant, these classics are undemanding to mix up, taste rich and gratifying, and, whether formed using a cookie press or pastry bag and tip, look very special.

If you have a cookie press and enjoy working with it, by all means use it to form these cookies. But, if you wish, a pastry bag and tip will yield equally handsome (though slightly different) results, and, in my opinion, is easier to use. In either case, the "spritzing" will go quickly so long as the dough is the right consistency.

Baking Preliminaries: Position a rack in the middle of the oven; preheat to 350°F. Line a large baking sheet with baking parchment.

In a large bowl, beat the butter on low speed (use a paddle-shaped beater if available) until smooth and the consistency of sour cream. On low speed, beat in the sugar, milk, and vanilla until well blended and the sugar dissolves. Beat in the egg yolks and salt until very evenly incorporated. Gradually beat or stir in the flour just until evenly incorporated; if the dough is stiff, stir in enough more milk, ½ tablespoon at a time, to yield a slightly soft but not batter-like consistency.

Test for the correct consistency by putting a small quantity of dough in the cookie press tube fitted with a decorative plate, or in a pastry bag fitted with a ½-inch-diameter open star tip. If the dough is too stiff to readily press or pipe, add a little more milk and try again. When the dough can be pressed through the plate or piped but is not soft, fill the tube or half-fill the bag.

Press or pipe the cookies into 1½-inch pressed cookie shapes or 1½-inch rosettes, spacing about 1½ inches apart on the baking sheet. Press a garnish into the center of the cookies, or sprinkle lightly with decorating sugar, if desired.

Bake (middle rack) one pan at a time for 15 to 18 minutes or until the cookies are just firm when pressed in the centers and their edges are lightly tinged. If necessary for even browning, rotate the sheet from front to back halfway through baking.

Yield: Makes thirty to thirty-five 2- to 2½-inch cookies

Storage: Store these, airtight, up to 10 days. Or freeze, airtight, for up to 1 month.

FROSTINGS, FILLINGS & FINISHING TOUCHES }

For the past several years I've been coming up with assorted fresh, au naturel ways of decorating cookies to supplement the usual old-fashioned techniques most of us have always used. In this chapter and in photos in the book you'll see some of the results—icings and buttercream frostings, homemade decorating sugars, and even homemade sprinkles that get most or all of their color and flavor from natural ingredients, including vanilla, fruits and fruit juices, berries, spices, herbs, citrus zests, and even fresh and crystallized *edible* flowers. Of course, you'll still find the expected traditional toppers and fillings, but in case you'd like to try the au naturel ones, they are noted as such at the top of the recipe.

These alternative recipes make it possible to create beautiful, eye-catching cookies without relying much on purchased decors and sugars full of commercial food colorings, especially red and yellow ones. For one thing, many folks (including me!) have discovered they're allergic to certain red and yellow dyes. (Many of the red and yellow shades are classified as azo dyes, synthetic petrochemical formulations known to be allergens or irritants for some people.)

Since a lot of people bake cookies either with or for their family and some of these *entirely optional* additives are iffy, it seems wise to employ them sparingly or skip them altogether. (Several manufacturers do sell all-natural food color sets and sprinkles, and I've successfully worked with them. See page 300 for a rundown of the various options and sources.) In case you're wondering, using all natural colorants *does not* mean having to settle for ho-hum results: *All* of the iced cookies shown in this book are enhanced with only botanically based colors, most often from readily available frozen fruit juice concentrates, occasionally from purchased all-natural dyes (discussed on page 300).

With the exception of several new flavored sugars (mentioned in the source list, page 300) most store-bought decorating sugars, sprinkles, and food coloring products have another important drawback: They're added only for looks and contribute *nothing* whatsoever to taste, other than sweetness. So, for cookies that taste their absolute best, opting for tempting homemade toppers just makes sense. (Don't worry—they're easier than you might imagine!)

You probably won't be surprised to hear that garnishing sugars made by quickly grinding citrus zest, vanilla beans, spices, fresh herbs, dried berries, and even edible flowers in a food processor with granulated sugar are vastly superior to those just tinted lemon yellow, beige, lime green, raspberry red, or rose pink with food color. Plus, the decorating sugars have ground flecks that lend subtle texture and extremely pleasing *natural* color. Whole fresh flowers and flower "confetti," page 330, can both add stunning touches of vivid color and form, too.

Of course, glazes, icings, and homemade sprinkles (yes, sprinkles are quite doable at home!) that get their cheerful hue from natural ingredients such as orange juice or cranberry juice concentrate are likewise far more appetizing than ones merely tinted with flavorless yellow, orange, or crimson dyes. For specific details on how to capitalize on fruit juice concentrates and cocoa powder to create strikingly colorful looks, check out the "Au Naturel" Rainbow of Powdered Sugar Icings and Homemade Decorator Sprinkles, page 305, as well as the "painted daisies" icing recipe on page 310.

Incidentally, I've come to routinely reach for frozen (thawed) cranberry juice concentrate and orange juice concentrate (they're conveniently stashed in my freezer in little plastic jars) when I want to tint my buttercreams pink, red, and yellow. The juices are usable as is so are fuss-free, plus they are concentrated enough to lend fairly intense colors. They also have a neutral flavor and slight tartness that enhances but doesn't dominate in most frostings, glazes, and such.

Do check out the large selection of buttercreams in the book—all of which can be used as *either* cookie sandwich fillings or toppings. Choose from classic vanilla, lemon, almond, and chocolate as well as from more exotic chocolate-tarragon; fresh lavender (it's truly amazing!); ginger, citrus, and green tea; intensely raspberry or strawberry; and even rose petal (yes, really!).

ROUND-UP OF COMMERCIAL ALL-NATURAL FOOD DYES AND COLORED SPRINKLES

I'm predicting that the demand for food dyes and decorating sprinkles that feature natural botanical colors instead of the synthetic petroleum-based ones is going to increase to accommodate the growing consumer interest. Here are the au naturel commercial products now available to home cooks and bakers.

India Tree "Nature's Colors" Red, Yellow, & Blue Liquid Dye Set—No, these colors aren't as vibrant as the typical little supermarket four-bottle sets. But they have the advantage of containing only concentrated color pigments from beets, purple cabbage, other vegetables, and turmeric. In contrast to the synthetic dyes, these avoid tar derivatives, long chain hydrocarbons, and other petrochemicals banned as unsafe in a number of countries and considered suspect by some American health advocates.

I've found the blue and yellow shades much more useful than the red, which eventually faded to brown. (Note that the blue lends a pleasant but muted denim hue.) The three-bottle sets can sometimes be found in gourmet shops and health food stores and are available from online sources. The dyes will hold their color better if refrigerated.

India Tree "Nature's Colors" Decorating Sugars & Sprinkles—These are similar to the usual colored coarse crystal sugars and opaque sprinkles sold with supermarket cake and cookie decorating supplies except that all the colors are botanically based. Find these in gourmet and health food stores and online kitchen supply venues.

Seelect All-Natural Liquid Food Colorings—The Seelect brand line of fruit, vegetable, and flower-based food colors is only occasionally found in retail stores, but if you have your heart set on a particular shade, it's likely on the company's website at www.seelecttea.com. Click on "organic food color" in the navigation bar. The dyes are individually sold in 2-ounce or larger bottles (the 2-ounce size will likely be more than you'll ever need) in a full palette of attractive, vivid colors; or come in a slightly more economical five-bottle Rainbow Pack (cherry red, orange, melon green, yellow, blue). The descriptions of the choices are detailed, not only noting the shade, but indicating whether that particular formula is heat and freezer stable. I refrigerated the bottles as directed, and the colors have remained stable over several years.

Essential Cane All Natural Flavored and Colored Cane Sugars—Featuring only cane sugar and a flavoring element ranging from raspberry, blueberry, tangerine, and lime to habanero, clove, espresso, and cocoa, the "Essential Cane" sprinkling sugars provide a hit of flavor, and sometimes a little color as well. Occasionally grocery stores, gourmet shops, and online purveyors carry Essential Cane naturally flavored sugars, but to find the full line of offerings go to the manufacturer's site www.flavorstorm.com and click on "Sugars."

ChocolateCraftColors "Natural Colors" Food Colors, Sparkle Sugars, and Sprinkles

Available mostly through the Internet, the various offerings at www.chocolatecraftcolors.com include a very appealing "Natural Colors" line of plant-based food colors (in liquid, paste, or powder form), plus colored crystal sugars, sprinkles, and "shimmer gels" in quantities geared for the home baker. All the products are gluten-free, dairy-free, synthetic dye–free, and vegan.

The 1/2-ounce liquid dyes come in nifty dropper-tipped bottles and can be purchased in a three-bottle primary colors (red, yellow, and blue) set, or a six-bottle assortment including red, yellow, orange, green, blue, and purple. The blue is the only color that's muted; it's a soft blue-gray. The liquid colors keep best in the refrigerator. The sprinkles and sparkling sugars come in a range of attractive colors as do the decorating gels.

ROUND-UP OF ALL-NATURAL COOKIE GARNISHES

You have likely either seen or used many of the au naturel cookie garnishes called for or pictured in *Simply Sensational Cookies*. But just to remind you, here are the naturally beautiful options that, depending on the particular cookie, can be spectacular replacements for the commonly employed artificially colored items.

—Chopped or shredded dried fruits and candied and fresh citrus peel

—Fresh herb leaves, sprigs, "confetti," and homemade sprinkling sugars

—Chopped or sliced nuts, chopped chocolate or baking morsels, crushed cookie crumbs, and candy shards, and shredded coconut

—Whole, crushed, grated, and ground seeds and spices

—Dried fruit, berry, herb, green tea, cocoa, coffee, vanilla, and spice dusting powders and sprinkling sugars

—Vanilla, chocolate, and naturally colored icing drizzles, frostings, glazes, and homemade sprinkles

—Naturally colorful coarse crystal salts and sugars (such as pink salts, demerara and turbinado sugars)

—*Edible* flower petals, tiny blooms, "confetti," and flower garnishing sugars. Use only the following unsprayed (and gently but thoroughly washed and dried) edible flowers as decorations:

Violets (not African violets, which are not true violets)

Pansies and johnny-jump-ups

Carnations, pinks (dianthus), and sweet William

Roses

Lavender "bloomlets" and/or whole flower heads

Marigolds

3   cups powdered sugar, sifted
     after measuring, if lumpy, plus
     more if needed
1   teaspoon light corn syrup
½   teaspoon vanilla extract
⅛   teaspoon almond extract,
     raspberry extract, or real
     coconut extract, optional
     About 3 to 4 tablespoons water
     Food color (either synthetic
     or botanical) as desired,
     optional

Tip

If you are working with very bright colors and don't want them to bleed together during storage, set the color by adding 1 tablespoon of commercial meringue powder or dried egg white powder to the powdered sugar before incorporating the other ingredients.

Tip

To avoid all commercial dyes, use the completely "au naturel" powdered sugar icing on page 305. All the colors come from frozen (thawed) fruit juice concentrates found in supermarket freezer cases.

TRADITIONAL POWDERED SUGAR ICING

This is the go-to recipe when you want an easy icing that spreads smoothly and dries with a sheen. Depending on the amount of liquid incorporated, it can be used to glaze entire cookies, or thickened enough to add quick swirls to their tops. If spread in a thin layer, it firms up enough that the cookies can be stored together without sticking, but unlike royal frosting it does not become flaky-dry and hard. It's quite sweet, so it is best applied in moderation and on cookies that aren't too sugary to start with.

This recipe calls for optional food coloring, but if you wish to minimize the use of synthetic dyes, substitute botanically based dyes (discussed on pages 300–301) instead. (I particularly prefer to limit the petrochemical dyes in the red-yellow color range because many of them, including red dye #40, yellow #5 [aka tartrazine or hydrazine yellow], and yellow #6 are azo compounds, which can cause irritation or allergic reactions in some people, including me.)

In a medium deep bowl, vigorously stir together the powdered sugar, corn syrup, extract(s), and 2½ to 3 tablespoons water until very well blended and completely smooth. Adjust the consistency by adding more water to thin the icing or powdered sugar to stiffen it as desired. Thoroughly stir in the food color, if using. Or, if desired, divide the mixture among several bowls and tint each a different color.

For frosting cookies: Stir in more powdered sugar until the mixture holds some shape and is completely smooth. Using a table knife, spread it out over the entire tops of flat or mounded cookies or just add a swirl to the center tops, if preferred. For thinly glazed cookies: Thoroughly stir in drops of water until the mixture flows readily but is not runny; be sure the water is *fully incorporated* or the glaze may be streaky. Using a table knife, small pastry brush, or clean artist's paint brush, spread a thin but even layer of icing over flat cookie surfaces. Domed cookies may also be dipped in the icing; shake off the excess and let it drip back into the bowl. Double dip for a thicker coating.

For piping onto cookies: Stir in enough powdered sugar so that the mixture is completely smooth and holds its shape but is not too stiff to pipe through a pastry bag fitted with a fine writing tip or through a paper piping cone (or sturdy plastic bag with a small opening cut in one corner). Pipe accents such as fine zigzags and squiggles or outlines that can then be flooded as desired.

If you wish to top the frosting or glaze with sprinkles or other accents, do it right away while the frosting surface is still wet.

Let the cookies stand after decorating for at least 45 minutes and up to 1½ hours, until the icing sets and firms.

Yield: Makes about 1½ cups, enough to generously frost fifty to sixty 2½-inch cookies

Storage: Store this, airtight, for up to 3 days. Stored icing may thicken, so thin with a small amount of water, if necessary; stir it in very thoroughly.

These icings were all readied with botonical food colors.

1½ cups powdered sugar, sifted after
      measuring, if lumpy, plus more
      if needed
1½ teaspoons fresh lemon juice
¼   teaspoon vanilla extract or
      ⅛ teaspoon almond extract,
      optional

Tip

If a colored drizzle of icing instead
of white suits your fancy, feel free
to add a drop or two of synthetic or
botanical food coloring to the icing.

QUICK POWDERED SUGAR DRIZZLE

This makes a very quick yet attractive drizzle or white garnishing icing for cookies that just need to be dressed up a little, or perhaps that simply benefit from a touch of extra sweetness. If allowed to dry thoroughly, the drizzle sets up hard, so the cookies can be stacked, stored, or even shipped without any danger of stickiness. It won't noticeably soften crisp cookies, either.

The drizzle looks best if piped into very fine squiggles, zigzags, spirals, dots, or thin crisscross lines. A pastry bag fitted with a fine writing tip or a parchment paper cone with a small opening works particularly well, but you can squeeze out and drizzle using a small, sturdy zip-top plastic bag if necessary. Just snip the tip of one corner to form a tiny opening, seal the bag, force the icing into the corner, and drizzle away! (If the hole gradually enlarges, switch to a fresh bag.)

In a medium deep bowl, stir together the powdered sugar, lemon juice, extract, and 1 teaspoon water until well blended and smooth. If necessary, stir in enough more water to yield an icing stiff enough to hold some shape but thin enough to pipe. Or, if necessary, stiffen the mixture by adding a little more powdered sugar. Put it in a small pastry bag fitted with a very fine writing tip, or a paper parchment cone, or a sturdy plastic bag with one corner snipped open; don't fill the bag or cone more than half full or the drizzle may squeeze out the top.

To garnish: Line up the cookies, slightly separated, on a rack set over paper to catch the drips. Lightly pipe decorative lines, dots, or other accents on the cookies as desired. Let stand until the icing completely sets, at least 1 hour.

Yield: Makes about ½ cup, enough to heavily accent thirty 2-inch cookies or lightly accent 40 to 50 cookies

Storage: Store this, airtight, for up to 3 days. Stored icing may thicken, so thin with a small amount of water, if necessary; stir it in very thoroughly.

Easy
Quick one-bowl mixing.
Versatile recipe.
Au natural recipe.

1 cup powdered sugar, sifted after measuring, if lumpy, plus more if needed

1 teaspoon commercial meringue powder or pure dried egg white powder, optional (omit if preparing sprinkles to be added before baking)

2 tablespoons frozen (thawed) cranberry, orange, Concord grape, raspberry-white grape, or cherry-grape juice concentrate (or a combination), plus more if needed

½ teaspoon light corn syrup
½ to 3 teaspoons unsweetened natural (non-alkalized) cocoa powder or Dutch-process cocoa powder, sifted after measuring, if lumpy, optional

Tip

Leftover frozen juice concentrates can be made up into juice (or blended for a fruit punch) as directed on the package; diluted by half with water and turned into tasty popsicles; or placed in small storage containers and refrozen so that au naturel food colors are always at the ready for tinting your icings and buttercream frostings.

"AU NATUREL" RAINBOW OF POWDERED SUGAR ICINGS AND HOMEMADE DECORATOR SPRINKLES

If you are interested in creating very eye-catching decorated sugar cookies, but wish to completely avoid using the traditional synthetic food coloring products and commercial decorator sprinkles tinted with them, I'm proud to offer you this special, yet very doable au naturel recipe. Simply by relying on the gorgeous natural colors of frozen (thawed) fruit juice concentrates from the supermarket (and on occasion incorporating cocoa powder as well), you can create a whole rainbow of tempting and tasty cookie icings and, yes, even pretty homemade cookie sprinkles!

To create au naturel icings, just combine the appropriate thawed pure fruit juice concentrate or a custom blend or several concentrates (for example, yellow orange juice and red cranberry to produce a light peach-orange shade) with powdered sugar and a small amount of corn syrup. Don't skip the corn syrup; it promotes smooth flow and yields a glossy finish. Though it is optional, you may want to stir a little purchased meringue powder or dried egg white powder into the powdered sugar before mixing in other ingredients. This sets the colors so that strongly contrasting shades don't bleed together as the decorated cookies stand. (Many discount department stores stock the Wilton brand of meringue powder with cake decorating supplies. Supermarkets and nutrition stores sometimes carry the Deb El "Just Whites," product or another brand of pure dried egg whites in their baking aisle.)

Creating the homemade sprinkles (shown page 306) is remarkably easy, too. In this case, do not add any meringue powder to sprinkles that will be baked as it will cause them to darken. Just squeeze fine lines of the icing through a piping bag fitted with a fine tip (or a baggie) onto parchment paper. Let the lines stand and dry thoroughly, then just chop them into sprinkle-sized bits. If desired, just make sprinkles by piping the dribs and drabs of icing left over after decorating sessions. This is not only convenient and avoids waste, but means that a whole rainbow of sprinkles can be readily prepared in the small quantities needed. These can be stored in little bottles and used like purchased sprinkles, but since they contain no additives, after a few months their colors will begin to fade a bit. Their colors also fade from lengthy exposure to high heat, so it's best to use them for sprinkling over icings or frostings, or on sugar cookies or other cookies that bake fairly briefly and at moderate temperature.

The usual assortment of naturally colorful pure fruit juice concentrates normally sold in supermarket freezer cases works well in this recipe. However, be sure to read labels, as some frozen juice products are tinted

with the same commercial petrochemical food dyes you're trying to avoid! I've found cranberry, orange, Concord grape, raspberry-white grape, and cherry-grape all produce lovely, unique shades (see the leaf cookies, page 309). Many more hues can be created by blending the shades together or adding a tiny amount of cocoa powder. I've provided a starter list of blends and the resulting colors they produce below, but, like an artist, you can mix and experiment to create many more custom hues. The directions call for using the maximum amount of juice to produce the brightest colors, but if paler shades are preferred, simply substitute some water for part of the juice concentrate called for.

In case you're wondering, the juices do flavor as well as color these icings—most tasters find this actually enhances and adds dimension to the frostings. Note that bottled juice concentrates often stocked on shelves in health food stores are not a good choice. The au naturel color pigments tend to fade at room temperature, so the frozen concentrates are much better for decorating.

On the assumption that you'll want to make several colors of icing at once, the basic recipe yields enough to fully decorate around 12 to 15 cookies. I normally make up at least three or four colors to provide an appealing "rainbow" array for decorating a batch of sugar cookies. But feel free to double, triple or even quadruple the recipe to decorate an entire batch in a single color.

In a small deep bowl, vigorously stir together the powdered sugar and meringue powder, if using. Stir in the juice concentrate (or desired blend of concentrates) and corn syrup until very well blended and completely smooth. If a brown color or brownish tint is desired, stir in cocoa powder as needed at the same time. Adjust the consistency by adding more juice concentrate to thin the icing, or powdered sugar to stiffen it. Adjust the color by adding in more of the desired juice or cocoa powder or by incorporating a little water for a less intense shade.

For icing cookies: Thoroughly stir in the juice concentrate until the mixture flows readily but is not runny; be sure any added liquid is fully incorporated or the icing may look streaky. Using a table knife, small pastry brush, or clean artist's paint brush, spread a thin, but even, layer of icing over flat cookie surfaces. (If you're an "advanced" decorator, feel free to pipe outlines that can be flooded, first.) Domed cookies may also be dipped in the icing; shake off the excess and let it drip back into the bowl.

For piping onto cookies: Stir in more powdered sugar until the mixture is completely smooth and has some body; it needs to be stiff enough not to run but thin enough to pipe through the small opening. Put the icing in a piping cone; or a piping bag fitted with the desired tip; or for simple piping or drizzling, into a sturdy baggie with a corner snipped off. Fill the bag or cone only half full. Pipe accents such as fine zig-zags and squiggles or outlines that can then be flooded, as desired. For accents that blend into the base color, as for the leaf veining shown on page 309, pipe or brush on while the first layer of icing is still wet. For accents that stand out and hold their shape, wait until the base layer completely dries.

For making decorator sprinkles: Pipe very fine lines of icing lengthwise onto a long sheet of baking parchment, spacing them far enough apart that they don't run together. Let stand uncovered at least 12 hours and 18 hours if the weather is humid. Slide the parchment sheet with icing lines onto a cutting board. Using a large knife or a pizza wheel and working across the piped lines, chop the lines into ¼-inch or shorter sprinkles. Let the sprinkles stand at least 4 hours longer, or until completely dry. Then pack into airtight bottles or storage jars. Note that because their colors fade with long exposure to intense heat, they are best sprinkled on as cookies are being iced, although they can be sprinkled on sugar cookies (and other kinds that bake at low heat and quickly) before baking with satisfactory results.

If you wish to top any icing with sprinkles or similar accents, do it right away while the surface is still wet. Let iced cookies stand after decorating at least 1½ hours and up to 8 hours until the icing sets and firms.

Yield: About ½ cup icing, enough to generously decorate twelve to fifteen 2½- to 3-inch cookies or to make about ¾ cup of homemade decorator sprinkles.

Storage: The icings will keep, airtight and refrigerated, for up 1 week. Stored icing may thicken, so thin with a small amount of water, if necessary; stir it in very thoroughly. Store the sprinkles airtight in a cool spot, away from bright light, for up to 6 months.

Add these natural colorants to the basic recipe on page 305 to produce the colors of the leaves shown at the right, the daisy cookies on page 311, plus the others listed below.

Bright fuchsia: Cranberry juice concentrate

Light yellow: Orange juice concentrate

Light orange or peach: About half orange and half cranberry juice concentrates

Purple red: Concord grape juice concentrate

Lavender Pink: 1 to 3 teaspoons Concord grape juice concentrate combined with water

Burgundy red: About 1 tablespoon plus 1 teaspoon Concord grape juice concentrate and 2 to 3 teaspoons cranberry juice concentrate

Maroon: Concord grape juice concentrate plus ½ to 1 teaspoon cocoa powder

Bright medium pink: Raspberry-white grape juice concentrate or cherry-white grape juice concentrate

Mahogany: Cranberry juice concentrate, plus ½ to 1½ teaspoons cocoa powder as desired

Cocoa brown: Cranberry juice concentrate plus 2½ teaspoons cocoa powder

Tan or golden brown: Orange juice concentrate plus ½ to 1½ teaspoons cocoa powder as desired

4¼ cups powdered sugar, divided,
plus more if needed

1 teaspoon light corn syrup,
divided

½ teaspoon vanilla extract, divided

2 teaspoons corn oil, canola oil,
or other flavorless vegetable
oil, divided

1½ to 2 tablespoons frozen
(thawed) orange juice
concentrate, plus more if
needed

1½ to 2 tablespoons frozen
(thawed) cranberry juice
concentrate, plus more if
needed

1½ to 2 teaspoons unsweetened
natural or Dutch process cocoa
powder, plus more if needed

Turbinado sugar, or white crystal
sugar, for optional garnish

Tip

The sugar cookie dough on page
112 is an excellent choice for making
painted daisy cookies, because it
isn't overly sweet.

"PAINTED DAISIES" POWDERED SUGAR ICINGS

I dubbed this recipe "Painted Daisies" because it's designed to simultaneously make four different icings appropriate for decorating three kinds of daisy-shaped sugar cookies at the same time. The end result: an eye-catching "bouquet" containing white Shasta daisies with yellow button centers, and pink and yellow painted daisies with contrasting brown "eyes."

Not only do the colors look very cheerful and realistic, but they also come from orange juice and cranberry juice concentrates and cocoa powder, all of which subtly heighten flavor and introduce color without requiring any food dyes. A daisy cookie cutter will most closely mimic the real flowers, but simpler petal-edged or scalloped round cutters look fine and are easier to use and find. (Of course, you can use the naturally colored icings to top cookies in other shapes you like as well.)

The icings flow and set so smoothly and easily that even kids can produce very attractive cookies. My elementary-school-age grandchildren had great fun decorating a batch of daisies with me for a summer birthday party. The only help they needed was with piping the yellow and brown flower "eyes."

Put 1¼ cups powdered sugar in each of three medium bowls and ½ cup powdered sugar in a smaller bowl. Add ¼ teaspoon corn syrup, ⅛ teaspoon vanilla, and ½ teaspoon oil to all four bowls.

To one medium bowl, add 1½ tablespoons thawed orange juice concentrate. To the second medium bowl, add 1½ tablespoons cranberry juice concentrate. To the third medium bowl, add 1½ tablespoons water. To the smaller bowl, stir in 1½ teaspoons cocoa powder and 1½ teaspoons water. Stir each icing until thoroughly blended and smooth, adding in a little more juice or water if too dry to mix together or more powdered sugar if needed to stiffen the icings to a slightly fluid and spreadable but not runny consistency.

To decorate cookies: Using a table knife, spread a light, smooth coating of white, yellow, or pink icing over the cookies until all are decorated. Let stand on racks set over wax paper to catch drips until set, 10 to 15 minutes. Then add the yellow eyes to the white daisies and brown eyes to the yellow and pink daisies as follows: Stir cocoa powder into the leftover white frosting until smooth and stiffened enough to pipe but not run, stir enough more powdered sugar into the yellow frosting until stiffened enough to pipe but not run. Put the cocoa and yellow icings into sturdy plastic bags with a small hole clipped from one corner; or if preferred, use a disposable plastic piping bag. Then squeeze out small portions of either the yellow or chocolate to

form eyes in center tops of the cookies. Immediately sprinkle a little coarse sugar over the eyes to add texture, if desired.

Let the cookies stand for at least 2 hours until the icing sets. Then pack, airtight, preferably in one layer or with wax paper between the layers. Iced cookies will generally keep for up to 10 days, depending on the cookie. Or freeze for up to 1 month.

Yield: Makes enough to generously frost fifty to sixty 2½- to 3-inch daisy cookies

Storage: Store this, airtight and refrigerated, for up to 3 days. Stored icing may thicken, so thin with a small amount of water, if necessary; stir it in very thoroughly.

Tip

Keep cranberry and orange juice concentrates stashed in plastic jars in the freezer so you'll have these all natural colors on hand whenever needed to tint icings and buttercreams pink or yellow. To create au naturel icings in other colors see the "Au Naturel" Rainbow of Powdered Sugar Icings and Homemade Decorator Sprinkles recipe, page 305.

⅔ cup egg whites (4 to 5 large whites), completely free of yolks, at room temperature

1 teaspoon fresh lemon juice
Pinch of salt
4½ to 5 cups powdered sugar, plus more if needed
Liquid or paste synthetic or botanically based food colors, optional

Tip

For icing that is free of risk to those with compromised or weakened immune systems, buy pasteurized eggs specifically designed to be safe when used raw. Note that whites from these will require much longer beating than unpasteurized egg whites. Or use dried egg white powder (meringue powder) and reconstitute the ⅔ cup of whites needed following the package directions.

ROYAL FROSTING

The following recipe makes enough icing to elaborately decorate a very large batch of rolled cut-out cookies. It pipes beautifully and dries hard, so it is the icing to turn to when durability and appearance are your highest priorities. It's by far the best choice for decorating cookie ornaments or cookie houses. Once the icing is dry, the colors are set and will not bleed together during storage. Note that if you are using botanically based food colors, it's best to test a small sampling of icing with the color selected first. Some natural dyes change color in the presence of lemon juice.

In a large mixing bowl (using the wire whisk attachment), beat the egg whites, lemon juice, and salt on medium speed until frothy and opaque. Raise the speed slightly and beat for 30 seconds. Gradually beat in 4½ cups powdered sugar until fully incorporated and the frosting is free of lumps.

Raise the speed to high and whip until the mixture increases in volume and stands in stiff peaks, usually 3 to 5 minutes. If the mixture is too stiff to pipe or spread easily, thoroughly beat in water a teaspoon at a time; if too runny to spread or pipe, beat in more powdered sugar until completely smooth and stiffened slightly. The icing may be used immediately or refrigerated for later use. If stored, let warm up slightly, then stir well, before using.

If the icing stiffens upon standing, thin it with a few drops of water. Keep a damp kitchen towel draped over the bowl to prevent the icing from drying out as you work.

To tint the icing: Divide it up in as many bowls as needed, then thoroughly stir in drops of liquid or paste food color until the desired color is obtained. For very intense shades, paste colors work best. Food colors can be mixed together for virtually any custom color desired.

Yield: Makes 3½ to 4 cups frosting, enough to generously decorate 40 to 60 medium rolled cookies

Storage: Store this, tightly covered and refrigerated, for up to 4 days. Stir well before using.

1½ cups powdered sugar
¼ cup unsweetened natural (non-alkalized) cocoa powder or Dutch-process cocoa powder
¼ teaspoon instant coffee granules dissolved in 1 teaspoon hot water
½ teaspoon light or dark corn syrup
¼ teaspoon vanilla extract

Tip

The amount of water needed will vary considerably depending on the brand of cocoa powder—some are much drier and more absorbent than others. Don't leave out the corn syrup; even though the amount is small, it gives the drizzle its sheen.

GLOSSY CHOCOLATE DRIZZLE

Like the Quick Powdered Sugar Drizzle (page 304), this recipe makes a simple, eye-catching accent and looks most appealing piped into fine (thread-like) decorative lines and squiggles. It can enhance almost any chocolate cookie or other cookie that pairs well with chocolate. I especially like it to add pizzazz to biscotti, and other suggestions for using it appear throughout the book. It sets up very glossy and firm and, unlike many soft chocolate frostings, won't cause crisp cookies to soften. It is fairly bold and bittersweet, so it won't add too much sweetness to cookies.

For a drizzle with the darkest color, use a Dutch-process cocoa; for one with the deepest chocolate taste, use natural (non-alkalized) cocoa powder. The recipe may be doubled if you like.

Sift the sugar and cocoa powder into a small deep bowl. Add the coffee mixture, corn syrup, and vanilla. Gradually stir in 2 to 3 tablespoons water or more until well blended, smooth, and fluid enough to pipe. If the drizzle stiffens upon standing, thin it by thoroughly stirring in a bit more water until fluid enough to pipe (if the water is not evenly incorporated, the glaze may be streaky).

To decorate cookies: Line them up in rows, slightly separated, on a rack set over paper (to catch drips). Place the drizzle in a piping bag with a fine writing tip, a parchment cone, or a small, sturdy plastic bag with one tiny corner snipped open; fill the cone or bag only half full. Pipe very fine squiggles, dots, crisscross lines, zigzags, spirals, or wavy lines as desired. Let the cookies stand until the glaze sets, at least 45 minutes and preferably 1 hour.

Yield: Makes enough to generously accent forty 2½-inch cookies or lightly accent 50 to 60 cookies

Storage: Store this, covered airtight, for 2 to 3 days; if necessary, thoroughly stir in a little more water until fluid before using.

2 tablespoons cold unsalted
   butter, cut into chunks
4½ ounces extra-bittersweet (70
   to 85 percent cacao) chocolate,
   coarsely chopped
1⅓ cups commercial or homemade
   (page 323) dulce de leche
2 teaspoons vanilla extract
2 tablespoons light or dark corn
   syrup

Tip

If you don't have an extra-bittersweet chocolate with a high cacao content on hand, in a pinch substitute a combination of 3 ounces of regular supermarket semisweet chocolate and 1 ounce of unsweetened chocolate.

CHOCOLATE DULCE DE LECHE

In this variation on the usual dulce de leche theme, dark chocolate helps balance the characteristic sweetness of the caramel, and the caramel flavor mellows the bittersweetness of the chocolate. The recipe is designed to go with the Brown Sugar Alfajores (page 126), although it can also be paired with most any sugar or shortbread wafers for equally easy and succulent sandwich cookies.

While you can make your own dulce de leche (also called "cajeta," "manjar," or "milk caramel") following the recipe on page 323, here it's perfectly fine to start with a tin or jar purchased in a Latin American market or supermarket. Be sure to look for a brand made with cow's milk; goat's milk has a stronger taste that competes with the chocolate.

Put the butter and chocolate in a large microwave-safe bowl. Microwave the mixture on high power for 30 seconds; stir well. As necessary, microwave the mixture on 50 percent power, stopping and stirring at 20-second intervals, until mostly melted. Let the residual heat finish the melting, stirring occasionally.

If the dulce de leche is stiff or looks separated, stir well. Add the dulce de leche and vanilla to the chocolate mixture, but don't stir them into it. Microwave the bowl, covered, on 50 percent power for 30 seconds. Add the corn syrup, then vigorously stir the mixture until very well blended and smooth. If it looks separated and oily, vigorously stir in up to 1½ tablespoons hot water until the filling smoothes out and becomes readily spreadable.

To prepare sandwich cookies: Immediately spread enough warm dulce de leche on the underside of half the cookies to yield a ¼-inch-thick layer. Top the filling layer with a similar-size cookie, underside against the filling. Press the two together until the filling squeezes to the edges. Let cool to room temperature before serving the sandwiches.

Alternatively, cool and cover the chocolate dulce de leche, then refrigerate it. Rewarm on medium power in a microwave oven, stirring every 30 seconds, until spreadable again before using.

Yield: Makes enough to fill about 25 small cookie sandwiches

Storage: Store this, airtight in the refrigerator, for up to 1 week. It can be frozen, airtight, for up to 1 month. Thaw in the refrigerator; rewarm slightly using a microwave oven, then stir well.

1¼ cups (6 ounces) 70 to 90 percent
    cacao coarsely chopped
    bittersweet chocolate
1 tablespoon unsalted butter,
   slightly softened
1 cup minus 2 tablespoons
   granulated sugar
2 tablespoons light corn syrup
1 teaspoon vanilla extract, or
   ½ tablespoon Grand Marnier,
   or ½ teaspoon raspberry
   extract, or ¼ teaspoon almond
   extract

PURE SATIN CHOCOLATE ICING

If you're one who believes that nearly every brownie or bar cookie can benefit from being topped with a very sumptuous, super-chocolatly icing, take note of this recipe. It has a clear, clean, supremely tempting chocolate taste, plus it flows and sets up with a satiny finish. It is a superb topper for the Simple Shortbread Bars (page 166), and it makes a fine garnish for almost any other bars or brownies you wish to lend a rich chocolate finish. Its only slight drawback is that the directions are a little fussy and must be followed carefully.

You can modify the recipe to suit your own taste simply through the choice of chocolate: One with 70 percent cacao will produce a semisweet glaze; an 85 to 90 percent cacao chocolate will yield one with a slight bittersweet bite. (It's possible to take a cue from pastry chefs and create your own particular signature blend by combining, say, a 70 percent cacao chocolate with a 90 percent one.) It's also possible to tailor the flavor to suit various bars and brownies by incorporating one of the optional extracts or flavorings suggested in the ingredient list.

The recipe produces enough icing to generously top a 9 by 13-inch pan of brownies or bars. If you're using it for an 8- or 9-inch square pan, use half of the icing. Save the second half and reheat it to cover a second batch of brownies. Or thin the leftover portion with hot water to a syrupy consistency and use it as a decadent sauce for ice cream!

In a medium microwave-safe bowl, microwave the chocolate and butter for 45 seconds on high power. Stir well. If necessary, continue microwaving on medium power, stopping and stirring every 20 seconds, just until barely melted.

In a small, heavy saucepan, bring the granulated sugar, ⅓ cup hot tap water, and the corn syrup to a boil over medium heat, stirring with a wooden spoon. Wash any sugar from the pan sides with a wetted pastry brush (or damp paper towel). Without further stirring, heat the syrup just until it comes to a full boil, lifting the pan and swirling the syrup once or twice. Immediately cover and boil for exactly 1½ minutes.

Immediately pour a generous half of the syrup into the chocolate mixture. With a clean wooden spoon, stir until the mixture is well blended and beginning to thicken. Pour the remaining syrup into the chocolate; don't scrape the last of the syrup from the pan, as it may be gritty or overcooked. Add the vanilla (or other desired flavoring) to the chocolate. Vigorously stir the mixture until the icing is completely blended, silky smooth, and just beginning to thicken. If it is thick, gently

A chocolate with 90 percent cacao will yield a stiffer icing than one with 70 percent simply because, as the cacao percentage increases, so does the natural starch in the chocolate. This means that an icing with a higher cacao percentage will likely need to be thinned with more water to obtain the fluid consistency required for easy spreading. The icing sets fairly rapidly as it cools, so make sure the bars or brownies being topped are at room temperature and smooth it on promptly. If it does stand for too long and becomes too stiff to spread readily, gently warm it until fluid again; a few seconds in a microwave on low to medium power should do the trick. (For more information on the complexities of chocolate, see page 15.)

but very thoroughly stir in hot water a teaspoon at a time until it's thin enough to flow readily; thin it until quite fluid, as it will thicken a surprising amount as it cools and sets.

Immediately pour the icing over the barely warm or room temperature (never chilled) brownies or bars. Quickly spread it out with a long-bladed spatula or table knife. If only half the glaze is used, cover the remainder and refrigerate for later use. (Reheat it in a microwave oven on 50 percent power, stopping and stirring every 30 seconds, until fluid enough to spread, then use immediately.)

Yield: Makes enough to amply glaze a 9 by 13-inch pan of brownies or bars.

Storage: Store this, covered and refrigerated, for up to 1 week. Gently re-warm, stirring, before using.

6 tablespoons heavy (whipping) cream
1½ cups (8 ounces) 50 to 65 percent cacao semisweet or bittersweet chocolate morsels, discs, or chocolate chunks
½ teaspoon vanilla extract, or ¼ teaspoon almond extract, or ¼ teaspoon raspberry extract, or 1 to 2 teaspoons instant espresso powder dissolved in ½ to 1 teaspoon warm water
1½ tablespoons clover honey, optional

Tip

If you're looking for a topping that sets up smooth, very glossy, and firm, use the Pure Satin Chocolate Icing on page 316.

Tip

You can adjust the sweetness slightly through your choice of chocolate and by adding or omitting the honey. Modify the flavor by choosing to incorporate vanilla, almond, or raspberry extract, or a little instant espresso powder dissolved in water.

CHOCOLATE GANACHE GLAZE, FILLING, OR ICING

This full-flavored chocolate ganache is easy to make and versatile enough to serve as a glaze, filling, or piped or swirled on frosting. It's best used with slightly soft shortbreads and butter cookies, or chewy cookies or bars, as the moisture in it can cause very crisp cookies to soften slightly. Over a few hours the ganache gradually firms up, but initially cookies topped with it need to be stored in a single layer.

In a 2-quart saucepan, heat the cream almost to a full boil over medium heat; do not boil longer. Remove from the heat; immediately stir in the chocolate and extract. Continue stirring until completely melted and smooth; if necessary to complete the melting, return the pan to the burner over low heat for up to 1 minute, stirring continuously. Taste, and if a sweeter ganache is desired (or a honey flavor is desired), thoroughly stir in the honey. Or if it is very thick, thin it with a teaspoon or two of warm water.

To use as a glaze: Immediately pour the warm ganache over the surface of room temperature bars, spreading evenly thick to the edges. Let stand until completely cooled and set, at least 1½ hours.

To use for dipping: Put the warm, fluid ganache in a small, deep bowl. If necessary, thin it with a teaspoon of water; stir it in very thoroughly. Set a large cooling rack over a baking sheet. Dip the cookies until coated halfway across the tops into the ganache (or as specified in a cookie recipe), then shake and scrape off any excess onto the bowl side. (The dipping is easiest if the ganache bowl is tipped so the mixture flows partway over each cookie top.) If desired, garnish further by sprinkling some chopped almonds or other nuts, or toasted coconut over the dipped portion immediately after it is dipped. Space the cookies, top sides up, slightly separated, on the rack; arrange so the dipped portions overhang the rack if you don't want any rack marks on the undersides of slices. Let stand until the ganache is cooled and firm, at least 1 hour.

To use as a frosting or filling: Refrigerate the ganache, covered, for at least 1 hour and up to 4 days. Transfer it to a large bowl. Beat on medium speed, occasionally scraping the bowl sides, until it lightens in color and is smooth, fluffy, and spreadable. If it seems too stiff to spread or pipe, beat in up to 4 teaspoons warm water. Spread out or swirl over the surface of cooled, uncut bars. Or put the ganache into a piping bag fitted with an open star tip, then pipe rosettes onto cookie or cut bar tops. Or, spread generously over the undersides of half the batch of cookies or French Macarons and top each with another cookie to form sandwiches.

Yield: Makes a scant 1 cup, enough glaze to cover a 9 by 13-inch pan of bars; or fill about 25 medium-sized cookie sandwiches; or to pipe rosettes onto 30 to 35 small bars or butter cookies.

Storage: Make ahead and store this, covered and refrigerated, for up to 4 days. To use as a glaze, reheat until fluid, stirring constantly over low heat. If necessary, thin it with a teaspoon of warm water.

1¼ cups powdered sugar, plus more if needed

1 cup (2 sticks) unsalted butter, slightly softened and cut into chunks

1 cup (2 sticks) solid white vegetable shortening, at room temperature

2 teaspoons vanilla extract

⅛ teaspoon salt

2 7-ounce jars or one 16-ounce jar marshmallow crème

Tip

If you're opposed to using solid white shortening, feel free to use 2 cups of unsalted butter and omit the shortening from the recipe. This will yield a cream-colored rather than a traditional white marshmallow filling, and it will have a noticeable butter flavor rather than the usual neutral taste. It will also become slightly greasy-soft if allowed to stand in hot weather, while the version with shortening will be completely heat stable.

EASY MARSHMALLOW VANILLA CRÈME FILLING

This is the classic filling for chocolate whoopie pies, but it's also nice tucked around other cookies. If making whoopie pies, use the filling very generously, as these treats are all about overindulgence. For more novel filling flavors, see the variations below.

Combine the powdered sugar, butter, shortening, vanilla, and salt in a large bowl. Beat on low, then medium, speed until very light and well blended. Scrape down the sides as needed. Beat in the marshmallow crème until evenly incorporated. If the filling looks too soft, beat in more powdered sugar until stiffened as desired.

Spread enough filling on the undersides of half the whoopie pies to yield a ⅓- to ½-inch-thick layer. Cover them with similar-size rounds, top side up, gently pressing down until the filling spreads to the edges.

Yield: Makes about 4 cups, enough for eighteen 3- to 3½-inch whoopie sandwiches or 24 madeleine-whoopie sandwiches.

Storage: Store this, airtight in the refrigerator, for up to 1 week. It can be frozen, airtight, for up to 1 month.

Variation: Raspberry Crème Filling Add 1 teaspoon raspberry extract; 2 to 4 drops red food color, optional; and 4 to 5 teaspoons freeze-dried raspberry powder (page 336), when the powdered sugar–butter mixture is combined.

Variation: Mint Crème Filling Add ½ teaspoon mint extract, plus 2 to 3 drops green food color (if desired), when the powdered sugar–butter mixture is combined. For a mint–chocolate chip filling, fold in ½ cup finely chopped semisweet chocolate morsels at the end of mixing.

Variation: Peanut Butter Crème Filling Beat in 1 cup smooth peanut butter along with the butter. Increase the powdered sugar initially added to 1½ cups.

Variation: Mocha or Mocha-Orange Crème Filling Dissolve 2 tablespoons instant espresso powder in 2 tablespoons warm water. Add the espresso mixture, ⅓ cup unsweetened cocoa powder, and 1 teaspoon finely grated orange zest (optional for mocha-orange flavor) when the powdered sugar–butter mixture is combined.

2⅓ cups powdered sugar, plus more
if needed
Pinch of salt
½ cup (1 stick) unsalted butter, just
slightly softened but still cool
1½ teaspoons vanilla extract or
½ teaspoon almond extract
combined with 1 teaspoon
vanilla extract

Tip

Any number of vanilla, chocolate, and butter cookies in the book can be paired with this buttercream; Delicate Vanilla-Cream Sandwich Cookies (page 116), Vanilla Shortbread Buttons (page 118), Chocolate-Cocoa Wafers (page 129), and French macarons (page 289) are just several possibilities.

VANILLA OR ALMOND BUTTERCREAM

It's amazing how a simple buttercream can dress up cookies and turn them into truly sumptuous treats. By adjusting the consistency slightly, you can pipe or decoratively spread this buttercream over the tops of cookies, or use it as a filling and create elegant little cookie sandwiches. The basic recipe can also be turned into a coffee-buttercream; see the variation. The recipe may be doubled.

Stir together the powdered sugar and salt in a large bowl. Add the butter, vanilla, and 1 teaspoon cool water. With a mixer on low, then medium, speed, beat until very well blended, about 1½ minutes. Scrape down the sides as needed. If the mixture is too stiff, beat in a few drops of cool water; if too soft, beat in more powdered sugar.

To use as a filling: Put a scant teaspoon of buttercream on the undersides of half the cookies (or use enough to create a ¼-inch-thick layer). Cover each with a similar-size plain or cutaway cookie, top side visible, gently pressing down until the filling peeks through the center cutaway and/or spreads almost to the edges.

To use as a swirled or piped icing: If necessary, adjust the buttercream to a spreading or piping consistency by thinning it with up to 3 to 4 teaspoons water. Put tiny dollops of the buttercream on the cookie tops, then swirl it slightly with the tip of a knife. Or spoon the icing into a pastry bag fitted with a ½-inch-diameter open star tip, then pipe rosettes onto the cookie tops. Let stand until the buttercream sets, at least 45 minutes.

Yield: Makes a scant 1½ cups, enough for twenty to thirty 2½-inch cookie sandwiches (20 generously, 30 scantily)

Storage: Store this, airtight in the refrigerator, for up to 1 week. It can be frozen, airtight, for up to 1 month. Thaw completely before using.

Variation: Coffee-Vanilla Buttercream Prepare the recipe exactly as directed, except reduce the almond extract to ¼ teaspoon. Also, dissolve 1½ teaspoons instant coffee granules in 1 teaspoon hot water. Add when the extract(s) are added. (For an orange-coffee flavor, add ¼ teaspoon finely grated orange zest along with the coffee mixture.)

2 cups powdered sugar, plus
   more if needed
5 tablespoons cream cheese,
   slightly softened
1½ teaspoons fresh lemon juice
¼ teaspoon corn syrup, optional
¼ teaspoon vanilla extract

Tip

If you don't have corn syrup, you
may omit it. However, it's what gives
the glaze its sheen.

CREAM CHEESE GLAZE (OR FROSTING)

A cream cheese glaze or frosting often garnishes carrot cookies (page 70), but it is also a luscious finish for some fruit-studded cookies, pumpkin cookies, and moist or cake-like spice cookies. It's not a good choice for snaps or other hard, crunchy cookies, as it can cause them to lose their crispness.

You can drizzle or pipe the glaze over cookies. Or apply it by dipping the tops of domed cookies into the glaze, then shaking off the excess. Another option: Stiffen it to frosting consistency with a little extra powdered sugar and swirl it over cookie tops with a knife. The glaze sets up firm but not hard.

In a food processor, process the sugar, cream cheese, lemon juice, corn syrup, if using, and vanilla until smooth and well blended, stopping and scraping down the bowl sides as necessary. (Alternatively, in a large bowl beat the sugar and cream cheese on low, then medium, speed until completely free of lumps; scrape down the beaters and bowl sides as needed. Beat in the lemon juice, corn syrup, if using, and vanilla until evenly incorporated.)

If the glaze is too runny to hold its shape, add a tablespoon or two more powdered sugar until stiffened just slightly; if too stiff, thoroughly incorporate a few teaspoons water. Use immediately, following the directions the individual recipes, or as desired in other recipes in your repertoire.

Yield: Makes about 1 cup glaze, enough to generously glaze 30 to 40 medium cookies

Storage: Store this, covered in the refrigerator, for 3 to 4 days; stir before using.

2 14-ounce cans condensed
   milk
2 teaspoons vanilla extract
   Pinch of salt
   Pinch of ground cinnamon,
   optional

Tip
Some shortcut dulce de leche
recipes in circulation call for placing
unopened cans of condensed milk
in a pot of water and boiling them,
but canned milk manufacturers
warn against the method, as the
cans can explode!

Use the dulce de leche in the
Coconut Alfajores on page 100 and
the Congo Bars on page 157, or in
any other recipes calling for the
product.

HOMEMADE DULCE DE LECHE

If I hadn't come upon this virtually effortless way of preparing the popular
Latin American milk caramel filling dulce de leche, I doubt that I'd ready it
myself. Yes, the homemade is definitely fresher tasting than canned, but it
usually involves spending hours at the stove. Like most folks today, I'm just
too busy to slowly boil down milk and sugar into a spread.

But this very safe alternative method completely eliminates the tedium:
Sweetened condensed milk (not evaporated milk) goes into a baking dish,
which is then set in a shallow hot water bath. Over several hours in the oven,
the condensed milk gradually bakes down and turns into milk caramel on
its own. Other than stirring the mixture once or twice and replenishing the
water bath, the cook literally doesn't have to do a thing.

Baking Preliminaries: Position a rack in the middle of the oven; preheat
to 375°F. Set out a 9 by 13-inch baking dish (or roasting pan) and a 7 by
11-inch (or similar) glass baking dish that can sit in the larger dish. Spray
the 7 by 11-inch dish with nonstick spray.

Pour the condensed milk into the 7 by 11-inch dish. Shake the pan to
spread out the milk. Tightly cover the dish with foil. Set it in the larger
baking dish. Place on the middle oven rack. Add enough hot water to the
larger dish to come two-thirds of the way up its sides.

Bake for 1½ hours. Stir the milk to redistribute it, as the edges will cook
faster than the interior. Re-cover the dish. Add enough more hot water
to the larger pan to come two-thirds of the way up the sides. Continue
baking, stirring and checking once or twice, until the milk is thickened
and has darkened to the color of slightly dark caramel candies, 1 to 1½
hours longer. Turn off the oven. Let the dulce de leche stand in the oven
to cool for 20 to 30 minutes. Transfer the dulce de leche pan (but not the
pan of water) to a wire rack. (Let the pan of water stand in the oven until
completely cooled before removing it from the oven.)

Stir the vanilla, salt, and cinnamon (if using) into the dulce de leche. If it
is lumpy, stir vigorously and mash out any lumps with a spoon. Store it in
a clean, dry, wide-mouth 1-pint glass canning jar or similar storage jar.

Yield: Makes about 2 cups dulce de leche

Storage: Store this, tightly covered in the refrigerator, for up to 2 weeks.

QUICK COCOA BUTTERCREAM (OR COCOA-BERRY BUTTERCREAM)

This easy, lightly chocolaty buttercream can be used as a filling or piped or swirled icing for almost any butter cookie, French macaron, or chocolate cookie. You can prepare the plain cocoa or the cocoa-berry version, or several slightly exotic variations found at the end of the recipe. The buttercream pipes readily, holds up well, and doesn't make the cookies soggy.

For cocoa-*berry* buttercream, you'll need to incorporate either freeze-dried raspberry or raspberry-blackberry powder. The details and the recipe is on page 336.

¼ cup good-quality unsweetened natural (non-alkalized) cocoa powder or Dutch-process cocoa powder
2 cups powdered sugar, plus more if needed
Pinch of salt
1½ to 2 tablespoons raspberry powder or raspberry-black-berry powder, optional (add if a cocoa-berry buttercream is desired), to taste
¼ teaspoon raspberry extract, optional (add for a cocoa-berry buttercream)
½ cup (1 stick) unsalted butter, slightly softened and cut into chunks

Sift the cocoa into a large mixer bowl. Thoroughly stir in the powdered sugar, salt, and berry powder, if using. Sprinkle the extract (if using) and butter over top. Beat on low, then medium, speed until well blended. Scrape down the sides as needed. Gradually beat in 2 to 5 tablespoons water until evenly incorporated and the mixture is creamy-smooth. (Some brands of cocoa gradually absorb more moisture than others, so continue beating in water until the buttercream is soft enough to spread or pipe readily.) It normally stiffens further upon standing.

For filling cookies: For French macarons or other small rounds, spread a scant teaspoon of buttercream on the undersides of half the cookies. For larger cookies, use enough to yield a ¼- to ⅓-inch-thick layer. Pair them with similar-size cookies, top side visible, gently pressing down until the filling spreads almost to the edges.

For decorating cookie tops: To swirl, put little dollops of buttercream on the cookie tops, then swirl each slightly with the tip of a knife. To pipe, spoon the mixture into a pastry bag fitted with a ½-inch-diameter open star tip; don't fill the bag more than half full and twist tightly to close it. Pipe rosettes onto the cookie tops by holding the tip vertically and squeezing the bag and rotating the tip at the same time. Let stand until the buttercream sets, at least 45 minutes and up to 1½ hours, if desired.

Yield: Makes about 1⅓ cups, enough for filling twenty-five to thirty 2½-inch cookie sandwiches

Storage: Store this, airtight, for up to 1 week. It can be frozen, airtight, for up to 1 month.

For a frosting or filling with a deeper chocolate taste use the ganache on page 318.

Variation: Tarragon-Grapefruit-Cocoa Buttercream Add 1½ teaspoons finely pulverized dried tarragon leaves along with the powdered sugar. Omit the berry powder. Add 2 teaspoons very finely grated grapefruit zest when adding the butter. Omit the extract; proceed exactly as directed in the original recipe.

Variation: Cocoa-Cardamom-Orange Buttercream Add ¼ teaspoon ground cardamom along with the powdered sugar. Omit the berry powder. Add 1 teaspoon very finely grated orange zest when adding the butter. Omit the extract; proceed exactly as directed in the original recipe. (Allspice can substitute for cardamom, though the taste won't be the same.)

Extra Easy
Quick mixing.
Au naturel recipe.

2⅔ cups powdered sugar, plus more
if needed

½ cup (1 stick) unsalted butter,
slightly softened and cut into
chunks

3½ to 4 tablespoons freeze-dried
strawberry powder or
raspberry powder, or half of
each, or blend of two-thirds
raspberry powder and one-
third blackberry powder

1½ to 2½ tablespoons water or
cranberry juice cocktail

1 teaspoon raspberry extract

INTENSELY STRAWBERRY, RASPBERRY, OR BLACKBERRY-RASPBERRY BUTTERCREAM

Right off, let me say that these intensely flavored buttercreams (shown on page 287) require pure, freeze-dried raspberry powder, strawberry powder, or a blend of berry powders. But not to worry—these can either be purchased (they're becoming more readily available all the time) or quickly made at home using the recipe on page 336. Besides instantly contributing amazingly intense, natural berry flavor and color (and thus completely avoiding the use of synthetic food dyes), the powders have the advantage of not making the frostings overly soft or soggy, a big problem in buttercreams that call for fresh berries.

The following buttercreams can serve as a decorative piped and swirled frosting and topping, as well as a filling for French macarons, delicate vanilla-cream cookies, and many other sandwich cookies. The recipe may be doubled if desired.

Combine the powdered sugar, butter, berry powder, 1½ tablespoons water or cranberry juice, and the raspberry extract in a large mixer bowl. Beat on low, then medium, speed just until very well blended; scrape down the sides as needed. If necessary, gradually beat in a little water or a little more powdered sugar as needed for a smooth spreading or piping consistency; don't over beat.

For filling cookies: Spread a scant teaspoon of buttercream on the undersides of half the cookies (or use enough to create a ¼- to ⅓-inch-thick layer). Pair the rounds with similar-size cookies, top side visible, gently pressing down until the filling spreads almost to the edges.

For decorating cookie tops: To spread, put little dollops of buttercream on cookie tops, then swirl it slightly with the tip of a knife. To pipe, spoon the mixture into a pastry bag fitted with a ½-inch-diameter open star tip. Pipe rosettes onto the cookie tops by holding the tip vertically and squeezing the bag and rotating the tip at the same time. Let stand until the buttercream sets, at least 45 minutes and up to 1½ hours, if desired.

Yield: Makes about 1¼ cups, enough for lightly topping or filling about thirty 2½-inch cookie sandwiches

⅔ cup granulated sugar or 1⅓ cups powdered sugar

1 4- to 5-inch-long whole, dry vanilla bean, broken or chopped into ½-inch pieces

2 teaspoons crushed cinnamon stick or 2 teaspoons dried lavender, optional

Tip

If possible, use a dry, firm to brittle vanilla bean for this recipe. A fresher bean will make the sugar too moist or even soggy. It's fine to use one that has had the seeds removed.

INTENSELY VANILLA, VANILLA-CINNAMON, OR VANILLA-LAVENDER DECORATING OR COATING SUGAR

My homemade garnishing sugar habit first started when I discovered a bottle containing several very dry yet still fragrant vanilla beans in the back of my cupboard. They were so brittle I couldn't split them to scrape the seeds out as I'd intended, but they were too pricey to even think of throwing away.

After researching to confirm that the *whole* beans were in fact edible, I decided to create a garnishing sugar by grinding broken pieces of bean in a food processor with either granulated or powdered sugar. Both turned out so much more aromatic and flavorful than vanilla sugar I'd either bought or made by just tucking a scraped-out bean into a jar of sugar that I've used this technique ever since. The same recipe can also be used to produce a vanilla-cinnamon or vanilla-lavender sugar.

Use the powdered sugar versions wherever you want a smooth, dusty texture and the granulated for a sandy consistency. The vanilla-flavored sugar can enhance almost any not-too-sweet butter cookie; the vanilla-cinnamon works with all kinds of molasses and spice cookies; and the vanilla-lavender is nice with lemon, berry, and lavender cookies. Note that the powdered sugar is lighter and only about half as dense as the granulated, so it can be used to garnish or dredge cookies in greater abundance.

In a food processor, process the sugar, vanilla bean, and cinnamon or lavender (if using) for 2 to 3 minutes or until the bits are very finely chopped. If the mixture looks at all moist or clumped, gradually add more sugar until it looks dry. Stir the mixture through a very fine-mesh sieve onto a sheet of baking parchment. Discard the coarse bits, or save them to ready another batch of sugar.

If the sugar seems thoroughly dry and unlikely to clump during storage, simply pack it in a jar or zip-top plastic bag. If it is moist, turn on the oven for 1 minute, then turn off again. Put the baking parchment with the sugar on a baking sheet and let the sugar stand in the oven to dry out for at least 1 hour. If it is clumped, return it to the processor and process until fine again. Let cool, then store airtight.

Yield: Makes about ¾ cup granulated garnishing sugar or 1½ cups powdered garnishing sugar

Storage: Store this, airtight in a cool spot, for up to 1 year.

Easy
Versatile recipe.
Easy food processor mixing.
Excellent flavor.
Au naturel options.

1 tablespoon very finely grated lemon, orange, lime, grapefruit, or tangerine zest (colored part of the peel), plus more for optional decoration

1 teaspoon finely grated or very finely minced peeled fresh gingerroot, optional

2 cups powdered sugar, divided, plus more if needed

½ cup (1 stick) unsalted butter, cool and slightly firm, cut into pats

1 teaspoon fresh lemon juice or thawed orange juice concentrate

  Tiny drops of synthetic or botanically based food color, optional

Tip

Be sure to use only the colored part of the citrus skin; the white part underneath is bitter.

CITRUS OR FRESH GINGER-CITRUS BUTTERCREAM

I use this versatile recipe to create a whole array of buttercreams, from plain lemon, orange, lime, grapefruit, and tangerine to various citrus–fresh ginger combinations—lemon-ginger and orange-ginger are especially nice. The basic recipe can also be modified even further to produce several more exotic buttercreams; see the tarragon-grapefruit and ginger–green tea variations at the end of the recipe.

These buttercreams make excellent fillings for cookies such as the French macarons (page 289), the Delicate Vanilla-Cream Sandwich Cookies (page 116), or other choices suitable for creating elegant sandwich cookies. The buttercreams are equally appealing used as frostings; simply pipe them on top of cookies (or swirl with a knife) to add a luscious, decorative finish. (Suggestions on which cookies pair up best with buttercreams appear along with the cookies throughout the book.)

The first step of the recipe—thoroughly processing together the zests (and gingerroot, if using) with a little of the sugar—accounts for exceptional flavor because it fully infuses the sugar with the volatile oils in the zests. The infusing process also lends an appealing natural fruit color, although you can boost it with drops of food colorings if you wish. I prefer vegetable- or fruit-based food dyes; health food stores and online vendors most often carry them. Or, I often toss in a teaspoon or two of finely chopped *edible* flower petals, such as fresh yellow pansy or orange marigold petals or tarragon leaves (no stems), along with the zest to brighten the yellow, orange, or green hues. See page 338 for more on the novel yet effective technique of using flowers and herbs in cookie decorating.

The recipe may be doubled. Or, make two different flavors and colors for an eye-catching variety.

Combine the zest, ginger (if using), and 1 cup sugar in a food processor. Process until the mixture is very well blended and paste-like, 2 to 3 minutes; stop and scrape the mixture from the bowl bottom and sides as necessary.

Sprinkle the butter, juice, and 1 cup more sugar and food color (if using) over the top. Process until very smooth and well blended, stopping and scraping down the sides as needed. If the mixture is too fluid to spread or pipe, gradually add more powdered sugar until stiffened; if too dry, gradually add a few drops of water until the buttercream is spreadable and well blended.

For filling cookies: Spread a scant teaspoon of buttercream (or enough to create a $\frac{1}{4}$- to $\frac{1}{3}$-inch-thick layer) on the undersides of half the cookies. Pair them with similar-size cookies, top side visible, gently pressing down until the filling spreads almost to the edges.

For decorating cookie tops: If necessary, thin the buttercream by gradually adding in water until a spreading or piping consistency is obtained; or thicken it by gradually adding in powdered sugar. Put little dollops of buttercream on the cookie tops, then swirl it slightly with the tip of a knife. Or spoon the mixture into a pastry bag fitted with a $\frac{1}{2}$-inch-diameter open star tip. Pipe stars by squeezing the buttercream onto the center tops or pipe rosettes by squeezing and rotating the tip at the same time. If desired, add a tiny strip of zest, attractively curled, or place 2 short strips crisscrossed in the center tops. Let stand until the buttercream sets, at least 45 minutes and up to $1\frac{1}{2}$ hours, if desired.

Yield: Makes a scant $1\frac{1}{2}$ cups, enough for twenty to thirty $2\frac{1}{2}$-inch cookie sandwiches (20 generously, 30 scantily)

Storage: Store this, airtight, for up to 1 week. It can be frozen, airtight, for up to 1 month.

Variation: Tarragon-Grapefruit Buttercream Add 2 teaspoons finely crumbled dried tarragon leaves to the grapefruit zest and sugar and mix until smooth and paste-like and the tarragon leaves are finely pulverized. Proceed exactly as directed in the original recipe.

Variation: Ginger, Citrus, and Green Tea Buttercream Incorporate the optional 1 teaspoon grated or finely minced fresh gingerroot and 2 to 3 teaspoons powdered green tea (sencha) along with the sugar. (For more green color, add in 1 teaspoon chopped fresh tarragon leaves, too.) Proceed exactly as directed in the original recipe.

3   cups powdered sugar, divided,
    plus more if needed

2   tablespoons chopped fresh,
    well-washed, then patted dry
    pink or red rose petals or 1
    tablespoon chopped fresh
    lavender blooms and bracts
    (no stems)

¾   teaspoon finely grated lemon
    zest (yellow part of the peel)

6   tablespoons (¾ stick) cold
    unsalted butter, cut into pats

1½ teaspoons rose flower water if
    making rose frosting or
    ½ teaspoon vanilla extract if
    making lavender frosting

    3 to 5 teaspoons frozen
    (thawed) cranberry juice
    concentrate, as needed for
    pink color

1   drop of blue liquid food
    color (for lavender frosting),
    or 1 to 2 teaspoons frozen
    (thawed) Concord grape juice
    concentrate, optional, for pale
    lavender color

Tip

Fresh blooms or confetti will begin
to wilt within an hour, so add only
shortly before the cookies are
served.

FRESH ROSE PETAL OR LAVENDER BUTTERCREAM

I'm excited to share this recipe with you because these very charming and unusual frostings capture the exquisite floral flavor and aroma of fresh roses or lavender better than any other versions I've ever tasted. Modestly, I have to say I think the sensory experience will be memorable and should not be missed. (If you are a fresh mint, tarragon, or basil fan, you'll be interested in the variations for these at the end of the recipe.) The buttercreams can be either swirled or piped onto cookies or tucked between them for sweet little sandwiches.

The secret is in using either fresh pink to red rose petals or fresh lavender blooms and infusing the powdered sugar with their essence. (Use only unsprayed blooms.) Although I call for fresh rose petals and much prefer to use fresh lavender blooms in this recipe, in a pinch, I've used dried culinary lavender with pleasant results. (I actually freeze the fresh lavender flower heads in little plastic bags so the herb will be available to make this frosting in winter!)

Since I'm always eager to create eye-catching frostings that minimize the use of food coloring (especially red and yellow azo dyes), I incorporate some cranberry juice concentrate to heighten the natural color of the flowers. (Its hue is vivid and its acidity also helps spark the frosting flavor.) On occasion, I add a very small drop of blue food color or a teaspoon or two of Concord grape juice concentrate to lend the lavender buttercream a pale purple shade. But when fresh woodland violets or purple pansies are in my garden, I just chop up a couple teaspoons of the petals and grind them along with the lavender to lend the right hue. (For more on decorating with edible flowers, see page 338.)

It's also fun to dramatize the unique and surprising appeal of frostings featuring real flowers by garnishing the cookie tops with snippets of fresh rose petal "confetti," crystallized rose petals, or the tiny lavender "bloomlets" removed from their bracts first. The results are striking and always create a stir. For special occasions, I've made half a batch of rose and half a batch of lavender and served two kinds of cookies together for an even more razzle-dazzle presentation. And once for a large spring gathering, I served a platter of pink rose, soft purple lavender, and pale green mint frosted cookies all at once—beautiful!

Combine 1 cup powdered sugar, the rose petals (or lavender blooms and bracts), and the lemon zest in a food processor. Process for 3 to 4 minutes, until the flowers and zest are as fine as possible; scrape down the bowl sides halfway through. If the mixture seems wet rather than

powdery, add in more powdered sugar and keep processing until it is powdery.

Stir the processed mixture through a very fine-mesh sieve set over a bowl until the sugar and only very fine flower particles pass through; stop before any coarse bits are forced though the sieve, but push through enough fine bits to fully flavor the frosting.

Wipe out the processor, then return the sieved mixture to it, along with the remaining 2 cups powdered sugar. Process until just well blended. Sprinkle over the butter. Process in on/off pulses just until it is cut in and no clumps of butter remain; the mixture should not be coming together.

Through the feed tube, add the rose water or vanilla; pulse several times. Gradually add in the cranberry juice concentrate and, if desired, a tiny drop of blue food color or Concord grape juice concentrate mixed with it through the feed tube until the desired lavender color is achieved. Then, as necessary, add a little water or more powdered sugar until the desired spreading or piping consistency is obtained; remember that the frosting will stiffen slightly as it stands. Its flavor will also intensify.

To frost cookies: Spread a $\frac{1}{4}$-inch-thick layer of frosting over the cookie tops using a table knife, then swirl it attractively with the knife tip. Or add just a little dollop to the center top of cookies, and swirl with a knife tip.

To pipe frosting onto cookies: Put the frosting in a pastry bag fitted with a $\frac{1}{2}$-inch-diameter open star tip. Either pipe out simple stars, or rotate the tube slightly as you pipe to form rosettes. If serving promptly and adding flowers or flower petals, dip their undersides into some slightly moistened frosting, then lightly press them into place on the frosted tops.

Serve the cookies immediately or place in a single layer, in an airtight container. Store refrigerated for up to 3 days or freeze for up to 10 days. Let come to room temperature before serving.

Yield: Makes about $2\frac{1}{2}$ cups frosting, enough to pipe 1-inch-diameter rosettes into the centers of 45 to 50-small cookies

Storage: Store this, airtight in the refrigerator, for up to 1 week. It can be frozen, airtight, for up to 1 month. Allow it to return to room temperature and stir vigorously before using.

Variation: Fresh Mint Buttercream Prepare exactly as for the rose frosting, except substitute 3 tablespoons finely chopped very flavorful fresh mint leaves (no stems) for the roses or lavender. Substitute $\frac{1}{4}$ teaspoon peppermint extract for the rose water; add it when the vanilla is added. If desired, add a tiny drop of green food color in place of the blue food color; omit the cranberry juice concentrate. Garnish mint-frosted cookies with dainty mint leaves.

Variation: Fresh Tarragon or Basil Buttercream Prepare exactly as for the rose frosting, except substitute 3 tablespoons finely chopped fresh tarragon or tender basil leaves (no stems) for the roses. Substitute $\frac{1}{4}$ teaspoon anise extract, if desired; add it along with the vanilla. If desired, add a tiny drop of green food color in place of the blue food color; omit the cranberry juice concentrate. Garnish tarragon- or basil-frosted cookies with herb confetti.

Easy
Au naturel recipe.
Quick food
processor mixing.

⅓ cup granulated sugar, plus more
   if needed
1 tablespoon finely grated lemon,
   lime, orange, tangerine, or
   grapefruit zest (colored part of
   the peel)
   About 1 tablespoon chopped
   fresh yellow or orange pansy
   or marigold petals or a few
   tiny drops of synthetically or
   botanically based food color,
   optional

LEMON, LIME, ORANGE, TANGERINE, OR GRAPEFRUIT DECORATING SUGAR

A while back, it occurred to me that I was missing a huge opportunity when it came to lending cookies truly vibrant flavors and aromas. Like most folks, I often garnished baked goods with commercial colored sugars and nonpareils, which, while visually appealing, added absolutely nothing taste-wise. I'd also occasionally garnished cookies with cinnamon sugar, or vanilla sugar, and noticed that these, on the other hand, boosted taste appeal enormously.

This eventually led me to devise a whole array of flavored and scented garnishing and decorating sugars, from citrus to dried berry to fresh herb and edible rose petal. They turned out to be so simple to prepare and delivered such spectacular results that I now use them often. The sugars (some are shown on page 334) all serve the same basic purpose, but the preparation methods and ingredient quantities vary a bit, so to avoid confusion I've provided separate recipes for the various kinds.

Decorating sugars infused with fresh citrus zest are particularly amazing flavor boosters because the colored part of the skin possesses pungent volatile oils that miraculously capture and concentrate the essential character of each particular fruit. Sprinkling a little zest-infused sugar over the tops of cookies announces "lime," or "lemon," or other citrus flavor even better than the often-used technique of incorporating zest into the dough. That's because the distinguishing sensory elements are right out there for the mouth and the nose to enjoy, not buried in the dough. As a bonus, the fine flecks of zest in the sugars contribute tiny bits of texture, plus subtle *natural* fruit color that I think is quite beautiful.

Yes, you can certainly boost the colors of your decorating sugars with appropriate food dyes. But there is an alternative au naturel way to go: For a brighter green color, add a tablespoon of chopped fresh tarragon, mint, or basil leaves when you process the lime zest. For brighter lemon, orange, or tangerine colors, add chopped unsprayed yellow or orange pansy or marigold petals when you process these zests. (Wash the flowers and pat them dry first.) Don't worry; the flower and herb additions never overpower the citrus—they just blend in and lend subtle taste notes and pleasing natural color. For a list of which flowers are edible, see page 301.

This recipe makes enough to decorate about two batches of cookies. You can double it if desired, but remember that the bright flavors, aromas, and colors will gradually fade, so homemade citrus sugars are best used within a month or two.

Combine the sugar, zest, and petals or food color (if using) in a food processor. Process for 2 minutes or until the sugar is evenly infused with color and the zest is very fine; stop and scrape the sides and bottom as necessary. If the mixture is very wet and clumped, gradually add in several tablespoons more sugar while processing.

Spread out the sugar on a parchment-lined baking sheet. Turn on the oven for 1 minute, then immediately turn it off again. (A too-warm oven will cause the bright flavors and colors to fade.) Let the mixture stand in the oven for at least 45 minutes and preferably 1 hour, until thoroughly dried and cool.

Scrape the sugar into a dry, clean food processor and process just until all lumps are removed. Use immediately in place of commercial decorating sugar. Or place in a clean, dry, airtight container for later use.

Yield: Makes ⅓ cup to ½ cup decorating sugar

Storage: Store this, airtight at cool room temperature, for up to 2 months; or refrigerate for up to 4 months. (The flavor and aroma will fade after that.)

Variation: Orange-Spice Decorating Sugar Add ¼ teaspoon ground cardamom or ¼ teaspoon ground allspice along with the orange zest. Continue exactly as directed.

Variation: Grapefruit-Tarragon Decorating Sugar Add ½ tablespoon chopped dried tarragon leaves (no stems) along with the grapefruit zest. Continue exactly as directed.

Au naturel garnishing sugars shown at left: Rose petal, lime, lavender, dried raspberry, and orange.

2 tablespoons powdered sugar,
   plus more if needed
⅔ cup freeze-dried strawberries,
   raspberries, or a combination
   of ½ cup raspberries and 3
   tablespoons blackberries
   1 to 1½ teaspoons dried
   lavender blooms and/or bracts,
   to taste, optional

Tip
Berry colors tend to darken and fade
from heat, so garnish your cookies at
the end of baking or after they are
out of the oven.

FREEZE-DRIED BERRY FLAVORING POWDERS (OR DECORATING SUGARS)

For decades home bakers have depended on extracts like vanilla, almond, lemon, and so forth to crank up cookie flavor. But now there are some nifty new freeze-dried fruit powder products on the market that can be used with equally impressive results.

Currently, the most readily available of these flavor enhancers is pure raspberry powder. This is nothing more than unsweetened freeze-dried raspberries ground and then sieved to remove the seeds. For the cookie baker, the great advantage of this and other berry powders is that they can contribute intense, natural fruit taste and color without making doughs, frostings, and fillings soggy or seedy. The powder can even be sifted over baked cookies, macarons, and buttercream for a naturally colorful dust.

The only catch is that these powders aren't yet easy to obtain (though I predict they will be fairly soon). Raspberry and, very occasionally, strawberry powders are sold in some stores, but more often they have to be ordered online. Another drawback is that manufacturers generally sell them only in very pricey 1-pound or larger containers designed for commercial bakeries. Even the busiest home baker can't use up that much before the product grows stale and loses its oomph (though keeping it in the freezer will help)!

The very simple solution is to buy consumer-size containers of whole unsweetened, freeze-dried berries, now stocked in many health food markets and gourmet shops. Then just grind them in a food processor and sieve them to make your own berry powders. The most readily available brand, from the Just Tomatoes, Etc! company, is called Just Raspberries, or Just Strawberries, and so forth depending on the product featured.

Once ground and sieved, these are then at the ready for tossing into frostings, fillings, and some doughs or for sifting over the tops of *baked* cookies. Another possibility: Sift a tablespoon or so of berry powder together with ¼ cup powdered sugar, then either coat or dust fully baked cookies with the delectable pale pastel berry dredging sugar. Or create a more granular decorating sugar using the variation at the end of the recipe.

Note that you can create your own unique, customized berry blends: such as half raspberries and half strawberries or two-thirds raspberries and one-third blackberries. (Blackberries have a very muted color and flavor, so aren't attractive used solo.)

It's also possible to enhance the aromas and flavors by adding in some dried lavender before processing—this herb has a particular affinity for both raspberries and blackberries. Be sure to use a brand harvested for culinary use; some are suitable for crafting purposes only.

The recipe calls for a small amount of sugar to facilitate grinding the dried berries to a powder. If the ones you're processing seem very dry and powdery (this varies considerably from brand to brand), use the minimum amount of sugar called for. If they seem slightly moist or begin to clump together during processing, just add more sugar as necessary. Don't try to completely grind up the seeds as they are bitter; once the berries are powdery, sieve the mixture to remove the seeds.

Double the recipe if desired. Just remember that the powders lose their intense flavors and bright colors fairly quickly, so they are best made in quantities that will be used within a month or so.

In a food processor, process the sugar, berries, and lavender (if using) for about 1½ minutes or until very finely chopped; don't try to grind up the seeds or small bits of pulp. If excess moisture causes the berries to clump, keep adding more sugar and continue processing until the mixture is dry enough to sift. Press and stir the powdery mixture through a very fine-mesh sieve (one that the seeds and coarse bits won't pass through) to obtain the berry powder; stop before you force through every bit of sugar and pulp, as seeds may be forced through in the process.

Use the powders immediately, or to prevent them from clumping during storage, place them on a baking parchment in a heatproof dish in a barely warm oven (turned on for 1 minute, then turned off again). Let stand until completely cooled and dry, about 30 minutes. Stir well, pressing out any clumps or returning to the processor and processing away any lumps, then store airtight in a clean, dry bottle or jar.

Yield: Makes about ⅓ cup berry flavoring powder

Storage: Store this, airtight and in a cool, dark spot, for up to 2 months. It can be frozen, airtight, for up to 6 months; let warm up to cool room temperature before using.

Variation: Berry Decorating Sugar Substitute 2 to 2½ tablespoons granulated sugar for the powdered sugar called for.

⅓ cup granulated sugar, plus more
if needed

⅛ teaspoon grated lemon zest and/
or rose water; or peppermint
extract if desired; or anise
extract (if making tarragon
sugar)

¼ cup lightly packed fresh lavender,
tarragon, or mint leaves (no
stems), fresh rose petals, or
lavender blooms

About 1 tablespoon chopped
fresh purple pansy, garden
violet, or purple rose petals for
color or tiny drops of the
appropriate synthetic or
botanically based liquid food
color, optional

FRESH HERB AND EDIBLE FLOWER DECORATING SUGAR

Homemade decorating sugars infused with fresh (*not dried*) herbs and *edible* flowers may seem novel, but in certain recipes they can lend extraordinary and quite unexpected appeal. I started experimenting because these enabled me to produce au naturel decorating sugars in green, pink, and lavender shades. But actually they heighten flavor and aroma as well.

I'm particularly thrilled with the garnishing sugars created using fresh lavender, tarragon and rose petals: These are aromatic, pretty, and perfectly complement many cookies. Though a mint-scented sugar might seem an obvious choice as well, use only fresh mint that has a clear, bold, minty character; some kinds are too grassy. It's also best to boost the flavor with a drop or two of mint extract. And since the mint flavor is quite distinctive, the resulting sugar is best used only on mint cookies.

If you happen to have amassed enough tiny lavender blooms, you can create a fantastically fragrant decorating sugar that also has a faint purple tinge. Lacking an abundance of blooms, use them along with their bracts. The sugar will taste and smell just as good and can be colored by adding a few well-washed deep purple fresh garden pansy, spring violet (not African violet, which isn't edible), or purple-hued pinks (dianthus) or purple rose petals in with the lavender. (These are all mild tasting and won't detract from the lavender itself, and in fact, pansies can be used alone for a beautiful purple sugar.) Or you can go the food color route and tint the sugar purple with tiny amounts of red and blue liquid food color. (Several brands of botanically based food dyes are sold if you wish to avoid the typical synthetic food colorings.)

Fresh tarragon leaves hold their color surprisingly well, so the resulting decorating sugar is a pleasing soft herb-green shade that really needs no tinting. The tarragon flavor is subtle, with a faint hint of anise that nicely accents both many citrus and vanilla-flavored cookies. Boost the anise notes by adding a few drops of anise extract, if desired. (If you can't obtain tarragon, basil leaves, which also have anise notes, can be substituted with satisfactory results; the green color is just not quite as pretty.)

Rose garnishing sugar will have a pale to bright color depending on whether the petals used are soft pastel or medium pink or burgundy or deep fuchsia. The intensity of the floral aroma will depend on the fragrance of the roses themselves. For a more distinct rose-like character, add in a little rose water; for a more neutral garnish that lends mostly color to the cookies, leave it out. For obvious reasons, use only unsprayed home garden roses or organically grown purchased ones. Incidentally, these and other petals will stay fresh and colorful packed in an airtight plastic bag and stashed in the refrigerator for several days.

Note that adding in a little fresh lemon zest enhances the aroma of all these sugars.

Combine the sugar, zest, extract, and the herbs and/or flower petals in a food processor. Process for 2 to 3 minutes or until the herbs or petals are chopped as fine as possible; stop and scrap the sides and bottom several times as necessary. If the mixture seems very wet, gradually add more sugar, processing until the sugar is a bit drier and less clumped. Add drops of the appropriate food color, if using, and process until evenly incorporated.

Spread the sugar mixture on a parchment-lined baking sheet. Turn the oven on for 1 minute, then immediately turn it off again. (An overly warm oven will cause the flavors and colors to fade.) Put the sugar in the oven and let dry for at least 45 minutes and up to 1 hour, until thoroughly dried. Scrape the sugar into a clean, dry food processor bowl. Process just until thoroughly pulverized. Use in place of purchased decorating sugar whenever a natural garnish is preferred. Place thoroughly cooled leftover sugar in an airtight jar or zip-top plastic bag.

Yield: Makes about ½ cup decorating sugar

Storage: Store this, airtight and away from heat and light, for up to 2 months; or refrigerate, airtight, for up to 3 months. (The color, aroma, and fragrance will fade with longer storage.)

INDEX

Page numbers in **bold** indicate recipe location; page numbers in *italics* indicate photos; **(V)** following a recipe page number indicates variations for that recipe.